"This is cool! *New York on $1,000 a Day (Before Lunch)* is music to my ears. It's my kind of book."

CAB CALLOWAY

"Outrageous, witty, and fun. If it had music, it would be a long-running hit on Broadway. In fact, I may write the music myself—'Tomorrow' "

CHARLES STROUSE

"The Big Apple is bigger and more delicious than ever after reading *New York on $1,000 a Day (Before Lunch)*. I loved it."

ADOLFO

"Growing up in Winnipeg, Canada, during the Depression, I lived on $1 a day. After reading this book, I know how to do something I could never even have dreamed of then, how to spend $1,000 a day—before lunch yet! Only in America."

MONTY HALL

"Something for every taste, mood and moment filled with all the pleasures and treasures that New York has to offer."

ARLENE DAHL

"Forget your filofax, *New York on a $1,000 a Day* has it ALL. Whether you've got a million or just 20 bucks to spend, this book will show you how to do it with real New York style. Now that's worth singing about!"

PATTI LA BELLE

NEW YORK
on $1,000 a day
(before lunch)

What celebrities are saying about *New York on $1,000 a Day (Before Lunch)*

"The perfect guide to a lifestyle of champagne wishes and caviar dreams in the world's best city. A handy, almost biblical book to insure your new decade in New York City is cram-packed with dazzling delights."

ROBIN LEACH

"A lavish, witty, informative—absolutely irresistible—guide to New York$$"

VICTORIA PRINCIPAL

"I loved it, but now the whole world knows my secrets for looking like a millionaire! *New York on a $1,000 a Day (Before Lunch)* really tells it all."

EILEEN FORD

"If you want to save yourself a grand a day and still have a great time in New York, try this book—before or after lunch. You'll love it."

REGIS PHILBIN

"After reading this book, I am reminded of the fact that I have been poor, and I have been rich—rich is better."

TONY RANDALL

"*New York on a $1,000 a Day (Before Lunch)* sings with the rhythm of my city. They are both glamorous, fun, and exciting."

BARBARA COOK

"This book is a definite *must*. I'm going to sample all its treasures—even if I gain weight doing it!"

SYLVIA MILES

NEW YORK
on $1,000 a day
(before lunch)

FERNE KADISH
SHELLEY CLARK

PASSPORT BOOKS
a division of *NTC Publishing Group*
Lincolnwood, Illinois USA

Given the fact that no two people can totally digest the bounty that is New York City, we sought help from experts in certain areas. Most of the galleries featured here were selected and researched by noted art writer Deborah Gimmelson. For antiques we relied upon the taste and experience of decorator Grady Cooley who researched the section.

cover photo: Jake Rajs/The Image Bank

Published by Passport Books, Trade Imprint of National Textbook Company, 4255 West Touhy Avenue, Lincolnwood (Chicago), Illinois 60646-1975.
© 1990 by Ferne Kadish. All rights reserved. No part of this book may be reproduced, stored in a retrieval system, or transmitted in any form, or by any means, electronic, mechanical, photocopying or otherwise, without the prior written permission of National Textbook Company.
Manufactured in the United States of America.
Library of Congress Catalog Card Number: 89–62887

0 1 2 3 4 5 6 7 8 9 ML 9 8 7 6 5 4 3 2 1

Dedication

*This book is dedicated to the memory of my
beloved parents, Bessie and Lewis Wolner, who
in their lifetime bestowed upon me riches beyond
measure—their unconditional love—and to my
children Ilene and Michael to whom I give this
legacy.*

F.W.K.

*For my mother, Margery—always loving,
always supportive of a daughter who, on
occasion, has given her plenty of reason to be
otherwise!*

S.M.C.

Contents

CHAPTER TWO

Hotels 14
Or a hotel is not a home?

CHAPTER THREE

Restaurants 52
Give my regards to a great paillard

CHAPTER FOUR

A Sudden Yen for . . . 157
Something for every taste, every mood, every moment

CHAPTER FIVE

Shopping   183
If it's not here, it doesn't exist

CHAPTER SIX

Jewelry 290

Baubles, bangles, and big bucks

CHAPTER SEVEN

Art and Antiques 314

Pleasure vs *treasure*

CHAPTER EIGHT

Beauty and Health 338
From ear to there

Introduction

New York on a $1,000 a Day (Before Lunch) is about how to enjoy New York in style. We've tried to cover every conceivable indulgence, whether you have a particular passion for shopping, dining, or entertaining—or simply prefer to experience extravagant lifestyles vicariously by reading about where international movers and shakers stay, what they buy, and where and what they eat. New York is a city of extraordinary contrasts with unlimited temptations seductive enough to separate you from your money in very short order, as well as innumerable opportunities to fashion memories for free. The key is time, that most precious of commodities. This is a guide to not wasting any.

We've outlined much of the best of the city to serve as a basis for your own exploration, your own discoveries. You'll know what to expect from many of New York's finest and most interesting hotels, restaurants, shops, galleries, and service enterprises. You'll find out which are the privileged sections of restaurants such as 21 and La Grenouille, which are designated Siberia and how to avoid being seated in those desolate areas. Those special characters known as Sirio, Karen, Gilbert, Frank, Frankie, Monty, and Dario will become as familiar to you as they are to their regular guests. You'll discover the secret to resurrecting that beloved tie after its unfortunate encounter with the soup, and you'll become intimate with the tailors, furriers, jewelers, and custom shoemakers who put people on the world's best-dressed lists. Some of New York's most entertaining secrets are revealed to make you the host or hostess with the most or mostess. And there are tips on shopping for trinkets to treasures, from $5 to millions or for just the sheer pleasure of indulging in flights of fancy or fantasy as you marvel at all that New York has to offer.

Did we cover everything? Of course not. We're talking about a city that, by some calculations, supports over 25,000 restaurants and countless shops. No doubt we missed some special places here and there—we leave it to you to fill in the blanks. And we *know* we skipped a few establishments that usually appear on the pages of guides to New York—some fell by the wayside because of time and space restrictions, others because, quite frankly, we don't feel they're worthy of our time or yours. We invite you to divine which is which as you explore the city using this book as a resource of places and people you can be sure of—safe havens from which to launch a more hit-and-miss approach to the city.

In the process, you'll be struck by the vibrancy of this city we're proud to call home. It's constantly on the go, undulating with change. New York and New Yorkers are not inclined to leave well enough alone—renew, restore, replace are the three R's here, as part of the conversational standbys of restaurants and real estate. By the time this book is published there will be any number of exciting, commendable new businesses and services that you can add to your list of ways to spend $1,000 a day before lunch. By the same token, rates and prices quoted may have changed. But the good news is that where hotels and restaurants are concerned, they're not likely to increase by much. Hotel competition at the luxury end of the market is heating up, and restaurants are still reeling from the October '87 crash—they're trying to hold down prices, and some are even rolling them back in search of clientele.

So, whether you're in town for a weekend, a week, a lifetime or only in your imagination, thinking about your next jaunt to the Big Apple, help yourself to all the opportunities for indulgence, to all the possibilities of excitement that make New York one hell of a town!

Ferne Kadish
Shelley Clark

CHAPTER ONE

Transportation

Up, down, and around the town

*G*etting there, they say, is half the fun. Not in New York it isn't. But it may be the start of the adventure that's New York City. It may also be a good start on the thousand dollars a day you can spend, without any trouble at all, before lunch. But if you've got it, flaunt it. And transportation-wise, there's lots to flaunt getting to and getting around New York.

Because of all it is and whom it hosts, New York is fortunate in that, more than any other city in the country, it's serviced by entrepreneurs dedicated to getting you there fast and protecting you from any traveling travails.

That's why, darling, chartered planes and helicopters were invented, not to mention the special first-class service on regularly scheduled flights from just about anywhere. There's no problem getting to New York—the question is, how? By plane, by train, by automobile, it doesn't matter; just do it in style. Our motto is first class or not at all. Just keep in mind that the most reliable carrier has been known to lose a bag or two, so come dressed for dinner. You *are* anxious to take a bite out of the Big Apple, aren't you?

And make arrangements for "a car," which in New York means a hired conveyance with a driver, be it an understated town car or overstated limo. Quite frankly, if we have to spend forty-five minutes crossing town, we insist on doing it in comfort and style, with a wet bar and television, a telephone and fax, and a driver who speaks English and knows the Bowery can be a bank as well as a strip of flophouses.

Of course, there's always that one most efficient mode of transportation that especially suits New Yorkers—walking. Indeed it's the one we tend to rely on as much as possible, but only in the interest of getting someplace on time, or what passes for on time in New York—there's a good fifteen-minute grace period built into any appointment.

For dramatic entrances, though, there's nothing like a limousine, the more stretched, the better. Color is key. Black is best, though increasingly difficult to come by. Navy blue will do. Gray is okay in a pinch, but white? Save it for weddings in Brooklyn.

Why is transport so important to New Yorkers? Everyone's always on the move. It's part of the energy and the pace of this town that never sleeps. It's the tension in the air, not to mention the fumes. It's the fabric that holds the city together—the warp and woof of life. And it's certainly a good chunk of your thousand dollars a day before lunch.

SCHEDULED SERVICE

Amtrak

(800) 872-7245
(212) 582-6875

One thing about airports; they're never any place you want to be. Instead they tend to be at the end of the earth, or at least a good forty-five minutes from anywhere that could be described as civilization. So even though we have some suggestions about the best way to fly, even the most convenient way to get to and from New York's airports, we still feel honor bound to tell you about an alternative—the train.

Not just any train. We have a specific class of service on a particular kind of train in mind—the club car on Amtrak's Metroliner between Washington, New York, and such points as Baltimore and Philadelphia. The D.C.–Manhattan trip takes what Amtrak calls two hours and fifty-five civilized minutes. When you consider the crucial downtown-to-downtown element of the trip, it's about the same time you'd be likely to spend getting to National (which in all fairness is one of the few major airports within shouting distance of the city it serves), grabbing the Trump Shuttle to La Guardia, and schlepping to midtown Manhattan.

And with all due respect to Donald Trump and his admirable efforts to transform the former Eastern Shuttle into luxury transportation, the train is really more comfortable than the plane. For one thing, you don't feel so confined to your seat. You can take a stroll and belly up to the bar. Although, in the club car (read *First Class*) there is a waiter, so you really don't need to.

In fact, in the Club Car, you don't need to do much of anything except sit back and relax in your oversized seat and wait to be served your meal with complimentary beverage and a newspaper. Now a word about the food—it isn't bad. And it's nicely presented, topped off with a hot towel that does refresh and invigorate. If you must, you can conduct business on the telephone, more reliable and infinitely more satisfying in its private booth than those available on planes.

The current one-way fare is $115.50, but fares tend to have short life spans, so call to check and make the required reservation. Without a booking, even regular Amtrak travelers like William F. Buckley, Jim Lehrer, and Pearl Bailey aren't allowed on the train.

We imagine that, like us, they ride Amtrak for the comfort and convenience. Still, for us there's another very appealing factor—the social possibilities. We don't know exactly what it is, but there's a feeling about the train that brings out a sense of camaraderie. Instead of studiously avoiding any human contact by burying our heads in a magazine or pretending to be asleep, as we do on planes, we find ourselves chatting away with neighbors. We've actually met people on the train—people we like and have made our friends. When was the last time you had that experience on a plane?   🍂

British Airways

530 Fifth Avenue   (800) 247-9297
New York, NY

British Airways claims to be "the world's favourite airline." We have no way of verifying that typically bold British assertion, but there's no question that as far as we're concerned British Airways' supersonic Concorde is the only way to fly—at least between London and New York. Yes, it's glamorous. Yes, having one of the Concorde's leather identification tags on your briefcase is a status symbol. But our reason for flying the Concorde (indeed the only reason for anyone in his or her right mind to do this) is that it's fast—very fast.

The transatlantic flight, Concorde-style, averages only three hours and twenty-five minutes. There are four crossings daily, two originating from Heathrow, two from JFK. A 10:30 A.M. departure from London means an early morning arrival in New York in the nick of time for a power breakfast at the Regency, Carlyle, or 21, with a whole business day ahead. The 7:00 P.M. departure allows a full day in London, but arrival in New York in time for dinner. By the same token, leaving New York in the morning gets you to London in time for dinner, while the lunchtime departure allows plenty of time for a morning meeting Stateside with an evening arrival in London. Best of all, when you get there, you can look forward to a full night's sleep.

Time, as they say, is money, and all this time-saving doesn't come cheap. A round-trip ticket is $7,212, half that for a one-way fare. But that includes VIP treatment from check-in to baggage claim and some first-class food. At both airports there are ticket counters reserved for the exclusive use of Concorde passengers. After check-in, travelers relax in a special lounge, where complimentary libations and snacks, appropriate to the time of day, are served. Once on board, the gracious flight crew tempts you with delicate canapés, accompanied by vintage champagne. Brunch, lunch, or dinner follows, the creation of British Airways' master chefs and served on damask table linens and fine Wedgwood china. For dinner, the meal might consist of smoked Scottish salmon and grilled filet of Angus beef. Of course, any dietary restrictions will be catered to, if you call in advance. In any case, it's bound to be the best in-flight meal you've ever had.

Now, you should know that despite all of British Airways' admirable efforts, there is a slight discomfort factor associated with supersonic travel. The Concorde is on the narrow side, the cushy leather seats lined up very closely in pairs on either side of the aisle. The headroom reminds you of a forty-foot yacht—adequate, but barely. It's not for the claustrophobic. (You will find seats far forward—in front of the wings—less noisy.)

Still, the close quarters are a small price to pay for such a quick, convenient flight and an end to the miseries of jet lag—another sensible reason for flying the Concorde. As we settled into our seat one recent morning, we recalled the seventeenth-century English poet Andrew Marvell: "But at my back I always hear Time's wingèd chariot hurrying near." He must have had a vision of the Concorde, rapidly becoming one of life's more delectable necessities. ❧

MGM Grand Air, Inc.

(213) 640-2700
(800) 422-1101

Remember when traveling was a glamorous adventure? It still is, between Los Angeles and New York on MGM Grand Air. For $975 one way, about the same as full-fare first class on most other airlines, you can experience MGM's commitment to eliminate the stress and hassle associated with flying.

It starts curbside where bags are whisked away while you are directed to a lounge with all the serene comfort of a private club. Phones and fax machines are available, as are conference rooms for that last-minute meeting. A concierge deals with any travel arrangements you might want made or changed, while a waiter serves complimentary beverages.

The adventure begins when you look around at your fellow passengers, all thirty-two of them. You never know whom you might meet on MGM. It has become the airline of choice for a host of notables whose business takes them back and forth from coast to coast—Eddie Murphy, Elizabeth Taylor, Michael J. Fox, or Sammy Davis, Jr., might be among your traveling companions.

You'll know why as soon as you step on board any of the airline's three reconfigured 727-100s. Built to accommodate 110 passengers, each has been luxuriously refitted to carry only 33 in very high style. Three cabins are separated by beautifully etched Lalique-like glass panels. The forward cabin holds nine large leather-and-velour swivel seats, a large television screen to view any of the six films available on each flight, and a leather-trimmed powder room.

The middle section serves as bar and buffet. Used for food preparation, it also acts as a fully functional flying bar-cum-gathering-space. Four more swivel chairs and a love seat make up the seating arrangements. And there are stowable tables for a friendly game of cards. The best seats are 4A, 4D, 5A, and 5D.

The aft cabin features four private staterooms, each with four large seats and two television monitors. To take advantage of the privacy offered by these self-styled staterooms, you have to purchase all four seats for $3,900. It's an amount gladly paid by some like Johnny Carson, who prefer to sleep their way across the continent, or Mary Tyler Moore, whose dogs, Dash and Dudley, find the accommodations superior to the space allotted four-legged passengers on other airlines.

If you've been counting and wondering about the other four seats, they're the oversized variety, two on either side of the aisle, and are located in front of the group of cubicles, facing the bar. Wherever you sit on the plane, you can look forward to quick and efficient service—there are five flight attendants. And you're never very far away from any of the three telephones.

You can also look forward to the food service, which MGM likens to a "five-star restaurant in Paris." The comparison is more than a tad ambitious, but we can't quibble too much because the food is good, indeed peerless at 40,000 feet (the Concorde cruises at 50,000 to 60,000). Stuart lead crystal and Frette linens lend a touch of elegance to every meal, as does the Moët & Chandon that's standard. A dinner menu might consist of sevruga caviar, smoked salmon, beef Wellington stuffed with veal mousse, and espresso fudge-nut brownies for dessert. For lunch, the choices could include stuffed clams, grilled veal chops, fettuccine with lobster, or ginger-poached sea bass prepared in white wine and lemon. If you take either of the morning departures, one each from LAX and JFK, you can sample what must be the only cooked-to-order eggs in the sky.

There are four flights daily, 9:00 A.M. and 3:30 P.M. from L.A., 10:15 A.M. and 7:00 P.M. from New York, a schedule with a convenience factor similar to most of the major airlines. And MGM has even instituted a frequent-flyer program—one free flight for every ten taken. It's a very generous reward indeed for having the good sense to pamper yourself by flying what really is the world's only completely first-class airline. 🐛

New York Helicopter

(800) 645-3494
Heliport: 34th Street
and East River Drive

Schlepping out to JFK is a drag under any circumstances and when time is, shall we say it, on the wing, the trip can turn into pure torture. Sitting on the Van Wyck Expressway in bumper-to-bumper traffic while the minutes to flight time tick away can be very nerve-wracking. But wait! There's a quick, comfortable, reliable alternative provided by New York Helicopter. Ride in style in one of their four fourteen-passenger Sikorsky choppers. With thirty-six scheduled flights daily, there's bound to be one to suit your agenda.

It's only $65 one way—unless you're traveling business or first class on most major airlines, in which case it's "free." Likewise, if you're flying a foreign carrier in from Europe, the service is generally included. Even full economy fares on many airlines allow substantial discounts or free rides on New York Helicopter.

Book the chopper flight at the same time you book your airline reservations—they're connected to all major airline computer systems—whether you're coming or going. When going, you check in at the heliport located at 34th Street and the East River Drive. Luggage is checked through to your final destination. If, on the other hand, you're arriving, a New York Helicopter representative will meet you at the gate, help you retrieve your luggage, and escort you to the TWA terminal, which serves as their JFK facility.

It's just a ten-minute flight into Manhattan, fast, easy, and fun. For an additional $20, they'll arrange for a limo to whisk you from the heliport to your final destination, providing that rarest of experiences: truly hassle-free traveling.

In fact, there's only one way to make the trek any easier—charter a New York Helicopter for your very own. The Manhattan-JFK route, either way, can be exclusively yours for $300 to $1,200. For $300 you get a tidy little four-passenger BellJet Ranger; $1,200 rents a Sikorsky. The folks at New York Helicopter liken the former to picking you up in a Ford station wagon, while the latter is more akin to riding in a Rolls-Royce. For security reasons, they're reluctant to cite high-profile types who use their service, let alone who opts for the Ford and who goes for the Rolls, but they do allow that private charter tends to be the way most celebrities choose to make the JFK–Manhattan jaunt.

Bear in mind, however, that New York Helicopter charter services are by no means restricted to runs back and forth from the airport. They are regularly called on to take private parties to the Hamptons or to fly a group to any of the tristate area's elite country clubs for a friendly game of golf.

Call Bob Ettinger for any such special requests. Charter rates are by the hour—$475 each for the little Bell helicopter, $1,600 for the big Sikorsky, with several sizes and prices in between. With thirty aircraft, New York Helicopter operates the largest fleet in the East.   ❧

The Trump Shuttle

(800) 247-8786

For years Eastern Airlines had a lock on the Washington–New York–Boston corridor, shuttling the truly important, the self-important, and just plain folks among the three cities. It was run more like a bus line than an airline—hourly departures, no reservations, and no assigned seating—and you could always get the flight you wanted because a second (or third) plane would be added if needed. People knew they could show up at their convenience and, weather permitting, be on a plane to the city of their choice within an hour. What's more, they knew it was likely they'd run into (or at least see) someone they knew or would like to know—The Washington–New York run was particularly fertile celebrity sighting territory and, indeed, became famous for its networking possibilities. Articles were written about it, and any number of references were made to it in the press, in books, and in movies. Popular legend has it Barbara Walters sewed up some of her best interviews on what in those days was simply referred to as The Shuttle. Eastern's was the only game in town.

Then along came New York Air and Pan Am with their versions. Eastern lost its hold on the market. Meanwhile the airline was losing its grip in some other areas as well, and by 1988 was in serious trouble. The Eastern Shuttle, while no longer the only game in town, was still a profitable cash cow and it was put on the block to generate much-needed revenue to bolster the rest of the company's operations. Enter Donald Trump. Enter the Trump Shuttle, the latest player in the northeast corridor shuttle shuffle.

"The Donald" as wife Ivana refers to him, paid $365 million for the privilege of owning his first airline and God knows how much more he'll end up putting into it to meet his goal of making it "the best transportation system in the world." You see, Eastern's planes and facilities had seen better days by the time he got hold of them, but knowing Donald, he'll spend whatever he has to to make his shuttle service "the diamond" he envisions.

The complete overhaul and refurbishing of the twenty-one jet fleet, as well as the terminals at Boston's Logan, New York's La Guardia, and Washington's National airports, is in the works. The new interiors of his Boeing 727s are done in burgundy and saddle tones with chrome and bird's-eye maple veneer accents. The seats have been re-covered in soft leather and airfones installed in each row. The same colors figure in the upgraded terminals, along with a fair amount of foliage to give them a suitably lush look. Donald wants an airline worthy of himself and his millionaire pals.

Despite amenities like seat assignments, guaranteed seating to any customer arriving at the gate prior to the scheduled departure time, complimentary beverages, and genuinely edible, even enjoyable, snacks, fares are a competitive $99 one-way during peak hours, $69 off-peak. Weekday departures run hourly on the hour from 7:00 A.M. to 9:00 P.M., with weekend schedules differing slightly.

Our guess is that The Donald has another winner on his hands. We wonder when he plans to set his sights on the space shuttle. ❦

CHARTERS

Jet Aviation Business Jets, Inc.

(212) 868-1122
(800) RENT-JET

It can be *so* tiresome worrying about getting to the airport in time to make a scheduled flight. You break your neck getting there, only to discover it's been delayed—worse, canceled. Even if it does take off on time, there's that dreary food to contend with. Jet Aviation to the rescue! Theirs is really the only way to go. They've been in the business of supplying private planes and jets for charter for the last twenty-two years.

With 120 aircraft, over 200 flight personnel, and facilities in the U.S., Europe, and the Middle East, Jet Aviation operates one of the world's largest executive fleets. If it flies, they have it—from a five-passenger twin-engine King Air turbo-prop for those quick jaunts to Washington or Boston at $625 a flight hour to a sixteen-passenger Gulf Stream jet with a range of 4,800 miles and a fee of $4,500 an hour.

They even have 727s for charter, in several different configurations seating up to a hundred. The pride of the pack is an Executive B727, complete with full working galley stowing Baccarat crystal, Puiforcat silver, and Limoges china, two bedrooms with king-size beds, and an elegant salon area outfitted with couches, club chairs, telephones, fax machine, and VCR. It can take about twenty-five of your very closest friends anywhere in the world for about $7,000 an hour.

Jet Aviation's very professional staff (no tipping, ever) employs considerable resources to make flying as painless as possible. All major newspapers and periodicals are routinely supplied, and the food alone is worth the price of admission—cold lobster salad and champagne for lunch, or perhaps a little beluga washed down with chilled vodka just before landing, which does tend to soothe even the most white-knuckled flyers.

While most of Jet Aviation's charters use the Teterboro, New Jersey, airport, only twenty minutes from midtown Manhattan through the Lincoln Tunnel and just beyond Giants Stadium, arrangements can be made to fly into or out of any of the area's facilities. If you've set your sights on one of the 727s, it's easiest to pick it up at Newark as many CEOs do. Wish we could tell you who, but confidentiality is of paramount importance to Jet Aviation, for security and business reasons. Use your imagination. We're sure you'll think of one or two people who rely on their twenty-four-hour dispatch service—and on their discretion.   ❦

CAR / LIMO SERVICES

Dav-El

(212) 645-4242
(800) 922-0343
National Reservations
(800) 543-5719
New York Reservations

A decade ago Scott Solombrino blew his $600 savings on a limousine rather than his year's college tuition. Both he and the car were 19 years old. His gamble allowed him to work his way through school. His books stayed under the front seat, so he studied whenever he had a break. In the process, he managed to build a tidy little business. By 1987 his Boston-based Fifth Avenue Limousine had a 32-car fleet and annual revenues of $3 million. In 1988, he blew his savings again, but there was considerably less risk involved. Scott, along with partner Ralph Caruso, purchased the already well-established Dav-El Limousine Service. Founded by the late David Klein, it is one of the world's largest with an international network of over 5,000 cars.

Dav-El, which now includes the Fifth Avenue Company that bought it, and boasts 300 cars in New York alone, has long had an enviable reputation for polite, efficient service and beautifully maintained cars. One of the first services to have phones and writing desks in every car, it is especially popular with busy corporate types, who Scott says now spend 90% of their time in his cars on the phone. Big-time celebrities like chatting on the phone, too, but it's Dav-El's discretion and respect for their privacy that's of even greater importance to them. Limo drivers are traditionally a great source for gossip columnists—but not Dav-El's limo drivers.

Scott and Ralph insist that, in addition to keeping their mouths shut, their drivers be well-groomed and well-versed in the goings-on of the cities they serve. In fact, a Dav-El driver is generally as helpful as some of Manhattan's best concierges when it comes to suggesting places to dine and dance. Most know all about the in spots of the moment and are happy to share the knowledge.

And speaking of concierges, Dav-El has its own fleet of those too, who service area airports. Upon request, they will meet you at the airport to assist with all your travel arrangements and anything else you might need. There's no charge for their services, but Dav-El does tend to be the most expensive act in town when it comes to cars. Sedans (Lincoln town cars) are $38 an hour, or $1.30 per mile, whichever is greater, while the deluxe variety (stretch limos) are $50 or $1.60 a mile. A gratuity is automatically added to the bill—15% for the sedans, 20% for the deluxe cars.

Interestingly enough, Dav-El, in keeping with our assertion that limo-wise bigger is better, has eliminated formal limousines altogether. They only offer stretches and only in approved colors: black, navy, and silver. Each comes equipped with oriental carpets, phone, moon roof, bar, television, VCR, and radio/tape player. CD players are available on request, but it's the VCRs that hold the greatest appeal and are giving Dav-El an edge in this highly competitive market. Scott sees corporate execs as "video-conscious," now demanding VCR-equipped cars as insistently as they once demanded those with phones. He says they now forego reading the paper in favor of reviewing tapes of meetings or seminars.

All major credit cards are accepted, but house accounts are so much more convenient—no bothering with tearing up those troublesome carbons, and you can say charge it in any of the 300 cities worldwide that they service.

While we can personally attest to Dav-El's commitment to confidentiality where their clients are concerned, we do happen to know of one international celebrity who wouldn't dream of driving with anyone else. We think Madame Hanae Mori's worldwide reputation as a stickler for excellence may be just about the best testimony to the quality of Dav-El's service—they do deliver on Scott's edict of "clean cars on time."

K.A.L.

(212) 979-9393
(718) 392-8633

Theirs was a marriage, or at least a partnership, made in heaven. Frank Bernhard had been a driver for a decade, so he knew all about difficult clients and their even more difficult demands. Frank Ward had been in the limo business for a quarter of a century, so he knew even more about satisfying their every need. They teamed up to put together a very good, very reliable, and very reasonably priced car service.

Like a lot of marriages, the Bernhard-Ward union broke up, leaving Frank Bernhard custody of the business. Nothing about the quality of the service has suffered from Frank's single-parent status. The fleet is large and varied. Twenty-five stretch limos alone, at your service for $40 an hour, plus twenty percent gratuity.

Of course, the more secure among us prefer the anonymity of an ordinary black sedan to tool around the city at $25 an hour. Either Lincoln or Cadillac town cars, they are quiet luxury personified, and all are equipped with telephones. Take one to JFK for the flat rate of $35, plus tolls and tip—not much difference between that and the cost of a taxi. But the difference in comfort is immeasurable. And there's bound to be no comparison between the drivers. Frank requires his to be well groomed, to wear a coat and, even more important, to have an excellent command of the English language.

In fact, service is so important to Frank that he puts all his drivers through a rigorous training program. He makes them study the city to get to know every nook and cranny. Then he tests the new drivers by having a veteran ride shotgun to make sure they can find every charming-but-difficult-to-find restaurant and out-of-the-way tourist attraction.

Polite is a big word in Frank's vocabulary too. You can be sure his drivers will be friendly and courteous, no matter how long you've kept them waiting at the airport. In actual fact, you won't have held them up because they make a habit of checking flights—no airport waiting charges from K.A.L.

No wonder Grace Jones depends upon K.A.L.'s services, as do executives from Citibank, Merrill Lynch, and the New York *Post.* In fact, *Post* owner Peter Kalikow hired K.A.L. to deliver the very first run of the Sunday edition. His glamorous wife uses their cars to go shopping. And we've been known to call Frank to ask him to take the dog to the vet or pick up a few parcels at Bloomingdale's. He's happy to dispatch drivers to run those time-consuming little errands for us, and for you too.

Call Anna Pawlyk to set up an account. Of course, cash or credit cards are also graciously accepted. That Frank, he's just *so* accommodating.

CHAPTER TWO

Hotels

Or a hotel is not a home?

*D*espite the fact that we use words like *comfy*, *cozy*, and *homey* to describe some of our favorite New York hostelries, none of them is really anything like home—nor should they be! Hotels should be exciting, magical places, where anything can happen and often does. (Get the Mayfair Regent's Dario Mariotti to tell you about the honeymoon couple, the roaring fire in the fireplace, the air conditioner, and the fire department.) There's a sense of romance, a dash of suspense about these elegant properties dedicated to spoiling their guests with sumptuous surroundings and impeccable service. Why, it's all enough to make you feel as though you're got this city of eight million stories and people at your feet.

So it's not surprising that some of the most amazing of New York's doyens are turning into hoteliers. After all, if that's where power and influence come together, that's where you'll find the Trumps and their breed. When Donald and Ivana can bounce Eloise from the Plaza, when Queen Leona can stand guard at the Palace, and when the Kaskels start putting new life into Doral properties you can be sure New York's rental beds and baths will never be quite the same again.

If they're not bed-and-breakfasts, it's only because of the scale. Everything in this city's larger than life—and the plaza suites and their rates are by no means an exception. Indeed they're certainly a very real exception to the rule that "what goes up must come down." New York hotel prices, in fact New York hotels themselves, never have come down and never will. The hotels just get remodeled; the prices just escalate. Today there are more luxury hotel rooms here than in any comparable piece of real estate in the world—especially any that originally sold for $24 worth of beads. And there are more every day.

New Yorkers, of course, don't stay in hotels, we just visit them. We visit them to eat, to socialize, to show off our latest gowns and jewels, our latest coiffures and beaus. But that's why they've become so important. When we're "seen" in public, we want the background to be just right. You are, after all, where you visit, so of course you are where you stay.

"You'll find me at the Pierre (or the Carlyle or the Mayfair or the Plaza or the whatever)" may be as much a social (or a business) statement as a way of reaching you when you're "in town." Each is a different look, a different feel, a different statement of who you are, where you're from, what you'll be doing, and what you're all about. We New Yorkers are always sizing you up. Consider this just another way of taking your measure.

The Carlyle

Madison Avenue at 76th Street	(212) 744-1600
New York, NY 10021	(800) 227-5737
	FAX (212) 717-4682

Often referred to as the "grande dame" of New York hotels, even by managers of rival properties, the Carlyle's 185 rooms make it neither the largest nor the smallest, and its fifty years make it neither the oldest nor the newest. Still, the Carlyle has carved a special niche in the city's hotel hierarchy. Its quiet luxury and large, protective staff make it an elegant, safe haven for the most discriminating world travelers, not to mention high-profile "bolters" like Annette Reed and Sid Bass.

Tucked away in a peaceful residential neighborhood on upper Madison Avenue, the Carlyle caters to a devoted international clientele. They've been going to the Carlyle for years, together with family and friends; they all regard the hotel as somewhat of a private preserve. You sort of have to know about the Carlyle, because owner Peter Sharp does very little to promote it. He feels his money is better spent ensuring his guests' comfort—better spent on the little touches like a staff of four hundred, which gives the Carlyle one of the highest guest-to-staff ratios in the city.

Individually and as a whole, the Carlyle's staff is one of its greatest assets. Led by the charming Frank Bowling, the vice president and manager who learned his trade at London's famed Connaught, they are unfailingly discreet and sincerely accommodating. They are also fiercely loyal to the hotel. Frank is fond of telling the story about the young man who came to the Carlyle to apply for a position as a bellman.

He was told, "Your mother had to have put you on the list at birth, and someone has to die." Therefore, he was not destined to join the ranks of a staff dedicated to making the hotel worthy of the likes of Prince Philip.

When he's in town, the prince opts for Suite 2701, with its broad views across Central Park to the West Side. We don't know if Prince Philip plays, but a grand piano is at his disposal in the huge living room. The suite goes for $900 if just one bedroom is required; $950 includes the second, optional bedroom.

For less princely sums there are the single or double rooms from $240 to $325. All boast VCRs and well-equipped bathrooms complete with scales, real hair driers (not those nasty no-power jobs attached to the walls in some hotels), and portable makeup mirrors. Most even have Jacuzzis. We are particularly enamored of one of the Carlyle's little extras—the breakfast tray tucked away in the closet of every room. What a treat to cope with New York's Sunday-morning ritual of poring through the *Times* while enjoying breakfast in bed.

Room 305 is another pleasant place to play the person of leisure. A warm and cheerful double, it has a nice foyer and overlooks Madison Avenue. Most impressively, its closet space is outlandish. All for only $280 a night.

The Carlyle is very much an integral part of its tony neighborhood. Indeed, the hotel is considered by many New Yorkers to be a civilized retreat from their manic city. It offers excellent food in an elegant, timeless setting, so inviting that many area residents consider its dining room an extension of their own. The hotel bar, called Bemelman's, serves as a local pub—the drinks generous, the service attentive, the dusky lighting just dim enough to lend a sense of romantic intimacy, just bright enough to observe regulars like Senator Pat Moynihan holding court.

The Cafe Carlyle offers some of the best entertainment in town, especially during May, June, November, and December, when the legendary Bobby Short is in residence. The pied piper of café society never fails to charm with his witty renditions of popular songs, old and new. Bobby does two shows a night, at 9:30 P.M. and 11:30 P.M. There's a $30 cover (but no minimum) and reservations are hard to come by, so plan ahead.

Of course, if you are a guest at the hotel, the resourceful head concierge, John Neary (a rookie by Carlyle standards with only ten years in service here), will make every effort to help with reservations. Similarly, maître d' Armand will do his best to oblige you for breakfast in the dining room, which is always crowded with neighborhood types who've made this the ultimate of the city's power breakfast sites. We know of one hotel guest who arrived at Armand's station at the same time as Henry Kissinger. The good doctor was politely told he would have to wait a bit for a table. The guest was seated first!

While bent on maintaining the Carlyle's unique brand of Old World sophistication, Peter Sharp and Frank Bowling do bow to current trends. They have recently installed a fitness center on the third floor for their guests' convenience. Predictably, it is small, understatedly elegant, hospitable, well equipped, and efficient—in a word, a microcosm of the hotel it serves.   ❦

The Doral Tuscany Hotel

120 East 39th Street	(212) 686-1600
between Lexington and Park	FAX (212) 779-7822
New York, NY 10016	

Robert Boyle, general manager of the Doral Tuscany, loves to remind people that his is a hotel at which "neither the past nor the present is forgotten." He's referring to the fact that the dual themes of then and now are intertwined throughout this delightful property hidden away in a residential neighborhood, yet conveniently midtown. It flaunts all the modern amenities expected of a fine hotel, as well as the old-fashioned personalized service so often forgotten by other luxury properties.

The Doral Tuscany is located in the historic Murray Hill section of the East Side, nestled between brownstones, courtyards, and mews. It's small (136 rooms and 16 suites) but elegant, catering to an upscale corporate crowd, attracted by its proximity to the centers of New York's business, entertainment, and fashion—all within just a few short blocks.

The rooms tend to be large and sunny, with push-button drapes, exceptionally good lighting, and walk-in closets. They have refrigerators stocked with complimentary beverages. All have marble bathrooms with immense tubs suitable for good, long, relaxing soaks—just the ticket at the end of a pressure-filled day of high-powered negotiations. The bathrooms are also thoughtfully equipped with phones, scales, hair driers, and magnifying mirrors.

Exercise bikes are just a phone call away. And newspapers arrive at the doorstep every morning as a matter of course.

Our favorite suite is 1501, with its welcoming foyer and large living room. A pleasing combination of overstuffed sofas and good reproductions makes it cozy and comfy; the large desk makes it practical. And the Jacuzzi and television in the bathroom make it fun. It rents for $400 a night.

Regular room rates run $195 to $220. One-bedroom suites range from $350 to $700, and there is a two-bedroom suite at $650.

Don't be surprised by a knock on the door just after you check in. The hotel believes in the practice of sending up tea. If you're a regular, your preferences in things like flowers and room service will be solicited and duly noted, ready thereafter for your arrival. Should you become a special favorite of Robert's, he might have some of his beloved chocolate popcorn delivered. It and a good book have kept us company through many an evening—delicious, but addictive.

Robert's remark about things past and present comes to mind when you enter the Doral Tuscany's restaurant, Time & Again. Designed to evoke turn-of-the-century New York, it is extremely attractive. The antiques, chandeliers, etched glass, and beveled mirrors truly recapture the style and grace of a bygone era. However, while Time & Again may favor the decor of yesterday, the food is definitely that of today. As conceived and executed by Derrick Dikkers, formerly the chef of the renowned Le Bel Age in Beverly Hills and chef saucier of Maxim's de Paris, the food has earned the Zagat guide's respect as one of the best hotel restaurants in the city.

The sweet potato soup with bacon, scallions, and sour cream followed by pheasant breast stuffed with foie gras, truffle, and vegetable julienne wrapped in a cabbage leaf is representative of the kitchen's flair. Open for breakfast, lunch, and dinner, Time & Again can accurately be described as moderately expensive, or just about what you would expect at a good hotel restaurant. Breakfast, including complimentary newspaper, pads with pens, and the use of tape recorders or portable telephones, starts at $7.50. Dinner is at least $90 for two, if you include a reasonably priced bottle of wine from the rather impressive list.

For private parties, Time & Again sets up the hotel's uniquely spectacular two-level Renaissance Room on the roof. The upper level is encased in glass, allowing the sun or the moon and the stars to join the fun. And the view is terrific.

Finally, you should know the Doral Tuscany owns a fitness center right around the corner at 90 Park Avenue. The facility is available free to hotel guests and opens at 6:00 A.M. for early-rising fitness buffs.

Whether you're more comfortable with the past or with the present, this sophisticated little enclave of civilized living enchants.   ❧

Grand Bay Hotel at Equitable Center

152 West 51st Street	(212) 765-1900
between 6th and 7th	(800) 237-0990
New York, NY 10010	FAX (212) 541-6604

If you want to give your regards to Old Broadway, there's no better place to do it than the Grand Bay Hotel. It's the one truly great hotel in the theater district. Before the 1920s-vintage tattered old Taft Hotel was reincarnated as the Grand Bay in August 1987, the great stars went to work in the area's theaters, then fled after the show for luxury digs scattered all over town. Now there's a convenient hotel up to their exacting standards.

Indeed, it's up to a lot of people's standards, especially its 178 rooms and 52 suites. First, they tend to be unusually large—an average 450 square feet. They triumph with marble foyers, sitting areas, TVs in the marbled bathrooms, multiline telephones, hair driers, Frette linens, and elegant architectural details like coffered ceilings and crown moldings.

We're rather fond of the mauve and black Art Deco look of Suite 512. A junior suite, it rents for $385 a night. Suite 635 looks like a stage set for a Noel Coward play with its theatrical black-and-white, large-checked marble floor, overstuffed sofas, bold black lacquer, gilt, and cherry coffee table, striking black moldings, and dramatic lighting. The powder room off the living area is graced by an enchanting Deco sculpture of an antelope. An enormous sleigh bed dominates the bedroom. The closets benefit from thoughtfully placed sachets, while the bathroom offers something truly unique—a toddler-sized robe to go with the ubiquitous monogrammed terries for adults. It's all very grand at $675 a night.

Addressing the bang-for-the-buck issue, singles start at $255, doubles at $275, with junior suites from $365. One-bedrooms begin at $475 and two-bedrooms at $925.

As for dining, there's Bellini, owned and operated by the fabled Harry Cipriani of Venice. Harry's quite a character and has quite a following; when not at Bice, fashion's famous can often be found here. Open for lunch and dinner, Bellini serves what it describes as innovative Northern Italian cuisine. We call it mediocre, served with much too much attitude. Still, it's a stylish, energetic place that's good for celebrity-sighting.

The hotel's Mezzanine Café, overlooking the elegant lobby, serves only breakfast. Otherwise, it is available for private functions, seating up to sixty people.

For less private affairs, there's the lobby lounge, an intimate and gracious setting for cocktails. Harold Danko tinkles the ivories most evenings from 6:30 to 11:30. If he's not available there's always a substitute player, so you can count on the lounge for an entertaining after-dinner or after-theater drink seven nights a week.

In addition to the show-biz crowd, the hotel is very popular with English, French, and German businesspeople, who take advantage of the complimentary limousine service to Wall Street. They also like the beepers the hotel offers each guest so there's no missing those important calls from home.

The Grand Bay is yet another sign of the West Side renaissance that will irrevocably change its character. At least, the hotel is a better, more necessary, and more welcome addition than most, so much so that Park Lane Hotels International out of Hong Kong is considering buying it and changing the name to Parc Fifty-one.   ☙

The Helmsley Palace

455 Madison Avenue	(212) 888-7000
between 50th and 51st	(800) 221-4982
New York, NY 10022	FAX (212) 355-0820

While Leona Helmsley claims the title of Queen in those seemingly endless ads that go on and on page after page, it is general manager Freeman Hill who really sits on the Helmsley Palace's throne. He appears a benevolent monarch, ruling his kingdom in a dignified manner, with a sparkling sense of humor.

The humor is especially important when overseeing a hotel of this size—1,180 rooms. Despite the hotel's ability to accommodate large groups and conventions, you'll be pleased to know that neither the Queen nor Freeman will allow them.

The *Palace* in the name of this flagship of the Helmsley-owned hotels refers not to its palatial size, but to the origins of the Stanford White–designed mansions that form the nucleus of its public rooms. Built in 1882, the former Villard Houses, a cluster of townhomes, were inspired by the Palazzo della Cancelleria in Rome, and in true Vatican style, once served as home for the Archdiocese of New York on one side, the venerable publishing house of Random House on the other. Real estate tycoon Harry Helmsley (husband to Leona) united the once-private residences, restored many of the rooms to their original splendor, and added a dark bronze glass, fifty-one-story tower to create the Helmsley Palace in 1979.

Today, you can marvel at the ornate gold-leafed carved wall panels, the vaulted two-story-high gilt ceiling, the stained-glass windows, and the John La Farge murals of the aptly named Gold Room, where princes of the Church as well as mere mortals once strolled. True to its roots as a music room, a harpist or string quartet is usually on duty in this exquisite sanctuary where breakfast and tea are served.

A former dining room now functions as the Palace Bar. Its dark carved walnut paneling and huge deep-red marble fireplace seem suited to an exclusive men's club. The unusual sliding doors embellished with tiny nailheads in intricate patterns add to the reassuring masculinity of the room, which probably should have been a bar in the first place!

The cocktail lounge just beyond the bar and overlooking Madison Avenue is another beautifully restored room. Designed as a triple drawing room, it is preserved as an elegant space for socializing. The walls bear the original framed panels depicting royalty at play, painted by the French artist, P. V. Galland. Given Leona's weakness for elaborate designer gowns, we wonder if she's ever noticed that these royals are portrayed in peasant costume.

The historic wing of the Palace also boasts a restored library as conference room, two restaurants, and a ballroom. All the sleeping quarters are found in the adjoining tower, despite the fact that only two hundred are specifically designated as "Tower" rooms or suites. Since those designated "Tower" are on the higher floors, they tend to be larger and benefit from "private" (read *faster*) registration desk and elevators. We suggest you book one of them.

Of course, you pay a bit more, but it's worth it. Take Suite 4109, with its view across Rockefeller Center all the way to the Hudson River—truly spectacular. You can gaze to your heart's content from almost anywhere in this one- (or two-) bedroom beauty. There is even a window in the full-scale kitchen, a feature considered to be one of *the* New York status symbols. Done in the same rusty-rose colored tones the glorious sunsets outside reflect, this suite rents for $695 with one bedroom, $950 with two.

Single and double rooms, regular and Tower, range from $230 to $320. Suites start with juniors at $395 and go through several categories to the "two-bedroom corner" at $950.

However, if you really want to live quite literally high on the hog, reserve one of the triplexes that take up significant portions of the top three stories of the hotel. Nestled in the tower's four corners, they were the first triplex apartments offered in New York for long-term lease or transient occupancy. As such they were an immediate hit and remain booked six to eight months in advance, even at $2,500 a night. Michael Jackson always stays in one, although his chimp (presumably chaperoned) usually stays across town at the Parker Meridien.

The triplexes are the closest we've seen to the sort of hotel suites Fred Astaire and/or Ginger Rogers always occupied in the movies. They are nothing short of drop-dead glamorous. In 5301, the marble foyer opens into a two-story glass-walled living room, suitable for entertaining seventy-five or so of your closest friends. The formal dining room seats twelve with room to spare. The spacious kitchen is fully equipped to deal with virtually any food-related activity.

A curved staircase perfect for very noticeable entrances sweeps up to the two bedrooms on the second level, with its balcony surveying the living room scene; there is a third bedroom on the first floor. For more furtive and less strenuous comings-and-goings, there is a Lilliputian private elevator linking all three levels.

The third floor is devoted to a wonderful solarium. Its woodburning fireplace, full bar, powder room, and private rooftop terrace make it a very special place indeed.

Standing on that terrace with all of Manhattan spread out below, beckoning with the exhilarating combination of sights and sounds that is the city's siren song, you can't help but feel regal. Suddenly, Leona can almost be forgiven her excesses. As owner of this palace, they may just be part of her royal prerogative!

The Lowell

28 East 63rd Street   (212) 838-1400
between Madison and Park   FAX (212) 319-4230
New York, NY 10021

There's a little bit of England on a pretty, tranquil tree-lined street between Madison and Park Avenues—the Lowell, a hotel owing much of its sumptuous graciousness of a grand English country house to Martin A. Hale. As operations manager, he learned all there is to know about running a memorable hotel at Claridge's in London.

Not surprisingly, it's a particular favorite with visiting Brits, but the hotel also serves as New York base for Americans who treasure the luxurious, quiet privacy the Lowell affords its guests—people like Stephanie Powers and Shelley Long.

With only sixty rooms, fifty of them suites, the Lowell ranks as one of the city's smallest hostelries. The relatively large staff, two to each guest, enables resident manager Lynn Hunter Gray to pamper every guest, to humor every whim.

The elite landmark building, former home to the likes of Scott and Zelda Fitzgerald, Dorothy Parker, and Noel Coward, has recently undergone a $25 million facelift. The boutique-sized lobby echos the Lowell's original Art Deco splendor, with a rare console signed by Edgar Brandt and palatial doors connecting it to the Post House restaurant next door. But a French Empire influence predominates. Pale gray silk swathes the walls, which are adorned with *faux* marble wainscoting accented by gold-plated bronze moldings and period appliqués. A French carpet inspired by one originally in Empress Josephine's bedroom covers the polished marble floor.

Perhaps taking their cues from the origins of that carpet, the staff cheerfully works at making you feel like royalty. A liveried doorman ushers you into the hotel with pomp and circumstance. The charming reception staff, appropriately dressed in formal morning attire, greets you by name. They even escort you to your room which is eclectically furnished with French and Oriental pieces, punctuated by the presence of the occasional Art Deco lamp.

Each room and suite is different. Many have working fireplaces (logs are supplied for $3.50 each) and terraces with stunning cityscape views.

All have Italian marble baths and double-thick casement windows that may make the Lowell a site for the most restful nights in town.

We're especially fond of Suite 16A at $460 a night. Its peach walls, lush taupe carpet, rich green drapes, pink and gray chintz sofa, and black lacquer furniture harken to the Lowell's Art Deco days. The entrance foyer doubles as dining area with a black marble table surrounded by four black leather chairs. The kitchen, typical of Lowell suites, lends new meaning to the description of "fully equipped"; it's truly complete with a stocked refrigerator, dishwasher, oven, and most impressively, pots, pans, china, crystal, and silverware.

For such a small hotel, the rate schedule is a bit convoluted. There are singles and doubles at $260 and $280, respectively. A junior suite is $360, while one-bedrooms are $460 and something called the Lowell Suite is $520. Two-bedrooms go for $640. The marvelous three-bedroom penthouse rents for $1,200 a night.

Although the independently owned Post House, one of New York's most celebrated chophouses, serves as a nice appendage next door, the real culinary gem of the Lowell is the Pembroke Room. Discreetly and unusually tucked away on the second floor, there are no signs to direct you to its whereabouts. Best categorized as a traditional English tea sa-lon, this exquisite little room seats only thirty-two. Open for breakfast, lunch, tea, and cocktails, its faithful clientele tend to regard it as their discovery, one they're loath to share. Dustin Hoffman often holds break-fast meetings here, presumably because he knows he can deal with busi-ness uninterrupted by well-meaning fans.

Surrounded by needlepoint carpets, yellow chintzes, crystal wall sconces, and upholstered chairs in a "nice English stripe," you can par-take of such delicacies as beluga caviar or duck with wild mushroom sauce. For breakfast, there's a choice of Continental for $11 or full-English for $15. Tea is $15.50 and the à la carte menu for lunch and hors d'oeuvres ranges from $8 to $26.

The Pembroke Room is truly fit for the English country squire who might indeed find himself very much at home in the Lowell, his little bit of England in old New York.

The Mark

Madison Avenue at 77th Street   (212) 744-4300
New York, NY 10021   FAX (212) 744-2749
(800) THE MARK

Just when we thought we'd covered all the city's best luxury hotels, another player burst on the scene—The Mark on the Upper East Side in territory formerly dominated by The Carlyle and The Stanhope. Now they've got serious competition in this 186-room property, the result of a much-heralded $30 million renovation of the old Madison Hotel.

The entrance, on a lovely tree-lined street between Madison and Fifth, is distinguished by the building's landmark tower and four brass flagpoles, which are lit at night to emit a welcoming beacon. A striking retro entry and marquee are accented with brass. Elegant black vitroglass makes up part of the facade with the doorway opening onto the Neoclassical lobby. The decor was inspired by the rich style favored by eighteenth-century English architect Sir John Soane—Italian marble, eighteenth-century Piranesi prints, and floral motifs, all lending a delicate refinement to the English-Italian elegance.

Beyond the marble entrance and reception area with its intimate little forty-seat bar is the multilevel Mark's Restaurant, graced with brass-topped wrought-iron balustrades, marble columns, and ebony and gold-leaf moldings. Done in tones of champagne, salmon, and oyster, it is quite lovely and likely to be a well-received addition to the East Side dining scene, once the kitchen is finished. Actually, the Mark built three kitchens in the formerly kitchenless building (the Madison and its predecessor, the Hyde Park, were residential hotels). One kitchen will serve the restaurant, another room service, and the third banquets. It would seem management takes food service very seriously indeed.

Actually, service, period seems to be the hallmark of the Rafael Group, whose motto is "Your demands, our obsession" and whose other world-class properties include the Breidenbacher Hof in Dusseldorf, the Turnberry Isle Yacht and Country Club in North Miami, the Hôtel du Rhône in Geneva, Hotel Bora Bora in Tahiti, and the Hotel Pierre Milano in Milan. Head concierge Giorgio Finocchiaro is a prime example of the hotel's commitment to first-class service. If he looks familiar, it's because for years he took the best possible care of The Pierre's discriminating and demanding guests. He was spirited away and is now working the same miracles for The Mark's guests.

General manager Raymond Bickson, a graduate of the prestigious Lausanne Hotel Management School, is further proof. His goal is to have The Mark "represent the basics of what the hotel business is and should always be about—to achieve a level of personalized service where the guest feels genuinely at home. I want to ensure that the Mark establishes a reputation as the kind of hotel one keeps returning to."

Given the level of the service and amenities such as double-line phones with fax capabilities, VCRs, gleaming black pantries with refrigerators, marble or tiled bathrooms with tubs and separate glass stall showers, heated towel bars, heat lamps, bathroom scales, and ceramic bowls of potpourri, we're betting on Raymond fulfilling his ambitions for the hotel.

The Presidential Suite is nothing short of spectacular with its brown-and-white marble circular foyer dominated by graceful columns. The corner living room, overlooking both Madison Avenue and East 77th Street, is sumptuously decorated in beige and blue. It boasts a wet bar, antique prints, and access to a terrific terrace. The kitchen makes entertaining so much easier on the staff, and the library/den is perfect for curling up with a good book (preferably this one). The master bedroom and bath are spacious, as are the closets. There are three televisions—living room, bedroom, and den—as well as a VCR and a CD player. The hotel's extensive video and CD library service both. It's all yours for $900 a night.

If you arrive in the winter and think you can forego the terrace, Suites 1510 and 1610 are otherwise identical to the Presidential. With one bedroom, one and a half baths (the library/den has a powder room), they rent for $725. A second bedroom can be added for $285.

Number 1418 is called the Terrace Suite. Its large living room in shades of doe and forest green leads out to a glorious terrace outfitted with pretty patio furniture and flower boxes. The bedroom on the other side of the graceful double set of French doors features a king-size bed and window seats. The enormous bathroom is divided into three sections, one for the double-sinked vanity, one for the tub, and one for the shower. Tough to beat for $550.

Any of what The Mark calls its deluxe rooms at $285 are on the special side. A cozy feeling prevails in these large double rooms with the table and chairs placed by the window for in-room dining. There's also a writing desk ample enough for real work and a comfy sofa.

The hotel is so new that it hasn't had much of a chance to develop that regular clientele that Raymond wants. But we feel comfortable speculating that The Mark will attract a sophisticated international crowd with more than its share of celebrities who will appreciate the hotel's discreet elegance. As for The Carlyle across the street—watch out!   ☙

The Mayfair Regent

Park Avenue at 65th Street	(212) 288-0800
New York, NY 10021	(800) 223-0542
	FAX (212) 737-0538

A number of New York's current crop of deluxe hotels can lay claim to long histories, but only The Mayfair Regent's Dario Mariotti maintains his is a "hotel with soul." As general manager and resident since Regent International Hotels purchased the former Mayfair House in 1978, he should know. In fact, we suspect he is the very embodiment of that soul.

Certainly, he has imbued The Mayfair Regent with the elegantly intimate feel of a posh European hotel, the sort of place that used to be the seat of a noble family before inheritance taxes. There is something reminiscent of an Italian palazzo about the exquisite lobby. Perhaps it's the lush tones of sienna, ochre, and terra cotta that manage to harmonize what might otherwise be considered a compilation of fifty years of decorating trends—Tudor beamed ceilings and a baronial fireplace alongside Moorish arches. It's very grand, yet warm and inviting. It begs to be sat in, and is in fact one of the few hotel lobbies truly conducive to meeting and greeting.

Like any palazzo worth its salt, The Mayfair Regent plays host to royalty—of several varieties. There's the regular garden variety like the King of Spain. Then there's the Hollywood strain like Barbra Streisand. The Mayfair's special brand of luxury is also appealing to Issey Miyaki and members of the Missoni family, representatives of fashion royalty.

So what exactly does draw them to the hotel? We imagine it's all those little thoughtful touches Dario provides. Take the gray umbrella tucked away in every one of the eighty rooms and 120 suites. Actually, feel free to take it—Dario expects it and delights in telling tales of Mayfair regulars recognizing each other on rainy streets all over the world by their umbrellas.

Dario equips his guests to deal with dry spells as well. There is a humidifier in every room. Practical matters aside, the decor is complemented by roses, but never red roses. Dario prefers a softer touch—shades of peach and coral, which he laughingly describes as being much more flattering to everyone.

The level of service that Dario affords his guests is another element of the palacelike quality of the hotel. It's as if you have been assigned your own personal staff during your stay—standard operating procedure in any palace—including your affable doormen, capable of cab-hailing miracles in even the foulest weather. Likewise, the gloved elevator attendants, who are there only to ensure that you get to your room as quickly as possible. Surely that puller of strings par excellence, concierge Bruno Brunelli, must be part of your personal entourage. And there's Mel, for whom everyone clamors. Mel oversees the hotel's laundry. He has such a way with shirts that many guests make it a regular practice to send them to The Mayfair Regent for Mel's tender loving care from wherever they happen to be, even from their homes!

With so much to offer, it's little wonder the hotel is often full, particularly in September, October, April, and May. So try to book well in advance.

When you call, you might want to reserve Suite 1015, if you're in the market for a one-bedroom number with a rate of $405 per night. Tones of celedon green abound. The living room has a plush yet homey feel to it, with its mirrored bar all set up for entertaining. Another favorite in the one-bedroom category is 206, complete with wood-burning fireplace and dining area at $800.

If you prefer a two-bedroom suite, try 803, which runs $1,700 a night. It, too, has a fireplace, not to mention a Jacuzzi, enormous closets (a Mayfair trademark), and delightful views of Park Avenue.

Less spectacular but equally elegant single and double rooms can be had from $255 to $275.

No discussion of The Mayfair Regent is complete without mentioning the hotel's tea, which has become a New York institution. Admittedly, almost every luxury hotel in the city now engages in the practice. But when Dario started it as one of the European traditions he brought to the Mayfair, it was considered novel. It remains the best tea in town, attracting a glamorous crowd of natives. They happily nibble away at the delicate finger sandwiches and sinful pastries while comparing notes on the day's news as reported by Suzy, Liz Smith, Billy Norwich, or Cindy Adams. Dario relishes their presence. He knows a little gossip is good for the soul, and particularly good for his beloved Mayfair Regent.   ❦

Morgans

237 Madison Avenue	(212) 686-0300
between 37th and 38th	(800) 334-3408
New York, NY 10016	FAX (212) 779-8352

No question about it, Morgans is different. There's no impressive porte cochere (not even an awning) and no sign outside to distinguish the building as a hotel. Furthermore, Morgans does not advertise.

Yet, since the faded former Executive Hotel was renovated and reopened in 1984 as Morgans (in honor of the legendary J.P., whose nearby home now serves as the Pierpont Morgan Library), it has enjoyed an occupancy rate that makes other hotels green with envy.

By breaking all the rules, Morgans attracts a glitzy, showbizzy crowd— Cher, Billy Joel and Christie Brinkley, Farrah Fawcett, and Oprah Winfrey. And, only a hop, skip, and a jump away from fashion's fabled Seventh Avenue, Morgans is a favorite with visiting designers like Giorgio Armani and Azzedine Alaia.

But then, what would you expect from Ian Schrager and the late Steve Rubell, the boys who revolutionized the club scene with the now-historic Studio 54? They broke a few rules there, too, and for their pains, served some time in prison, courtesy of the IRS. Having paid their debt to society, they were once again its toast (until Steve's recent death) with a burgeoning hotel empire that prides itself on breaking with tradition. Along with partner Philip Pilevsky, the Rubell/Schrager partnership also owns the Royalton, and plans were afoot for more properties. The settling of Steve's estate, however, may shake things up a bit. It's bound to take a while.

In the meantime, the Morgans difference is clear from the moment you step across the unadorned threshold and into a lobby like no other, thanks to Andrée Putman, who designed all Morgans' interiors. Predictably, the "French empress of style" had never done a hotel before, which is exactly why she was commissioned. Putman created a striking environment in stark black and white, softened by shades of gray and hints of beige, green, and melon.

Likewise, the friendly, eager, and self-consciously attractive staff was hired because of its lack of previous hotel experience. Trained never to say no, they cheerfully cater to your every whim—from the truly radical notion of orchestrating the delivery of a meal from your favorite New

York restaurant (no restrictions on room service hours or menu here) to arranging for an in-room massage.

Beyond the efforts of the accommodating staff, there are plenty of creature comforts to keep you from venturing forth from any of Morgans' 112 rooms and 28 suites. Down pillows and comforters are the norm on the low-profile beds, along with Oxford cotton sheets. Of course, each room features the standard-issue goodies of any luxury hotel in New York—two-line telephones, stereo color television, refrigerators, etc. It's their unique, strangely serene surroundings that make the difference here—Putman's blend of Art Deco, high tech, and Oriental motifs lend a personal touch.

Nothing about the decor suggests "hotel." Rather, you feel as if you are in a home worthy of the pages of *Architectural Digest*. Indeed, the powerful black-and-white photographs Robert Mapplethorpe created for each of the rooms may make you feel as if you are the guest of a fabulously wealthy collector.

But you don't have to be a J. P. Morgan to stay here. Singles start at $195, doubles at $215, and suites start at $380.

Still, you can spend a lot of money, if you so desire—just ask for Penthouse 1909. It's quite spectacular, resembling the Hollywood version of what a New York apartment should be—two stories separated by a grand curving staircase, elegant living room, dining room suitable for formal entertaining, kitchen, three spacious bedrooms with magnificent baths, den/library boasting a desk larger than most CEOs, and two terraces showcasing panoramic views of the city. At $1,200 a night it's a bargain—a year's stay would barely make a down payment on a comparable piece of Manhattan real estate! ❦

Peninsula Hotel

700 Fifth Avenue	(212) 247-2200
at 55th Street	(800) 262-9467
New York, NY 10019	FAX (212) 903-3949

Just when we'd all but given up on the once-proud Gotham ever seeing the light of day again as a world-class hotel, the Peninsula Group stepped in like a knight in shining armor. Their purchase of the property was truly the perfect happy ending to a long story full of twists and turns. First there was the mysterious Swiss investor who bought the Gotham and set about renovating it, spending huge amounts of, apparently, other people's money. The city was agog with tales of lavish expenditures and questionable taste. Plans for purple marble Jacuzzis in the rooms (not the bathrooms—the rooms) were cause for particular comment.

In any case, the project faltered and the Gotham faced an unfinished and uncertain future. Things looked a little brighter when Pierre Cardin and the Hotel Maxim's de Paris group took over, actually opening the hotel in December 1987. Reviews were mixed, prices high, and business never very good. Rumors of its imminent demise circulated almost from the beginning. People began to wonder if the site, seemingly so perfect for a hotel right on the corner of 55th and Fifth, was jinxed.

Enter the Peninsula Group and their first foray into the American market with the $127 million purchase of the hotel in October 1988. Enter a major new player on the city's hospitality industry scene.

The Peninsula New York, latest sister to the venerable Peninsula Hong Kong, has 250 rooms and suites, two restaurants, and a trilevel fitness center, that is the largest, most extensive such facility of any New York hotel. Predictably, rooms feature two-line telephones, writing desks, oversized marble bathrooms with six-foot tubs, silk-padded hangers, and refrigerators. All very nice and very comfortable, but what truly makes the Peninsula stand out is the service. It's unparalleled.

General manager Manfred Timmel has assembled a young and enthusiastic staff trained in the traditions of the Hong Kong property, which has been celebrated for its incredible service for over sixty years. True, in New York, twin white-liveried doormen don't fling open the double glass doors on your arrival as they do in Hong Kong, where there's also a white-liveried floor attendant to wait on your every need. In fact, a number of staff were sent to the flagship property to learn first-hand the Peninsula style of gracious attention to detail. They learned how to anticipate guest needs and how to enjoy providing attentive assistance.

Still, the staff at the Peninsula New York will routinely pack and unpack guests' clothes, as well as park their cars and do their laundry seven days a week. Room service is offered twenty-four hours a day, with only a fifteen-minute wait for breakfast if you order in the morning. Of course, instructions left on the hang-tag on the door the night before assure its delivery precisely when you want it, along with *The New York Times* and any other paper you might request. They'll even bring it on a tray if you desire, so you won't have to spend the morning banging into a large, bulky serving cart. Most impressively, fresh buckets of ice are placed in each room twice a day, so refreshments from the minibar can actually be acceptable substitutes for a drink in the main bar downstairs.

Still, we do recommend you check out the stately Gotham Lounge with its grand piano playing softly in the background. Overlooking 55th Street on one side and the lobby's imposing double staircase on the other, it's a lovely, sophisticated room.

The Belle Epoque decor of the Adrienne Restaurant reminds you of the Maxim's regime, but the food is vintage Peninsula—Franco/Swiss accented by Oriental influences, classic but not too heavy, with an emphasis on seafood—a tribute to the Swiss hotel schools where many of the Peninsula Group's executives learned their art, and the Asian capital where they've practiced it. For less formal dining there's Le Bistro d' Adrienne, featuring traditional brasserie fare.

However, we tend to rely on room service, because we just love to be pampered. Besides, it means spending more time in the pretty Art Nouveau–decorated rooms. We think Suite 1601 is one of the best at $850 a night. The living room is done in soothing tones of rose and celedon and benefits from a large powder room and a wet bar. There's a small dining area that doubles as a respectable work space. The bedroom is good size, the bathroom large with one of those big tubs you can stretch out in and a separate stall shower.

Room 1805 is another winner with its extra large foyer leading to the bedroom, which has a cozy sitting area overlooking Fifth Avenue. The view is spectacular, great for parade watching. There's even a window in the bathroom, so you won't miss a step—all for $430, the top rate for a deluxe room.

Others described as superior start at $220. Executive suites at $510, with one-bedrooms between $750 and $850. Two-bedrooms go for $1,205, and the price of the Presidential Suite, luxuriating in over 2,500 square feet of living space, is quoted upon request.

Besides the service, the other true distinction of the Peninsula is the fitness center on the twenty-first through twenty-third floors. Including a rooftop swimming pool, whirlpool, steam room, sauna, massage facility, weight training and aerobics rooms, and hair salon, it's a full-service, glass-enclosed spa surveying the New York skyline. Automatically available to hotel guests, it also offers corporate memberships to area businesses.

Forgot to bring your bathing suit or workout togs? Once informed of your plight, concierge Renato Della Noce will quickly remedy the situation. Typical of Peninsula efficiency, he'll even satisfy your taste in color and style!

Having whipped this property into shape and with plans to open a second hotel in Beverly Hills, the Peninsula Group is well on its way to becoming a serious competitor for America's major luxury hotel groups.

The Pierre

Fifth Avenue at 61st Street	(212) 838-8000
New York, NY 10021	(800) 332-3442
	FAX (212) 758-1615

In real estate they say that "location, location, location" is everything. In the hospitality business it's "service, service, service." At The Pierre you get the best of both worlds—an unbeatable site on the corner of 61st and Fifth within walking distance of the city's best museums, restaurants, and shopping. And, the service is impeccable. It's no wonder that much of the Pierre is devoted to private residences—only 205 rooms and suites are available for transients.

Built sixty years ago by Charles Pierre (with a little help from friends like E. F. Hutton and Walter P. Chrysler), the hotel was described in a 1929 *New York Times* article as exclusive and "characterized by its simplicity and refinement." The Pierre remains all of those things under the regime of Four Seasons Hotels Ltd.

Elite is the best way to describe the clientele here, be they guests or the locals, who use The Pierre's extraordinary catering facilities for some of the city's most talked-about parties. The ballroom is a gleaming jewel, the food perfection. Just ask catering director Herb Rose to do what he regularly does for the likes of Barbara Walters and Merv Adelson. Their recent Pierre soirée was dubbed by several columnists "the Party of the Year." (Though Henry Kissinger's birthday party was nothing to sneeze at either!)

Should you enter The Pierre from Fifth Avenue, don't be put off by the rather pedestrian institutional look of this lobby-cum-corridor. Keep moving and look to your left, where you will be enchanted by the sight of the Rotunda. It's one of the prettiest public rooms in New York. Round, as its name suggests, the Rotunda envelops you in whimsy—muraled walls soar two stories to meet the domed ceiling. Cherubim frolic with pagan gods. Toga-clad men converse with women in Renaissance garb.

Speculating about the story line of the murals and spotting all their historical contradictions can amuse you for hours. We recommend doing it over tea, which is a particular treat here.

Just beyond the Rotunda is the Café Pierre, a luxurious culinary oasis. Dignified in its soothing tones of gray, enlivened by lovely crystal chandeliers and wall fixtures, it is an intimate room. The food lives up to the setting and the little bar is the perfect place to cap any dinner. Actually, it's a popular place to repair to after a lot of activities—work, for instance. The daily 5:00–7:30 "Happy Hour" is made happier by complimentary hors d'oeuvres. The Café Pierre also attracts the posttheater crowd, who relax in the comfortable armchairs and love seats (real furniture, not the kind usually found in bars) while they review the show.

The real lobby is entered from 61st Street and is appropriately refined. The wing chairs arranged in conversational groupings are the perfect place to camp while doing a little people-watching.

There's plenty to watch. The Pierre is a favorite with Hollywood's old guard A list—Jimmy Stewart, Audrey Hepburn, Red Buttons, and Charles Bronson. The hotel also attracts an international clientele. Indeed, vice president and managing director George Schwab, who presides over The Pierre with such thoughtful, meticulous care, maintains that only forty percent of his guests are American. The remainder include the likes of Princess Michael of Kent and Prime Minister Brian Mulroney of Canada, who's doing his patriotic though certainly pleasant duty by staying at The Pierre. After all, Four Seasons is a Canadian company.

He's also doing his not-inconsequential bit for the balance of payments with rooms from $295 a night, suites at $520 to $2,000. One of our favorites is 2804, a one-bedroom for $1,200, with its wonderful view across Central Park to the Wollman ice-skating rink and beyond to the grand old buildings lining Central Park West. Highly polished marble floors and regal English furniture make it feel very grand. The bedroom is a cheerful delight in lemon yellow and sea green, while the dressing area doubles as den or office with a large desk capable of supporting any number of piles of important papers. The black-and-white marble bathroom is nothing short of magnificent.

For something cozier, there are several "Boudoir" suites—3708 for instance. The bedroom benefits from the warm glow of tones of peach and blue and is augmented by a very large dressing area with lounge chair and desk set. There's a nice view here too, facing north up the East Side. It rents for $520.

Life at The Pierre is indeed sweet, made all the more so by George Schwab's edict that guests' needs should be anticipated and satisfied before they have a chance to voice them. With a 2.5-to-1 staff-to-guest ratio, his philosophy is not just lip service, it is a reality. Concierge Tito Fornari, who speaks six languages, has been catering to the needs of the Pierre's clientele for the past five years. Even if you're out of New York and need something done in the city, call Tito. He works miracles.

Service and location. Location and service. Two hallmarks so many hotels strive to attain and so many fail. Thank goodness for The Pierre!

Plaza Athénée

37 East 64th Street	(212) 734-9100
between Madison and Park	(800) 225-5843
New York, NY 10021	FAX (212) 772-0958

Given the frenzy produced by a public sighting of such glamour queens as Elizabeth Taylor and Joan Collins, we can forgive the rather forbidding presence of the three security guards permanently installed in the small lobby of the Plaza Athénée. They keep a watchful eye on the hotel's single entrance, allowing the Plaza Athénée a right to its claim as the most secure hotel in New York. Everyone has to pass the guards' not terribly friendly, though always polite, scrutiny for the privilege of appreciating this sister hotel of Paris' renowned Plaza Athénée.

Rest assured, it's worth the effort. After all, this intimate property (only 160 rooms) had a formidable reputation to live up to. Every effort was made to ensure that the New York hotel captured the ambience and spirit for which its Paris counterpart is so beloved—not an easy or an inexpensive task. The vintage 1927 former Hotel Alrae had been declared a landmark. So no exterior changes could be made; creative solutions had to be devised to deal with basics, like the installation of central air conditioning. Furthermore, the internal structural beams typical of 1920s construction made transforming the interior an equal challenge.

The bilevel lobby is the first clue to the extraordinary success of the project. While relatively small, its division into two levels by a *faux* marble balustrade and a set of shallow steps lends a sense of grandeur. The decor is magnificent—Italian marble floor, French antiques, large gilt mirrors, Oriental rugs. The classical and pastoral scenes of the specially commissioned tapestry wall coverings are reminiscent of the priceless Gobelins hanging in the long gallery of its Paris counterpart.

After registration at the eighteenth-century desk, management escorts guests to their rooms. The ride in one of the lovely leather-lined elevators is a clue to the delights of the hotel's rooms and suites, decorated in shades of peach and mushroom, mint-green and coral, mauve and beige. A variety of paisley Swiss fabrics coordinate the richly elegant look, complemented by specially designed Navarian carpets imported from Ireland. Most rooms have practical little pantries with a refrigerator and two-burner Corning stove. The rose-colored Portuguese marble bathrooms sport the usual luxury amenities like hair driers, makeup mirrors, scales, and designer toiletries (Lanvin, in this case), but general manager Bernard Lackner insists on a very special touch too—fresh flowers.

Room prices start at $265, going up to $395 for a deluxe double, like 1510 with its captivating little terrace. One-bedroom suites are $590. If you want one with a dining room and solarium, you're talking $975. For $895 you can get a two-bedroom. The rate for either of the two duplex penthouse suites with rooftop terraces is $1,950 a night.

The penthouses are truly majestic. How fitting that Princess Diana stayed in one during her triumphant solo visit to New York. The sumptuous living room with its marble floors and silk moiré walls is certainly fit for a princess, as is the dining room, which easily accommodates a dinner party for twelve. Of course, Di didn't have an opportunity to entertain during her stay, but the room may have come in handy for storing all those trunks of fabulous clothes that she used to dazzle the city. It will take New Yorkers years to stop talking about her dramatic entrance at the Brooklyn Academy of Music benefit in a glorious Victor Edelstein beaded satin evening gown.

Talk about eclectic clientele—Richard Pryor loves the Plaza Athénée so much, he onced stayed for three months! Julio Iglesias is also a fan, due in part to the singular treatment Bernard Lackner offers his guests. During their stay, charming treats arrive routinely, courtesy of Bernard— a sampling of smoked salmon, caviar, or perhaps a bottle of Dom Perignon. He also delights in sending up a tray of canapés and a half bottle of wine for what he describes as a little respite before dinner. Lee Rosenberg, founder of Triad Artists, Inc., wouldn't dream of staying anywhere else. He just wouldn't give up the food, the telephone services—yes, messages are taken accurately—or the impossible feats accomplished by head concierge Eugenio Chinigo.

And isn't it wonderful that you only have to go as far as the hotel's three-star restaurant, La Regence, for a superb meal in an exquisite setting! Dominated by a twelve-foot vaulted sky-blue ceiling, fancifully adorned with fluffy painted clouds, the eighty-five-seat restaurant features the Continental cuisine of chef Jo Rostang and his sons, Michel and Phillipe. The Rostangs represent a culinary dynasty, having been at it for five generations. In addition to their duties as executive chefs and managers of La Regence, each still retains celebrated multistarred restaurants in their native France.

The à la carte luncheon is popular with those seeking a quiet meal in what seems more like a private dining salon than a public restaurant. Barbara Walters is among the regulars who happily pay $40 apiece (at least). We can't speak for her, but we have found the smoked duck salad with red fruit and apple at $16 a perfect starter. Cholesterol considerations aside, we've been known to follow it with the absolutely sublime calf's liver (always our measure of a truly great French restaurant) for $19.

Dinner, often enjoyed by Woody Allen and his significant other, Mia Farrow, not to mention Ryan O'Neal and his main squeeze, Farrah Fawcett, is prix fixe at $59.50. Try the salad of warm duck foie gras with arugula, turnips, and crisp potatoes, followed by the cream of zucchini soup and quail eggs and beluga caviar. For the main course, we like the roasted sea scallops from Maine, served in tomato butter. If you're hungry and adventurous, undertake the *menu degustation*, a seven-course feast of the chef's favorites for $77.50 a person.

We've all had the experience of agreeing with Robert Louis Stevenson's assertion that "to travel hopefully is a better thing than to arrive." The Plaza Athénée may be the exception that proves the rule. To arrive here is to satisfy, indeed exceed, even the most grandiose of expectations. 🍏

The Plaza Hotel

768 Fifth Avenue	(212) 759-3000
at Central Park South	(800) 228-3000
New York, NY 10019	FAX (212) 759-3167

The venerable Plaza Hotel has been invaded by a new Eloise. Fairer, a little older, and presumably a great deal wiser than her elfin predecessor, Ivana Trump has embraced the eighty-two-year-old landmark purchased by her husband ("The Donald," as she calls him) in 1988. And she's set about putting her personal stamp on it. Bent on making The Plaza "the greatest hotel in the world," Ivana has swept away the vestiges of a succession of somewhat unfortunate management styles; gone are the dowdy chairs in the lobbies and the hordes of tour groups that had overrun the elegant public spaces.

A massive restoration and renovation project is in the works and it's winning kudos for the Trumps. They have taken great pains to ensure that the improvements are true to the spirit and intention of the original architect, Henry Janeway Hardenbergh, who also designed the famous (*and* infamous) Dakota. As befits what many consider to be New York's most beloved cultural monument, unsympathetic alterations made to The Plaza's interior and exterior are being corrected: elaborate ornamental plaster ceilings long hidden by acoustical tile will again be revealed; the Tiffany ceiling of the celebrated Palm Court, destroyed during one unfortunate era under the Hilton folks, will be reconstructed; mosaics concealed years ago will reappear in the Oak Room; the exquisite room once known as Rose, later as Persian, and most recently as the site of a garish dress shop, will be resurrected; the charming cast-iron canopies marking the entrances are being stripped of modern trimmings, as are the lamps and flagpoles that adorn them. The Trumps have even raised $3 million from the community to restore the city-owned landmark fountain that separates the hotel from Fifth Avenue.

In keeping with the 1907 advertisement proclaiming the opening of "the world's most luxurious hotel," every bathroom in the "new" Plaza is being redone in marble; all of the beds are outfitted in Frette linens; supplies of bottled water from an Australian source called Plaza Spa are constantly replenished in each room; and kitchenettes have been installed on each floor to ensure prompt delivery of every Continental breakfast.

While the execution of all these plans is scheduled to take at least two years, some areas of the hotel have already benefited from the Trump era, notably two spectacular suites.

The Vanderbilt is named in honor of Mr. and Mrs. Alfred Gwynne Vanderbilt, the first guests to sign The Plaza's register when they moved into a $10,000-a-year apartment eighty-two years ago. We imagine that they would quite happily move into the three-bedroom suite that bears their name, though at $4,500 a night the rent is considerably higher than that of their former abode! With 2,400 square feet, there is room to roam or to do some very lavish entertaining. The living/dining room is beautifully done in rose and celedon, accented by striking moldings, and made most comfortable by remarkable Empire reproductions resting on the three-hundred-year-old rug. The topiary trees flanking the fireplace are a nice touch. Indeed an abundance of lush flowers and plants in all rooms are rapidly becoming a trademark. Each of the suite's bedrooms exults in a different and very definite color scheme, but the master bathroom is the real eye-catcher. More like a boudoir, its white leather chaise lounge, hand-painted screen, and huge marble Jacuzzi tub make it very glamorous indeed.

Somewhat smaller at "only" 1,500 square feet, the Frank Lloyd Wright Suite is so named because Wright actually lived in the space while he was designing the Guggenheim Museum. No doubt he enjoyed the twelve-foot ceilings, the three fireplaces, and the wonderful Fifth Avenue views. Today, its occupants may also savor fine reproduction Wright furniture and accessories, complemented by a few originals like the high-backed chairs in the corridor leading to the two bedrooms. The marble floor in the entry is also worthy of note. It is a pattern created by Wright, but never actually used in the Guggenheim, or anywhere else for that matter. The Trumps found it while researching the Wright archives and had it specially commissioned and installed. With both bedrooms, the suite sells for $3,000. Should you only require the use of the master bedroom you can save $500.

Alternatively, if you want to experience the unique Wright ambience on a budget, you can rent the second bedroom on its own for only $500—a bargain when you consider its extra-large proportions, two queen-size beds, the fireplace, and the grand desk that doubles as an elegant dining table.

Other of the Plaza's 813 rooms and suites that are being decorated in traditional French or English country-manor style carry more modest price tags—singles start at $200, doubles at $260, and suites at $600. Whatever the cost, make sure you secure accommodations only on floors two through eleven, so that you can relish the spaciousness accorded by the high ceilings on these levels.

As The Plaza's president, Ivana's concerns go beyond overseeing the hotel's creature comforts. She is also determined to give her guests good old-fashioned service. To ensure that the needs of VIPs (like you) are properly attended to, she established the Office of the President. Its gracious staff is devoted to monitoring the stay of each of its eminent charges, extending every courtesy and service imaginable.

However, exceptional service is not the exclusive prerogative of designated VIPs at The Plaza. One only has to visit any of the hotel's dining establishments to experience feeling important, Plaza style. The Palm Court has for decades been a favorite gathering spot for New Yorkers, particularly for tea, when guests are serenaded by classical music—live, of course! A new kitchen solely dedicated to this sumptuous palm-garnished oasis has dramatically improved the quality of the service and the food.

Similarly, the clubby Oak Room, the saloon-like Oyster Bar, and the elegant Edwardian Room are profiting from a renaissance. They are reclaiming their long-lost standing as destinations of choice for natives as well as tourists.

Of course, not everyone is completely taken with the (Trump) Plaza. Plans for the addition of a new penthouse level of luxury suites have some preservationists up in arms, while the relagating of the legendary Trader Vic's to lounge status caused a near riot by the legions who sampled their first, and most likely illegal, drink in the restaurant.

However, we think that in the grand and seemingly glorious scheme that the Trumps are plotting for The Plaza, these are relatively minor transgressions. We think you will agree that The Plaza's new Eloise and her Prince Charming are just what the doctor ordered to bestow upon the hotel the life its creators envisioned. ❧

The Regency Hotel

540 Park Avenue at 61st Street   (212) 759-4100
New York, NY 10021-7385   (800) 243-1166
                                      FAX (212) 826-5674

The Regency stands proudly as the flagship of the Loews Hotel chain, controlled by the Tisch family. You know the Tisches. They emerged from wealthy obscurity to powerful celebrity a few years ago with a stronghold on communications in America; Preston Tisch was named Postmaster General not long after brother Larry bought CBS. Their offspring are making power waves too. Jonathan Tisch is considered the whiz kid of the hotel industry as vice president of Loews, and may have pulled off the dynastic merger of the century when he married corporate raider Saul Steinberg's daughter, Laura. Their multimillion-dollar wedding extravaganza stood usually jaded New York on its ear. Then there's

Steve Tisch, who's earning his own whiz-kid status Hollywood style as the producer of such hits as "Big Business."

The site of many a Tisch family breakfast, it's no surprise The Regency is considered the originator of the now de rigueur power breakfast. If you're a captain of industry, a CEO, a movie mogul, or an investment banker, chances are you've experienced the frenetic scene that is the Regency, 7:00 to 9:00 A.M. every weekday. It's Marie Hallas with her warm personality and knowledgeable charm who oversees the city's powerful— disseminating tables perfectly. We're sure she reads *The Wall Street Journal* and *Forbes* faithfully to keep up to date on the latest mergers.

However yummy and powerful it may be, breakfast is only one of The Regency's attractions. Having recently celebrated its twenty-fifth anniversary with a $16 million "enhancement" (a clever and rather charming euphemism for what other hotels call renovation), it is certainly worthy of flagship rank. As the name suggests, there is a Regency-period flavor to the decor throughout. But, it doesn't seem stuffy or institutional. Instead, the Regency's unpretentious elegance imitates a tastefully decorated, though very grand, home. And manager John Beier watches over every last detail of it perfectly.

In fact, you could easily move right into the peach and blue comfort of Suite 1831, a one-bedroom that can be converted to two. The living room is so vast the grand piano is almost lost in one corner. Equally large, the terrace overlooking Park Avenue readily accommodates seventy to eighty people for cocktails on a warm evening. With both bedrooms, it's yours for $1,050 a night.

In deference to The Regency's increasing popularity with the bicoastal set, another of the hotel's more lavish suites has been dubbed the California. Bleached wood floors complement dramatic but comfortable overstuffed furniture. George Hurell's photographic portraits of Tinsel Town greats add a glamorous touch. And the sauna explains why The Regency has assumed the nickname "Hollywood East"! With two big bedrooms, a night's stay here is well worth the $1,050 charge.

Other one- and two-bedroom suites range from $525 to $850. Single and double occupancy rates start at $260, up to $285, with junior suites at $350.

Regardless of size or price, all the Regency's 450 rooms offer several nifty features—ample (often more than ample) closet space, well-appointed bathrooms with mini-TVs and enough counter space to provide a home for all your toiletries.

Lest you be left with the impression that breakfast is the only food story at the hotel, you should know that executive chef Frank Champley spends virtually every waking hour of every day overseeing The Regency's kitchen. As a result, the 540 Park restaurant (yes, its name is its address) has been earning praise as a source of refined, decidedly American cooking, with maître d' William Annear overseeing lunch and dinner. For those watching their weight, there are daily low-calorie "Recommendations from the Fitness Center" at lunch and dinner.

If you are wondering which fitness center, it's the Regency's, of course. Designed for the exclusive use of the hotel's guests, it has an elaborate ensemble of state-of-the-art equipment, as well as whirlpool spa and sauna. The professional staff will show you how to take the best advantage of the facility.

For those who prefer their exercise bending an elbow with the world's power brokers, see John Mahon in the Regency Lounge, a popular watering hole for chic East Siders. John has been with the hotel since its opening, so he's seen and heard it all. Fortunately or not, he's very discreet. Still, he does engage his considerable wit to regale you with amusing stories while pouring his generous drinks.

And don't worry if you get a little too relaxed and forget that vitally important last-minute errand. The concierge team of Kathleen Nugent, Penny Wallberg, and K. Sezake will take care of it. Knowledgeable and unflappable, they routinely run the arranging gamut for their demanding guests—from chartering a Lear jet to doing Christmas shopping.

Lear jets, concierges, fitness center, California Suite, power suite— pretty heady stuff for two boys who got their start in the hospitality business by running a summer camp in Jersey. The elder Tisches' rise to fame and fortune would make a great story for Hollywood Steve's next movie! ❧

Royalton

44 West 44th Street	(212) 869-4400
between 5th and 6th	(800) 635-9013
New York, NY	FAX (212) 869-8965

In 1898 Manhattan sat up and took notice when The Royalton was built as an exclusive residential hotel. Now, almost a hundred years later, this small hotel is once again commanding attention after a complete over-haul.

Small wonder—the Royalton is another Rubell/Schraeger (formerly of Studio 54 and Palladium and currently of Morgans fame) production. And, once again, they made waves—this time with a hotel Steve liked to describe as "a new kind of gathering place." He predicted, before his death, that hotel lobbies will become the social hubs of the nineties, just as restaurants were in the eighties, and nightclub/discos were in the seventies.

Whether or not you agree with his prediction, you have to give him and Ian credit for creating a lobby where one might certainly gather, if one were so inclined. More specifically, you have to give them credit for hiring superstar interior designer Philippe Starck, who produced a fantastic stage set for a constantly changing cast of characters who really do seem engaged in the fine art of lobby socializing. (Perhaps they are guided by the spirits of such former Royalton lobby gatherers as the Barrymores, Mae West, Gertrude Lawrence, Noel Coward, Tennessee Williams, and W. C. Fields!)

Despite its block-long, 10,000 square feet of space, the room has a sophisticated, inviting warmth with its clever multilevel division into areas. There's the study, with the 20-foot library table and extensive selection of reading materials. *Vanity Fair* editor in chief Tina Brown has taken to conducting staff meetings here.

Beyond the study, and deliberately hidden, lurks the destined-to-become-legendary Bar-in-the-Round. Resembling a very blue padded cell, it was ostensibly inspired by Ernest Hemingway's favorite bar at the Ritz in Paris. However, we can't help but wonder if it might also be a takeoff on the already legendary Round Table of the venerable Algonquin, which just happens to be right across the street.

The Royalton subscribes to the theory that if you can't find the bar or if you don't know where it is, you don't belong there. Not to worry, there are other areas to explore. Take the living room, boasting Starck's specially designed visions of futuristic overstuffed furniture. Sink into a settee or armchair to survey the scene, but be wary of the three-legged chairs—they have been known to tip over, with great fanfare.

Then there's the recreation area, complete with a pool table and a rotating repertoire of board games. If food and drink are more your idea of recreation, the sushi-bar-without-sushi serves light fare on a 24-hour basis. For more serious eating, the dining room, otherwise known as the

Royalton Grill, presents breakfast, lunch, and dinner, though it was at times hard to find one of the black-clad waitresses on our last visit who was prepared to be of more than cursory service.

The idea, though, is that the Royalton is supposed to be more like a home than a hotel—albeit a somewhat futuristic home. The Royalton represents Rubell's and Schrager's notion of a "mansion hotel"—living/entertaining on the first floor, sleeping quarters upstairs.

And speaking of sleeping quarters, they are every bit as captivating as the lobby, all 157 of them. Forty of them have fireplaces. They all have VCRs and, of course, 24-hour room service.

Our fancy was particularly struck by 516, described as a "Loft Suite." Starck's sleek modern decor is executed in tones of gray, warmed by the glow from the fireplace, and punctuated by a single piece of art—a post-card that's changed three times a day. In addition, like all of the Royalton's sleeping rooms, it sports a cushioned window seat, a writing desk, a dining table, a stereo cassette deck, refrigerator, custom-made two-line telephones, and a glamorous bathroom.

At $375 per night, 516 is at the high end of the Royalton's tariff card. Minus the fireplace and the extra square footage, you can experience Starck's delightful environment in a regular double for $215 to $285.

Regardless of the size of your economic participation in the hotel's runaway success, you can be sure you'll be treated royally by the staff. Your every wish will be considered a command. Evening planned around a movie not part of the Royalton's large video library? No problem—a call to the front desk will send someone scurrying out into the night to find it.

Extraordinary decor, exemplary service (with a few lapses), and the opportunity to refine your lobby social skills—what more could one possibly want in a hotel? We might be interested in slightly larger closets, but we're awfully picky!   ❦

The Stanhope

5th Avenue at 81st Street	(212) 288-5800
New York, NY 10028	(800) 828-1123
	FAX (212) 517-0088

Small and quiet, reeking with sophisticated elegance underscored by a touch of nouveau magnificence here and there, The Stanhope is ever-so-suited to its Fifth Avenue address. Surrounded by some of the city's most expensive residences and just across the street from the Metropolitan Museum, The Stanhope is somewhat surprisingly a favorite of CEO types, particularly of the European variety. It's surprising, because it is a bit out of the way from most places where big business is conducted.

Maybe it's the residential quality that attracts them (most of the 142 rooms are suites) or the staff that prides itself on committing to memory guests' habits and preferences. Perhaps it's managing director Guenter Richter's soft-spoken manner. Certainly, The Stanhope's complimentary weekday limousine service to midtown doesn't hurt! Nor does the extraordinary service provided by the concierge team of Rick Cook and Vera Kovar—recently they purchased a car for a wedding gift on behalf of a client.

Still, you don't have to be intimately acquainted with the language of leveraged buyouts to appreciate The Stanhope's many charms. The quality of the eighteenth-century antiques in the lobby is self-evident. Indeed, lavish appointments are a Stanhope trademark. Real estate magnate Gerald Gutterman invested a staggering $26 million in the renovation of the classic Roaring Twenties building, once called the American Stanhope. Much of this investment was devoted to the custom-designed Baccarat crystal chandeliers and sconces for the Dining Room, the hand-loomed carpeting, specially commissioned made-to-order French furniture, Oriental rugs, exquisite trompe l'oeil walls, moldings accented by twenty-four-carat gold leaf, and museum-quality artworks.

All of this was meant to entice regular guests into buying a condominium suite or room for their permanent use. Unfortunately for Mr. Gutterman, the plan failed miserably, and he was forced to sell the hotel to the Japanese. Tobishima Associates purchased The Stanhope in January 1989 and brought in Grand Bay Management Company to keep up the high standards. As of this writing, the new owners have no plans to change the hotel substantially, except for the addition of a new one-bedroom penthouse that will rent for $4,000 a night. Our research indicates it will be the most expensive one-bedroom suite in town.

Fortunately, The Stanhope's other sleeping rooms are more modestly priced. Rooms start at $250, suites at $400 with a cap of $900 for a two-bedroom.

One of our favorites is the large and airy 1110. Done in warm tones of beige, it counts two full bathrooms among its amenities, and a plethora of telephones, three to be precise. Sinfully soft Italian leather binds all the desk appointments. Even the hangers are special—ladies' are padded silk. The gentlemen's are heavy wood, and all of them removable, for which we are eternally grateful.

For $250 less than the $650 charge for 1110, you can settle into 1008. It is smaller, but still very charming and quite peaceful with its sea green decor. In keeping with the French influence throughout the hotel, the suite's bathroom offers Chanel toiletries, as do all The Stanhope's facilities. A first among hotels, even in Europe, The Stanhope's lead in taking advantage of the quality and cachet of Chanel products is now being copied by other deluxe properties.

The French influence is pervasive, except in Gerard's, the bar off the lobby, which is finished like the inner sanctum of a very gentlemanly English men's club with its mahogany-paneled walls, Chesterfield sofas, leather-bound books, and hunt paintings. Gerard's is a warm and comfortable spot for a light lunch (served from noon) or for cocktails.

Gerard's stands in dramatic contrast to the rather intimidating formal French Dining Room. The Limoges china and Baccarat crystal place settings are well suited to their rich surroundings in which one feels compelled to whisper.

As lovely as the Dining Room is, we prefer the cozier ambience of Le Salon, where continental breakfast and a very respectable tea are served. We highly recommend taking tea here to rejuvenate the senses after exploring the countless wonders of the Metropolitan Museum across Fifth Avenue. For $18, indulge in a selection of delicate finger sandwiches, followed by hot scones with Devonshire cream and an array of tempting pastries. Of course, there is a selection of teas—Fortnum and Mason, House of Twining, Jackson's of Piccadilly, even Grace Rare Teas. In case you haven't tried it, a glass of sherry or one of The Stanhope's vintage ports makes a fine substitute for tea at tea!

While The Stanhope excels in providing luxurious accommodations, well serviced by an efficient staff, we do have a bone to pick. In an admirable effort to ensure security and privacy, the automatic elevators are key activated and will only take you to the floor where you are staying. Therefore, if you are inclined to visit friends or business associates on other floors, you have to go down to the desk and enlist the aid of someone on duty. He or she, in turn, has to call the object of your intended visit, announce your impending arrival, then escort you to the elevator and access the appropriate floor with a master key.

It's a bit of a nuisance. Hopefully, the new Japanese owners can come up with a better system—like good old-fashioned elevator operators!

The Waldorf-Astoria

301 Park Avenue	(212) 355-3000
between 49th and 50th Streets	(800) 445-8607
New York, NY 10022	FAX (212) 758-9209

Ever since it opened as the world's largest hotel in 1931, The Waldorf-Astoria has been associated with some of New York's grandest occasions. By the time Herbert Hoover made history officiating at the opening ceremonies via radio from the White House, the name *Waldorf* was already synonymous with the lavish frolicking of the upper reaches of New York society.

The legacy debuted in 1893 with the original Waldorf Hotel on the corner of Fifth Avenue and 33rd Street, the former site of the William Waldorf Astor mansion. This opening was a truly historic affair, inaugurating an institution that is now sacrosanct—the first charity ball ever held in a hotel. Furthermore, the evening proved significant on the culinary front—the Waldorf Salad made its debut. Created by the legendary maître d' Oscar, it was meant to lighten a heavy meal by combining fruit and greens as a single course.

Several years later, John Jacob Astor IV followed his cousin William's example and razed his mansion on the corner of Fifth and 34th to build the Astoria Hotel. The two hotels were linked by an enclosed walkway, hence the Waldorf-Astoria tie. And what a walkway it was! It became the promenade of choice for those showing off the latest fashions—lots of plumes in the late nineteenth century. The spectacle prompted one journalist to note, "They are like peacocks on parade." Whether he was referring to the plumage or their hauteur (or both) remains uncertain. In any case, the walkway was dubbed Peacock Alley, and lives on today as an elegant lounge and restaurant off the main lobby of the present Waldorf-Astoria. It is also immortalized in the hotel's official logo—a double hyphen illustrates the famous walkway.

Having recently benefited from a $150 million restoration courtesy of the Hilton Hotels Corporation, which has owned the property since 1977, the Waldorf is certainly worthy of its illustrious ancestry. But some parts of the hotel are more worthy than others, namely The Waldorf Towers, a hotel unto itself within the larger 1,692-room facility. Occupying floors twenty-seven through forty-two, the Towers has its own door-manned entrance on 50th Street, along with exclusive registration and concierge services.

For our money, the Presidential Suite in the Towers is the worthiest of all at $3,000 a day. After all, it's hosted every U.S. president since Herbert Hoover, who finally made it there in person, not to mention innumerable heads of state and more than its share of royalty. The suite's 3,000 square feet contain, among other amenities, four bedrooms with enormous closets and dressing rooms, and a palatial formal dining room with a table that can seat up to twenty-two. Like all the suites in the Towers, antiques and classical hand-carved moldings abound, illuminated by crystal chandeliers and fixtures. Art Deco ornamentation lends a touch of whimsy—actually more than a touch, as no less an authority than the Smithsonian Institution has designated the Waldorf as one of the three major Art Deco buildings in the country.

Representative of what the Towers refers to as one of its smaller suites is 30A. For $1,550 a night, you get a three-bedroom apartment—annual leases on such quarters have been taken by the likes of Cole Porter, the Duke and Duchess of Windsor, Herbert Hoover, and Douglas MacArthur—complete with a living room filled with French and English antiques, fully equipped kitchen, and dining room suitable for dinner parties for as many as twenty-four.

In addition to the incredible suites, the Towers offers singles and double rooms ranging from $260 to $310. Beyond the Towers, there is plenty of life at the Waldorf, with regular room rates starting at $190 and going up to $275 for a minisuite. Real one-bedrooms go for $325 to $425; two-bedrooms are $450 to $585. All rates depend on the location and decor of the room.

No matter where it is or how it's decorated, however, your room will be serviced by the mind-boggling Waldorf kitchen. An entire city block long and outfitted to serve 100 pounds of beluga caviar, 27,000 pounds of lobster, and 380,000 pints of strawberries each year, it has the capacity to feed nearly 10,000 guests on any given day. Indeed, it often does just that, since the Waldorf's public rooms host many of the city's most important functions. The Grand Ballroom alone, the only four-story ballroom in the world, can accommodate up to 2,000 people and is the site of innumerable contemporary incarnations of the first Waldorf hotel's earliest invention, the charity ball. No wonder the wine cellar boasts 300,000 bottles of fine wines and spirits, most of which are sold and re-stocked every month!

The amazing Waldorf statistics go on and on. Sixty-one languages are spoken by the employees, making it the United Nations of the city's hotel staffs. Appropriately enough, the UN has been known to borrow one of the hotel's 115 national flags.

The kitchen that serves all the official and unofficial occasions uses 500 pounds of chicken bones, 350 pounds of beef bones, and another 350 of veal bones each day for soups and stocks. And the Waldorf is the only place in the world to have available a complete gold china service for 1,600. Stored in a computerized safe, it is used daily for VIP room service and for afternoon tea on the Cocktail Terrace, overlooking the beautiful mosaics of the Park Avenue lobby. We couldn't get a count on the total supply of cutlery, china, and glassware, but there's no question it could service a small town. In addition to the twenty-five public rooms available for banquets (48,000 square feet in all), there are four restaurants and two cocktail lounges that keep the dishwashers busy. Peacock Alley serves American cuisine in a pretty floral setting, while the Bull & Bear, site of a former men's club, is an old-fashioned chophouse. For more exotic fare, there is Inagiku, which must be one of the best Japanese restaurants around, given the number of Japanese businessmen who are very much at home there every day. And finally, Oscar's satisfies cravings for sandwiches and salads in a coffee-shop atmosphere.

While we haven't seen a statistic on this either, we imagine a lot of guests check in and never leave the premises. Hugh Liedtke, chairman of Pennzoil, called it home while he negotiated the biggest legal settlement in history—the $3 billion he wrung from Texaco in 1987. And why shouldn't the Hugh Liedtkes of the world call it home? The Waldorf-Astoria is, after all, larger than life just like them—a self-contained world dedicated to their comfort and enjoyment.

A quick call to general manager Per Hellman will ensure you're getting a suite in the towers, and upon arrival concierge Herbert Tepper will already have stocked it with our favorite candy—M&M's—along with a bowl of fresh popcorn. The Waldorf may be large, but no detail is too small.

Maybe it's time for us to take a tip from Ginger Rogers and spend a *Weekend at the Waldorf*, appropriately, another Waldorf first—the first hotel to be featured in a major film.   ❧

Hotel Westbury

69th Street at Madison Avenue	(212) 535-2000
New York, NY 10021	(800) 321-1569
	FAX (212) 535-5058

If you have been wondering what Meryl Streep, Olivia De Havilland, Valentino, and Yves St. Laurent call home in New York, wonder no longer. It is the Hotel Westbury, a small hostelry in the midst of upper Madison's finest shopping, offering an incredible sense of privacy to its guests.

The lobby is small and, though gracious with its seventeenth-century Belgian tapestries and Chippendale furniture, is decidedly not a gathering spot. Instead, it is a quiet, dignified place to conduct business discreetly with the management at the unobtrusive mahogany desk or engage the efficient services of concierge Anthony Pike. It is a place to pass through as you leave the hustle and bustle of the city en route to your private oasis, one of the Westbury's 335 rooms and suites.

Entering any of the hotel's guest quarters is like entering one of the neighborhood's historic brownstones. It was built in the 1920s as a residential hotel, and the Westbury's rooms retain their individuality in shape and design. Over fifty themes are used in their decor, capitalizing on the handpainted wallpapers and fabrics from the world's most exclusive suppliers. No two are exactly alike; each has its own distinctive cachet.

There is the air of a gracious English country house about the Westbury's rooms. English chintz, cozy sofas, and a bright, cheery look make Suite 715 a favorite choice at $625 a night. We think the high four-poster bed has a lot to do with its popularity.

Despite the threat from the outside world posed by the two telephone lines that service each room, there is a charming tranquility here. Rates for standard to deluxe rooms range from $210 to $290. Junior suites are available at $325 and one-bedrooms start at $375. For $1,600 a night, you can get an entire one-bedroom apartment thoroughly outfitted with fireplace, formal dining room, kitchen, two bathrooms (one with Jacuzzi), and the latest in luxury hotel gadgets, a fax phone. Two-bedroom suites cost $585 to $1,200 for one with a balcony and sauna.

Although we consider the Hotel Westbury to be close to perfection, Trusthouse Forte Hotels, Inc., which owns the property, apparently still believes there's room for improvement. A massive renovation project is in the works, geared to making the hotel "one of the very best in the world." In the process, General Manager Stefan Simkovics promised us they wouldn't compromise the unique gentility of the Westbury.

Moreover, they aren't even going to attempt to tamper with the Polo, the hotel's restaurant; it's already just as chic and smart as it can be. Uncommonly attractive in an English horsey club sort of way, it serves uncommonly good food. (Isn't it wonderful that the days of entering hotel restaurants with fear and loathing have been banished?)

The Polo, named as a reminder that the Hotel Westbury was built by the family of an American player of the "Sport of Kings," is an outpost of civilized dining in the often too trendy Upper East Side. As such it is a favorite spot for breakfsat, lunch, and dinner for everyone from visiting Soviet dignitaries to New York City mayoral hopefuls. Sometimes, they even collide. On the last day of Mikhail Gorbachev's first visit to New York City, the top luminaries of the visiting Soviet press were breakfasting in the Polo before their trip to the airport and home. Faces were long, even of the likes of Soviet TV star Vladimir Posner and the head of Tass, clearly disappointed to be leaving their plush surroundings for the cold of a Moscow winter. At the next table sat New York City comptroller Harrison J. Goldin, then a prominent candidate for mayor of New York, breakfasting in his accustomed corner. Goldin's companion leaned over to Posner and suggested he might like to "meet the next mayor of New York." Posner beamed. Goldin smiled. East met West in the Westbury. ❦

CHAPTER THREE

Restaurants

Give my regards to a great paillard

*E*avesdrop, these days, on just about any conversation among New Yorkers and you're bound to hear talk turn first to restaurants. All New Yorkers, it seems, have become critics—restaurant critics. And the reason is simple—with the price of a Broadway show approaching the cost of a meal, New Yorkers now have a real choice of entertainment on any given evening—eats in a world-class bistro or seats in a first-class theater.

So today, with a top-flight restaurant critic carrying the same status that Brooks Atkinson carried in his day (though no restaurant's yet been named after a critic!) the new hype in haute cuisine is clearly having a major impact on the New York restaurant scene. Plain and simple? Everyone who's anyone or wants to be somebody is coming here to try to make it. When chefs begin closing two-star restaurants in Paris and opening up in New York, you know something important is happening. In New York these days it seems chefs are becoming celebrities and celebrities are becoming chefs.

It's always been that way in France. Now New York's truly become Paris-on-the-Hudson. But also Tokyo, Canton, Bangkok, Seoul, Delhi, Istanbul, Athens, Rome, Madrid, Copenhagen, and Kiev on the Hudson.

More to the point, you can eat well for an awful lot of money in New York (before, during, *or* after lunch). But you can also eat very well for an awfully small amount of money. Much of that has to do with the stage setting and the publicity surrounding the chef, the maître d', and the owner. All that ink costs *them* money, which they merrily pass on to their "guests."

But the *real* reason for all that hype? Well, if a hotel defines who you are or want to be for a visitor, restaurants perform the same function for us native New Yorkers. Though there's still the celebrity catering service for that occasional soirée you simply *must* give at home, or that pamper-yourself, candlelit dinner for one, most New Yorkers, constrained by those teeny tiny kitchens that are the norm in all but the most palatial Park Avenue palaces, are dining *out* these days.

Consequently, reservations can be a problem. We've given some hints about whom to call and how long in advance, but there are no hard and fast rules here. Concierges can work wonders as can dropping the name of a friend you know to be a regular. Persistence is also important. A restaurant that is fully booked two days before, can suddenly be depopulated by cancellations. And be advised that some restaurateurs think reservations are valued goods—the harder they are to get, the more people want them. They'll pretend to have nothing available just for effect. Watch how fast they suddenly discover a table when you mention, as one local reporter did in an informal poll of the city's poshest spots, that you're calling for Paul Newman, *the* Paul Newman.

Now don't look here for clubs. They change more quickly than first-run films on Third Avenue. "Here today, gone tomorrow," as the saying goes. Ask your concierge. Or if you don't trust his gray hair to guide you to the latest "in" scene, call a limo service. They know where the action is. Actually, call one in any case. Arriving in stretched style tends to assure you'll get past that black velvet rope.   🍂

NEW YORK CITY

Aquavit

13 West 54th Street   (212) 307-7311
between 5th and 6th
New York, NY 10019

Of course, you know aquavit is a clear vodka-like distillate usually infused with one or more flavors such as anise, caraway, fennel, and orange peel (but best in its natural state). We're sure you're well aware of the fact that it is the favored drink of the entire Scandinavian region. You probably can even speak to the translation of the name *aquavit* to "water of life." And we imagine you always drink it in the proper manner, neat and very cold, 34 degrees Fahrenheit, to be precise. But did you know that *Aquavit* is also the name of the first major Scandinavian restaurant to open in Manhattan since before World War II?

Occupying two levels of a landmark townhouse once inhabited by John D. Rockefeller, Jr., Aquavit is an unusually pleasing addition to the city's dining scene. There's just nothing else quite like it, with its split personality, five-story atrium, waterfall, and giant mobile by Richard Smith.

Split personality? Aquavit is really two restaurants. The upper level houses a seventy-five-seat casual café and long stand-up bar, offering an à la carte menu for all-day dining. The main room on the lower level seats 125 in the spectacular atrium, dominated by the incredible mobile and soothingly cooled by the twenty-foot waterfall cascading down a gray tiled wall.

Maître d' Steve Rosenbloom will guide you to the Aquavit of your choice. Regulars like to trade off—the café for the Danish open-faced sandwich *smørrebrød* ($14 for any two), the restaurant for the more formal prix-fixe lunch or dinner. Some even dine downstairs, then stop by the café for its take-out service—hors d'oeuvres for a pretheater gathering or the makings of a late-night snack. The juniper-smoked salmon at $7 per quarter pound is a popular take-out choice. All the smoked goods are processed right on the premises.

Should you opt for luncheon among the powerful publishers, lawyers, and bankers who tend to fill the atrium every business day, try the herring plate for the first course. With Baltic, maatjes, and mustard herring beautifully presented with västerbotten cheese, it's worth the $4 supplement to the $35 lunch. We suggest following the herring with either the gravlax served with dill-creamed potatoes or the poached halibut in brown butter and horseradish. The poached ginger pear sprinkled with powdered sugar and accompanied by homemade vanilla ice cream topped with a butterscotch sauce makes a sensational dessert.

We think the $60 dinner starts best with the salmon mousseline in a puff pastry napped by a tomato and dill sauce. The tasty salmon tartare with Beylon oysters is also hard to beat. The second course presents another dilemma, but we tend to stick to the game—some of the freshest and best in town. You can't go wrong with the peppered loin of Swedish hare with brussels sprouts and potato cake, the loin of Arctic venison in apple and juniper sauce with celery root puree, or the snow grouse in a cream sauce with a potato, carrot, and lingonberry timbale.

For somewhat lighter fare, Aquavit aficionados like Walter Cronkite, Woody Allen, Joan Rivers, and Geoffrey Beene graze through a menu that proposes (in addition to the sandwiches) Scandinavian shrimp soup for $5.50, baked creamed potatoes with anchovies for $8.50, and Swedish meatballs in a cream sauce with lingonberry and cucumber salad for $14.50.

Almost half a century is a long time for a world-class city like New York to wait for a new, truly first-class Scandinavian restaurant to add to its international culinary resources. In the case of Aquavit, it was worth the wait.   ❦

Arizona 206

208 East 60th Street   (212) 838-0440
between 2nd and 3rd
New York, NY

Not content just to tinker with their ever-evolving landmark restaurant on Third Avenue, the Sign of the Dove, the Santos family, Dr. Joseph, brother Berge, and his wife Henny, began fooling around with their Austrian restaurant on East 60th. Despite the fact that it had a corner on the market for Austrian food and was doing well, it just didn't feel right. About five years ago they began casting about for a new theme, preferably one that would work with the decor in which they had already invested a considerable sum—stucco walls, fireplace, specially commissioned wood tables, chairs, and benches. A trip to the Southwest proved to be a revelation and provided the answer. Tyrolean could be transformed into Santa Fe—stucco becomes adobe, European furniture becomes rustic American, après-ski fireplace becomes Indian hearth.

By happy coincidence, they were also genuinely fascinated by Southwestern themes. By hard work they are now the proud possessors of two restaurants—Sign of the Dove and Arizona 206—considered worthy of three stars by *The New York Times*. Indeed, as far as we know, they are the only two three-star family in town.

Now we admit that our sense of geography mirrors the famous *New Yorker* cover depicting everything west of the Hudson as sort of a jumbled mess. But in a way, so does Arizona 206's. The irony of this restaurant, which has set the New York standards for southwest cooking, is that the Santos' charge to their first chef, Brendan Walsh, was to create a cuisine using ingredients indigenous to the region—not necessarily to duplicate southwestern dishes. After all, Brendan had never even been to that part of the world.

Brendan succeeded in fulfilling the Santos' wishes; his successor and long-time second Marilyn Frobuccino has exceeded all expectations. The menu, both at lunch and dinner, has a limited number of choices, but each is a delight to read and contemplate. The unfamiliar combinations sound so exciting—it is a menu that truly whets the appetite for the exuberant food that follows. For lunch, starters include the $8 desert salad and the hot/sweet red chili corn cakes cooled by a pumpkin seed pesto sauce topped with a dollop of crème fraîche, also $8. Both are delightful taste sensations. As for what Arizona 206 calls "Mains," the grilled swordfish club sandwich on whole wheat with an avocado remoulade at $17 is our number one choice. But the $18 crispy striped bass sauced with warm gazpacho should not be ignored.

At dinner, often a crowded free-for-all which includes being corralled at the bar for a while, we can't resist buckwheat blinis topped with smoked salmon minced with peppers, ossetra caviar, and sour cream for $12. We also usually succumb to the $10 shrimp and catfish cakes with a pineapple salsa while waiting for the rib-eye of lamb with a smoky tomato chili sauce and sweet goat cheese ratatouille for $24—or achile chili pan seared shrimp combined with crabmeat in a rich gumbo for $25.

Personally, we don't think desserts are the strong suit here. It's not so much that they're not good, it's just that our tastebuds, all knotted up by chilied and peppered meat, don't cotton all that well to sweets afterwards—except, perhaps to the vanilla custard drizzled with a little fresh fruit.

Reservations? We don't have many about Arizona 206, despite a noise level and too-close-for-comfort seating arrangement we would find objectionable elsewhere. Here it seems part of the self-consciously informal (though not necessarily unpretentious) scene, right down to the casually attired waiters, who are nonetheless very professional. Of course, we always do *make* reservations for dinner, giving maître d' Larry the obligatory couple of days' notice. Still it is possible to enjoy Arizona 206 on a more spontaneous basis. You can often just pop in to the Café next door—same food, smaller portions, smaller prices, $4 to $12. The Café's is a tasting menu which changes daily, served in a very casual atmosphere. Here the food is meant to be shared.

Speaking of sharing, you may notice on the way to the facilities, at least the ladies will, that the Café, entered via Arizona 206, also seems to share space with two more restaurants, Yellowfingers and Contra Punta. It does—two more members of the Santos' family of restaurants, both quite acceptable for a quick Italian fix. Neither are anywhere near a three-star rating, but given the Santos' penchant for reincarnations, just give them time.   ❦

Aureole

34 East 61st Street   (212) 319-1660
between Park and Madison
New York, NY 10021

Ever since Charlie Palmer gave people a reason to go to Brooklyn's River Café for something besides the spectacular view, he's been a celebrity chef. So his announcement that he was leaving the barge-bound restaurant to open his own on terra firma was greeted with much interest and speculation by the culinary community.

The speculation is over—Aureole (*halo* in French) has arrived, but the interest is unabated. Charlie's got an unqualified hit on his hands in this almost self-consciously unpretentious addition to the midtown dining scene. In partnership with the already successful restaurant team of Steve Tzolis and Nicolette Kotsonui, who own Il Cantinori and Periyali, Charlie has created an environment and a cuisine that truly appeal— appeal to a stylish crowd that appreciates the informal atmosphere and Charlie's youthful enthusiasm in the kitchen (he's only 29). Ron Darling, Matthew Broderick, Daryl Hannah, Dustin Hoffman, Kate Capshaw, and Goldie Hawn have all been spotted savoring Charlie's somewhat playful inventions.

We can't speak for them, but we're smitten with the sea scallop "sandwiches" with crisp sauteed potatoes acting as the bread, and citrus juices filling the role of mayonnaise. The unique terrines of fresh foie gras and braised oxtails garnished with a confiture of onions and sundried cherries are pretty tempting too.

Both dishes are appetizers on the $50 prix-fixe dinner menu. Given the popularity of the place, not to mention excellent main courses like poached black sea bass with marinated eggplant and sweet peppers and pan-roasted baby pheasant with wild mushrooms embellished by a leek and zucchini tartlet, common wisdom dictates that the price will not be fixed at that level for very long.

Actually, Aureole's instant popularity is its one stumbling block. It can take one to two weeks to get a dinner reservation (the à la carte lunch is easier, but they do go through the ritual of calling you to reconfirm). Once the long-awaited evening arrives, you may be obliged to wait still longer at the tiny bar, especially if you insist on sitting downstairs, the preferred of the two rooms, done in soft, soothing beiges brightened by glorious clusters of flowers.

The two-story wall of glass that fronts the converted townhouse provides a dramatic window of opportunity for people-watching while you wait—watching people outside, watching you! A review of the plaster representations of various forms of wildlife adorning the cream-colored walls is another mildly amusing activity. It can also serve as preview of the specials that change every day or so in this restaurant that describes itself as being American, using the bounty our proud continent has to offer.

If you're here at lunch, be forewarned—the portions are so large that you may not want both appetizer and main course. Two appetizers easily suffice. Try the tasty combination of carpaccio of yellowfin tuna atop a salad of wild greens and mushrooms graced with a citron dressing for $10 and the $11 apple-smoked salmon with a roulade of Japanese omelet. A what? It's an exceedingly thin omelet rolled very tightly, many times over; it resembles a jelly roll and is simply divine.

So here's to Charlie, the kid who dreamed of being a professional football player. Instead of a helmet, he's wearing a chef's toque, but he's definitely scored with Aureole.   ❦

Aurora

60 East 49th Street   (212) 692-9292
between Madison and Park
New York, NY 10017

Aurora, goddess of the dawn, of new beginnings—what an appropriate name for a Joe Baum–owned restaurant. Joe's seen lots of new beginnings during the course of his illustrious career. He's acted as a consultant to more than 300 restaurants, coming up with scores of innovations along the way, some more successful than others. The technique of covering a full ashtray with a clean one as it's removed from the table is a Baum touch imported from France. We also have him to thank (or curse) for the custom of waiters introducing themselves.

Fortunately they don't do that at Aurora. It would be too out of place in this uncommonly (refreshingly so) quiet restaurant. The large tables are spaced far apart, and the burnished wood wainscotting, butter-soft leather chairs, and plush carpet do an admirable job of muting the noise level even when the place is crawling with the publishing types who frequent it at lunch. Many days it looks like Conde Nast's corporate dining room. The handsome Milton Glaser decor (he's also designed some of the magazines whose editors are eating in his surroundings) is rescued from being slightly stuffy by a whimsical bubble motif that manifests itself in the china, the carpet, the windows, even the waiters' teal mess jackets. Even the overhead lighting fixtures carry out the theme.

The configuration of a dozen or so of these double-tiered bubble shapes hanging over the bar looks like it's about to float away and lends a fanciful touch to this otherwise very serious, rather imposing-looking structure. With its granite top, the bar recalls the days when men were men, drinking their whiskey neat, and downing oysters by the dozens. As such it's a pretty nifty place to perch and sample the quite respectable bar menu—dishes like a serving of oysters with sautéed sausage for $10.50 and fresh-cured chicken breast with three salads for $20.

Gerard Pangaud is responsible for the food here, which is deliberately difficult to classify. Classic French techniques Gerard once embraced at his Michelin two-star restaurant in Boulogne-sur-Seine are in evidence, but he massages them with a unique appreciation for American tastes and American products. Whatever the cuisine is, you can be sure the food is good. Gerard, once the youngest two-star chef in France, is very serious about his work.

It was Pangaud who was chosen by François Mitterrand as chief chef for the first Western Summit the new French President hosted at Versailles back in 1982. He assembled a panoply of the leading chefs of France, each preparing a single course or plate. Pangaud personally decided that his would be a magnificent lobster mousse, in the shape of an enormous lobster. As this elegant perfection was about to be wheeled into the grand ballroom for the assembled Western leaders, a tough-looking hombre with mirrored sunglasses and an earpiece approached.

"Is President Reagan going to eat that?" he drawled.

"All the heads of state will be able to eat it if they desire," Pangaud said in his then halting English.

"Then I taste it first," said the Secret Service agent.

It took a member of President Mitterrand's personal bodyguard to explain to the secret service man that NOBODY touched the lobster mousse of a French two-star chef—over his dead body. Pangaud is still prepared to die for his guests' culinary pleasure.

There's no permanent menu at Aurora, with the possible exception of the prix-fixe pre-theater offering at $37.50. At least it doesn't change daily like its à la carte lunch and dinner counterparts. When we last visited, the three-course menu featured crown of zucchini filled with lump crabmeat, roasted rabbit with chanterelles, and an almond and apricot tart.

Luncheon will probably cost $40 to $45 per person, without alcohol. For dinner, plan on $65 apiece for a full meal. If it's on the menu, the lobster tart baked with fresh cèpes is an absolute must as a first course at $18. A portion of tournedos of beef with a crust of marrow, mushrooms, and herbs napped with red wine sauce for $35.00 is tough to beat as the main course. Desserts tend to be showy, fussy affairs for two, at $11 per, like cherries jubilee or crepes suzettes. Our advice? Skip it and get a kick out of watching somebody else's $22 sweet go up in flames.

Now that Joe is consumed by the many demands of the Rainbow Room, son Charles Baum is most often at the helm here. He went to the same charm school as dear old dad and goes out of his way to please. Call him for reservations. If Charles is unavailable, speak to Dawn Flannagan. We don't know what to tell you, if she's not around, but be sure to speak to someone because reservations are strongly recommended. Still, you shouldn't hesitate to stop by on a whim. Usually the worst that can happen is that you'll be seated at the bar, which we've already noted is not at all a bad place to be.   ❦

Ballato

55 East Houston Street   (212) 226-9683
between Moot and Mulberry
New York, NY 10022

If you've had it with the Upper East Side's temples of Italian chic and their large, loud restaurant-as-theater downtown counterparts—if you seek perfectly marvelous Italian food served in a comfortable, intimate setting, try Ballato.

Founded by John Ballato in 1957, it operated successfully on a frontier that few other serious restaurants dared to enter—the Lower East Side. Ballato is no longer the only reason to venture into the territory. The art galleries of the East Village and Soho have lent an aura of roguish chic, if not outright respectability. Indeed, such stalwarts of the Establishment as S. I. and Victoria Newhouse (they're the couple in the corner with the black pug dog that answers to "Nero") and Alan Alda are regulars at Ballato's twelve tables.

A more avant-garde, artsy crowd makes its appearance for Saturday lunch. The late Andy Warhol frequently held court here. His presence continues by virtue of the dramatic art that decorates the restaurant's walls—Andy's gifts over the years to the Ballatos.

Despite John Ballato's passing, this remains a family enterprise with his widow, Lucia, at the helm. She greets you with genuine warmth and treats you as if you are a guest in her home, rather than as a paying customer.

Actually, relatively speaking, you won't be paying much. The prices are quite reasonable—dinner about $35 a person, including wine. Veal scaloppine with a marsala mushroom sauce is a particular treat at $14.95. In fact, veal is somewhat of a specialty. If you don't see the veal dish of your dreams on the menu, don't hesitate to ask. Chef Vinko, a nineteen-year veteran at Ballato, will be happy to accommodate you.

No matter what you order—the sublime linguini with clams, the very special stuffed clams, or your veal request—be prepared to pay for it in cash. No checks or credit cards are accepted. ❦

Barbetta

321 West 46th Street   (212) 246-9171
between 8th and 9th
New York, NY 10036

Barbetta, dating from 1906, claims a lot of "oldests" and "firsts"—like the oldest restaurant in New York still owned by the family that founded it, the oldest Italian restaurant in New York, the oldest restaurant of any kind in the theater district.

Barbetta was the first to introduce the cuisine of the Piemonte, Italy's northwestern region, bordering on Switzerland and France, to the American public. The family maintains it was the first Italian restaurant to present dishes that were elegant yet absolutely authentic, though whether that's a local or national first is unclear. However, it is clear that Barbetta was the first restaurant in America to offer white truffles on a continuous basis; It keeps its own truffle hunters and hounds in Piemonte. Finally, Barbetta was the first U.S. importer of Barbaresco and Gattinara wines.

With all that hype, it's really surprising the food is also first rate. What's more, it is served in one of the loveliest and most romantic settings in New York. The bar, with its antique sienna-colored wood paneling and elaborately carved Baroque trim, sets the stage. Beyond is the warm dining room in palest peach, illuminated by a huge eighteenth-century chandelier liberated from a palazzo in Torino, the capitol of Piemonte. Through the French doors on the left a charming garden beckons. Designed by the current owner, Laura Maioglio, daughter of founder Sebastian Maioglio, Barbetta's garden has been a favorite New York dining oasis since it opened in 1963. Verdant with century-old trees and scented by magnolia, wisteria, oleander, and gardenia blooms, it is often peopled by such nature lovers as Elizabeth Taylor, Robert Redford, Walter Cronkite, and Leonard Bernstein, not to mention many of the top editors and executives of the nearby *New York Times*.

They feast on well-sauced pastas and Barbetta's regional specialties like Carne Cruda, raw fillet of veal alla Piemontese, for $28.95, or Bue al Barolo, beef braised in red wine with polenta, for $26.95. Count on spending $35 a person at lunch without wine, more like $55 at dinner. There is a reasonable pretheater dinner—four courses at a bargain $39, served until 7:30 P.M.

Should you be uncertain about your taste for Piemontese, the menu, which changes seasonally, also features dishes from more familiar Italian regions. Manager Paul Nunez or any of the very efficient staff will gladly serve as culinary guide.

In addition to the garden, the original dining room, drawing rooms, and library of the adjoining nineteenth-century dwellings that now house Barbetta also owe their special look to Laura Maioglio. Imposing and patrician with their ornate woodwork and marble fireplaces, the rooms are available for private functions, seating from six to seventy people.

Romantic tryst or corporate party, Barbetta offers a lot more than all those "oldests" and "firsts"!

Beau Geste

320 Amsterdam Avenue   (212) 724-2222
New York, NY 10023

Sal Guzay decided the Upper West Side was missing something vital to the quality of life in the area—a truly elegant, first-rate, and appropriately expensive French restaurant. Beau Geste is his solution to a problem that many neighborhood residents had not even realized existed. Indeed, many people choose to live on the West Side because it is not inundated by overpriced purveyors of ambitious food.

Is Beau Geste, like the ever-growing potpourri of fine boutiques dotting the district, a sign of things to come, a sign that the West Side will become virtually indistinguishable from the East Side? Perhaps. Whatever the future, Beau Geste is a current if somewhat qualified success.

The room is large, light, and airy, broken into two levels separated by only a very few steps. Columns of etched glass reflect the muted pastel patterns of the chairs and carpeting, not to mention the profiles of such aficionados as Malcolm Forbes, Sam Donaldson, and Kathleen Turner.

Bruno Tison is the chef, imported by Sal from his favorite San Francisco restaurant, Ernie's. Whatever Ernie's reputation (not very good in certain culinary circles), Bruno's classical training under the likes of Roger Verge and Michael Guerard is in evidence at Beau Geste. Terms like *terrine, quenelle, sabayon,* and *gratin* and ingredients like venison, foie gras, rabbit, morel, partridge, tongue, and endive spice up the menu.

Dinner with wine from the adequate but not terribly exciting wine list will probably run at least $100 for two. The fresh duck foie gras in sauterne jelly with caramelized onions and turnips on toasted brioche is a good appetizer bet at $24. Another winner is the quenelle of tuna tartare with marinated raw fish in lime and smoked scallops at $11. Among the main courses, we liked the $23 halibut sautéed with morels and beef marrow, accompanied by a chive sauce, and roasted rack of lamb with sautéed garlic cloves and eggplant cake at $45 for two.

So why do we describe the restaurant's success as qualified? Service. It's just a tad too affected for our taste. There's lots of solicitous hovering and yet some simple requests meet with long delays. Furthermore, many of the staff seem to be rather too obviously graduates of the Berlitz school of French accents.

Granted, Beau Geste is still relatively new. The service will probably improve, and the phony, difficult-to-understand accents might evaporate with the passage of time. Still, there's something just a trifle incongruous. Perhaps it's the decor—not quite serious enough for the cuisine, the prices, the almost studied pretentiousness of the place. And despite all their flourishes, despite the theatrically synchronized presentation of dishes (all too often accompanied by a self-satisfied "Voilà!"), the staff isn't very knowledgeable about the food they are serving. Or maybe it's just us. Maybe we're too provincial to accept a fancy first-class French restaurant on the West Side! ❧

Bice

7 East 54th Street	(212) 688-1999
between 5th and Madison	
New York, NY 10022	

In July 1987, the New York Transit Authority should have inaugurated a shuttle-bus service between Seventh Avenue and Madison at 54th. The always-strapped Transit Authority might have made some money. Ever since Bice hit town that summer, it's been a favorite haunt of the fashion crowd, especially at lunch. We know several members of that stylish population who've been taken to the restaurant so often by well-meaning ad-space salespeople that the mere mention of the name (pronounced bee-chay) makes them groan.

While the food is okay, it's not really responsible for Bice's popularity. Instead, that can be traced to the restaurant's origins as the American version of Milan's revered Bice, traditionally the first place journalists and buyers head when they're covering the Italian fashion shows. Having enjoyed many a meal there of truly superb Tuscan food, they rejoiced at the owner's announcement of an impending New York outpost. They eagerly awaited the opening; the press heralded it in advance. The rest is a classic success story based on expectation and hype. Bice was destined to be a hit, regardless of the uninspiring food.

Now Bice has even gone bicoastal with a Beverly Hills location, and we hear rumors about licensing agreements—a far cry from the informal, family-owned establishment in Milan, where the best seat in the house is actually in the open kitchen.

No open kitchen in New York, but there are lots of good and highly coveted seats, thanks to restaurant decorator of the moment, Adam Tihany. Bice is large and open with lots of light, good for people-watching all around—people like Calvin Klein, Oscar de la Renta, Versace, Oleg Cassini, and Valentino. Hollywood is well represented by Dustin Hoffman (who seems to go everywhere that is anywhere), Michael Caine, Kim Basinger, and Frank Sinatra. Then there's the publishing firmament, including virtually all the editors and all the publishers of all those very glossy magazines. The senior staffs of *Town & Country*, *Vogue*, *Harper's Bazaar*, and *Vanity Fair* are likely to be here at any given time, on weekdays at least.

On the weekends, when most high-profile New Yorkers are away (or pretend to be), a very "bridge and tunnel" (read *New Jersey* or *Long Island*) crowd descends, anxious to sample Bice's celebrated glamour.

They don't get much in the way of celebrities, but they do get a perfectly respectable, if expensive, meal. Lunch for two without wine is about $90, dinner at least $120. The lobster-and-arugula salad at $16 is a good starter, as is the Bice specialty salad of shrimp, avocados, and crabmeat for $16. One of the risottos is a good choice for the pasta course, so rich you might consider splitting one, particularly the sinful $19, four-cheese interpretation.

Main courses change daily, hence their designation as *Piatti del Giorno* on the menu, but you can generally count on the veal chop Milanese as a staple. A favorite at the Milan restaurant, it's a favorite here. Pounded to within much less than an inch of its life, it's covered with a tasty breadcrumb mixture and sautéed to perfection. It's a winner at $23, as is the grilled swordfish with olives and tomato Mediterranean style for $24.

Needless to say, reservations are a must and best booked a couple of days in advance. Even so, it's likely you'll have to wait in the small bar, which is usually packed right up to its redwood-paneled walls. There's some relief during the warmer months, when the bank of French doors fronting the street are thrown open and additional tables set up on the sidewalk.

Of course, if you're a regular or a somebody, i.e., anyone maître d' Maurizio or owner Roberto recognizes, your wait will be shortened. Furthermore, you have a better shot at being seated in the front room. The back is considered Siberia, despite the fact that it benefits from the same flattering lighting, pretty, green, and surprisingly comfortable chairs, and distinctive redwood accents.

Roberto, by the way, is an archetypical Italian charmer. So schooled, he named his restaurants after his mother—her nickname is Bice. He's another reason the restaurant is so popular. Alas, with his far-flung enterprises he is there less and less. We can't help but wonder if absentee management won't tarnish Bice's bright star.   🍒

Bouley

165 Duane Street   (212) 608-3852
New York, NY 10013

David Bouley stands out from the growing pack of Manhattan's chef/proprietors. Few among them have traveled so illustrious a route to their fame and their establishments. Born into a French-American family, David studied with Roger Verge and Paul Bocuse. He is a veteran of Le Cirque, arguably the chicest game in town. And his talents launched the fabulous success of Montrachet, putting Manhattan's TriBeCa neighborhood on the culinary map. Indeed, David's departure from Montrachet created a sensation among foodies, who considered it a defection and worried about the restaurant's ability to survive his treacherous action.

Happily, in this case all's well that ends well—Montrachet continues to thrive, and David's Bouley has been a hit since he first opened its doors in August 1987. And we do mean *he* opened the doors—in actual fact he installed them, along with everything else in this intimate restaurant that is very much a labor of love. David, his brother, daytime maître d' Melissa Bosnell, and a make-shift crew of helpers hammered every nail, painted every wall. The result is a very pleasant, romantically serene setting for outstanding dining. As Provençal as the pastel scenes of the French region that form the bulk of the decoration, the walls are whitewashed, the ceilings vaulted. Both glow from the discreet indirect overhead lighting and the charming little lamps on each table with their pleated shades. An 18-foot flower box runs beneath the front windows and is always bursting with seasonal blooms.

It's all very low key, very understated, elegant but somehow homey—a feeling that is reinforced by the selection of warm and toasting breads offered just after you're seated. While the waiters have a very professional demeanor, they are not at all pretentious or intimidating. Still, they manage, starting with the bread, to serve each morsel as if it were a precious jewel. And well they should—the food is quite extraordinary.

Lunch, overseen by Melissa and peopled primarily by men of the Wall Street and City Hall species, is served either as a five-course menu degustation for $32 or à la carte. If you opt for the latter, it'll probably run you about $40 per person. We suggest the menu, but not because it's less expensive. We like the fact it always represents David's best efforts and eliminates agonizing decisions, allowing concentration on the serious business of eavesdropping on power politicos like Ed Koch, Andy Stein, and David Dinkins. While straining to hear their plans for the city's future, you can enjoy a feast that might start with what at most other French restaurants would be a very unusual creamless butternut soup garnished by roasted chestnuts—David follows the very modern French style of cooking, never using heavy cream or copious amounts of butter in any of his dishes. After the soup, choose between delicacies like Maine monkfish in a tomato coriander sauce, accented with sweet roasted garlic and savory cabbage or roast Pennsylvania chicken with French flageolet beans. A salad course comes next—warm goat cheese, last time we checked—succeeded by a refreshing sorbet and dessert.

For dinner, we advise skipping the $65 eight-course menu in favor of the à la carte suggestions. It's not any less tempting than the luncheon version nor are eavesdropping opportunities any less compelling (Andy Rooney, Morley Safer, and Walter Cronkite, en masse and individually, enjoy dinner here). But since you're here for the evening, you should make the most of it—foodwise. Part of the fun is discussing all the selections, each more mouthwatering than the last, and enjoying bites of your companion's choices, as well as relishing your own.

Just when you and yours have settled on appetizers of panache of three salads—hot goose foie gras, grilled shrimp, and wild mushrooms—for $15 and roast Maine lobster served in its consommé with crisp asparagus, winter mint, and fresh black truffles for $16, you spot the extensive list of daily specials. All of a sudden you have to think long and hard about $12 Maine harvested sea scallops on a nest of sweet lettuce with mushroom and dill vinaigrette or the $14 fresh Maine smoked eel, peppered mackerel, and shark in a green mustard sauce.

Having delighted in a debate on the merits of each, you move on to the entrées. Here again, David always slides in seasonal specials, but we have developed a passion for the regularly featured rack *and* loin of lamb with port wine, puree of potatoes served with black olive zucchini for $28. We're equally enamored of the glazed duckling with Italian sweet onions, French lentils, and compote of Italian figs at $23.

Dessert provides another quandary. Although the $8 hot apricot soufflé and chocolate pear soufflé topped with homemade vanilla ice cream always gets our vote, along with the identically priced coconut and chocolate mousse mille-feuille and coffee opéra with bitter chocolate sorbet. And we have been known to look favorably upon the warm raspberry tart with caramel ice cream, which is also $8. Really the best solution is to ask the waiter for a sampling of each. Don't be shy about asking, they're used to it.

Always the innovator, in and out of the kitchen, David employs a computer to keep track of his patrons, their reservations, and their meals. On the downside, if you're one of that breed most despised by restaurateurs, a "no-show," Melissa or night-time maître d' Olivier will know it next time you call. Expect a chilly reception. On the upside, each of your Bouley meals will be kept on file so you can always track down the source of that unforgettable taste sensation and request it.

Indeed, requests, rather exceptional ones at that, are sort of a house specialty. Not too long ago David created a singular meal for a group of 25 wine merchants and their guests. They arrived at Bouley bearing a number of incredible wines. Before each course, they sent David a glass from the appropriate bottle. A sip or two inspired him to design a dish to complement the wine. He'll do the same for you, if you have a special bottle or two in your cellar. Give him a little advance notice via Melissa, who will discuss any possible corkage fee with you, and you're set for the experience of a lifetime.

Carnegie Delicatessen & Restaurant

854 Seventh Avenue   (212) 757-2245, 2246, or 2247
at 55th Street
New York, NY 10019

Carnegie Deli—the very name conjures up images of sandwiches piled high with savory meats, dripping with tasty condiments...and long lines. It's sort of a cause-and-effect situation.

While it is high on the list of many a visitor, this is no tourist trap. It's a New York institution, a place natives come to consume huge portions of traditional deli food, at all hours of the day and night, quickly and in not particularly comfortable circumstances. In fact, the chairs are decidedly uncomfortable and the tables are so close together that all your contortionist skill is required to unfold the giant menu without socking your neighbor in the nose. So why do so many people bother to come here so often?

Quite simply, the food is good and honest, the variety extraordinary. Where else can you find a whopping $12.95 Reuben to give you that much-needed second wind at three o'clock in the morning? And the crowded hustle and bustle is all part of the fun. Somehow you don't mind having your plate whipped off the table as you put the last morsel of food in your mouth. Apparently Jack Nicholson, Warren Beatty, Meryl Streep, Shirley MacLaine, and Dustin Hoffman don't either. They all come in—and yes, they have to stand in line like anybody else. Marvin Davis loved it so much on his visits to New York that he became the major partner in Carnegie West, located at the corner of Dayton and Beverly Drive in Beverly Hills—where else?

The owner in New York, Milton Parker, runs the Carnegie here, carrying on the traditions he and his late partner, Leo Steiner, established at the fifty-five-year-old landmark. His card says the Carnegie's corned beef and pastrami are rated "Number 1 in the World." We're not sure about the source of the rating, but who would question it? Feisty Senator Lloyd Bentsen certainly wouldn't. During his ill-fated run at the vice presidency, he paid a visit with pal Henny Youngman. It was all he could do to get his hands around the massive "combination" sandwich, laden with at least one and a half pounds of meat. He had to solicit Henny's advice as to how to eat it. When he finally mustered the courage to tackle it, he pronounced the sandwich well worth the effort.

But sandwiches aren't the only story here—the fabulous $9.95 blintzes are made to order. The broiled chicken livers at $10.95 with fresh vegetable and boiled potato are another big hit, as are the baked short ribs of beef, served with baked Idaho potato and fresh vegetable of the day for $11.45.

The service consists of a true cast of characters. One of our favorites is Jack Sirota, who started working here thirty years ago. He claims he doesn't look any different than the day he first set foot on the premises. But then, Jack has a reputation as quite a storyteller!

Now we haven't addressed the dessert situation, but maybe that's just as well. Perhaps we would do you a better favor by concluding this entry with directions to the nearest health club!   ❧

Chanterelle

2 Harrison Street   (212) 966-6960
New York, NY 10013

It's way downtown, not easy to find once you get there, and reservations are hard to come by. Still, Chanterelle is worth the trip to TriBeCa, even worth the effort of booking six to eight weeks in advance. Karen and David Waltuck have created a little restaurant magic in this somewhat obscure location. But then they've had some experience in this regard. Their former restaurant, also called Chanterelle, introduced Soho to world-class dining (and prices).

In fact, the closing of the first Chanterelle caused a near riot among foodies addicted to David's clever but never cutesy combinations of flavors and textures, enhanced by his classic, straightforward sauces. The panic intensified as the renovation of the new space took longer than anticipated; the city was Chanterelleless for a number of months—too many months. Finally, David and Karen were able to open in March 1989, just in time for the tenth anniversary of the annual Albert Dinner, the most celebrated stag gourmet feast in America. The new Chanterelle was inaugurated by thirty-two black-tied gentlemen, who spent seven hours feasting on ten courses.

On entering through the small foyer, you are struck by the fact that something is missing—the bar. Its absence is a welcome signal that your reservation will be honored in a timely manner. There's no long wait here despite Chanterelle's extraordinary success and the fact that it seats only sixty.

The entrance to the dining room, occupying the corner of Harrison and Hudson Streets, is majestic—light pours through towering windows facing both streets. The lofty, ornate, pressed-tin ceiling and the three brass chandeliers are the room's centerpiece. No art adorns the peach walls, no flowers clutter the tables. Chanterelle's is a studied, pure environment that forces focus on the food. This is a place meant for serious dining. Plan on three hours for dinner.

The menu is revamped every two weeks. Even the menu covers change on a regular basis. Saluting Chanterelle's first incarnation as a popular spot with Soho's artsy crowd, each cover features the work of a different master—Elsworth Kelly, Donald Evans, Cy Twombly, Merce Cunningham, Keith Haring, Louise Nevelson. Inside, the choices are outlined in a sprawling handwritten script. When we last visited, the $68 prix-fixe dinner featured a selection of four appetizers, six entrees, and four desserts.

We dove into the sublime grilled seafood sausage and unusual squab mousse with green peppercorns for the first course. The poached salmon in basil and softshell crabs in lime butter as main courses attested to David's daily forays to the city's markets. Of course, we're always tempted by the tasting menu, which, when last we saw it, featured both the sausage and the mousse, followed by red snapper with mint and tomato, and rack of lamb with tarragon, topped off by cheese and ice cream. All this for $87.

As we go to press, Chanterelle serves dinner only, Tuesday through Saturday. But Karen tells us that plans are afoot to open for lunch as well, so call to check. It will probably be easier to get a reservation.   🦞

Docks

Oyster Bar and Seafood Grill   (212) 724-5588
2427 Broadway
between 89th and 90th
New York, NY 10024

                                                      (212) 986-8080
633 Third Avenue
New York, NY 10017

Pals Howard Levine and Barry Corwin hit on the notion that what Manhattan really needed was a good, reasonably priced seafood restaurant. The instant success of their first stab at filling the void, Docks on the Upper West Side at 89th and Broadway, proved them right. So right that barely three years after the 1985 Broadway opening, another debuted on Third Avenue. It seems that East Siders had been clamoring for the same fresh fish, mollusks, and crustaceans that had been the draw on the West Side. Indeed, the menus, the printed and the daily chalkboarded specials, are identical at both locations, but the atmospheres are somewhat different.

For starters, the Third Avenue restaurant is considerably larger than its predecessor. And though Howard and Barry claim it was unintentional, it has a slightly more upscale look and feel to it—more and better prints on the walls, fancier lighting fixtures. Still, both Docks benefit from a handsome, unpretentious decor featuring lots of tile, brass, and wood. They are the visual version of onomatopoeia. They look exactly what they are—comfortable, old-fashioned, basic seafood houses where fish and their shelled brethren are cooked to pure perfection.

As such, they attract a cross-cultural crowd. Docks Broadway tends to draw from the neighborhood, which is an eclectic lot, while Third Avenue gets more than its share of legal, publishing, and garment industry types who find its just slightly east-of-midtown location handy for lunch and dinner. In fact, we must admit that while we hold a sentimental place in our hearts for the first Docks, the people-watching at its East Side offspring is better.

At 5:00 in the afternoon you see little old blue-haired ladies in search of their manhattans and broiled sole. Later on, the power-red-ties-and-suspenders group comes in for their belon oysters, 3-lb lobsters, and bottles of chardonnay. It's about this time that the Third Avenue Docks becomes a bit of a meat market (despite what it serves)—a single woman threading her way to her seat through the packed bar does run a gauntlet. Still, the regulars' ranks are enlivened by the frequent presence of William F. Buckley, Kathleen Turner, Robert Duvall, Paul Simon, Jerry Orbach, Jackie Mason, and Harrison J. Goldin.

We generally start our Docks seafood binge with a selection of the four varieties of oysters offered nightly. Priced per piece and according to market value, we've been known to mix them with some littleneck or cherrystone clams—they're all just so succulently moist and fresh. The fried calamari, just as light and scrumptious as it can be at $6, is another favorite starter. For the most part, fish is either simply grilled, broiled, or fried with an occasional sauced rendition among the specials. You can't go wrong with any of the grilled "steaks"—salmon, swordfish, tuna, snapper, or halibut, all in the $17 to $18 range. And the fried oysters served with a sublime tartar sauce are terrific at $14.50. All entrées are served with the sensational Docks slaw and a choice of potato (baked or fried) or rice, but order the French fried yams on the side for $2.50. They are a special taste treat indeed.

In case you're wondering, there are some "land locked" items on the menu like a $19 grilled New York shell steak and an $8.50 burger, but why bother? If you think fish belongs in the water and not on a plate, go elsewhere.   ❦

E.A.T.

1064 Madison Avenue	(212) 772-0022
between 80th and 81st Streets	
New York, NY 10028	

First the Zabar family conquered the West Side with the extraordinary food emporium that bears its name. Then, in 1973, they sent an emissary in the guise of Eli Zabar to colonize the East Side with E.A.T. Son and nephew of the founders of the legendary Zabars, Eli first set up shop on the corner of 72nd and Madison in part of the Rhinelander Mansion, where Ralph Lauren is now so luxuriously ensconced. A runaway success, E.A.T. quickly gained New York landmark status akin to its crosstown forebear.

In 1984, Eli moved up the street to larger quarters, which allowed him to expand on his theory that people would welcome the opportunity to consume his homegrown delicacies right on the premises. Today, E.A.T. is a delightful restaurant, while still clinging to the vestiges of its take-out roots.

Actually, it's a bit of a shock to drop $70 for lunch for two in a place that takes no reservations and most closely resembles a cross between a deli and an ice cream parlor, with marble-topped tables, bentwood-style chairs, lots of chrome and mirrors, and black-and-white marble floors. While there's something almost clinical about the decor, the food is anything but. Buoyant with freshness and exuberant flavor, it is positively addictive, which explains why people line up at the take-out counter for $12.99 chicken salad sandwiches. Garnished with a little side salad and served on a plate in the café, it goes for $14.00.

By now a neighborhood fixture, E.A.T. is open seven days a week for breakfast, lunch, tea, and dinner, starting at 8:00 A.M. Especially on weekends, it is a favorite haunt of many of the city's movers and shakers who live in the area. By noon on Saturday there is usually a line out the door, but it's not as bad as it looks. Only half the people are waiting for one of the seventy-five seats. The rest are queuing up to take out Eli's $24-a-pound creamy smooth liver pâté with pistachios and currants, or the Norwegian salmon version for $50 a pound.

Eli's bread is a most popular pick-up item. In fact, they bake four tons a day to supply over 200 restaurants and hotels. It's Eli's that fills the bread baskets of 21, the Four Seasons, the Pierre, and the Regency. If you want a loaf for your very own, it will cost $2.50 at E.A.T.

For dinner, Eli bows to restaurant convention by accepting reservations—a nice touch, considering that you'll probably spend $50 per person. If you visit between October and February, you can sample an E.A.T. New York exclusive—Nantucket scallops, succulently sautéed, for $24.

Save room for one of Eli's homemade desserts. We're always hard-pressed to decide between the luscious bread pudding and the wicked seven-layer chocolate cake.

One decision you won't have to make is what credit card to use. Eli accepts only American Express, but he will arrange for a house account if you choose to leave home without it!   ❦

Elio's

1621 Second Avenue   (212) 772-2242
between 84th and 85th
New York, NY 10028

There's nothing all that special about the hardwood floor and bentwood chair motif, certainly nothing that accounts for the nightly crowds here. Actually it's pretty difficult to pin-point exactly what it is about Elio's that makes it so popular. Maybe it's the hour-long wait for a table—and that's with a reservation. Maybe it's the hour-long wait for a bill at the other end of the evening. Still, the restaurant is one of those New York happening sort of places, with an energy that serves as magnet for the city's legions of over-achiever types—most of whom seem to know each other. Air-kissing and table hopping add to the throbbing hustle and bustle that is the scene at Elio's. Curiously, none of this seems to have much to do with the food. Food? You don't come to Elio's for food, for goodness' sakes. Really.

But yes, Virginia, there is an Elio—he and partner Anne Isaak gallantly try to maintain some order in the midst of apparent chaos. The bar, where you inevitably pass your hour waiting for a table, can be stifling with its extraordinary press of flesh. It's bearable only if you can worm your way into a position where you can strike up a conversation with the delightful Ida. Not only is she the bartender, but she is the reservationist during the day. She'll remember your name. Indeed knowing what you're in for, she may even have asked about your favorite drink so she'll be ready to whip it up when you arrive and identify yourself.

Is it worth the wait, worth the hassle? Well, the food is good, not over-whelmingly so nor particularly memorable, but perfectly acceptable (and by New York "in" spots' standards, reasonably priced). In fact, in some isolated cases, it borders on excellent—the pesto, for instance. Elio is Genovese and insists that his city's signature sauce is perfect. And on Thursdays there is always a better than good ossobuco. But our money's always on the $15.50 spaghetti puttanesca, the obvious pasta very spicily sauced with tomato, black olives, and anchovies. The nodino alla salvia, or split veal chop sautéed in sage and butter, is another winner at $24.

Anne's husband, Joe Fox, is a senior editor at Random House. So you can bet the literary crowd is in attendance—Joan Didion and husband John Gregory Dunne, Joan Buck, and Norman Mailer. The likes of *New York Times* publisher Punch Salzberger, Tom Brokow, Anne Bass, Peter Jennings, Diane Von Furstenberg, Woody Allen, and Paloma Picasso also show up with regularity. The celebrity ranks are augmented by an extended neighborhood crowd, many of whom consider Elio's home away from home on Sunday evenings. They come in early on their way back from the Hamptons or some other preserve of the rich and almost famous, having alerted Elio of their E.T.A. from their car phones. Indeed, Elio is probably the best source of Sunday in-coming traffic information, as he gets reports from every conceivable route.

If you're more interested in movie trivia than traffic jams, be sure to sit at one of Marvin's tables—Marvin the waiter, that is. He's an encyclopedia of old movie facts and graphically illustrates the menu too. He often carries samples of pasta (mercifully raw, as opposed to cooked) to prove his movie and menu points. We've often thought Elio and Anne should charge for entertainment when Marvin is on duty. He's terribly amusing.

But don't plan on being amused or fed at Elio's for lunch. It's dinner only—seven nights a week, from 5:30 to midnight. ❤

Ferrara

195 Grand Street   (212) 226-6150
New York, NY 10013

New York in the Gay Nineties had almost everything—everything except a place where an Italian opera singer (or anyone else for that matter) could sit, relax, and sip a few cups of espresso, chased by a sweet delicacy or two. Enter opera impresario Antonio Ferrara and his pal, Enrico

Scoppa. In 1892, they opened Caffè A. Ferrara. Caruso loved the place and put it on the map, so to speak.

But the neighborhood café didn't come into its own as a world-famous destination in New York's celebrated Little Italy until the arrival of Antonio's nephew Peter shortly after World War I. Peter had stowed away on a New York–bound ship. Ever enterprising, he married Enrico's daughter, thus creating the family dynasty that still owns what has become simply Ferrara.

Famous and commercial though it is with its mail-order catalog, Ferrara retains an Old World charm. The little rectangular marble tables are squeezed close together and the atmosphere depends on the crowd that comes from all over the city. It remains the sort of place you drop into on the spur of the moment, at almost any time of day or night. Current owner Alfred Lepore and sister Anna Maria open at 7:30 every morning and don't close until midnight or so, later on Fridays and Saturdays. It's busiest after 6:00 P.M. By nine o'clock there's a line outside—seating is on a first come, first served basis. If you show up late in the evening as many do, expect a fifteen- to twenty-minute wait.

Ferrara's so popular because it's the perfect "after" place—after lunch or after dinner. People like Lee Iacocca, Frank Sinatra, and the last three U.S. presidents come here to sample the decadent pastries, not to mention the best espresso and cappuccino in town. During the summer, they set up an ice cream stand, so you can stop by for a cone and then continue your stroll through Little Italy, on to Chinatown.

Light breakfasts and lunches are also served, but the allure of Ferrara is the desserts, all made on the premises. The cannoli, that most traditional of Italian pastries, is superb. At $2.25 each you can have as many as you wish. The cappuccino torte is nothing short of addictive—coffee custard-filled sponge cake, bathed in coffee punch, and topped with cappuccino butter cream. It packs a wallop for only $4!

The cookies can be packaged for take-out—$10 per assorted pound. They make great gifts and can be shipped anywhere in the world, as can all the rest of the Ferrara products outlined in the aforementioned catalog.

About to enter its second century, Ferrara has carved a unique niche in the heart and appetite of New York.

The Four Seasons

99 East 52nd Street   (212) PL4-9494
between Park and Lexington
New York, NY 10022

When Phyllis Lambert persuaded her father, the late Samuel Bronfman, founder of Joseph E. Seagram & Sons, of the wisdom of making Seagram's projected New York headquarters building an important architectural work instead of a conventional office monolith, little did she know that it would house what would become one the city's most important restaurants. Indeed, the original concept did not call for a ground-floor restaurant. But, however it happened, by 1958 Philip Johnson, who in conjunction with Mies van der Rohe designed the stunning Seagram's Building, was working on plans for a restaurant. The Four Seasons opened in 1959 and has played a major role in the city's restaurant scene ever since. Long recognized as a culinary landmark, it is now designated by the New York Landmarks Commission as an architectural one as well.

It certainly gets our vote. The restaurant is just as striking, just as contemporary, just as awe-inspiring as it was when it opened 30 years ago. The Four Seasons is essentially two large square rooms—The Grill Room boasting the bar and a lot of heavy hitters at lunch; and The Pool Room, or main dining room. Both are framed on two sides by walls of windows covered with hypnotically rippling chain draperies. The Grill's high, wide, and handsome two-level floor plan is warmed by French walnut paneling and dominated by the dramatic Richard Lippold sculpture of gold-plated brass rods.

The dining room, connected to the Grill by a corridor hung with a huge Picasso tapestry, is arranged around a central white marble pool with a comforting gurgle. Both rooms benefit from artwork and substantial plantings that are changed, like the menus, seasonally.

At lunch, Alex von Bidder holds the key to the prized tables in The Grill Room. Of course, the dining room is open, but only the uninitiated happily walk down that travertine lined corridor to Siberia. The regulars, people like John Fairchild, Bill Blass, Michael Korda, Kimberly and John Farkas, HG publisher Don Madden, *Vogue* publisher Verne Westerberg, Felix Rohatyn, Judy Licht, and a host of Japanese executives vie for seats in the Grill. Alex sets his daily stage with tact and decorum, two qualities particularly appreciated by his Japanese clientele. In fact, Alex went to school to learn their social customs to make them feel more at home, customs like not presenting the bill at the table. Japanese regulars at The Four Seasons receive monthly statements in the mail.

But you certainly don't have to be Japanese to feel comfortable here, literally and figuratively. The Mies van der Rohe designed chairs are downright restful, and the service, under the watchful eyes of owners Tom Margittai and Paul Kovi, is superb. And the food? You already know it's special. You would have to have been dead or living on another planet not to have heard of The Four Seasons' deserved reputation of excellence.

The menus are in a constant state of flux, both seasonally and daily, so there's always something new to try—perhaps in deference to the not inconsiderable number of people who make it a habit to dine here three or more times a week? In the dead of winter the menu might feature hearty items like lentil soup with sausage and roast duck with baked apple or spicy shrimp and scallop curry, while the summer months might prompt the sautéeing of succulent soft shell crabs.

The Grill Room has its own kitchen dedicated to what by Four Seasons standards is "basic" cooking, meant to be unassuming and uncomplicated. It is created *not* to compete with important lunchtime conversations as the focus of attention. As such the food is perfection, so perfect that real regulars call only when they don't plan on showing up. With wine, lunch for two in the Grill will probably edge into the $160 neighborhood.

You should consider ordering a bit of the grape here. The wine list is pretty amazing, with "Bottles of the Week" highlighted by asterisks. Because of The Four Seasons' buying power, they are often able to purchase some exceptional wines at good prices, which in turn they pass along with a relatively low mark-up as the weekly specials. You might find a Cabernet Sauvignon Reserve Beringer 1983 for $45, or a Château Latour, Pauillac 1980 for $56. Not highlighted but still special are bottles from the cellar, like a Dominus C. Moueix 1984 at $72; a Chablis, Pic Premier 1985 at $65; and a Château Petrus, Pomeral at $225.

For dinner you'll want to sit in the elegant Pool Room and sample its somewhat more sophisticated, more refined, and innovative à la carte menu. Winter choices might include a flavorful wild boar pâté with red currant sauce for $14.50 or marinated salmon with dill sauce for $15.50 as appetizers. For main courses, winter is, after all, game season, so look for medallions of venison with red cabbage and chestnut puree at $40, breast of pheasant with gorgonzola-laced polenta served with a juniper sauce at $37.50, and grilled quails with mustard and sage at $37.50. For a more domesticated meal, try the filet of veal with crabmeat and arti-chokes for $40. Dinner can easily run up to $250 a couple with a salad or vegetable, wine and dessert.

If all this sounds a bit heavy, and you know your doctor would wag his finger diaspprovingly, The Four Seasons always features a few low-sodium, low-cholesterol, and low-fat spa cuisine selections. Developed in accord with recommendations from the Columbia University School of Nutrition, the spa dishes might include seviche of red snapper with orange at $14 and grilled beef, lamb, and veal tenderloin with braised lentils at $37.50. There's also a $41.50 pre- and post-theater menu, which in addition to several regular choices for each of the three courses also offers spa cuisine items.

This is a restaurant that not only celebrates all seasons, but covers all bases. There's something for everyone here, and rest assured that every-one comes. For dinner in The Pool Room on the weekend, reserve a week in advance—three days should do it during the week. As for lunch in The Grill Room, call and hope for the best. If you want to be assured a table on relatively short notice, launch a campaign. Plan well ahead and book a week or two worth of lunches. Be sure to show up, on time, and do your best to infiltrate Alex's consciousness—that's our best advice on how to become a true Grill Room regular. After that, you're very much on your own! ❧

Fu's

1395 Second Avenue   (212) 517-9670
between 72nd and 73rd Streets
New York, NY 10021

In a city overflowing with elegant "gourmet" Chinese restaurants, Fu's stands out from the pack. The contemporary but surprisingly sophisti-cated and soothing decor helps—muted gray walls, pink linens, bur-gundy chairs, and tiny white lights glimmering in strategically placed mirrors. But it's Gloria Chu who makes the real difference.

A noted restaurant consultant and old friend of owner Michael Leung, Gloria was asked to help out when Fu's first opened in 1984. Somewhat to her surprise, she's been there ever since and has proved to be the mag-net for clientele who move and shake with the biggest. Always chic in her Adolfo suits and impressive jewelry, Gloria delights in telling you about who's who and what's what as she darts among the tables. She'll whisper conspiratorially that Paul Newman actually sat in your very seat the other night or that John Kennedy, Jr., is even better-looking in person. Gloria cites the fashion crowd as regulars, designers and execs alike—Missoni, Laura Biagiotti, Saks' Mel Jacobs, and Bloomingdale's Marvin Traub. And the broadcasting community is well represented by Mike Wallace and Barbara Walters.

Most habitués simply put themselves in Gloria's hands, telling her about dietary restrictions or allergies, never even bothering to look at a menu. (In fact, we'd never even *seen* a menu until we asked for one as part of our research.) If you're a first-timer, Gloria will ask a few questions about your taste in Chinese food, then proceed to custom-design a memorable meal. She never fails to please even the most doubting Thomas.

We once dined here with a gentleman who claimed to dislike Chinese food because he's acutely allergic to eggs, a common ingredient. He had previously taken ill at other restaurants, despite long, involved explanations about his problem that met with nodding heads and protestations of comprehension. Thanks to Gloria, at Fu's he enjoyed a Chinese meal for the first time in his life.

A long-time inhabitant and visitor to the Far East, he was still especially taken with the Peking Duck, as are most patrons. Unless you've indicated vegetarian tendencies, Gloria usually includes it as it is one of the house specialties. In fact, for the last three years, Fu's has provided Peking Duck to the La Chaîne des Rôtisseurs annual "View from the Vineyards" dinner—duck for 2,000 people. It's quite a show. The whole duck, all crispy golden brown, arrives tableside, where it is flamboyantly carved and served. At $32.50, one duck serves at least four.

If you leave it all to Gloria, you'll experience a rich variety of textures and flavors, generally four or five courses, not counting dessert, which she tends to ignore other than passing out the ritual fortune cookie. In addition to the duck, we always look forward to delicate steamed dumplings and the slightly crunchy but tender orange beef, complemented by the hot and spicy sesame chicken. All of it is beautifully presented and impeccably served, according to Gloria's exacting standards. She regularly takes her staff on outings to Lutèce, Le Bernardin, the Four Seasons, and Le Cirque so they can experience the level of service she expects of them.

Dinner for two, Gloria-style, will usually run about $70 for food. She makes no decisions about libations, so in that area, at least, you're on your own and in control of costs.   ❦

Grotta Azzurra

| 387 Broome Street | (212) 226-9283 |
| New York, NY | (212) 925-8775 |

Agonized groans are an all too common sound on Broome Street, uttered by Grotta Azzurra fans who arrive to find people packing the stairway leading down to the restaurant, spilling out onto the street, waiting. Lines are not uncommon in New York. What's unusual is that in the midst of Little Italy, cluttered with alternatives, most people don't reconsider their plans and wander down the block to another restaurant. Instead they groan and resign themselves to the wait.

Why? Why do they even bother making what is often a long trek to a restaurant that doesn't accept reservations? The two F's—Food and Fun. Grotta Azzurra has plenty of both, all of it good. It's a crowded, good naturedly noisy place, often enlivened by a roving guitar player who whips everybody into a sing-a-long frenzy. When not singing, or downing the generous portions of first-class Neapolitan specialties, patrons often busy themselves making new acquaintances. The coveted tables are so closely packed together that individual party boundaries are blurred. It's virtually impossible to get through a meal without engaging your neighbors in conversation.

As the walls attest—studded with autographed pictures of decades' worth of celebrities—the crowd tends to be interesting. On any given night you might run into Sergio Mendes, Neil Diamond, Dolly Parton, Barbra Streisand, Brenda Vaccaro, or Lainie Kazan. One night Sinatra called owner John Davino to announce he was coming down with a party of 25. John checked with wife/hostess/cashier Cathy about the feasibility of taking proper care of Ol' Blue Eyes. Since a number of regulars were already seated (and no one under any circumstance is ever rushed at the Grotta), people were lined up on that steep, almost treacherous stairway, they regretfully told him he better plan on going elsewhere. Now, rumor has it that Frank doesn't deal well with the "no" word, but in this instance he graciously accepted the decision. He might even understand that the Davinos treat everyone equally.

No doubt he figures they know what they're doing. After all, the Davino family has been running the Grotta for four generations—ever since it opened in 1908. John's been here for the last 38 years, 30 of which he clocked as the chef. These days, son Vincent mans the kitchen at lunch and daughter Connie is around in the evenings. So there's almost always a member of the immediate family on the premises. And most of the staff is part of the extended family—Tony the tall, terribly goodlooking, and ever-so-helpful waiter is a ten-year veteran. But that makes him a relative newcomer. Fellow waiters Giovanni and Frankie have been here for 25 and 27 years respectively. And current head chef Joe Amato has logged 40 years with the Davinos.

Joe's responsible for what may be the best lobster fra diavolo in town. Priced according to the size of the lobster, a very special treat, the restaurant is justifiably proud of it. But it's not the only star on the menu. The outstanding chicken, steak, and sausage contadino serves 3 to 4 people for $39.95. Try a side order of spaghetti with white or red clam sauce for $10.95, but plan on splitting that, too, since no half portions are offered. And don't miss the homemade minestrone at $5.95.

A satisfying and very good meal at Grotta Azzurra can cost as little as $15 a person, or as much as the traffic, not to mention appetite, will bear. But rest assured that the bill will not be inflated by the bar tab—there is no bar. The Davino family has always believed that good food and liquor don't mix. Only wine and beer are available, with a $22 bottle of Bardolino at the high end of the small list of imported wines. In the sparkling category, you can indulge in a $96 bottle of Dom Perignon, but bring plenty of cash. You guessed it; the Davinos believe credit cards and good business don't mix either.   ❦

Huberts

575 Park Avenue   (212) 826-5911
on 63rd between Park and Lexington
New York, NY 10021

Besides being one of the hottest restaurants in town, it is, next to the European imports, the best traveled. About 15 years ago Len and Karen Allison were living in a large Brooklyn brownstone, which on weekends they turned into a restaurant serving up Karen's cooking. Originally structured as an extra income producing venture to raise money Len needed to pursue his career as filmmaker, it changed their lives. Karen's talents and the reasonable prices ($10 for a three-course meal) began to attract a substantial following—they were making more money with their weekend enterprise than they were at their real jobs. They became restaurateurs and Huberts (no apostrophe, named after Karen's grandfather) was born.

While Karen held down the culinary fort, sometimes cooking in three kitchens simultaneously—hers and that of her neighbors on both sides— Len applied his considerable talent for promotion to their new business. Business thrived and the Allisons decided it was time to reclaim their home.

They leased and renovated an old tavern down the street. Huberts was beginning to acquire a real personality and a citywide reputation, built on solid reviews and a program of visiting chefs. The presence of some of the country's most notable chefs did two things for Huberts—it generated a lot of publicity and it taught Karen and Len a thing or two about cooking. Indeed their roles were beginning to switch; Len was spending more time in the kitchen, while Karen was dispensing her considerable warmth out front.

Four years later, in 1980, by popular demand and in search of greener pastures, they made the move to Manhattan, to the then unlikely location of 22nd and Park Avenue South. There they got their first taste of the big-time, the rave reviews from *The New York Times* and *Gourmet*, and the celebrity patronage. Len, now firmly ensconced in the kitchen, began attracting national attention for what he calls his "eclectic ethnic" food. Impossible to classify, it draws ingredients, preparation styles, and inspiration from a number of cuisines—Cajun, Japanese, French, and Mexican among them.

By 1987, despite a $55 three-course dinner menu in an area which was not supposed to be able to support such "uptown" prices, the 60-seat restaurant was proving too small. Too often they were turning away too many people. It was time to move once again.

In March 1988, they opened the current Huberts. The striking Adam Tihany–designed restaurant is a far cry from its Brooklyn brownstone origins. The main room with its hand-painted dabbled walls, Venetian glass lighting fixtures, paper screened windows, and decorative, curved teak beams resembles an intriguing cross between a Kyoto teahouse and the Art Deco dining parlor of an oceanliner. It's oriental sparseness is warmed by some deco glamour. There's a gracious, civilized serenity about the room, no matter how crowded it is. The space between the tables is as generous as their size, so you can have a real conversation with your meal.

And what a delightful meal it's likely to be, especially given the prices. Having moved "uptown," Len has recently instituted a "downtown" pricing policy. The luncheon tastings menu is $32.50 for three selections. Alternatively, you can order any of the choices, none classified as either appetizer or entrée, for $7 to $14 each. Light lunchers, we usually go the latter route, ordering the sensational smashed cucumbers smothered with shrimp in a sesame vinaigrette at $9 or the terrine of smoked salmon layered with cream cheese flavored by horseradish at $11, and a $7 endive salad.

The fixed price dinner is $45.00, a downright bargain for a restaurant of its caliber, with à la carte selections from $7 to $14 for appetizers, $18 to $26 for entrées, and an average of $7 for desserts. Go for the fixed price—it's so much easier for the waiters to add up the bill. But save room for one of pastry chef John Dudak's divine desserts. John has made his own journey with Huberts, having started out as a dishwasher. Now, after years of watching, experimenting, and practicing he makes a lemon tart that you'll never forget, not to mention a whole repetoire of other sweets like a chocolate mousse cake seemingly sent from heaven.

As for Len's food leading up to dessert, it remains innovative, distinctive, provocative, and, oh yes, perfectly marvelous. His signature dish, the spicy rabbit sausage with a bitter chocolate sauce hailing from Mexico called mole, makes an unforgettable appetizer as does the sweet/tart roquefort soufflée. While we don't usually make it a practice of ordering steak in such an establishment, the grilled Black Angus with an ancho chili mayonnaise is hard to resist. In the fish department, it's always a toss-up between the pan blackened salmon, spicy crisp on the outside, sweetly, succulently rare on the inside, and the grilled tuna with an endive ragout.

After dinner, if you're so inclined you can retire to the smoking room with its rich oriental rug and soft leather Chesterfield sofas. There you can settle down in style for an after-dinner drink, perhaps one of Huberts' excellent cognacs, ports, or Armagnacs. It's one of the only rooms in New York where gentlemen are actually encouraged to smoke a cigar, provided it's a good one—such a sophisticated uptown touch.

Actually the only thing we miss about the restaurant's downtown predecessor is Karen's presence in the dining room. These days she's on the Mommy track, so Len's dividing his time between cooking and greeting regulars like Peter Allen, Geoffrey Beene (who designed the waiters' handsome uniforms as a restaurant-warming gift), Dan Rather, Mimi Sheraton, Douglas Fairbanks, and Grace Mirabella. Grace chose Huberts as the site for the launch party of her sophisticated new fashion and lifestyle magazine *Mirabella,* the latest in the Rupert Murdoch publishing empire. No restaurant in New York had seen that many cameras and Somebodies with a capital *S* since the re-opening of 21. You can't get much more uptown than that!   ❦

J. G. Melon

1291 Third Avenue   (212) 650-1310
at 74th Street
New York, NY 10021

Since 1972, Jack O'Neil and George Mourges' bar/restaurant has been one of the Upper East Side's premiere watering holes. With a basic menu not recommended for those concerned about cholesterol (burgers, steaks, chili, and fries are the big movers here), Melon's, as it is universally called, is busy from the moment it opens at 11:30 A.M. until the kitchen closes at 2:30 A.M. The front barroom keeps hopping 'til four!

Egalitarianism is the rule. No matter who you are, if there is a line, you wait—there are no reservations. So you wait your turn along with Mayor Koch, Henry Kravis, Saul Steinberg, Kate Capshaw, John Kennedy, Jr. "The Boss" has been known to stop by, but Springsteen seems to have no patience and usually leaves before one of the coveted tables in the small dining room is available.

Besides eavesdropping on illuminating (and potentially profitable!) conversations while waiting at the bar, you can amuse yourself by counting the number of representations of melons that constitute the major part of the restaurant's decor. It seems that when Jack and George opened, they had only about $100 to decorate. In search of bargains, they wandered around the corner to an antique store about to go out of business—and happened upon four affordable prints, all melons. Voilà! Jack and George (J. G.) and Melons. They got a name and motif for their place in one outing!

Friends have been donating melon items to the decorating cause ever since.

Today, Melon's is a casual, comfortable place to share predictable but good food with friends at reasonable prices—$4.75 for a hamburger,

$17.50 for a sixteen-ounce steak. It's dark and cozy, with green-and-white checkered tablecloths, hooks on the walls for coats, sturdy and stiff dark wood chairs, and strategically placed blackboards as menus. At night it's a melting pot—a couple in jeans next to a party in black tie.

The service is informal and friendly. If you're dining alone, sit at the bar so you can chat with amiable Patrick or Dennis.

Be careful not to get carried away with the conviviality of the place and lose track of your cash reserves. Melon's does not take credit cards.

❦

Jim McMullen

1341 Third Avenue   (212) 861-4700
between 76th and 77th Streets
New York, NY 10021

Brick walls, bentwood chairs, planked wood floors, and Art Nouveau sconces make for an appealing atmosphere, but it's owner Jim McMullen who's the real attraction. A very visible host, who wisely associates himself with a number of the city's most worthy causes and their socialite supporters, Jim actively cultivates his Upper East Side clientele. Furthermore, his restaurant satisfies their basic need for a joint they can call their own. Not as preciously chic as Mortimer's, Jim McMullen (the restaurant) nonetheless has a certain élan that elevates it well above the neighborhood dive category, but mercifully keeps it out of the chichi sweepstakes.

Jim created an environment where trendy types can feel comfortable and at home, but still be "out" to see and be seen. The long, narrow bar is a popular gathering place for a young, stylish crowd. It's fun watching them pretending not to admire themselves and each other in the large mirrors that line the wall.

Three dining rooms flow behind and around the bar, forming a U-shape and seating 170 or so. With every seat usually filled, there's a noisy, informal conviviality—like a club where everyone automatically belongs simply by virtue of having the good sense to be here. Devotees like Blaine Trump, Joanna Carson, Cheryl Tiegs, Kim Basinger, Reggie Jackson, and even Mayor Koch casually acknowledge each other with a nod of the head or a glass raised in salute.

Social considerations aside, there's a lot to be said for the food; it's pretty good in a down-home sort of way. We call it nursery food, because it's soothingly familiar and somehow reminds you of Mom. There's just something about the warm corn bread and homemade biscuits. The mashed potatoes are refreshingly real, complete with lumps. Certainly you're reminded of Mom's admonitions about starving children in China, while you try to cope with the ever-so-generous portions! Even the prices are comforting—a reasonable $11.50 for succulent whole broiled flounder or for our favorite, buttermilk fried chicken. Dinner for two runs about $40. You can get away with $25 or less at lunch, though you may have to stay away from the delicious $13.50 cold poached salmon with watercress mayonnaise. The juicy hamburgers and fresh chef or chicken salads in the $6.50 to $7.75 range are great alternatives.

So when you have an urge to go out for some first-class mingling and reliably good food, but don't want to dress or have to upgrade the limit on your credit card, check out Jim McMullen.   ♥

Joe Allen

326 West 46th Street   (212) 581-6464
between 8th and 9th
New York, NY 10036

Opened in 1965 by theater buff Joe Allen, this is what Sardi's used to be—an integral part of the theatrical community serving up good food and better company. It's an informal, brick-walled, red-checkered table-cloth sort of place. Food is taken seriously here, but nothing much else is—the bathrooms are decorated with posters from Broadway's most disastrous flops. Joe reads the trades and the reviews just as faithfully as the actors, directors, and producers who dine here and the waiters with theatrical ambitions who serve. Ralph Waite was bartending here when he got word he'd won the part of the father in what was to become the fabulously successful series, "The Waltons." Joe laughs when he recalls, "Ralph never really finished his shift. He started celebrating and everybody felt they had to buy him a drink. You see, he'd been an out-of-acting-work actor for so long."

Set right in the middle of 46th Street's restaurant row, Broadway's traditional stomping grounds, Joe Allen is always packed before show time. The location helps, but the reasonably priced food is the real lure. Joe's daughter Julie oversees the open kitchen, which serves up reliable, down-home American cooking—sublime meatloaf with mashed potatoes and gravy for $12, a truly noteworthy $5.75 cheeseburger. The chicken salad with gorgonzola, white beans, chopped tomato, and olives is a great combination of flavors and textures, and the $13 serving is enough to feed a small army.

While a perfectly respectable dinner may cost you only $20, you should consider the reservation lead time here comparable to that of the fanciest, most expensive multiple-starred restaurants in town, especially for a pretheater meal. Think a week ahead and feel free to call early. Joe starts accepting reservations at 9:00 A.M. seven days in advance.

Joe Allen's is open every day from noon for lunch through late supper. The kitchen accepts orders 'til 11:45 P.M. On Wednesdays, Joe Allen's opens early—at 11:30 A.M.—in deference to the matinee performances. The downside is that you're liable to run into the to-be-avoided-at-all-costs bridge-and-tunnel crowd. Wednesdays aside, you'll get a glimpse of whoever happens to be headlining on Broadway at the moment, together with a legend or two like Lauren Bacall or Mike Nichols. Roy Scheider, Len Cariou, and Ken Howard also stop by, though whether they come for the food or the excellent selection of beers—"from Minnesota to Czechoslovakia"—is unclear. A popular New York magazine recently declared Joe Allen's one of the best places in the city to enjoy some of the world's best brews.

Not being beer connoisseurs, we cannot personally bear witness, but we do know the bar is usually full with a happy, boisterous crowd whose paws seem permanently attached to frosty mugs. We can state unequivocally, however, that Joe Allen's is one of the better acts in town—its agreeable plot, mixing satisfying food, convivial atmosphere, and ample opportunity for stargazing, makes it a perennial hit.

La Caravelle

33 West 55th Street   (212) 586-4252
between Fifth and Sixth
New York, NY 10019

When it opened in 1960, La Caravelle was the quintessential Camelot restaurant—formal and glamorous, serving classic French fare. Indeed, almost since Day One it was embraced by the Kennedys. Their regular patronage and the superb food assured its success for a decade or two.

But by the early '80s, La Caravelle seemed like a restaurant whose time had passed. Long considered a sacred temple of haute cuisine, it was a church without much of a congregation except some faithful aging regulars who returned week after week to order the same dishes. La Caravelle's formal glamour was considered stuffy and fussy, its classic food too heavy and old fashioned by a new generation of diners. They trekked to every corner of Manhattan to pay homage to French chefs of the nouvelle variety, but were conspicuously absent from this centrally located establishment.

Doomsayers predicted its imminent demise. La Caravelle disappeared from lists of the city's great restaurants. A lot of people thought it had closed. It was rapidly becoming a distant memory. But at least one person, Andre Jammet, a partner in the enterprise since 1983, was determined that La Caravelle would not fall entirely by the wayside. Indeed, since he gained sole proprietorship in October 1988, things have been looking up.

It is Andre's intention to revitalize La Caravelle. To that end he has elevated David Ruggerio from chief cook to chef and appointed himself as head meeter and greeter. Now everyone is treated to a genuinely warm welcome, which goes a long way in dispelling La Caravelle's formerly formidable intimidation factor.

By the same token, David has been busy shaking up the kitchen, infusing it with his youthful enthusiasm. At 26, he is one of the youngest chefs ever to assume control of a world-class kitchen, and almost certainly the only one ever to have been a professional heavyweight boxer. His approach to haute cuisine is in step with the times as the pendulum of foodie opinion swings back in favor of the classics—classics prepared with a late '80s twist, with a light hand, a concern for nutrition, and a passion for the freshest of ingredients. He steers clear of sauces clogged with cream and butter, relying instead on stocks and reducing sauces blended with vegetable purees and fruit compotes for both exuberantly intense and subtle flavors.

As a result, people are definitely sitting up and taking notice. La Caravelle, always brightly festive *looking* with its cherry red velvet banquettes and neo-Impressionist murals of Parisian landmarks, is once again a lively and convivial place, quickly regaining its status as a restaurant in which to see and be seen. In fact, it's set up better than most for a meal-long survey of the scene—a long narrow corridor-cum-dining annex (you don't want to sit there) opens into a large, almost square room lined with banquettes. From almost any seat you can keep an eye on any other, including the bar, which (oddly) is situated in the far corner. Anyone meeting someone there has to march across the room for the rendezvous, subject to scrutiny by a good-looking crowd, wearing serious clothes and jewels, and clearly enjoying the still-serious food.

The prices are appropriately serious too. The prix-fixe dinner is $59 with more than its fair share of supplements ranging from $6 to $75, making the pre-theater menu featuring a generous range of dishes from the main menu a great bargain at $37. For lunch, you can go the prix-fixe three-course route for $35 or à la carte. Some of David's new lighter dishes are gaining considerable popularity on their own—the poached fish du jour for instance priced according to market and the $18.50 marinated chicken breast.

At dinner, we can't resist the fresh grilled shrimps with mixed greens and the steamed ravioli filled with crabmeat as hors d'oeuvres as the menu describes them. But the real hors d'oeuvres are those served compliments of Andre shortly after you're seated, a dear little plate of surprises like a marinated mussel or two, a refreshingly light shrimp topped canape, and perhaps a mushroom stuffed with some flavorful concoction.

For the entrée, one of us swears by David's innovation of sweetbreads resting on a crisp bed of potatoes, while the other is taken with duck garnished differently every day. They make quite a spectacle of it, presenting the whole roasted fowl with a fair amount of fanfare before carving it tableside. David, ever the contender, challenges "anyone in the city to make a finer duck than we do."

A true French restaurant, no one bats an eye at La Caravelle when you ask for cheese for dessert. (It drives us crazy when waiters look at us like *we're* crazy when we make a request for cheese. There you all are in a restaurant with a menu boasting cheese in the salads, cheese sauces, gratins topped with cheese and cheese soufflés, yet some idiot with a perfectly straight face declares there is no cheese in the kitchen.) But at La Caravelle, there's a whole tray of cheese treats served with a full complement of breads, crackers, and bisquits. Another dessert delicacy is any of the soufflés, particularly the chocolate and coconut version—all have a $5.50 supplementary charge.

There's also an $80 six-course tasting selection, recently instituted by David. On any given evening it's a comprehensive sampling of the best of the kitchen's offerings—nightly specials always augment the printed menu. Fortunately, the waiters outline those specials out loud. As it is, La Caravelle's menu as a physical entity is one of the most cumbersome in the city, encased or rather upholstered in heavy, padded fabric. Actually, it's our one gripe, and we suspect we're not alone. Too often we've noticed the waiters straining with a heavy load of these behemoths.

La Côte Basque

5 East 55th Street   (212) 688-6525
between Fifth and Madison
New York, NY 10022

What's the old saying about pretty is as pretty does? Well, this very pretty restaurant does very nicely, thank you very much. The food, compliments of chef-proprietor Jean-Jacques Rachou, is nothing short of sensational and it's always very crowded with suitably pretty people. Remember, La Côte Basque served as the site of *Answered Prayers,* Truman Capote's wicked exposé of the antics, sexual and otherwise, of his jet-set pals who frequented it.

The book resulted in Truman's being brutally ousted from the company of his former friends, but did nothing to dampen their enthusiasm for the restaurant. In fact, it probably encouraged patronage among people desperate to establish themselves in that rarefied society. Today, there's often a paparazzi or two lurking about outside poised to snap away at Donald Trump, Gayfryd Steinberg (wearing Scassi or Galanos depending upon who she's with), Bill Blass, Lady Mary Fairfax, Alfred Taubman, Judy Peabody, Paul Newman, Diana Ross, and the list goes on and on. Consequently maître d's Gerard and Pascal are always at their wit's end trying to accommodate all the pretty somebodies at the nine tables in the bar and the seven tables in the front gallery. There may be plenty of room in the back, but no one we know would ever think of venturing into that unwashed territory.

Where is Monsieur Rachou in the midst of this seating frenzy that can border on being uncivilized at weekday lunches? He's in the kitchen, where we suspect he makes a point of staying until the boys out front have gotten everything all straightened out. He knows that once his guests have settled down to their prix-fixe meals—$32 at lunch, $55 at dinner—they'll forgive him anything, even being seated in what they consider Siberia. He seems to time his appearances for mid-second course.

As a first- or second-timer, give the maître d's a break and don't quibble about being led toward the back. The red leather banquettes and velvet chairs are just as comfortable there as they are up front. The David Stein murals on the walls, done when the restaurant was enlarged in 1984, are just as brightly scenic as the Bernard La Motte 1958 originals. The cunning little lamps with their crested silk shades grace every table in the back just as they do the front. Even the lavishly festive floral arrangements are virtually indistinguishable. Most important, the food is the same and that's *really* why everyone's here in the first place, isn't it?

Chef Rachou always offers daily specials in addition to the glorious (and large) menu. Furthermore, if there is something you have in mind that's not printed or mentioned, order it. He never refuses a special request.

At lunch, we tend not to experiment and stick to a couple of eagerly anticipated favorites—the asparagus beautifully arranged on an oversized plate (a $3.50 surcharge) followed by the Cassoulet du Chef Toulousian, a Gallic classic with sausage, lamb, duck, pork, beans, garlic, and whatever else is lying about the kitchen just waiting to be thrown into the pot. Hearty and flavorful, it's the best and one of the few genuine cassoulets in the city.

For dinner, our tastes tend to be more cultivated. The crab and lobster salad served with avocado makes a nice starter even with its $6.50 surcharge. So does the smoked salmon with green sauce at no additional cost. The quail "en croute" with a truffle sauce is sublime and our universal test of a *real* French restaurant is admirably passed by the veal kidneys, served here in a green peppercorn sauce. Dessert is easy, sort of—we always go for a soufflé. The problem then becomes deciding which one, since they're all divine. Usually, though, we opt for the Grand Marnier soufflé bathed in fresh raspberry sauce. With a surcharge here and there, dinner for two is bound to run at least $160 to $170, depending on the wine. For lunch, just leave a $100 bill.

Actually, plan on leaving several of those bills in the course of a week in order to gain the attention of the gentlemen doling out the seating assignments. Once they recognize you as a regular, you might, just might, get one of those dear little tables in the bar, but you'd still be well advised to make your booking several days in advance—a week if you've really got your heart set on basking at La Côte Basque.   ❧

Lafayette

---

65 East 56th Street   (212) 832-1565
New York, NY 10021

With 25,000 restaurants in New York, there's an awful lot of competition for "the best" honors. We wouldn't presume to declare any of them the absolute top of the heap, but this is one restaurant that seems almost flawless.

Only three years old, Lafayette's taken New York by storm, rating an unprecedented four stars the first time it was reviewed by *The New York Times*. Surprising, even difficult, you might think, in what is officially the dining room of a hotel owned by an airline. But you know the old saying about not judging a book by its cover. After all, the executive chef has to be taken into consideration. Louis Outhier was one of the most illustrious chefs in the history of France before he finally closed the doors of his three-star L'Oasis in La Napoule, just outside Cannes, packed up his toque, and headed off to make his fortune in the New World. His was the most celebrated restaurant on the French Riviera, so it is not too surprising that Lafayette would become the most celebrated in New York. And that's before we mention the full-time resident chef, Louis' protégé, Jean Georges Vongerichten. (In case you're wondering, an executive chef plans the menu, refines the recipes, and stops by every once in a while to make sure nothing's deteriorated in his absence.)

So on a day-to-day basis it's Jean Georges' culinary artistry that will astound you at Lafayette. And this is one instance where you'll be able to attach a face to one of the best meals you've ever had. The kitchen is glass-enclosed. Jean Georges works in full view of the restaurant's guests. In fact, those sitting at the "Chef's Table" right in front of the kitchen window come to think of him as their new best friend!

The rest of the room is timeless in its classic, tasteful decor—rose silk walls, French antiques, and wonderful paintings by Chris Anderson. The superb lighting is equally flattering to men and women. Of course, it's got a lot to work with in the handsome faces of Paul Newman, Mary Tyler Moore, Bill Cosby, Maury Povich, Rex Harrison, and Barbara Walters.

Most of the celebrity sightings though are at night. Lunch at Lafayette is consumed by heavy-hitter business types like Larry Tisch. In addition to the excellent food and service, they appreciate Lafayette's sense of

Old World discretion. The restaurant doesn't feed juicy items about who was dining with whom to Suzy, Billy, Liz, or Cindy.

The dinner crowd tends to be a delightful mix of locals and the international set, with telexes and faxes requesting reservations routinely arriving from all over the world. Some want the Chef's Table, others seek real privacy, like Table number 11. It's tucked away, almost out of sight, but positioned so that you can keep a watchful eye on the room. The tables by the window are also popular. Actually, there are no bad tables here, no Siberia. Most regulars, like us, ask for different tables, depending upon our mood or the purpose of the meal—number 11 for serious business discussions, the Chef's Table for festive occasions. Richard, the maître d'hôtel, seems to have a sixth sense about what will please people, seating-wise. So on your first visit, just leave it to him, but be sure to call for the reservation well in advance. Lafayette seats only eighty-five, so is almost always fully booked.

As to what to eat once you've been seated, we love the heavenly air-dried duck breast with foie gras and figs—simply out of this world. Once we've returned to earth, we have been known to move on to the grilled tuna (very rare, just the way we like it!) sitting on a bed of tomato and marinated fennel. For lunch, the prix fixe is $37.50.

At dinner, it's $65 per person, including a selection from a trolley laden with some of the most tempting confections you've ever seen, thanks to pastry chef Sonia El-Nawal. On your way to dessert, try the grilled squab broth with crayfish and girolle mushrooms, followed by roast lobster with polenta and rosemary honey vinaigrette. Extraordinary!

Seeking beyond extraordinary? Sample the Menu Lafayette at $85, with a two-person minimum. Otherwise known as a *menu degustation*, it's six courses, plus sorbet, of what the chef feels best represents his kitchen. For spring (the whole menu changes seasonally), this special dinner included tuna tartare with crisp spring vegetables; gyromitre-morel soup flavored with fresh herbs and asparagus; sea urchin flan with green pea pancake; caviar and halibut with fava beans, truffle, and yellow pepper. The sorbet breather intervened before the spit-roasted baby goat with chick-pea pancakes and marinated eggplant, followed by that sinful selection of desserts. While it may sound overwhelming, the portions are adjusted to allow you to amble through this meal without suffering overload.

All in all, a meal at Lafayette is an experience that Michelin might call *vaut le voyage*—worth a special journey.   ❦

La Goulue

28 East 70th Street   (212) 988-8169
between Madison and Park
New York, NY 10021

The moment you enter the petit bar, you know you're in a little bit of France lovingly transported to Manhattan. During the warmer months, you'll know before you enter by the white clothed tables lined up outside with their cane-back chairs, just like in Paris. In fact, owner Jean de Noyer did import all the restaurant's tables, chairs, decorative brass railings, beveled mirrors, and glass-globed sconces from his native country when he first opened back in 1973. The authentic bistro atmosphere, complete with hearty, flavorful fare, reasonable prices, and good service were an immediate hit. La Goulue has long since become an Upper-East-Side fixture, a favorite, familiar place for Madison Avenue shoppers and gallery hoppers.

For lunch, the crowd starts filtering in about 12:45, and it's usually jammed to its wood paneled walls by 1:30. If you're new in town, don't draw attention to the fact by showing up at noon. Bide your time and slide into one of the comfortably seasoned brown leather banquettes for a late, leisurely mid-day meal. And don't be miffed if Alain marches you through the front room to the one beyond. Ever since Jackie O. turned up one day for lunch and requested the back, the two rooms have enjoyed equal status. You're likely to spot any of La Goulue's regulars, Chuck Scarborough and Anne Ford, Yoko Ono and Paul Newman, anywhere in the restaurant, including the bar.

Actually, we like the bar the best. It gives new definition to cozy, glowing with warmth, from the ambiance or the delightful Louis, who's been here since the beginning. He mans his station, the tiny, antique zinc-topped bar, with Gallic wit and charm, endearingly remembering your favorite drink. In our case, he's got favorite dishes memorized too. Creatures of habit, at lunch we usually order the marvelous $14.75 cheese soufflé and maybe a house salad for $5.50. Occasionally, we've tried the tender chicken roasted with herbs at $16.50, and we're quite smitten with the classic $13.75 salade niçoise.

True to its bistro traditions, La Goulue doesn't attract much in the way of a dinner crowd till after 9:00 P.M. The neighborhood counts on it as a place to dine after an early movie or extended cocktails elsewhere. Every evening it's full of people who seem very much at home here, so at home that they don't even bother bringing along wallets. They simply sign the check and leave, a sure sign of their very regular rank as Jean doles out his house accounts judiciously.

We find ourselves frequenting La Goulue for dinner in the dead of winter when the thick, rich onion soup for $5.50 seems the best remedy to a bitter cold evening—that or the resplendently garlic laden escargots for $6.75. The $19.50 grilled lamp chops with a minted butter sauce is a fitting follow-up as is the roasted duck intriguingly sauced with a blend of stock, white wine, and olives, also $19.50. On the lighter side, you can never go wrong with any of the grilled fish, offered as daily specials according to market and seasonal availability.

La Goulue was a transplanted French bistro long before such establishments started enjoying their current trendy popularity. As such it is *magnifique, formidable, impeccable.*   ❦

La Grenouille

3 East 52nd Street   (212) 752-1495
between Fifth and Madison
New York, NY 10022

Any number of New York restaurants have national, even international, reputations for excellence to live up to. And many don't really make the grade. But La Grenouille is everything it's ever pretended to be, and then some. From the glorious symphony of color in the spectacular flower arrangements by owner Charles Masson to the excellent, formal (but never haughty) service, the scrumptious food, the extraordinarily high celebrity quotient, La Grenouille never disappoints.

Indeed, only the coat check is even vaguely disconcerting. It's a makeshift, sort of jerry-built operation hovering over the stairway that leads to the private dining room. In the dead of winter the tiny closet is always stuffed to overflowing. A number of coats end up on pegs along the wall of the stairwell, lending a rather startling flea market appearance to the place.

Whatever qualms you might have about leaving the family fur so seemingly vulnerable are quickly dispelled by the warm greetings of Charles, his lovely mother Giselle, or maître d'hotel Joseph. Even if they never laid eyes on you before, they welcome you like a long lost friend as they lead you to the back room—the hospitality effectively softening the blow of being seated in the room which prompted the coining of the term Siberia by the press. La Grenouille regulars and that large daily dollop of celebs sit only in the front.

We repeat ONLY in the front, preferably on the banquettes so intimately placed that they can all natter away at each other without raising the noise level unduly. Indeed, Charles is very careful about the seating. He places his guests as if he were seating them for a private dinner party, always sensitive to who knows whom, who *should* know whom, and who's feuding with whom. God knows it's a delicate business, when he's dealing with the likes of John Fairchild, Brook Astor, Georgette and Robert Mossbacher, Bill Blass, Pauline Trigere, Lynn Revson, Brian Marlowe, and Oscar de la Renta. Then there are the less well-known but still powerful business types like our pal Jim Kerwin who holds court at lunch on the first banquette to the left—he commutes almost daily from his New Jersey offices for his La Grenouille fix.

The first bite of the first course of your $37.50 "Prix du Dejeuner" or $68 "Prix du Diner" explains the attraction. Despite its classic French origins, there is a lightness, a delicacy about La Grenouille's food. The varied but not overwhelmingly extensive menu is augmented by daily specials, which may include fresh sole, turbot, or frogs legs flown in from France. At lunch, we often put ourselves in the capable hands of our waiter, allowing him to select a plate of assorted hors d'oeuvres from the always tempting buffet in the bar. When we're not in the mood for appetizer surprises we order the sublime Le Saint-Germain, cream of split pea soup, or the sinful La Crêpe de Mais et Foie blond de volaille, small corn blinis with chicken livers sauteed in sherry. Generally, we ask for the fish of the day as the main course and follow it with the deliciously comforting warm apple tart served with homemade vanilla ice cream.

At night La Grenouille takes on a richly romantic glow from the sweet little lamps with their silk shades—the flowers soften into a riotous blur complemented by the impressionist style paintings of Charles and his late father. The seductive atmosphere encourages you to throw calories and cholesterol to the winds, and linger luxuriously over a long, leisurely meal. Accordingly, we suggest the ravioli stuffed with lobster in a beurre blanc sauce laced with vermouth (Les Raviolis de Homard) to start. Then it's a toss-up between the fresh water pike mousse in a champagne sauce, the frogs legs sautéed in garlic butter and tomatoes, or the rib of beef braised in a red wine, foie gras, and shallot sauce. But there's no contest in the dessert department as far as we're concerned. The warm bittersweet chocolate torte is a must.

As much as we enjoy La Grenouille for lunch or dinner, one of our favorite times to visit is when nothing is being served at all. Every morning about 10:00 A.M., even on Sundays and Mondays when the restaurant is closed, Charles is bustling about, working his magic with the flowers. His artistry is fascinating to watch. Should La Grenouille ever flounder, he certainly has a future as a florist, perhaps even as an artist. His paintings, like those of his father, are really quite extraordinary, both having benefited from the inspiration of painter Bernard LaMotte whose studio used to occupy the upstairs room.

Charles has wisely refrained from remodeling the room, leaving La-Motte's wine racks and paintings lining the walls, with even his easel in its place. The high ceilings, leaded windows, and woodburning fireplace make it one of the most charming private dining rooms in the city. If you're considering a dinner party for up to thirty, by all means book it. Of course, for an occasion beyond special, you can always take over the whole restaurant as Mary Lasker does for her annual dinner dance.

Should that prospect be a little rich for your blood, you can enjoy a similiar experience once a year, the first Tuesday of every February, for $150 a person. La Grenouille celebrates Mardi Gras by throwing a black-tie bash—cocktails upstairs, dinner and dancing downstairs—masks required. It's just for seventy, though, so book now. Even regulars tend to reserve a year in advance to make sure they'll be part of one of New York's truly spectacular evenings. 🐸

Le Bernardin

155 West 51st Street   (212) 489-1515
between 6th and 7th
New York, NY 10019

Unlike other restaurants that hopped the Atlantic in an effort to "make it" in New York (the defunct Harry Cippriani and the still-going strong Bice come to mind), Le Bernardin arrived with little pre-opening fanfare in January 1986. Still, the day after brother/sister team of Gilbert and

Maguy Le Coze opened the New York translation of their two-star Paris establishment, the phone started ringing off the hook. Fed by an on-going series of rave reviews (*The New York Time*'s Bryan Miller has twice bestowed his maximum four stars), their number's never stopped ringing, and the restaurant's three telephone operators are kept busy from early morn to well after dusk.

The reason is a four-letter word—fish. Fresh, extraordinarily prepared, beautifully presented fish. The menu states that "non-seafood entrées" are available on request. But ordering a steak here would be a sacrilege. Gilbert gets only two hours' sleep nightly to be the first every morning at the Fulton Fish Market, the first to pick the best of the catch of the day. His duties as chef keep him at the restaurant till well after midnight. At 3:00 A.M. he's up and out the door searching for a taxi to take him to the market. Armed with a wicked looking fish hook and an ordering pad, he stalks through the stalls in search of succulent sea scallops, perfect pompano, tender tuna, and heavenly halibut. If a particular variety is not up to his exacting standards, standards set by a childhood in a village on the Brittany coast and a lifetime in the restaurant business, he doesn't buy it—whether it occupies space on the menu or not. A little star is simply placed by the entry, indicating that, today, it is unavailable.

His orders placed, Gilbert returns home for an early morning nap of an hour or two, before reporting back at Le Bernardin to oversee the preparation of lunch. As with the selection of his precious fish, he doesn't trust anyone else to cook it. His concern with and hands-on approach to his well-staffed kitchen pays off with food that has the critics frantically exploring their thesauruses looking for new superlatives.

Both lunch and dinner are prix-fixe, $45 and $65 respectively with some supplements ranging from $5 to $10. When it comes to appetizers, the menu is rather curiously arranged. Following the heading of "First Courses" are several mollusk selections. The next group is defined as "Simply Raw"—as opposed to the oysters and clams on the half shell? Besides, they're not so simple or entirely raw. With choices like flavorful black bass seviche and codfish marinated in an eccentric but very successful combination of juniper berry oil, salt, and sugar, this category could be more aptly described as "Cured." Next comes a list of "Lightly Cooked" items—don't miss the ethereal paper-thin sliced sea scallops quickly poached in a rich fish stock and served in a light chive sauce. Finally, there are three soups to choose from, including a sumptuous, chunk seafood chowder.

As far as we know there's not a miss among the main courses. You might consider leaving the choice to the gods, just close your eyes and point. Chances are better than good that you won't be disappointed. We can give personal testimony to the merits of the crispy black bass resting on a bed of cèpe-laced pureed potatoes and surrounded by a sublime lobster sauce. The codfish sautéed in a red-wine sauce layered with flavors and accented by fried shallots is also wonderful. Then there's the poached halibut napped with a warm vinaigrette and the, well. . . you get the picture.

Now if you're wondering what Gilbert's coquettish sister is doing while he's toiling in the kitchen, she's running a pretty tight ship out front. And what a lovely ship it is—spacious, gracious, posh, and plush, the dining room is strikingly elegant. The gray-blue velvet upholstered walls, approximating the color of the sea, soar up to a dramatic teak ceiling and are hung with what, next to the Four Seasons, is the city's best restaurant art collection—large quilt framed 19th century oils depicting fish and fishermen. Vaguely oriental table lamps cast a muted, flattering glow on patrons comfortably ensconced in the roomy armchairs, patrons like Warren Beatty, Mick Jagger, Dustin Hoffman (that boy does get around), Donald Sutherland and Klara and Larry Silverstein. All of them have wives or significant others, but as our hosts failed to mention them, perhaps the ladies don't like fish. In any case, the delightful Maguy Le Coze makes up for any lack of female companionship as she darts among tables, alighting here and there on the arm of a chair, casting her seductive spell.

Eager as she is to please, there's not much even she can do about the month-long wait for reservations. She tried adding a few more tables which did nothing but muck up the formerly uncluttered floor plan. Still, by New York criteria, Le Bernardin remains a sea of tranquility, fewer seats per square foot, and thus less noise, than any comparable restaurant.

As hard as Gilbert and Maguy were working to keep everything ship shape in New York, we were getting concerned about what was happening to their Paris restaurant. True, Maguy spent some time commuting back and forth, but this brother and sister are truly a team. They work best together. Apparently, the Le Cozes were also concerned about the effect of their absentee management on Le Bernardin-Paris and the effect of divided loyalties on Le Bernardin-New York. They recently sold

the Paris restaurant in order to devote their considerable and synergistic
energies to New York. ❧

Le Cirque

58 East 65th Street   (212) 794-9292
between Madison and Park
New York, NY 10021

What can we say about this most celebrated of New York restaurants that
hasn't already been said, ad nauseum? That Sirio is charming and attentive? That it's a hot-bed of rich and famous activity? That your social
standing can be measured by your ability to get a luncheon reservation
on short notice? That the food is okay but it's the scene that counts?
That Benito is a perfectly fine maître d', but it's too bad Sirio lost Bruno?
That it's almost impossible to get through a day's reading of Suzy, Billy,
Cindy, Liz, and James without one of them mentioning who was dining
here with whom? Since March 1974 when this French restaurant
opened just off the lobby of the Mayfair Regent, it has taken center stage
with no sign of relinquishing that position.

Of course, given the fact the food has traditionally not been exceptional, the decor not particularly memorable, and the location not even
all that fabulous, Le Cirque's dominance begs the question. Why? Quite
frankly we haven't the foggiest. And we readily admit that despite all of
the above, we enjoy Le Cirque just as much as anyone else. There's
something about being there that makes you feel socially secure, though
your day can be ruined if you're not seated on the banquettes alongside
Ivana Trump, Alice Mason, Barry Kieselstein-Cord, Barbara Walters,
Brooke Astor, or Judy Price. It really is a game, one that the contestants
play two to three times a week. Perhaps that's the secret—the Le Cirque
game may just be the most enjoyable in town.

To get into it, you have to make a reservation. No hard and fast rules
here. Some days or evenings five minutes' notice might be enough—
other times five weeks may not do it. When you show up to claim your
prize you're sure to be effusively greeted by Benito. Should owner Sirio
scurry over to offer his welcome and kiss a hand or two, you get two
points. Now comes the dreaded table assignment. If you're worried that
you won't rate a banquette placement, bring a party. There are no de-

merits for groups of four or more to be seated at a table in the center of the room, but the closer to the front the better. There, at dinner, you might find Regis and Joy Philbin with Ron Perelman and Claudia Cohen, Marilyn and Al Rush, or Victor Edelstein (Princess Di's preferred couturier) lunching with the ladies who do that sort of thing and who are in the market for his clothes fit for a (future) queen.

Once seated cheek by jowl (there are 28 tables jammed into this former doctor's office), you pretend to study the menu when in reality you're straining to eavesdrop on your neighbor's conversation. Ten points if you're seated next to Henry Kissinger telling Nancy Reagan what Ronny might have said to Maggy Thatcher, or Bill Blass trying to convince Michael Gross of the fashion worthiness of his latest line for his *New York* magazine column.

You don't lose any ground if you're seated next to a boring conversation; you're just better off genuinely devoting your attention to the menu, which since Daniel Boulud has been in charge is worthy of attention. The food has taken on a hearty, comforting bistro quality that's even encouraging pencil-thin Adolpho-suited ladies of a certain age to abandon their salads and dig in. You get more bonus points if Sirio drops by your table to proffer advice on the menu or suggest his favorite among the daily specials. He's most persuasive—you get an extra turn if you can stick to your guns and order what first captured your fancy rather than bowing to Sirio's counsel.

Lunch can be prix-fixe at $33, plus a $2 cover and supplements for dishes like sautéed sea scallops with tomato, fresh pasta, and basil and the delicious lamb stew with vegetables, rosemary, and orange zest. Or you can order à la carte—the cover stands regardless. We're fond of the lobster salad with vegetables and truffle dressing for $27.50 and the duck confit with wild mushrooms, sweet garlic cloves, and mashed potatoes for $22.

At dinner, plan on spending about $150 for two, including a $2.50 cover—plan on more if you start with the $27 Soupe Paul Bocuse, truffle soup with vegetables and foie gras, or go for the $75 four-course menu degustation. We recommend any of the "Roti à La Commande" for two, but believe the menu when it says there is a 45-minute *minimum wait*. For our $31 each, the classic châteaubriand is worth every minute of it. For lighter fare, try the braised red snapper with artichokes, coriander seeds, and sundried tomatoes at $29.50 or the roasted baby chicken with truffle under the skin, crisp potatoes, and mixed greens at $29.75.

If you'd rather be a spectator than a participant in the game, ask for a table in the sweet little bar, just behind the pretty glass wall. It's quieter there. Your conversation won't be overheard, but you can still, in all good conscience, use the visit to Le Cirque for points in the citywide game of drop-that-name played outside the restaurant.   🍎

Le Zinc

139 Duane Street   (212) 732-1226
New York, NY 10013

Owners Phillippe Bernard and Gerard Blanes have transformed a former shoe factory into an authentic French bistro, smack dab in the middle of TriBeCa. With its unusually high vaulted ceiling dotted by fans, original wood paneling, and rust-colored walls hung with artwork by famous and destined-to-be-famous patrons, Le Zinc is a handsome setting for a self-consciously hip, attractive crowd. They appreciate the rich, no-nonsense food and extended hours. Dinner is served until midnight on weekdays, 'til 12:30 A.M. on Friday and Saturday nights. But the bar that runs half the length of the restaurant doesn't shut down until the last person leaves, or 4:00 A.M.—whichever comes first.

Lunch is served from noon to 3:00 P.M. and attracts a very businesslike bunch who happen to have offices in the area, mostly attorneys. A little spice is added by the artsy types who saunter over from Soho. But the real people action here is at night when the likes of Jack Nicholson, Jim Belushi, Mimi Rogers, Robert Redford, and Prince Albert of Monaco are likely to show. Le Zinc is particularly popular with movie folks and recently even served as the setting for an Italian production directed by Francesco Rosi called "To Forget Palermo."

The menu reads just as you would expect—heavy on the calories and laden with cholesterol. There's foie gras and confit de canard, $11.50 and $7 respectively, to start. The steak tartare at $16 is a classic (though we suspect it does not follow the true bistro tradition of using horsemeat). Veal kidneys sauteed with gin and juniper berries at $14.50 is an example of chef Paul Emile Vandewoode's creativity. A native of Brussels, he subscribes to and often proves the theory that the Belgians taught the French how to cook.

In addition to his daily specials, Paul is justifiably proud of his cassoulet, one of the few served in the city. A time-honored peasant dish that utilizes the kitchen's most appetizing leftovers—duck confit and sausage in this case—and served with white beans, it's the regional favorite of southwest France. At $17.50 it's our southwest Manhattan favorite. We usually order the very respectable $20 house champagne, Domaine Chandon from the Napa Valley, to accompany our cassoulet. The refreshing bubbly lightens the intensity of the dish and makes for a very festive, very French meal.

Manager Lilliane Preux is the lady to call for reservations. A day or two in advance should do and make it for after nine o'clock. There's no difference where the food or service are concerned, but the people-watching potential improves as the night wears on.   💗

Lutece

249 East 50th Street   (212) 752-2225
between 2nd and 3rd
New York, NY 10022

Like a fine old wine from their impeccable cellars, Andre Soltner and his beloved Lutece just get better with age. They have dominated the ranks of New York's classic French chefs and restaurants for three decades with scarcely a successor (or even pretender) in sight. A number of what some ill-bred boors might be coerced into describing as competitors are more expensive. Many are certainly a lot fancier. But Lutece remains without question the finest. Therein lies the explanation for the month-long wait for reservations and the frequent visits of Richard Nixon, Malcolm Forbes, Lee Iacocca, Jackie Onassis, and Paul Newman.

In an era when the pedigree of a restaurant's designer seems to be as important as its chef in determining success, be prepared to be somewhat underwhelmed by Lutece's physical plant. On entering, you're struck by the fact that there is nothing elaborate, lavish, or even particularly elegant about this legendary establishment. "Cute," "quaint," even "dog-eared" spring more readily to mind. True, the miniscule bar sports a charming mural and very rattan chairs, but otherwise the first floor decor leaves something to be desired. The hand-painted walls of the front dining room look like they could use some new helping hands, and the stability of the trellis work in the "main" room (11 tables compared with four in the front room) looks a little dicey. Still, enormously high ceilings

of the room lend some drama, and the ambience quotient improves considerably as you mount the creaking, winding staircase to the second
floor.

There are two quite lovely rooms here, both small, both elegantly
refined—a Gobelin tapestry in one and a marvelous antique copper still
serving as repository for a magnificent floral display in the other. Despite
the obvious inequities in the decor, there is no real pecking order here.
No seating location defines your relative importance—no Siberia. It's
simply a matter of which room you prefer. Oddly enough, there are even
those who swear by the downstairs, just as we would never dream of sitting anywhere but upstairs.

Wherever you sit, we guarantee that the food and service will be superb and, considering the quality of both, rather reasonably priced—$38
prix-fixe for lunch and $60 for dinner. While you can't go wrong with ei-
ther one, dining at Lutece is an event of the highest magnitude, one that
should not be constrained by a busy schedule. Skip it for lunch. Go for
dinner and plan on spending the evening. The folks at Lutece expect it.
An 8:00 P.M. reservation means the table is yours for the night.

In addition to the printed menu, there are always three or four appetizer and main-course specials, mouthwateringly described to you by
your waiter. If he mentions lobster-filled ravioli as an appetizer, order it.
The same goes for the fresh baby lamb for the main course. For an absolutely unforgettable experience there's always the $85 tastings menu—six
courses selected for your delectation by Andre, in his considered opinion
the best of what his kitchen has to offer. While its specifics are in constant flux, the categories always include: soup, preappetizer, appetizer,
entrée accompanied by complementary vegetables, cheese and dessert
with a palate-cleansing sorbet thrown in here and there for good measure.

Naturally the wine list is as impressive as the food, doing justice to
dishes like foie gras in brioche, timbales of escargots, médaillons of veal
with morels, and sweetbreads sautéed with capers.

Now, we stand by our advice about the best way to experience Lutece
is to spend the whole evening there. But that can be easier said than
done, since reservations can be so difficult to come by. You might try
easing your way into the real dinner hours by opting for an early supper
once or twice—a 6 P.M. reservation is much easier to get. While you may
feel a tad rushed because your table will definitely be required again dur-

ing the course of the evening (unlike those of us who show up later for the rest of the night), you will get an opportunity to befriend the staff in order to establish yourself as a regular. Once you're a known quantity, it'll be somewhat easier to get a table in that coveted 8:00 to 8:30 neighborhood.

Under no circumstances, however, no matter how much of a regular you have become, should you ever even think about a meal at Lutece in August. During that month, Andre indulges in a time-honored French tradition and takes a well-deserved vacation. The restaurant is closed for the whole month, but the answering service will take reservations for September.   ♥

Maxim's

680 Madison Avenue   (212) 751-5111
between 61st and 62nd
New York, NY 10022

Maxim's is as much conglomerate as it is restaurant. There are the *two eateries,* L'Omnibus and Maxim's, not to mention the florist's, the bakery, catering, private parties, and of course, how could it be Maxim's without the cabaret. But what's most amazing about Maxim's is that it exists at all, let alone thrives, after its dismal 1981 debut. Owner Pierre Cardin spent gargantuan sums ($250,000 alone soundproofing the ceiling in the main dining room to mollify coop owners upstairs) transforming this prime piece of Madison Avenue real estate into a Belle Epoque approximation of its Paris namesake. But the much ballyhooed opening was a bust. Declared *the* most expensive restaurant in town, critics hated it.

Despite the investment, people wondered if Cardin would be forced to withdraw from the field. New York, after all, is a town where a bad review from *New York* magazine's Gael Green or *The New York Times'* Bryan Miller can kill a restaurant, fast. Maxim's was ranked "rank" by both. But Cardin persevered, bringing in the charming Monty Zullo as manager. After a number of staff changes and a lot of menu shuffling, Maxim's seems to have hit its stride—prices are down and the food is much, much better.

Maxim's has found a niche as a special occasion restaurant where no real occasion is necessary—just going there to dine and dance makes a special moment of any evening. It's so pretty and romantic. The stained glass glows, the burnished wood shines, and the brass decorations gleam. They radiate with color, casting a blush over the tables with their pretty bunches of pink roses.

The orchestra plays danceable music from a little proscenium stage at one end of the room from 8:00 P.M., Tuesdays through Saturdays. You feel like you're in the sort of place Fred and Ginger frequented in the movies. People really do get up to dance. These days, though, they're only doing it between courses. Otherwise they're too consumed with the results of Chef Marc Poidevin's labors. The appetizer salad or marinated raw tuna with caviar and asparagus at $16 and the butternut squash soup with duck confit at $7.70 are both excellent samples of his innovative flair. As an entrée, the sautéed dover sole wrapped in a crispy potato blanket topped by a confit of leeks and an herb sauce is, at $31.50, one of the city's most successful versions of the craze for combining fish and potatoes in a single dish. We also like the grilled $31.50 lamb chops with the dear little rosette of tomatoes and zucchini sitting on a bed of very tasty eggplant "caviar."

Still, should you elect to dine elsewhere, you can still enjoy the ambience and the music by stopping by later in the evening for a drink or coffee and dessert. While there is no music cover with dinner, there is a $15 charge per person if you just want to drink and dance. Whichever you do, you'll want to do it dressed. Coats and ties are a must, and Saturday nights are black-tie during the season. It's a place where you see a lot of pretty (or at least famous) people dressed to the nines—like Saul and Gayfryd Steinberg, Ron and Claudia Perelman, Frank and Kathie Lee Gifford, and George Schultz. With the exception of George, they're all New Yorkers. Unlike its Paris parent, Maxim's has not been relegated to the ranks of tourist trap, thanks mostly to Monty who's one of the world's great networkers.

For less formal dining, there's L'Omnibus downstairs with its own entrance on 61st Street. While not as lavish as Maxim's, it is nonetheless very attractive. If the wall murals of beautiful, glamorous women look somehow familiar, it's because they're by René Gruau, the artist who is also the world's preeminent fashion illustrator. You've seen his distinctive work just everywhere for years.

As for the food, it's lighter and less costly here. The number of interesting salads on the menu is indicative of its popularity with ladies who lunch. We always order the thinly sliced chicken breast with tomatoes and yummy xeres dressing on the side for $14.75 and the mixed greens and vegetables with a tangy mustard dressing for $12.50. Heartier appetites will be satisfied by the selection of meat and fish dishes—we're very fond of the fried calamari which melts in your mouth at $18. There's even a very respectable $12.50 hamburger.

Recently Monty instituted a $25 prix-fixe dinner, which makes it awfully tempting to hang around after one of our cocktail hours at L'Omnibus. It's a great place to stop in after work. The room sparkles with little votive candles and the convivial conversation encouraged by generous drinks and complimentary canapes.

Wednesdays through Saturdays there's another reason besides that bargain of a three-course menu to stick around—a cabaret featuring artists like Steve Ross, Barbara Cook, and Anne Hampton-Calloway. The intimate setting seems to inspire both performers and patrons, prompting a sing-a-long here and there. Generally speaking a good time is had by all, at both shows 9:00 and 11:00 P.M. with a cover determined by the act.

You should also know that Maxim's wonderful brioche and a number of other pastries are available for purchase or order. Beautifully bagged or boxed in white packages with Maxim's bright red logo and tied with red ribbon, they make great hostess thank-you gifts. The Maxim's de Paris florist shop offers an alternative with their bountiful and lavish bouquets. Their work is always on display in the form of two massive arrangements flanking the grand stairway leading up to that grand institution, Maxim's.

Melrose

48 Barrow Street   (212) 691-6800
New York, NY 10014

This outpost of California haute cuisine may not be named after L.A.'s trendiest avenue as owner/chef Richard Krause maintains, but it might as well be, given its popularity with the bicoastal set. No doubt the fashionable back room (the front is considered Siberia) with its look of an enclosed garden reminds them of their own dear Ma Maison. The food probably does too, since Richard used to work at that celebrated eatery.

Richard also used to work at Batons, where he perfected his signature potato pancakes, but he yearned for a place to call his very own. A chance sighting of a "restaurant for sale" ad in *The New York Times* lead him to Barrow street. Something told him this was it. He took it on the spot, never even looking at another site.

With partner Lee Friedman, who doubles as maître d', he has built quite an eclectic following for this small restaurant that serves only dinner. Raquel Welch, Jay MacInerney, Bianca Jagger, Rod Steiger, Daryl Hannah, Dominic Dunne, Ali MacGraw, Gael Greene, Rex Reed, and Gene Siskel—they all sit in the back room, preferably in the booths. With columns posing as birch trees twinkling with little white lights, an astroturf floor, and garden lanterns peeking through the foliage that tops the sideboards, it is the perfect setting for Richard's whimsical food.

The crisp potato pancakes napped with crème fraîche and three caviars for $12 are a must. And where else could you find something described as "Warm Sweet Curried Oysters with Cucumber Sauce and Salmon Pearls"? For $8, it's just as good and just as pretty as it sounds. In the main-course category, the grilled loin of veal with potato gratin, sautéed wild mushrooms, and a port wine cream sauce for $25 deserves high praise. We also liked the charred bluefin tuna served very rare and complemented by a sweet/tangy mango, tomato, and green onion vinaigrette. The presence of the $21 grilled Norwegian salmon nestled on black and gold pasta with Japanese miso and green onion puree makes it a very difficult choice indeed. Actually you'll notice that a number of Krouse's dishes rest on noodles—it's another one of his trademarks.

À la carte, dinner for two will cost about $70, if you skip the wine, which you shouldn't. Richard and Lee work hard on their wine list and are justifiably proud of their stock of fine California vintages.

There's also a three-course prix-fixe meal for $28. As good as it reads, we can't wholeheartedly recommend it because it doesn't offer those divine pancakes.

It does, however, feature any one of Melrose's dessert selections, which go for $6.50 apiece on the regular menu. The raspberry brown butter tart is heaven, the crème brûlée perfection.

End your meal with one of the excellent dessert wines, cognacs, or ports. Sit back, sip your favorite libation, and survey the very chic, the very sophisticated, the very downtown scene that is Melrose.

Metro

23 East 74th Street   (212) 249-3030
between Fifth and Madison
New York, NY 10021

Four gentlemen (not from Verona) share the ownership of Metro, but you need only concern yourself with two of them—chef Patrick Clark and maître d' David Coon. We're sure the other two partners, Jack Fuchs and Serge Rimpel, are very nice men, and we *know* they're smart. They had the good business sense to invest in a restaurant that's been playing to SRO crowds since opening in March of 1988. But you won't see very much of them. It's Patrick and David who make the Metro experience memorable.

Patrick apprenticed with Michel Guerard in France and was the chef of record when the trend-setting Odeon opened in 1980. Whether you call his food new-American or new-French-American, it's superb. The portions are healthy and so is the cooking—less cream, less butter. The emphasis is on fresh, so while there are several regularly featured dishes the menu changes every day.

Generally dinner runs about $55 a person, with lunch more like $25. Unless you're in the neighborhood however, taking in the latest exhibition at the Whitney, antiquing at Vito Giallo's, or shopping at YSL, it's a bit off the beaten path for lunch. Save Metro for dinner, when you might run across Leo Castelli, Joe Helman, Charlie Cowles, Dan Rather, Oprah Winfrey, Jodie Foster, or Judy and Michael Lasher. They all look so comfortable in Metro's decidedly elegant, but ever-so-relaxed atmosphere, courtesy of Adam Tihany (who may tie with Dustin Hoffman for the most number of mentions in the restaurant section of this book—Adam designs, Dustin eats).

We like most of Adam's work, but Metro is a particular triumph considering what he had to work with—the site of the old Adam's Rib. Dark and dreary, with the faded elegance of a men's club desperately in need of new and young blood, Adam changed all that. Today, Metro positively glows with beautifully carved Honduran mahogany paneling bathed in soft indirect lighting. The antique Venetian glass chandelier in the foyer is complemented by the French deco sconces in the bar and the sleekly handsome fixtures adorning the walls in the dining room. We might have gone so far as calling them unique, but they seem to be identical to those that decorate Huberts' dappled walls—another Adam Tihany–designed restaurant, which opened in its new uptown location just slightly before Metro made its debut. Wonder if Adam got a good deal on them?

At any rate, the synergistic food/atmosphere combination at Metro has made a reservation here a prize catch. Enter David, the most diplomatic and accommodating of maître d's. Getting him on the phone is the key to getting a prime time slot—8:00 to 8:30 P.M. And rest assured that he's very deft at booking his establishment properly. You may have to wait a bit in the usually crowded bar, but it will only be about 10 to 15 minutes. David won our hearts the evening he swept aside a flustered waiter who had been unable to deal with the concept of turning our table for four into a table for five. In a matter of minutes, with grace and aplomb, David managed to accomplish what the waiter had sworn was impossible.

Partner Patrick and his chef de cuisine Scott Barton are equally adroit in their handling of the kitchen. Courses arrive on time and practically leap off the plate with just-prepared vitality. The salad of sautéed sweetbreads mixed with wild lettuce, endive, and mushrooms in a hazelnut olive vinaigrette at $12.50 and the sautéed dungeness crab cake with a tomato butter and bell pepper compote are particularly good examples in the appetizer category. As for entrées, we've sampled $28.50 grilled Norwegian salmon with lentils, bacon, and horseradish cream and the $23.00 clay pot roasted chicken with potato pancakes, roasted garlic, and herbs. But it was the roast rack of lamb with a garlic custard, vegetable couscous, and baked eggplant napped by natural lamb juices for $32 that really captured our fancy.

Desserts are as sinfully rich as you might imagine. But somehow Metro is not the sort of place you want to linger over dessert, coffee, and an after dinner libation. It's a tad noisy and boisterous. Give into your desire for dessert if you must, then head over to Bemelman's in The Carlyle for a drink and quiet conversation.   ❦

Montrachet

239 West Broadway   (212) 219-2777
New York, NY 10013

Any attempt to experience the renowned food and ambience of this smallish TRiBeCa spot is an invitation to at least a $10 cab ride and some degree of adventure. Actually the cab fare and adventure are closely tied; the longer the driver wanders aimlessly through Montrachet's dismal-looking neighborhood, searching for the small hanging sign over an old storefront that rather too quietly announces the restaurant's existence, the larger the fare.

We like to think of the adventure and the cab ride as stimulating; all the attendant anxiety seems to spur our appetite to deal with Montrachet's excellent French cuisine steeped in Provençal traditions. Once settled in the stark but comfortable and oddly cozy front room (there are two others, but we never sit in them and neither should you) the travails of the trip quickly evaporate. We nestle into one of the rust-maroon colored banquettes beyond the mahogany and onyx bar, and gaze at the unadorned pale aqua walls, awaiting a surprisingly well-priced meal courtesy of visionary owner Drew Nieporent and chef Debra Ponzek.

Drew rates visionary status because of his courage to venture into TRiBeCa five years ago with an ambitious French restaurant. He also had the courage to persevere in the face of daunting adversity—the departure of his original and highly regarded chef, David Bouley, now proprietor of a delightful restaurant bearing his surname. Drew promoted Debra from the ranks of the sous chefs, and Montrachet has marched merrily forward, ever expanding its reputation for an exciting array of game, organ meat, and seafood selections designed to appeal to the adventuresome diner.

There is one area, however, where Drew's irrepressible courage may have failed him. Rather than risk offending any of the gallery owners like Max Davidson, Leo Costelli, and Ivan Karp, whom he counts among his regulars, he has chosen to leave the walls of this former industrial loft space totally blank. Still, with a high celebrity-quotient clientele— Jeremy Irons, Dustin Hoffman, Robert De Niro, Keith Hernandez, Geoffrey Beene—there is plenty to keep your eyes entertained, once you've studied the deliberately small menu.

Drew keeps it small, while changing it seasonally and always supplementing it with a number of daily specials, because he feels it enables him to "guarantee quality and interest." Regardless, there are always three prix-fixe menus—$25, $29, and $45—as well as the à la carte choices. While the $25 menu, which might feature a Roquefort salad with bacon and endive followed by pasta with wild mushrooms and a chocolate terrine covered by coffee sauce, is a perfectly acceptable way to sample Montrachet's wares on a budget, you're really cheating yourself. After all, you'll probably spend that and more in cab fare, so you might as well go whole hog and order from the right side of the menu.

Even so, you're likely to get away with about $115 for two with wine, which isn't bad for food of this caliber.

The salad of roast pigeon with wild mushrooms at $14 is a good and unusual starter. There's always a $28 lobster special and it's always a sure bet; Debra removes the meat from the shell and presents it in an inventive manner that changes daily according to her whim. She might slice the tail into medallions and set them, with the claw meat, on a bed of diced carrots, tomatoes, and pea pods glazed with a saffron butter sauce . . . or she might not. If her whim doesn't suit yours, go for the roast kidney with Chiroubles wine for $19, the baby pheasant with orzo and olives at $27, or the salmon with lentils and red wine for $23.

Whatever you choose, it's sure to reflect Drew's philosophy that "the best things are the simple things. The food doesn't have to be complicated." His may be a philosophy that is catching on among some of the city's most celebrated chefs. We've spotted Arcadia's Anne Rosenswieg and Huberts' Len Allison here. Both are known for their sophisticated, rather elaborate food with layered, complex flavors. Could some very serious uptown restaurants be taking a cue from the downtown upstart? Only time will tell.   ❦

Mrs. J.'s Sacred Cow

228 West 72nd Street   (212) 873-4067
between Broadway and West End
New York, NY 10023

There may be better steakhouses in town, certainly some more famous, but none more entertaining. Start with the name. Cute, huh? Except that when Ruth Jeffries named her restaurant 42 years ago, she wasn't thinking cow as in meat; she was thinking cow as in Franklin Delano Roosevelt. It seems he had a plane by the name of "Sacred Cow." A big Roosevelt fan, she adopted the name but added the possessive Mrs. J's, presumably to distinguish her restaurant from his plane.

But what really distinguishes Mrs. J.'s (as the restaurant is universally called) is the singing staff. You get a side order of Broadway with your steak. *Chorus Line* kids, one and all, they're aspiring singer/actors temporarily (they hope) consigned to life as waitpersons. And believe us when we tell you each and every one of them is good enough to be in that longest running of Broadway shows. Every singer in town going through that difficult "temporary" phase wants to work here, where they can practice their craft while earning a living. The competition is fierce, and only the best are given the nod by Mrs. J., who's still here and still very much in charge.

Actually, she's a bit of a drill sergeant, who makes sure her chorus line is as good at serving as it is at singing. Service doesn't suffer from the entertainment element. Your waiter will make sure you're covered before taking his or her turn at the mike. We always get misty-eyed when *ours* takes the spotlight—imagine our little Bobby (or Kevin, or Kelly, or Shelley, or . . .) up there singing in front of all those nice people. To think Mrs. J. has even given him a glamorous stage set, all dolled up in deco. She re-did the place about five years ago with lots of mirrors, etched glass, and theatrical lighting. The small restaurant really sparkles, with or without the star quality of patrons like Liza Minnelli, Shirley MacLaine, Janet Leigh, Chita Rivera, and Diahann Carroll.

Food? You want to know about the food? It's a great accompaniment to the show. In all fairness, a lot of it stands up pretty well on its own. A recent $5.50 soup special, a creamy clam, corn, and red pepper chowder, was downright dazzling. And the Caesar salad at $6.75 is a classic rendition of this traditional favorite. As for main dishes, there are a number of "Fresh Only" (the quotes are the menu's, not ours) seafood selections, but we always head for the beef, lamb, and veal choices. The "Dune Deck" steak, sliced sirloin topped with sautéed onions, red and green peppers, and mushrooms for $26.50 is a good choice. We also like the $26.95 veal chop stuffed with prosciutto and cheese, served with bordelaise sauce.

There are some good, rich desserts, like the heavenly chocolate terrine sitting on an intricately swirled glaze of crème anglaise and raspberry sauce. Since the portions tend to be on the healthy size, however, we generally opt for something a little lighter. It's fresh berries or melon in the $5.50 neighborhood for us.

Speaking of neighborhood, Mrs. J.'s is an Upper West fixture, almost always packed. If you show up with a reservation, you'll end up at the bar for a while waiting for a table in the main room—you do not, repeat not, want to sit anywhere else. Actually, it isn't so bad. At least here you get entertained while you wait. Even when no one's singing, the ivories are being skillfully tinkled. Somehow it all seems very New York—the glamorous setting, the piano player, the Broadway tunes, the prime meat. Guess that's why Fred Ebb is such a regular. He's so attuned to New York—he wrote it's theme song, "New York, New York."   ❧

Natalino

243 East 78th Street   (212) 737-3771
between 2nd and 3rd
New York, NY 10021

We have a surprise for you—it's Natalino, one of the smallest, best, and most reasonable restaurants in New York. Open only for dinner, it seats a mere thirty-two. Reservations for either the 6:30 or 9:00 seating are imperative. Occasionally, if you call well in advance you can secure a time somewhere in between, but regardless, owner Frank Davi won't book the reservation unless he's quite sure that you won't have to wait more than a few minutes.

Frank's wife, Frances, is the miracle worker in the kitchen, with a little help from her assistant, Jesus, and, in the summer, from twelve-year-old son Vincent. Elder son Natalino, for whom the restaurant was named, along with daughters Grace and Margaret, help Frank overseeing the minuscule dining room.

Don't come here expecting ambience—there isn't any. But you should expect uncompromisingly good food and family friendly atmosphere. Dinner for two runs about $60, including a modest wine and tip. Appetizers are either $4.95 or $5.95, while all the pastas are $7.95, except the spaghetti with olive oil, garlic, and anchovies, which is $6.95. The chicken dishes are extraordinary. Try the chicken and sausage sautéed in olive oil with marsala and mushrooms for $12.95.

Frank began his career in the food business as a butcher. Maybe that's why the veal at Natalino is so succulently flavorful—Frank knows what to look for when he buys. The $16.95 veal chop is superb, pounded paper-thin, then dipped in eggs and breadcrumbs. It's lightly fried and topped with sautéed radicchio, endive, and arugula.

As for seafood, the lobster fra diavolo is sensational at $18.95—half a lobster tossed with an assortment of fresh seafood specialties. All the main courses are accompanied by a selection of vegetables.

Although the menu is concise and easy to decipher, many regulars, like Neil and Leiba Sedaka, Peter Marshall, and Yvette Grubman simply put themselves in Frank's capable hands, leaving the ordering up to him. Frank, his family, and Natalino never disappoint. 🥄

Orso

322 West 46th Street   (212) 489-7212
New York, NY 10036

Like most producers, Joe Allen wasn't satisfied with one show; unlike most, he managed to produce two smashes in a row. With his namesake restaurant a long-running hit, Joe decided what New York really needed was another Italian restaurant. He was right. Orso, right down "restaurant row" from Joe Allen's, has been playing to SRO crowds since it opened in March 1983.

In case you're wondering, the name means "bear" in Italian, which in this instance is really irrelevant. As far as Joe is concerned, Orso doesn't mean "bear," it means "dog." More specifically, the name refers to one particular Italian dog befriended by Joe on his frequent trips to Venice. Orso, the dog, had the good sense to hang out at the Gritti Palace, which is where he met Joe. His picture hangs on the wall to the left, just as you enter.

Looking down from doggie heaven, Orso must be very proud that he's been immortalized by what is one of the very few and certainly one of the best authentic trattorias in town. Relatively small, with only nineteen tables, and decidedly casual, there is nonetheless a sense of elegant spaciousness conveyed by the split-level floor plan and lofty skylit ceiling in the back (read *lower*) room. All tables have a good view of the activity in the open kitchen, which takes up the rear.

Given the varied menu, there's a lot to watch. The antipasti section lists ten selections, to which daily specials are often added, all very suitable for serious grazing in the $7 to $8 price range. The cauliflower and white anchovies with caper anchovy sauce goes beautifully with the mussel salad with mixed peppers, black olives, tomato, and lemon. Top off the meal with one of the small zesty pizzas for $8.50 and you will have foraged quite well.

For a more conventional meal, thin noodles with swordfish, olives, red onions, garlic, and tomato sauce at $13 makes a nice pasta first course. We're always torn between the $16 pan-fried calf's liver and the roasted lamb sausage with garlic, polenta, and arugula at $17 for the entree. All dishes are served on pretty, playful Italian pottery that lends a festive touch to any meal.

The menu's the same for lunch and dinner, but the crowd changes dramatically. At lunch, Orso is filled with *New York Times* execs (who apparently have a thing about Italian food—if they're not here they're at the far grander Barbetta across the street), or Seventh Avenue types like Donna Karan and Geoffrey Beene. Later the eclectic pretheater-goers assemble, packing the house every night. Later still, representatives of the entertainment industry take over. Folks from the David Letterman show pop over, as do their cohorts from "Saturday Night Live." Theater greats Adolph Green and Betty Comden often visit, and we once engaged in a none-too-graceful ballet with William Hurt at the top of the steep steps leading downstairs to facilities. We were anxious to get where we were going. He was presumably anxious to get back to his party, which included Stockard Channing, and we just couldn't seem to get out of each other's way.

Of course, lately Joe's gotten a little annoyed about the way we hover over those steps, hoping against hope for another glimpse, whenever we come in for a little of daughter Julie's Italian cooking (yes, same daughter who directs the culinary action at Joe Allen's). We're determined that next time, Mr. Hurt won't get away.   🍏

Parioli Romanissimo

24 East 81st Street   (212) 288-2391
between Fifth and Madison
New York, NY 10028

Located in one of the best residential neighborhoods in New York, Parioli Romanissimo is further distinguished by the fact that it occupies its own dear little brownstone. The moment you pass through the massive wrought iron ornamented door you know you've arrived—at a very understatedly elegant, extremely sophisticated, and extraordinarily special place.

You enter into the tiny bar, where you might be asked to wait a moment or two. Somehow you don't mind, as it gives you time to adjust to your serenely sublime surroundings. The stroll through the passageway on the way to the dining room offers a preview of what's in store. You pass an elaborate dessert display and a fabulous arrangement of 50 or so cheeses on a trolley.

The original architectural details, intricate moldings, and lovely fireplace, along with the soaring ceilings, lend a sense of quiet grandeur to the dining room. The lighting, focused as it is on the flowers on each table, diffuses beautifully, shedding a complimentary glow on every patron. There's an opulent harmony about the atmosphere with its subtle peach, cream, and natural tones, that makes it very romantic, without being cloying. Even the so-called Garden Room beyond the dining room avoids the decorative pitfalls common to its breed. Originally it really was a garden, and dining there now is like enjoying the privacy of your own terrace.

Host and owner Rubrio Rossi is an elegant, refined gentleman. His exquisite taste is reflected everywhere, from the decor to the wine list, which must include the most impressive gathering of Italian wines in the city. It runs the gamut—modestly priced Pinot Grigio, Santa Margherita at $30.50 to the outrageously tagged Brunello di Montaleino, Riserva, Biondi Santi 1925 at $4,350 (well, the original cork *is* available). Rubrio says it's the only Italian red that can stand up to a century of aging, so he's still got a few years left to sell it.

The cuisine in this restaurant—which is to classic Italian food what Lutece, La Grenouille, and La Cote Basque are to French—certainly lives up to the wine. The Carpaccio de Agnello, filet of baby lamb cooked to a turn and served with a cream of red peppers, is a spectacular appetizer for $12.50, as is the $23.75 ravioli stuffed with porcini mushrooms and served in a light cream sauce. The 21-day-old chicken roasted with black truffles for $30.50 is a must and veal chop fans should order the tarragon sauced version here for $32. It literally melts in your mouth. As for dessert, one of us can never resist a $10 slice of the sinful-beyond-belief chocolate cake, while the other always dives into the cheese trolley for an $11 entrance fee.

It's dinner only at Parioli Romanissimo, Tuesday through Saturday, served by formal, attentive waiters in starched white jackets sporting red carnations. They service only about 70 prized seats, so you'll have to call a week in advance like Diane Sawyer and Mike Nichols, who adore the risotto here. They're in good company—Jackie Onassis, Lee Radzwill and bridegroom Herb Ross, David Rockefeller, and Mario Cuomo are fans too.

The menu changes two or three times a year. In season, be sure to order the fresh venison, pheasant, or partridge. During any season, your meal will be topped off by a plate of chocolates and cookies, with the warm compliments of Mr. Rossi. As a result, you feel as if you've been entertained by a close friend (who has a dynamite chef) in the sanctity of his own home. And guess what? You really have been. 🌰

Petrossian

182 West 58th Street	(212) 245-2214
at Seventh Avenue	Delicacies Shop (212) 245-2217
New York, NY 10019	FAX (212) 245-2812

Some sixty years ago, two young Russian brothers literally introduced caviar to the world. In 1984, their sons wrapped it in an intriguing art deco package—an exceptionally beautiful restaurant—and presented it to an eager New York, like a gift from heaven.

After fleeing to Paris in the wake of the Russian Revolution, Melkoum and Moucheg Petrossian discovered that their respective legal and medical credits from Moscow University would not be recognized by schools in their adopted city—they would have to start their training all over again. Even more disturbing, their beloved caviar was unheard of in the City of Light, yet with so many Russian emigres descending on Paris, there was certainly a demand. They determined they could fill the void and make a living if they could import the precious eggs. By phone they struck a deal with the new Russian government and subsequently loaded a suitcase with their life savings, which they deposited, as instructed, at the embassy in Paris. Then they waited, and waited. It was over two months before they got their first shipment that reassured them the Russians were honoring the deal. It is a deal that's held ever since. The Petrossian family is the exclusive agent for Russian caviar in France, the U.S., Canada, and Switzerland.

Furthermore, the Petrossians, with their very special and privileged relationship with the Russian Ministry of Fisheries, is the only firm allowed to actually participate in the Caspian Sea sturgeon catch. Petrossian Incorporated chooses its caviar lot by lot as it is caught, and oversees the preparation of the eggs. As a result, Petrossian has a well-deserved international reputation as purveyor of the world's finest caviar, and accounts for a large percentage of the total Russian export.

The store Melkoum and Moucheg founded on the Boulevard de Latour Mauborg has been a mecca for connoisseurs of caviar, smoked salmon, foie gras, and other delicacies ever since the 1930s. The restaurant and shop the founders' sons Christian and Armen established in New York is virtually assured a similar destiny.

Unabashedly fans and practitioners of living the good life, the Petrossian boys have created an environment celebrating that fine art. To enter Petrossian is to enter a lovely, lavish, utterly fantastic, and totally decadent atmosphere. We're told Christian and Armen instructed architect Ion Oroveanu to design "the most elegant, frivolous, unique place in the world." With his extravagant decor featuring polished pink and gray granite, burled walnut, gold-capped columns, stunning bronze sculptures, a gray leather banquette edged with mink, and a snail-shell chandelier originally made for Mme. Lanvin, we'd say he succeeded—admirably. On the occasion of his first visit to the restaurant for his 92nd birthday, the celebrated Erté-inspired etched mirrored walls prompted the Franco-Russian designer-artist himself to turn to Christian and exclaim, "This is me!"

No doubt Erté was even more at home once he sat down at one of the luxuriously appointed tables (China by Limoges, custom designed flatware by Christofle) and sampled the sinfully sensual food. Now we use the word food here advisedly. Yes, Petrossian does serve real, recognizable meals of the French persuasion. But we don't know much about them. We seldom get past the caviar, with occasional forays into the smoked salmon or foie gras. This is grazing at its grandest.

Petrossian serves four kinds of caviar—beluga, ossetra, sevruga, and pressed. The first three are named after their parent sturgeons, each of which produces a roe with a distinctly different look, taste, color, and texture. "Pressed" refers to the method of preparation. Eggs that are already broken or too mature and therefore liable to break when packed in tins, as is the norm, are pressed—four pounds of fresh caviar are condensed into a pound of pressed caviar, making a very concentrated product with a strong flavor.

Any of the caviars can be ordered individually, the size of the portion determining the price—$19 for 1$\frac{1}{16}$ ounces of pressed caviar, up to $210 for 4$\frac{3}{4}$ ounces of beluga. But we think that ordering the Royal Gourmet, 1$\frac{1}{16}$ ounces each of sevruga, ossetra, and beluga with toast points for $115 is the way to go. Take it one step further and indulge in the Les Années Folles (the crazy years) for $140. This decadent extravaganza begins with the Royal Gourmet presentation, followed by pressed caviar accompanied by light, puffy blinis with a dollop or two of crème fraîche. Their succulent smoked salmon, sliced more thinly than paper, on toast is the final course until you get to choose from the selection of predictably lavish desserts, which really do seem like overkill. We've been known to pass and have another glass of the refreshing champagne "Cuvee Speciale" for $11.

Petrossian is expensive, but it's special and truly unique, so who cares?! Certainly not Candice Bergen and Louis Malle, Raquel Welch and Andre Weinfeld (now more likely Raquel *or* Andre), Melanie Griffith and Don Johnson, Mike Nichols and Diane Sawyer, and Sean Connery (presumably, in this context, Mrs. Connery too, but nobody actually mentioned her). They're all habitués and they've probably learned that you can enjoy the hedonistic experience that is Petrossian without spending a small fortune.

Order the $19.50 selection of "teasers" for the main course—it consists of lots of tasty little tidbits like roulades of smoked sturgeon with wild mushrooms, truffled foie gras en croute, and smoked trout wrapped in lettuce. Alternatively, you can have the $22 smoked salmon or the $21 whole goose foie gras from Perigord. Either makes a perfectly respectable meal, when complemented by borscht or a garden salad, both $6.50. There's also a $35 pre-theater menu served from 5:30 to 7:30 P.M., featuring pressed caviar served with blini of foie gras, a teaser assortment, and a choice of desserts.

Despite the fact that dinner and after-theater reservations are a must (lunch is less problematical), you can enjoy Petrossian's finest on the spur of the moment. Just pop into the boutique at the entrance to the restaurant and pick up a little of this and a little of that—you can even taste before you buy. And you don't even have to be in New York to buy or taste. A phone or fax order will dispense any of their estimable comestibles anywhere in the world. Furthermore, the Petrossians have expanded their American presence with shops in Miami, Boca Raton, Chicago, Dallas, San Francisco, and Washington, DC.   🐦

P. J. Clarke's

915 Third Avenue	Reservations (212) PL9-1650
at 55th Street	Front Room Phone Booth (212) EL5-8857
New York, NY	Back Room Phone Booth (212) EL5-9307
10022	

P. J. Clark's. Is it a bar? A restaurant? A saloon? Well, yes—to all three! What's more, it's an institution, and a time-honored one at that. Since

1864 or 1892, depending upon whom you talk to, the bar, restaurant, saloon has been occupying this bit of prime real estate at the corner of
Third Avenue and 55th Street. Indeed, the site is so prime and the establishment so cherished that a highly unusual real estate deal was struck
in 1967. P. J. Clarke's property was sold to a giant development company, but allowed to retain its sacred and independent status. A new
forty-five-story skyscraper was designed and built around the tiny building.

Clarke's is open 365 days a year, from 10:30 in the morning to 4
o'clock the next morning. Stopping in for a little sustenance in the wee
hours is a New York tradition as are maître d's Leo and Frankie. The $5
hamburgers are legendary, grilled on an open fire, thick and juicy. Of
course, there are other delectables on the blackboard menu—a respectable steak for $14.70, chicken pot pie (just like Mom's) for $9.30, and a
bountiful $6.20 spinach salad. (Odd prices are a Clarke's trademark.)

There's nothing odd or cutesy about the decor, though. It's good old-
fashioned, no-nonsense, turn-of-the-century American bar, with the patina that only decades of smoke can produce—the pressed tin ceiling may
once have been a real color. Now it's an indescribable sooty brown. Likewise the bar, which some claim to be mahogany, has been transformed to
a black hulk. Only the white tile floor gleams. It's so utilitarian, so easy
to wash down.

One of the most fascinating things about Clarke's and one of the secrets to its unprecedented ongoing success is that there really was a P. J.
Clarke, who built the business and gave the place his personal stamp.
Patrick Joseph "Paddy" Clarke, a native of Ireland, started working in
what was already an existing saloon in 1904. When the owner died in
1920, Paddy took over and remained in charge until his death in 1948.
During his tenure the establishment became indelibly engraved on the
American imagination as the quintessential bar by Billy Wilder's classic
film *The Lost Weekend*, starring Ray Milland. One lone scene was actually
shot in Clarke's. The rest of the bar sequences were filmed in a replica
built on a Hollywood soundstage.

Typical of the timelessness and tradition associated with Clarke's, Paddy's nephew Charlie acted as manager until just recently, though the
family no longer owns the place. Paddy's immediate heirs sold it to Daniel H. Lavezzo, Sr., who already owned the building and operated an antique business in what is now Clark's large rear dining room. The
Lavezzo family moved their antiques to the second floor, added the din-

ing room, and have been part of the Clarke's scene ever since. Dan, Jr., is the current owner and his son, Dan III, is usually on the premises making sure everything is as it should be—like the purchase of fresh meat, fish, and vegetables every day (there are no freezers here, except one reserved for bags of ice cubes). He also makes sure those little white pads are on each table—at Clarke's you write your own order. It's another tradition, one instituted by Dan, Jr., when he discovered one of his waiters was illiterate. The poor fellow was trying to get by memorizing the orders, but his memory wasn't too terrific. Lots of customers were unhappy about getting something they didn't order and not getting something they did. Rather than fire him, Dan solved the problem by declaring that henceforth all orders were to be written by the guests, who presumably would get it right!

Indeed, we hear that some of those orders have been real literary tomes. After all, Clarke's is home away from office for the publishing, journalism, and advertising crowd. There are tales of people who have conducted their business from the back room—phone messages really are reliably taken and transmitted here, and the bar bills are considerably less than the cost of midtown office space.

Over the years regulars have run a broad gamut—Jake LaMotta to Jackie Onassis—indicative of the unique quality about Clarke's. There's something satisfying about it for virtually every taste—even yours! 🐞

Primavera

1578 First Avenue   (212) 861-8608
New York, NY 10028

It's always a relief to us to come across a bar as small as Primavera's— usually a tiny bar is a fair indication that you won't languish endlessly waiting for your so-called reservation. Primavera is no exception to this general rule of thumb. After all, owner, and Regine's alumnus, Nicola Civetta has devoted his life to the fine art of sumptuous *dining*, not drinking. The trick here is to get the reservation in the first place. It requires a call several days in advance (at least) and speaking directly with Nicola or maître d'hotel Paolo.

Now, when we maintain Nicola has devoted his life to fine dining, we don't say it lightly. At the tender age of fourteen he entered hotel school in his native Italy to study cooking and restaurant management. From there, he went on to work in a number of top rated establishments in

Switzerland, Germany, France, and England before descending on American shores in the early '70s. In New York he put in some time as Regine's captain where he refined some of his finesse at dealing with the sort of ultra chic crowd that now hails his Primavera as one of the best of the city's legion of Italian restaurants—a crowd that includes Mike Nichols, Jack Nicholson, Anthony Quinn, Richard Avedon, Herbert Allen, and Bill Cosby.

They delight in the warm, intimate tone of the place set by the rich wood paneling and softly muted lighting. The sensible spacing between tables in the small dining room (it only seats 70) is also appreciated. How pleasant, how unusual to have a truly private conversation in such a popular place. Indeed, there's a sort of purity about Primavera's decor—the unadorned white linens, the smooth clean lines of sparkling crystal, and the fresh yet minimal flower arrangements on the tables. Indeed, much of it is even authentically Italian to the degree that the paneling, windows, doors, and bars were handmade in Italy, then shipped to New York to be installed under the watchful supervision of their designer, Carone, the renowned Italian architect.

Italian craftsmanship aside, the Italian cooking of a contemporary though somewhat traditional nature is the real star here. The menu is relatively standard in that it's only changed twice a year. But the captain will apprise you of any seasonal delicacies like the grilled Italian wild mushrooms that are a specialty, or the truffle dishes Nicola features from late September to early January. Pasta with white truffles is a fabulous, if costly, appetizer at approximately $39.50—"approximately" because the truffle market tends to be on the volatile side. As a main course, it'll run at least $49.50, but Nicola says that only the nouveau riche in Italy would ever order such a dish as an entrée.

Baby eels with oil and garlic are usually on the menu, but not always available. They, too, are priced according to the market. But you can count on Spiedino alla Romana, fried mozzarella on bread topped with an anchovy sauce, being $12.50 and a great choice as a starter. Or you might want to begin with Bill Cosby's favorite Penne all'Arrabbiti for $19.50. Sometimes when Bill craves this spicy red-sauced dish in the privacy of his own home, he sends his driver over for an order or two. Of course, Nicola doesn't really encourage take-out, but Bill is, after all, The Cos and he often sends along a gift in the form of his own chef's special home-baked bread.

Entrée-wise, we've been seduced by the thinly sliced beef with rosemary and rugola for $29.50 and the $26.50 rolled veal stuffed with prosciutto and spinach. We've also wondered if Nicola has a thing about the number 50—with the exception the excellent risotto with wild mushrooms (cunningly priced to sound like a lot less than $25) at $24.95 and the fresh fruit for two at $14, everything on the menu is "ex" number of dollars and 50 cents.

You can happily add up all those 50 cents every night at Primavera, even Sunday when many other fine restaurants are closed. For that very reason, Sundays here tend to be a madhouse from 7:00 P.M. to about 9:30. This is definitely a night for regulars, so book your first Sunday supper reservation early, like at 5:00 P.M., in order to get one.   ❦

Primola

1226 Second Avenue   (212) 758-1775
between 64th and 65th Streets
New York, NY 10021

We checked the dictionary and it seems that primroses don't have to be yellow. What a relief! We'd been worried that Franco Iacoviello and Giuliano Zuliani had made a dreadful mistake on their menus. The rose that dots the *i* in *Primola* (Italian for "primrose") is decidedly hot pink. It had bothered us—until we turned to Webster's.

However, the seeming incongruity of a pink primrose is about the only disturbing trait of this charming restaurant. Light, contemporary, and casual with its bleached floors and bentwood-style chairs, it's an unusual hybrid—part power-people place, part neighborhood niche. Monday through Thursday it belongs to the politicos, financiers, and socialites. On the weekends the locals take over.

They all come for Franco's tasty renditions of Italian favorites. Many followed him from the site of his former gastronomical triumph at the popular Elio's. A native of the Adriatic coast of Italy, Franco has developed a distinctively delicate touch with his specialties—pasta, fish, and veal.

We particularly recommend the risottos—one infused with fresh seafood, the other with spinach, $19 and $18 respectively. There are eleven more pastas to explore, but make sure you get past them to the entrées. In season, Primola flies in a Mediterranean fish called *branzino*. A white fish reminiscent of sea bass, it's prepared with fresh herbs, garlic, and balsamic vinegar. Priced according to the market, Franco's *branzino* is divine.

Another favorite is the roast loin of veal with three kinds of mushrooms. You won't actually find it on the menu; you sort of have to know it's there. And it helps to call ahead, because it takes a good forty-five minutes to prepare.

When he opened Primola to instant success in 1986, Franco had the good sense to make sure the front of the house would perform as well as his kitchen by making Giuliano his partner. Another Elio veteran, Giuliano juggles the neighborhood crowd and the power set with equal aplomb. He does a terrific job of seeming to please everyone, although the front room simply isn't equipped to handle all the people who want to sit there. The back room tends to be a bit quiet, too quiet for the likes of Donald Trump, Dustin Hoffman, Clint Eastwood, Ronald Perelman, Joanna Carson, Barbara Walters, and Polly Bergen.

With dinner reservations hard to come by and requiring at least two or three days' notice, lunch might be a good introduction to Primola. It's easier to get a table, and you have the choice of the $19.50 prix-fixe luncheon or the regular menu. À la carte, a full lunch or dinner can easily run $60 a head, with a moderately priced wine.

It occurs to us that Franco and Giuliano could justifiably add the Italian for *path* to Primola. After all, theirs is a restaurant that certainly encourages actions of pleasure and self-indulgence—Webster's definition of *primrose path!*   🍒

The Quilted Giraffe

550 Madison Avenue   (212) 593-1221
between 55th and 56th Streets
New York, NY 10022
(in the AT&T Arcade)

The name is on the cutesy side; the restaurant is anything but. Rather it is the site of very serious dining—and spending. The prix fixe is $75 for a four-course meal, but that's just for the basics. Supplements for delicacies like fresh foie gras sautéed with warm lettuces, Petrossian caviar beggar's purses, or rack of lamb with Chinese mustard can escalate the tariff considerably.

Still, you don't get into the restaurant's pricing stratosphere until you wander into the left side of the menu. It takes a stout heart to follow the instructions and order the tasting menu for everyone in your party at $110 a pop. The menu maintains that otherwise these special dinners, consisting of many courses "including several of our specialties and most of our desserts," cannot be served properly. But to really test your credit card limits, try the Kyoto-style Kaiseki dinner. Chosen by the chef, this multicourse meal is the only one we know of that is described as costing "one hundred thirty-five dollars and up"!

Worth it? The international business crowd, armed with healthy expense accounts, that keeps the Quilted Giraffe's eighty seats constantly occupied for lunch and dinner, apparently thinks so. Presumably owner Barry Wine thinks so too, though there is a devilish twinkle in his eye as he asserts, "You just have to bring it all down to earth again. After all, it's just food."

Of course it's not just food—it's extraordinary food, adventuresome food, serious food. On the prix fixe you can start with sweetbreads and chips with a caramel soy and sesame sauce, followed by Norwegian salmon grilled with sweet hot mustard. Sample the selections from the cheese cart before deciding on dessert—the chocolate chip Napoleon or the butterscotch mousse with caramel.

Don't forget the wine. Even if you don't drink, ask to see the wine list. It's very entertaining to pore through the pages of computer printout—the only continuous-feed paper we've ever seen that has the feel and look of expensive bond, complete with water marks. Predictably, it reads like a who's who or what's what in wine, from the tempting 1982 Clos-Fourtet Saint Emilion at $60 to the astounding 1976 Louis Roederer Cristal at $1,000!

Ambitious food commanding astronomical prices has overtaxed more than one kitchen in town. Barry and his wife, Susan, have gone to great pains and expense to make sure that the Quilted Giraffe does not suffer such a fate. Fifty percent of the restaurant's space is devoted to a kitchen manned by fifteen chefs, personally directed by Barry, a former attorney who turned a talent for inventive cooking into a new career.

He made the switch fifteen years ago with the first Quilted Giraffe in upstate New York. The second incarnation was on Second Avenue for eight years. In 1987, he and Susan moved into the Philip Johnson–designed AT&T world headquarters building on Madison Avenue with its lush gray granite walls, and added the dramatic gray leather and stainless steel interior. Sleek and chic like the crowd it attracts, the decor is striking, unusual; critics went so far as to describe it as avant-garde when it opened. At first glance it is by no means warm and cozy, yet there is an intimate quality about the Quilted Giraffe. Perhaps it's the lack of the large bar that many trendy New York restaurants use as a holding pen. Reservations are honored in a timely manner. So there's no tiresome languishing in the Quilted Giraffe's tiny gesture of a bar. Or maybe it's the number of obvious regulars, enthusiastically greeted by Barry, Susan, and Wayne, the maître d' who has been with them since they became restaurateurs. In fact, the Quilted Giraffe goes out of its way to cater to those whose patronage can be frequently counted upon. The kitchen staff gathers every afternoon at 4:30 to discuss who's coming to dinner and what they habitually order.

Barry may have forsaken the former source of his livelihood, but his lawyer's training has stood him in good stead when it comes to splitting hairs. The one he splits the finest is the eighteen percent service charge that is automatically added to the bill. It is not, strictly speaking, a gratuity—it does not go directly to the highly professional service staff. Barry maintains that he pays them very well, thank you very much. We guess the eighteen percent, which might be more properly described as a cover, is what enables him to be so generous!

The Rainbow Room

30 Rockefeller Plaza   (212) 632-5000
50th between Fifth and Sixth
New York, NY 10112

The Rainbow Room first opened in 1934 and set the standard by which all other glamorous rooms should be measured in New York. Conceived as a formal supper club, it had, despite its two floors of windows, three terraced levels of seating, soaring domed ceiling lit by a rainbow of colored lights, and a revolving dance floor 32 feet in diameter, an intimate atmosphere—where New York's elite could gather to dine on fine cuisine and dance to the strains of legendary big bands. Over the years, some of the stardust wore off. Among other disappointments the dance floor stopped revolving.

But after a massive $20 million renovation that saw the space razed and cleared right to the outer walls, The Rainbow Room is back—not bigger, but perhaps better than ever.

Given his hand in the success of a number of the city's similarly high profile establishments (The Four Seasons, Windows of the World, and Aurora among others), it's not surprising that Joe Baum is credited as creator and operator of the new Rainbow Room. He is immensely proud of his role in returning it "to New Yorkers as their spot to dine, dance, and romance" and is almost always hovering near the entrance greeting old friends and making new ones feel welcome.

While some have quibbled that Joe has produced a restaurant with more style than substance, grumbling that the food is not what it could be, that there's an interminable wait for the second course, no one denies that the setting is the city's most spectacular. Occupying the entire eastern end of the 65th floor, the views to the north, east, and south seem endless during the day. At night, the lights of the city and beyond, way beyond, seem to be drawn into the room creating an undeniable air of romance.

There's simply no place else like it in this or any other city. And though an evening here will likely hit upwards of $100 a person with cocktails and wine, we think it's money well spent. The entertainment value alone is worth it. In addition to the views, the people-watching is unparalleled from tables that are set up to afford great sight lines to the dance floor, which once again revolves. When you're not tripping the light fantastic, there's usually someone on the floor worth keeping an eye on and musing about. People dress up here, and we have seen some amazing outfits—some fashion successes, a lot of dismal failures. We won't place them in either category, but we've spotted Farrah Fawcett and Ryan O'Neal, Marilyn McCoo and Billy Davis, and Phil Donahue and Marlo Thomas gliding around the floor.

As for the food, we think it's just fine. No question about what to start with—Oysters Rockefeller, of course, at $15. For even richer tastes, try the steak tartare "iced" with sevruga for $25. The $56 roast rack of lamb for two makes a great, and appropriately festive, main course. We've also been favorably impressed by the tournedos of salmon au poivre (no, the pepper does not deaden the taste of the salmon) for $26. This is a dessert kind of place, necessary in order to lengthen the evening and keep the table as long as possible. So go for it—baked Alaska for two at $18 and spectacularly flamed at your table, washed down with a $9 glass or two of Piper Heidsieck Extra Dry.

Early- and late-evening meals are available too. With the pretheater menu for $38.50 you run the risk of missing out on the dancing, assuming you really are going to the theater. Otherwise, you can stick around and pay the $15 per person music charge that gets tacked onto every bill after 8:00 P.M. The three course dinner includes selections like truffled paté of veal and lobster bisque with whiskey for appetizers, followed by grilled swordfish steak with a red wine sauce or escalope of veal with spinach and goat cheese tortelloni.

The supper menu, available after 10:30 P.M., is an encapsulated version of the dinner offerings with the addition of omelets and several substantial salads. You can sup to your heart's content for about $75 per person, including music charge.

Because it's so special, people are flocking to The Rainbow Room. Unless you're an old pal, don't bother trying to call Joe for a reservation. You'll simply have to hold on the line while a recorded voice asks you to wait "until the next available operator" can take your call, just like the rest of us. It does give you pause. For a moment you wonder if you dialed an airline instead of a restaurant. Once you get to talk to a real person, be prepared for a shock. He or she is likely to tell you there's a six-week wait for a reservation, and they only begin taking reservations six weeks in advance! Talk about planning ahead! Just call at 9:00 A.M. six weeks to the day before you want to dine, and you might get lucky. If you find yourself in New York unexpectedly and are just dying to go, test the mettle of your concierge with a request for a reservation.

Alternatively, you can try getting a taste of The Rainbow Room experience, minus the dancing, on Sundays. The $34.50 brunch here is a well-kept secret. You get the food, the view, and the entertainment—a string quartet one Sunday, a choir the next. And best of all you can usually get a reservation on fairly short notice. The menu presents a number of choices for each of the three courses—scrambled eggs with smoked salmon and goat cheese, or the cobb salad with turkey, smoked ham, endive, and roquefort are the most popular selections as main dishes.

As if all this weren't enough, there's more you should know about the *complex* that is called Rainbow and is attached to The Room. Called the Promenade, the bar stretches along the south face of the building, lower Manhattan spread out below. In addition to being a dynamite spot for a drink while you marvel at the view, it serves food. Described as "little meals," the menu features $8 dishes like fried calamari with two sauces, $10 dishes like two brochettes of shrimp and Cajun sausage, and larger dishes for $12 to $16. The $16 omelet with foie gras, mushrooms, and cheese makes an exceptional late-night snack—no reservations necessary.

The final Rainbow option, not including a number of rooms available for private functions, is Rainbow and Stars. It's a jewel of a 100-seat cabaret presenting established stars like Tony Bennett, Rosemary Clooney, Phyllis Diller, and Lorna Luft. The room, new to the complex and built to be a good-old-fashioned nightclub, has a fabulous view to the north. But here, the view plays second fiddle to the entertainment. The room surrounds the star of the evening, creating a feeling of intimacy, of relating one-on-one with the performer.

There are two shows a night, one at 9:00 and one at 11:15, each with a $35 cover. Cocktails and dinner are served from 7:00 to 10:30 P.M. The limited à la carte menu is intriguing, particularly the "Lobsters on Parade" section, five different dishes featuring our favorite crustacean. From lobster cocktail at $15 to roast lobster at $37.50, they're all marvelous and add to the sense of occasion you get at Rainbow and Stars. How many other restaurants do you know with silver lamé tablecloths overlayed with white netting and sprinkled with glittering stars? Predictably, reservations are necessary, but usually obtainable, especially at the beginning of a run before the rave reviews hit the paper.

Everything about the Rainbow—The Room, the Promenade, Rainbow and Stars—evokes images of another era without feeling like a monument to that possibly more glamorous time. Rather, the Rainbow complex today is very much alive, creating new memories for a whole new generation. 🌱

Rao's

455 East 114th Street	(212) 534-9625
New York, NY 10029	(212) 722-6709

The first thing you should know about Rao's is that you absolutely have to have a reservation to be admitted and it's going to take you at least three months to get one—honest! This information is vital because Rao's neighborhood is not the respectable Italian one it was when the restaurant was founded in 1896. It's not a place you want to be stranded because you didn't have a reservation.

Despite the change in the area's fortunes, which appears not to have affected business one iota, the Rao family remains steadfastly implanted. Their small, wood-paneled, four-booth, five-table restaurant is filled every week night (they're closed Saturdays and Sundays) with people who give a whole new meaning to the term "regulars." At Rao's, certain tables are permanently booked on a weekly or monthly basis. Their red leather chairs or banquettes are held for the "owner" or his designee, come hell or high water. And there's only one seating here, no matter when a party arrives, 6:30 or 9:30 P.M., the table is theirs for the night.

The Friars' Club maintains a table for six. Members sign up at the club for a time slot. Once there, they're likely to rub elbows with Woody Allen and Mia Farrow, Yvette Grubman, Michael Korda, Howard Kaminsky, or Mort Janklow, all of whom are probably delighted that Rao's authentic, flavorful sauces will soon be available in specialty food stores. But that won't stop them from making the almost ritual trek uptown (waaay uptown!). Where else can they dine on splendid southern Italian cooking *a la casalinga* ("of the housewife") in a quirkily romantic setting run almost like a private club? Where else can they enjoy Christmas decorations year round? Then there's the jukebox, which *New York* magazine declared one of the ten best in the city, and, most important, there's Anna and Frankie.

Anna, the wife of eighty-three-year-old Vincent Rao, whose father and uncle started the place, acts as the cooking housewife—duty she clearly adores. Frankie is her nephew and mans the front of the house, discussing the menu with all those regulars who have really become members of his and Anna's extended family.

As for the food, we like the roast peppers as a starter—$7.50 with or without anchovies. Served sprinkled with pinoli nuts and raisins, they're divine. The fish salad with calamari, scungilli, crab, and lobster is another good selection, also at $7.50. Don't miss the $6.50 escarole and bean soup.

For the main dish, we find the chicken with lemon mouth-watering, and Frankie's very proud of the veal parmigiana. Both are $13.50. Dessert? Try the cheesecake made expressly for Rao's by a lady in the Bronx who's an old friend of the family.

With such modest prices Rao's won't put a dent in your wallet, and it probably won't even disturb you that they don't take credit cards. What will drive you nuts is getting the reservation in the first place. You have to be persistent, sometimes calling daily to see if there's been a cancellation. Or, if you can, identify a Rao's regular and persuade him or her to invite you as their guest—it's the best way to go. 🌰

Reginette

69 East 59th Street   (212) 758-0530
between Park and Madison
New York, NY 10022

Leave it to Régine. No matter where she opens a club or restaurant, no matter what its style, shape, or form, it's sure to be a smash hit. She's got the Midas touch. In New York she's hit pay dirt twice, with her namesake club and with this charming bistro, so pert and pretty with its dark forest green carpeting and rose peach walls.

Opened in 1977, Reginette ever since has been a favorite haunt of the Euro-set as well as of savvy, sophisticated New Yorkers. It's one of the few places in New York for couscous—the real thing, the Moroccan national dish that is a staple of real French bistros. We know a number of French expatriates who have standing reservations every Saturday for lunch, when it's always the special. They claim it's not only the best couscous in New York, it's about the best they've ever had anywhere.

Régine's husband, Roger Choukroun, is usually around chatting with regulars like Omar Sharif or greeting newcomers. Occasionally, you'll even spot Régine herself, the redheaded whirlwind. But her international empire keeps her traveling, so don't count on it.

You can, however, count on the consistently good food at Reginette. The paillard of chicken with mustard sauce is done to perfection at $14.75. And the hamburger resting on a bed of sautéed potatoes for $12.75—it beats a burger on a bun any day. True to time-honored bistro tradition, Reginette serves food all day long. You can pop in any old time after they open at noon for a bowl of their excellent $5.25 onion soup or the terrific $11.50 poached eggs with red peppers and spinach. Lunch or dinner for two is about $40, if you stay away from the bar.

Lunch is always busy. So make a reservation, especially if there's a two o'clock sale at Christies, the famous auction house that's right around the corner. Our favorite table is on the terrace level in the left-hand corner. Other people insist on sitting by the windows so they can people-watch outside as well as in the restaurant. There are always plenty of comings and goings worthy of scrutiny—like Barry Manilow, Frank or Kathie Lee Gifford, and George Segal.

They frequent Reginette because it's good, quick, easy, and on the cozy side. Come to think of it, that's why we stop by, too!   ❦

Rosa Mexicano

1063 First Avenue   (212) 753-7407
at 58th Street
New York, NY 10022

Josefina Howard is a woman with a mission. She wants people to recognize the intricate color, flavor, and variety (over 3,000 native dishes) that is the cuisine of Mexico. Her passion for this mission is all the more interesting when you consider that she's not even Mexican. Josefina was born in Cuba, raised in Spain, and spent her early adulthood in New York before moving with her American husband to Mexico. She spent 34 years there and fell in love with the food, which she found "beautiful and moving like art."

On her 1979 return to New York, she was dismayed that she couldn't find any authentic Mexican food. So she opened a lunch café called La Fogata specializing in *real* tacos—soft tortillas filled with charcoal grilled meat. Josefina often had to mollify first-time customers, who thought their taco order had been replaced by something else. She would patiently explain that the ubiquitous hard taco shell was unknown in Mexico, and that if they didn't like the authentic version, it was on the house. Suffice it to say she was never obliged to pick up a tab, and soon she was serving more than 300 lunches a day.

After a brief stint as head chef at Cinco de Mayo, she opened Rosa Mexicano in 1984. It is truly her own creation, from design (she was a successful interior decorator in both New York and Mexico City) to dessert, and sparkles with her presence as she darts among tables apprising guests of the day's "goodies."

The subtly dramatic decor—the black slate foor, the pink and plum tiles, the open grill beyond the bar, the heavy rustic-looking wooden furniture—provides a fitting backdrop to Josefina's special brand of showmanship. Order the guacamole and you'll know what we mean. Starting with the whole avocados, it's prepared at your table with lightning speed by a waiter who delivers a running commentary and solicits your preference for mild, spicy, or hot. Served in the molcajete, three-legged mortar made of volcanic rock, in which it was made, Rosa Mexicano's guacamole is a rich, chunky mixture. A couple of $8.50 orders and a margarita or two (pink and piquant with Josefina's addition of pomegranate juice) has served us well at lunch on several occasions.

For a more substantial and arguably healthier lunch, there's a prix-fixe $18 menu, which includes a platter of the house's selection of appetizers, a choice of entrées, coffee, and dessert. The Pollo en Escabeche, grilled chicken served in a hot vinaigrette with rice, and Alambres de Camarones, skewered marinated shrimp with onions, tomatoes, and serrano chilies on rice with a vinaigrette sauce, are terrific, even though they may not coincide with your vision of Mexican food. Indeed, Josefina still finds it necessary to explain her penchant for authenticity—a notice at the top of the menu says, "In order to maintain Rosa Mexicano's desire to present classic Mexican cuisine, you may not find some of the popular Americanized dishes associated with Mexican food on our menu." Here! Here!

That suits most people just fine, and the restaurant is almost always crowded, except perhaps for Saturday lunch. Otherwise lunch and dinner reservations are a must. For Sunday brunch, call a few days in advance as it's one of the hottest tickets in town. Setup as a buffet on the 15-foot-long grill, the glorious array of food is a treat for both the eye and the palate. For $24 a person, you can dive into the bounty which may include platters piled high with seafoods (there are over 6,000 miles of coastline in Mexico, so fish and shellfish are an important part of the national cuisine), suckling pig, chicken with mole and chilies, duck with green tomato sauce, a variety of salads, and a selection of desserts. Ice cream is homemade and the flan is out of this world.

As for dinner, in addition to the guacamole, you might try the tart ceviche of bay scallops at $8.50 or the unusual chili poblano flan served on a tomato sauce at $6.50 to start. The $4 soup made of garlic and bread in a chicken broth is also good. From the grill, the pork chops marinated in a paste of ground chilies and spices served with Mexican rice and fried beans for $16.50 is a great choice. We also like the Budin Azteca as a $16 platillo principal. It's a tortilla pie layered with shredded chicken, cheese, and a chili poblano sauce.

As much as she likes to talk, Josefina gets a little circumspect when it comes to her clientele. Her eyes light up, but her voice drops as she claims the French, the Italians, the Japanese, as well as home-grown Americans and celebrities galore among her guests, but she declines to be all that specific. She is, however, pleased when we inform her that Rosa Mexicano is the first place Princess Diana's favorite couturier, Victor Edelstein, heads when he hits town to work with his American clients. Victor says that he and his assistant Sarah spend much of the plane ride plotting what they're going to have after they have downed an order or two of that divine guacamole. We know what he means—Rosa Mexicano produces food that fantasies are made of.

The Russian Tea Room

150 West 57th Street   (212) 265-0947
New York, NY 10019

A focal point for the famed and famished for over 60 years, The Russian Tea Room is a bona fide legend in a city where "in" restaurants fall out of favor with the speed of the Concorde. The RTR (as it's known to regulars) really did start out as a tea room in 1926. It was founded by members of the Russian Imperial Ballet who had fled to America during the Bolshevik Revolution. A meeting place for Russian emigres, the RTR only served tea, pastries, and ice cream until 1932, when Prohibition became an unpleasant memory. The soda fountain was transformed into a bar specializing in over 20 varieties of vodka from around the world, and the former tea room started serving full meals.

After World War II, a group of investors, lead by former high school chemistry teacher Sidney Kaye, took over the restaurant. In 1955 Sidney bought out his partners and devoted himself to preserving its unique Euro-Russian charm, while adding touches of his own—it was Sidney's idea, for instance, to keep the Christmas decorations up year round.

Sidney died in 1967, leaving the RTR to his widow, Faith, with the stipulation that she had three months to decide whether to keep it or sell it. Faith, a former actress, says it was a difficult, even frightening decision, but she took the plunge. She has since successfully combined her show business flair with what has become an in-depth understanding of restaurant management to insure the longevity of one of the country's most famous dining establishments. Indeed, for Faith, "The Russian Tea Room is a form of theater. It's like being on stage all the time."

It's an exuberant green-walled, red-leather-boothed, pink-table-clothed and art-adorned stage often filled with stars of the highest magnitude. The small booth in the bar at the front of the restaurant, as well as the first three tables along both walls, are traditionally reserved for the movie moguls and Broadway biggies who regularly transact business here. It is no coincidence that a couple of years ago Elizabeth Taylor chose the RTR to show off what was then her fabulous new figure. She waltzed into the restaurant with her agent, sending a clear signal to show business movers and shakers that she was at fighting weight, ready to work. Her agent returned to his office to find his phone ringing off the hook.

Of course, you can't count on spying Liz, but it's likely you'll spot at least one Somebody—Cher, Connie Chung, Michelle Pfeiffer, Carol Burnett, Tony Randall, Oliver Stone, and Garson Kanin frequently decorate those front tables. And the regular presence of Mikhail Baryshnikov and Rudolf Nureyev harkens back to the restaurant's origins. Still, some Somebodies prefer to stay out of the limelight. Like Alan Alda, they dash up the stairway to the Café Room upstairs. Open Wednesday through Sunday, the Café tends to be less crowded and considerably quieter. There you can enjoy the à la carte luncheon (served downstairs too) along with a serious business conversation. The borscht at $6.50 is a must—one of the great joys of summer is the arrival of the cold variety, which is truly sublime. Soup and salad types at lunch, we generally follow the borscht with either the $14 salmon or $11.50 chicken salad platter. Authentically fresh, the latter can be ordered tossed with the special house dressing or served plain with a vinaigrette on the side.

Like the cold borscht, the reservation schedule here is seasonal. For lunch during the season, call maître d' Ona DeSousa a week in advance and plan on groveling for a 12:30 to 1:00 P.M. slot. During the summer two or three days notice will suffice.

Richard Baron is in charge of the evening's festivities. With a $39.50 fixed price dinner menu and a location just "six minutes and 23 seconds from Lincoln Center and slightly to the left of Carnegie Hall," the RTR is a mighty popular pretheater spot. Lately, thanks to chefs Jacques Pepin and Anthony Damiano, that menu features innovative new dishes that cater to today's health-conscious tastes alongside the RTR's classic (and rich) Russian specialties. Gravlax and smoked fillet of trout are new to the list of appetizers. But Woody Allen can still start his meal with his beloved blini with two ounces of red salmon caviar and sour cream, for a $30 premium.

Even the classics like the superb chicken kiev and beef à la stroganoff are now prepared with a lighter touch. But for a real walk on the light side, you need to wander through the à la carte supper menu, served from 9:00 P.M. to closing (about 11:45). The RTR's special, Zakushka, an assortment of little bite-sized Russian hors d'oeuvres, makes a great late-night snack for $19. And if your idea of supper is eggs, there's a good selection—scrambled with smoked trout or smoked salmon for $18 or whipped into an omelet filled with red caviar for $24.75 are the best choices.

Recently, the RTR instituted a take-away menu with an emphasis on the "take-away"—no deliveries. But they'll happily turn over your order of $9.50 mushrooms à la Grecque, $17.75 eggplant à la Russe, or $6.00 baklava to a designated driver. Where Woody's favorite $30 blini with red caviar is concerned, however, we don't trust anyone but ourselves to take it away—same goes for the beluga, ossetra, and sevruga that are also available at "an additional cost."

Still, as good as the RTR's food may taste off-campus, it just isn't quite the same or quite as good as when you consume it on the premises. The you-never-know-who-you-might-see atmosphere adds an extra dash of flavor—a borscht and chicken salad lunch was never as good as it was the afternoon it was enhanced by the Andrews sisters. Dressed in identical suits and hats, they ordered identical plates of beluga caviar and blinis and then burst into song. We guess they took a cue from Liz; they've been hot on the come-back trail ever since!   ❦

San Domenico

240 Central Park South   (212) 265-5959
between 7th and Broadway
New York, NY 10019

The installation of the pretty, peachy-orange awnings was the first outward sign of new life being pumped into this formerly moribund restaurant site, despite its seemingly prime location. For as long as anyone can remember it had been home to Alfredo, a dark, dreary-looking sort of place that no one ever dreamed of talking about, let alone visit. All that has changed now. With the opening of San Domenico, everyone's talking about it (*Esquire* named it one of the best new restaurants in the nation in its 1988 annual round-up), and now everyone's coming to visit. Just goes to show you what can happen when you put together a first-rate team.

This particular team is headed by the owner—renowned Italian restaurateur Tony May, proprietor of several popular establishments including the very successful, but in our humble opinion overrated, Palio. This time, it was his intention, as he put it, to create a "luxurious and comfortable environment where one can relax amid warm colors and great art while enjoying wonderful food and wine...and the team we have gathered together, led by Bruno Dussin to orchestrate the dining room staff, has all the credentials to make this one of the most exciting restaurants in New York." Amen to that. And, indeed, the choice of Bruno was inspired. After a career as the much-beloved meeter and greeter at Le Cirque for 13 years, Bruno knows everybody who's anybody, and then some.

In fact, Bruno has quite a following. They followed to his brief stint at Bellini, where some may have found the food wanting. They've followed him now to San Domenico, where no one could possibly quibble about the quality of the cuisine. Here, Bruno's winning ways (he's a world class hand-kisser) are backed up by the talented Valentino Marcatilli, who grew up at San Domenico. Not this San Domenico, of course, but the Guide Michelin two-star original located in Imola, Italy. It was there that Valentino apprenticed himself at the age of 16, and it is there that Tony May got his inspiration for the New York version. To turn inspiration into reality he recruited Valentino and the man who first recognized his culinary promise, Gianluigi Morini, founder and owner of the original San Domenico.

It was Morini who first put Valentino to work in his kitchen peeling onions and boiling potatoes and who encouraged the boy's association with the restaurant's chef. As Valentino's latent talent developed, Morini determined that he should be sent to some of the great kitchens of France to refine his skills. The strategy was an unqualified success—in 1979 as chef at Italy's San Domenico, Valentino was awarded Michelin's two-star accolade. At 25, he was the world's youngest internationally ranked master chef ever so honored. A decade later, in charge at the New York San Domenico, he is facing his "greatest challenge—and excitement."

Deciding what to order from the pumpkin-orange menus, which match the tablecloths, may be your greatest challenge and excitement. First of all, you have to choose between the à la carte and the fixed price route—$29.50 at lunch and $55 at dinner. Go for the à la carte and take a journey through the best of Italian cooking traditions. Start with any of the $14.50 antipasti. The cured tuna roe with mixed greens in a lemon dressing is as unusual as it is good, while medallions of pan roasted sweetbreads scented with garlic is just as rich and wonderful as it can be. And the warm shrimp with bean salad with Tuscan oil is hard to beat too.

On to the pasta course, each $18.50 except for the sublime egg-filled raviolo with hazelnut butter and white truffles which carries a $10 surcharge (blame the truffles). You can't go wrong with either the seafood ravioli (as opposed to raviolo) and broccoli in white wine or the risotto with butter, parmigiano, and beef glaze. As for the main course, fish is $27.50, the meat $26.50. Sea scallops baked in an herbed crust and the roast veal chop in a smoked bacon and cream sauce tend to be our choices. But when we feel like throwing cholesterol caution to the wind and have a hankering to dine like Italian nobles, we order the goose liver sautéed with onions—yes, *goose* liver (if this were French, we'd be tempted to call it "foie gras d'oie"), not calves liver. Apart from the goose liver, there's nothing borrowed from the French here. This was, in fact, a time-honored favorite of Venetian nobility.

Today, San Domenico's classic yet delightfully original food is enjoyed by another kind of nobility—Claudette Colbert, Arnold Scassi, Kenneth Lane, Oscar de la Renta, Arlene Dahl and her husband Marc Rosen, Shirlee Fonda, Michael Douglas, Zubin Mehta, Candice Bergen, Harry Belafonte, and Lee Iacocca among others, many others. Indeed, the cast of characters here is nearly as rich and colorful as the decor—the bright (really bright!) orange tableclothes, burgundy-brown leather chairs, terra-cotta floors, and ochre-tinted stucco walls, all punctuated by the scurrying waiters in drop-dead red blazers.

As for the guest dress code, there isn't really one. But most evenings, i.e., Monday through Saturday, gentlemen will probably feel more at ease in a tie. This is after all a restaurant sporting not inconsiderable prices and a 900-label wine list. If you're constitutionally opposed to ties, save San Domenico for Sunday dinner when the atmosphere takes on a decidedly more casual air.

And if you really want to feel at home here—so at home that you don't even have to reach for your wallet when the check arrives—ask Bruno about opening a house account. He's so amiable and accommodating, that once he gets to know you, it will simply be a matter of course. ❦

Sarabeth's Kitchen

423 Amsterdam Avenue at 80th Street New York, NY 10024	(212) 496-6280

1295 Madison Avenue at 92nd Street New York, NY 10128	(212) 410-7335

Dubbed the breakfast queen of New York by no less an authority than *New York* magazine, Sarabeth and her kitchens produce the things of which very sweet dreams are made. In 1981, with a little bakery on the Upper West Side, she began carving out a modest breakfast territory on the culinary front, while others were entering the power sweepstakes. She quickly gained a city-wide reputation for her fresh-baked breads, muffins, cookies, and cakes, as well as her delicious orange-apricot marmalade.

Based on a 200-year-old family recipe, Sarabeth credits the marmalade with launching her business. As demand for it and her baked goods grew, so did her interest in expanding her repertoire. She began serving light meals at the bakery. The few available tables were soon overbooked with a clientele eager for her reasonably priced, ingenious concoctions. Sarabeth and husband/partner, Bill Levine, decided it was time to expand. They set up an East Side branch kitchen on Madison Avenue and moved to a larger location on the West Side.

A warm and fuzzy feeling comes over you when you enter either of Sarabeth's Kitchens on Amsterdam. Is there anything more wonderful than that fresh baking smell? You see, Sarabeth is a woman with a fetish—a fetish for fresh and perfect. You can depend on her food being both.

You can also count on your appreciation of all those fresh smells not being distorted by smoke. Sarabeth doesn't allow any smoking in either of her restaurants. She never has and never will. She also has a thing about baby carriages—not babies, just their transportation. They have to be parked outside. There's simply not enough room in either of her popular establishments to harbor them.

Both restaurants are open for breakfast, lunch, tea, and dinner. For breakfast, you can't beat the apple-cinnamon French toast with bananas for $7.95 or the cheese blintzes with sour cream and apple butter for

$7.75. At lunch we like to sample any of the salads or homemade pastas, but are especially fond of the poached Norwegian salmon tossed with spinach, arugula, and Belgian endive in a sour cream dill dressing at $10.50 and the fettuccini with fresh mozzarella, mixed vegetables, olive oil, garlic, basil, and rosemary at $8.50.

At dinner the tablecloths go on and the lights get dimmer, but the cheerful, informal atmosphere remains. Try the $19.75 roasted rack of lamb with fresh mint, green beans, carrots, and whipped sweet potato or the $18.50 grilled Norwegian salmon in a lime ginger sauce with seasonal vegetables and a golden squash flan. As at lunch, the pastas are succulently fresh; any of them is a first-rate choice.

While both restaurants have a pretty, pleasant country-kitchen look, embellished by paintings of rural scenes painted by friends of Sarabeth and Bill, the East Side location tends to attract a slightly dressier crowd than the West Side. But then, that's the East Side versus the West Side, and Sarabeth is equally at home on both sides of the divide. At either location, any day of the week, you'll find more than a sprinkling of actors, some famous, most not. Sarabeth's low-key, no-muss, no-fuss approach makes her kitchens a haven for them. We also expect they appreciate the touch of fantasy supplied by the Mother Goose theme that turns up here and there in the decor.

Reservations are accepted for dinner. For any other meal, stand in line like everybody else. While you're waiting, you can scan the shelves of bakery products and condiments to decide what Sarabeth goodie you're going to take home as a souvenir. On our first visit to the Amsterdam Avenue kitchen, our hostess, the inimitable Selma Weiser of Charivari, presented us with a jar of Apricadabra, a blend of apricots, pineapple, and currants. It must have truly magical properties, because it inspired even us to make like Sarabeth and do a little cooking; at $8, it's a great glaze for chicken, duck, or roast pork.   ❦

Seryna

11 East 53rd Street   (212) 980-9393 or 9394
between Fifth and Madison
New York, NY 10022

If you think all Japanese restaurants are alike, think again. Seryna is like no other Japanese establishment in New York. It's fancier and more expensive. Furthermore, the food is different, more refined, much of it prepared at your table.

Seryna announces its uniqueness from the outset, located as it is in a mid-town office tower. It is fronted by a two-story wall of glass punctuated by an imposing brass canopy—not the typical little unassuming storefront. The bold brashness of the outside is in sharp contrast to the calm serenity of the interior. A gracious cocktail lounge with an undulating banquette, reminiscent of one of Elsa Perretti's curvaceous shapes, and striking lacquer table serves as a place to gather your party before being seated. As attractive as it is, it's not meant for any serious drinking—that's saved for the tables in the two-tiered dining room where cocktails are served the old-fashioned way. The alcohol comes in little carafes, with mixers on the side. So if your drink isn't quite right you have no one to blame but yourself—you made it.

As is their national custom, the Japanese executives who populate Seryna at lunch and dinner tend to consume the contents of a number of those little containers. But that doesn't seem to dampen their enthusiasm for the food or for business. The substantial blond wood tables and banquettes are generously spaced allowing for serious and private conversation. The decor may have a soft, subtle appeal, but the atmosphere is electric with the talk BIG deals are made of. Manager Toshiaki Oikawa estimates that the bigwigs of every major Japanese company in New York show up at least once or twice a week—visiting executives and CEOs from the homeland are known to show up twice a day during their stay. We're sure that Malcolm Forbes, man of the world that he is, believes in the axiom that any ethnic restaurant with this many ethnics must be good, but we suspect there are multimillion dollar reasons, other than exceptionally good Japanese food, that prompt his visits.

A wide staircase guarded by a heavy and decorative wooden bannister leads to a mezzanine hanging over much of the dining room. This is the place to conduct very serious business or hold an intimate surprise party for a special someone in one of the traditional tatami rooms. Each seats six at low slung tables protected from prying eyes by wood framed paper screens. Of course, shoes are left outside, but the backs of the legless chairs resting on the floor help assure comfort—no emergency call to your chiropractor when you leave. Plan on reserving one of the tatami rooms two weeks in advance and remember that there is a $40 room charge in addition to the meal tab. There's also an "American style" private room—conventional table and chairs by Western standards—for 6 to 8, but why bother?

Lunch or dinner is likely to land in the $60 a person neighborhood, depending upon the number of cocktail carafes or porcelain sake jars that show up at your table. While the sushi and sashimi are achingly fresh and beautifully prepared, they are not the main attraction here. We suggest starting with the splendid Crab Kohra Age for $9—a large crab-shell filled with crabmeat doused in a lovely white sauce and delicately fried to form a crispy crust, served with a tangy sweet-and-sour sauce on the side. Alternatively, do dip into the sashimi column with an order of Usuzukuri. At $13.50 it is not your garden variety assorted sashimi. Instead it's a breathtakingly beautiful presentation of delicate fluke filet, pearly-white and sliced so thin as to appear transparent and served with a delicious lime and shoyu dipping sauce.

If there's someone in your party who claims not to like Japanese food, steer him or her toward the main courses. The obvious choice for such a barbarian is the Ishiyaki Steak, melt-in-your-mouth tender slices of either New York sirloin or filet mignon prime beef which you sizzle to taste on a red-hot rock brought to the table. Served with two delectable sauces—chili and garlic soy—it's fun and will satisfy even the most hardnosed meat-and-potato type for $29.50. For those with more sophisticated tastes, try the Shabu-Shabu, a time-honored Japanese dish. For $24.50, paper-thin sliced beef simmers, along with vegetables and noodles, to perfection in the traditional copper pot on your table.

In all good conscience, we have to also mention the $22.95 seafood tempura. It's a large and particularly good rendition of this staple of Japanese restaurants. The fried batter encasing shrimp, lobster, fish, and vegetables is just as light, delicate, and flavorful as it can be. Finally, for the daring, we suggest the eel teriyaki. At $19.50, the teriyaki-style dish features the unique and very successful combination of eel and avocado.

While there is no official dress code at Seryna, the management does admit a preference for men with jackets and ties and for women described as "smart." And you'd be wise to remember that unlike Chinese food, Japanese food is not meant to be shared. Nor is there any take-out here or delivery.

Sfuzzi

58 West 65th Street	(212) 873-3700
between Central Park West	
and Columbus Ave.	
New York, NY 10023	

It's too bad that a restaurant with a name promising "fun food" (the translation of *Sfuzzi*—don't pronounce the "f") has let success go to its head. This once-welcome addition to the Lincoln Center area has developed a serious attitude problem—the staff is just too impressed with itself for words. Of course, they have had a lot to cope with since opening last May. There were all those rave reviews and mentions in the gossip columns; Madonna, Arnold Schwarzenegger, Carly Simon, Robin Williams, and Billy Joel were actually lining up to get in, and you know how demanding superstars can be!

So maybe Sfuzzi can be forgiven its "and who are you" approach to reservations and seating—maybe. After all, there is much to like about Sfuzzi. It is a large, extremely attractive place, designed to suggest a Roman archeological dig. Interior columns look as though they belong in the Forum. Trompe l'oeil friezes in classical motifs adorn the walls.

The fun food starts with the fresh, crispy bread called focaccia placed on the table, sans butter. Instead, Sfuzzi serves a unique and healthy dip of extra virgin olive oil, spiced with pepper, shallots, basil, and garlic, otherwise known as a basil pesto sauce. Wash it down with a Frozen Sfuzzi, a little too cutely described as being "Un-Bellini-Able," and made with sparkling wine, peach schnapps, and "secret" ingredients. It's slushy, refreshing, predictably strong, and comes in small, medium, or ridiculous portions—a "goblet" of Frozen Sfuzzis serves twelve.

The brainchild of two Long Island–bred boys who have been lifelong pals, the New York restaurant is the second in a planned national chain. Brian Galligan and Patrick Colombo first opened a Sfuzzi in Dallas. Their out-of-town success encouraged them to bring their concept to Manhattan, the site of their youthful extravagances, where it was promptly embraced by a young, stylish crowd. The nightly bar action is ferocious, and it takes several days to get a dinner reservation, even if you've done your homework and cultivated maître d' Carlos Ascencio.

Sfzuzzi's proximity to Lincoln Center has made it a must on the theater circuit. If you can get in, take advantage of the $29 pretheater dinner. Otherwise, wander through the regular menu, which inspires grazing with primi plates, small pizzas, and pastas, all in the $5.50 to $14.50 range. Specialties or entrees include grilled chicken with goat cheese and oven-roasted peppers for $18.50 and pan-seared salmon with basil citrus sauce and crisp leeks for $23. The grilled veal chop with roasted shallot marsala butter at $24.50 is particularly good.

But if you're here for the fun, stick with the starters, the pizzas, and the Frozen Sfuzzis. The fried calamaris are just as light and tender as they can be. The hefty $6.50 portion serves two and is garnished with a spicy marinara sauce and a smooth garlic aioli. The $14 smoked salmon with pancetta and mascarpone cheese is another winner.

Of course, if you get too enamored of the Frozen Sfuzzis, it won't matter much what you eat—you'll just be soaking up the fun!   ❦

Sidewalkers'

12 West 72nd Street   (212) 799-6070
between Central Park West
and Columbus Avenue
New York, NY 10023

And they do walk sideways—crabs, that is. This is the home of the "Maryland Crab-Bash," the only outpost of the land of pleasant living worth mentioning in New York City. If you've never bashed a steamed Chesapeake Bay bluepoint crab to get at the sweet, succulent meat inside, don't miss this place. It's an experience you'll never forget and one you're likely to become addicted to.

The drill is you sit at a table swathed in paper (very necessarily disposable), order a pitcher of beer (just on principle), and decide how many dozen medium, large, or jumbo crabs you and your party are going to consume. And we do suggest you go to Sidewalkers' with friends—this is a great group activity. Now, as far as we're concerned, there's no sense fooling around with the mediums—too small, all that work for such a little reward. Go for the large at $19.50 a dozen or the jumbo, priced according to market.

When the bright red crustaceans arrive coated with a spicy mixture of seasonings known as Bay, they're respectfully but unceremoniously dumped onto the middle of the table, and the fun begins. Armed with wooden mallet and a knife, you attack. If you're unfamiliar with the procedure, any of the pleasant young staff will show you the ropes. Be forewarned. There's no avoiding making a colossal mess. Relax. Enjoy the opportunity to make like Tom Jones, eating with your hands, sucking seasoning off your (or whomever's) fingers, and tossing bits of shell over your shoulder (hopefully) into the buckets stationed at every table. Look around. Everyone's really into making a mess, even the patrician Sigourney Weaver, the Japanese Yoko Ono, and the hunkiest of hunky soap stars, Glen Ritchie from "One Life to Live."

While we wait for the main event, we usually whet our appetites with the $7.95 American Seviche, a tart, refreshing combination of shrimp, scallops, and tile fish marinated in citrus juice and peppers. To accompany the crabs, we order the chunky homemade cole slaw at $2.75 and the yummy sweet potato fries at $2.50. For those who just can't stomach beating their food, the menu has lots of offerings of a less participatory nature. They include a large list of fresh fish—broiled, sautéed, deep fried, poached, or blackened—that changes daily depending upon availability. In fact, Sidewalker's is a darn good seafood restaurant in general, but it's the crabs that make it truly special.

Indeed, as the only real crab game in town, it's very popular. Despite the restaurant's informality, showing up without a reservation is not advisable. Usually a call early in the day will do it for dinner that night (no lunch is served). When you call, ask managers Scott or Curt to save you a dozen or so of the large (make it jumbo if they have them). Otherwise, without a crab reservation, you may have to settle for the smaller, more frustrating ones.

And when you get there, don't be put off by the dim, almost seedy looking entrance corridor and bar. Beyond, lies a large, cheery, though somewhat startling, dining room. The sharp contrast between the purplish-red walls and the glaringly white decorative moldings and embossed ceiling takes a little getting used to. But once settled the convivial atmosphere washes over you. Food and fun, rather than decor, become your main concerns, Sidewalkers' delivers plenty of both, all of it good.

Sparks

210 East 46th Street   (212) 687-4855
between Second and Third
New York, NY 10017

When you've had it with the fru-fru-sauces and food too preciously presented for words, when some inner primeval force cries out for good old-fashioned, good old-basic red meat, head straight for Sparks. Do not pass Go. Do not collect $200—although you could probably use it to dine properly at this venerable chop house.

For almost a quarter century, brothers Pat and Mike Cetta have been serving up some of the best properly aged and oh-so-very prime meat in town, not to mention respectable seafood and monster lobsters. Admittedly, other members of the special breed of New York steakhouses are older and traditionally more famous, but for our 75 bucks a head (standard for a full meal with modest wine at any of them) none is better. And Sparks has enjoyed higher visibility ever since a reputed gangster was gunned down out front. Now, don't let that put you off. You should consider the late gentleman's patronage an endorsement of the Sparks' quality—mob types are notorious for their appreciation of fine food.

Given its proximity to the U.N., rest assured that most of your fellow diners will be most respectable, even international. And Sparks is considered a favorite hangout by the advertising crowd, who don't have to worry about seating protocol here. The two large dining rooms have equal status, both benefitting from the truly superior art on the walls—all from the Hudson River School and all signed. Of course, you'll have to look closely for those signatures, because the light is on the dim side. We've complained to the Cetta boys that it would be more flattering if it had a pink instead of amber glow, but they laugh and claim it looks soft enough to them. Theirs is, after all, a proudly substantial establishment, nothing the least bit prissy about it—from the massive portions to the large, comfortable red leather chairs. Nor should there be.

Any meat lover worth his (or her) salt would feel ridiculous consuming one of Sparks' "about a pound" $29.95 boneless prime sirloin steaks in a room awash in pastels and flowers. Steak houses should have a masculine air and Sparks is no exception. Still, unlike some of its competitors, women are not treated like second-class citizens. Mike and Pat know the fairer sex can hold their own when it comes to eating and to running up sizable tabs. And our tab is invariably hefty. When we stop in, we can't resist working our way through the familiar menu—*all* the way through.

Generally, we start with the lump crab meat and bay scallops, a hot (literally and figuratively) appetizer at $12.95, and the baked clam, shrimp scampi combination for $10.50. Then it's on to the main event and the inevitable question—to steak or not to steak. The three double-cut, extra thick lamb chops for $29.95 are a tempting alternative to the sirloin. And then there are those amazing lobsters. They start at 3¹/₂ pounds and $47, with 4¹/₂ and 5¹/₂ pounders always available.

Whichever way we go, we can't resist the $3.95 hash browns and we know people who save room for the pretty terrific New York cheese cake at $5.50. But that really is too much, even for us. We usually settle on whatever fruit is in season, from the $4.75 to $8.50 neighborhood. We've also been known to beg for a slice of Roquefort (on hand to top one of the steak selections on the menu) to accompany one of their outstanding port wines.

Indeed, no discussion of the merits of Sparks would be complete without a mention of the extensive wine list. It is extraordinary—the dessert selections alone would put most other wine cartes to shame with 20 sauternes, 23 ports, a number of Rieslings, and a Madeira or two. As for wines complementary to lunch or dinner entrées, the world's best vineyards are represented. Tours of the cellar aren't usually offered, but maybe they'll make an exception if you order #800, the Pauillac Château Lafitte Rothschild 1970 for $198. If you go for the $450 bottle of Paulliac Château Latour 1945, you should *demand* the grand tour. Should you be inclined to stay seated, lean toward the lower and end of the list, starting at about $25.

Speak to Rami or Walter about dinner reservations and be forewarned that 7:30 to 9:00 P.M. are the busiest hours. So be prepared to settle for earlier or later—the kitchen is open till 1:00 A.M. To get a table for lunch, speak with Mike's son Steve. But don't bother to speak to anybody on Sunday's—they're closed.   🍂

21 Club

21 West 52nd Street   (212) 582-7200
between Fifth and Sixth
New York, NY 10019

It's name says club, but contrary to popular wisdom it isn't and never quite has been. What it was when it first opened on New Year's Eve 1929 was a speakeasy. The only people admitted were those known personally to the management, specifically to Jack Kriendler and Charlie Berns, who had operated a succession of such establishments in the city. So if you could call Jack and Charlie's friends a club, then, yes, indeed, "21" was a club. When they moved from their former location at 42 West 49th (known as Punch & Grotto, Jack and Charlie's, or simply 42), they did so with the help of New Year's reveling regulars who picked up furniture and bottles and merrily marched the three blocks north to the new site.

So to some degree, 21 does come by its club designation honestly. Over the years it has carved a niche in the social fabric of the city unlike any other restaurant. It is a place that gives new meaning to regular patronage—some people practically live there. The stories of childhoods spent at 21, of romances begun and ended, deals done and undone, chance meetings, engagements, weddings, births celebrated, and deaths mourned are legion. We know one young lady who even claims to have been conceived at 21.

Naturally, with so many people feeling so proprietary about 21, there was a fair amount of grumbling when the founding families sold out to Marshall Cogan in 1984. It got worse when he closed the restaurant for extensive renovations and reached a crescendo when he re-opened. It just wasn't the same old 21. Marshall had dandified it. People complained that the walls needed some smoke. Worse, the food had been gentrified with dishes like fricassee of wild mushrooms in puff pastry and paillard of chicken breast with chili butter and mustard. At first people stayed away in droves, but they couldn't resist the lure of 21 for long. Scouts pronounced the new food quite good and now the tide of popular opinion has turned decidedly in the restaurant's favor.

The bar room, all three sections (formerly numbers 21, 19, and 17 West 52nd Street), is once again full of notable regulars like John Pomerantz, Bowie Kuhn, Jamie Niven, Dixon Boardman, Ralph Destino, Rand Araskog, Marty Raynes, Neil Walsh and Pete Rozelle—a heavy hitting, man's man crowd. And a new, younger group is embracing 21 as well, adopting its traditions like the superb chicken hash ($23 at lunch, $24.00 at dinner) and dining in the bar as their very own. Do they really know that the bar has always been considered prime seating territory, or are they just attracted to the enchanting collection of toys that covers the ceiling? After all, those "toys" represent the heart and soul of 21—each one comes from a CEO or that ilk with a tie, close and personal, to the company it stands for.

The bar itself has been immortalized in story and film, especially film. It's the bar at "21" where Gordon Gecko in "Wall Street" instructs his young protégé to "go get a nice suit." Then there's the immortals who frequent it. Frank Sinatra always gets the prime table in the front room.

Actually, the main dining room upstairs is nothing to sneeze at. It's warm and inviting with lots of wood paneling punctuated by red leather banquettes and the marvelous array of Kriendler family silver lining the plate rail. The rather formal men's club look has been softened a bit by one of the Cogan regime's touches, colorfully printed chair covers that change seasonally. Up here you might run across Ambassador Maxwell Rabb or Jackie Onassis enjoying the room's quiet atmosphere, as opposed to the rather rowdy bar. The tables are far enough apart to conduct serious conversations, business or otherwise, and of course the outside world is just a phone jack away. There's one at every table in the restaurant and a staff of telephone operators to make sure you don't miss that important call.

The third and fourth floors are devoted to a series of private dining parlors, including the aptly named Remington Room sporting the restaurant's museum quality collection of the artist's work. It's perfect for dinner for 20—or 21. That's where Harrison J. Goldin, New York City's Comptroller, had his 21st wedding anniversary, with 21 friends, at, of course, 9:00 P.M. (2100 hours). There's plenty of room for larger functions on these floors too; just describe your needs to Banquet Manager Brad Reynolds.

As in life, as much as things have changed at 21 just as much remains the same. The staff still boasts members of the Kriendler family. Pete Kriendler and Jerry Berns are still around for those who remember that Kriendler and Berns were "21." Harry and Shaker still usher you through the door. Vice president Bruce Snyder still visibly presides from his vantage point next to the stuffed horse, while Walter with his twinkling eyes and shock of gorgeous silver hair still acts as maître d' in the bar.

Such 21 veterans must be intrigued by the special events the restaurant has been sponsoring of late. They've been putting together exciting package evenings including dinner, orchestra seats for a hot show, and transportation to and from the theater for about $125 a person. If you want to put together your own package, sample the $37.50 pretheater dinner menu, served from 5:30 to 6:30 P.M. It consists of three courses with several choices in each. We've found that oysters on the half shell, followed by veal medallions with thyme and caramelized baby onions, topped off with homemade ice cream puts us in just the right mood for an evening of culture.

But if dining at 21 is the evening's principal amusement, we never fail to order the first rate tartar of black angus for $29.00. It's such fun to watch the waiter prepare it tableside. The superb $23.00 sunset salad, chopped tongue, chicken, cheese, and assorted greens mixed with a tasty dressing at the table is equally entertaining. Among the dishes defined as entrées on the menu, we recommend the grilled Dover sole at $38 and rack of lamb with tomatoes Provençal $39. The bottom line? Expect to spend about $150 for a complete dinner for two (marginally less at lunch depending on the bar tab).

The 21 Club—it's a certified New York institution that like the city it has served so well for so long continues to evolve and thrive...and throb.   🍎

OUT OF TOWN

The Bird & Bottle Inn

Nelson Corners   (914) 424-3000
Route 9
Garrison, NY 10524

Bird & Bottle sounds as though it should be nestled in England's Cotswolds in a village called Stowe-in-the-Wold. Instead it's in the highlands of the Hudson River Valley outside a town called Garrison, and only fifty miles from Manhattan. But it's always best to call for directions. One of the country's older inns, founded in 1761 as Warren's Tavern, it doesn't rate a claim of oldest because it has not continually operated as a hostelry; from 1832 to 1940 it served as the main house of a prosperous farm.

In 1940, the structure was restored to its eighteenth-century origins and opened as the Bird & Bottle. While for years the inn has been a popular day-in-the-country destination, it did not have a reputation for particularly fine food until 1982, when hotel and tourism consultant Ira Boyer purchased the property. Until Ira came along, the Bird & Bottle had relied on being quaint and charming (rather *too* quaint and charming) to attract clientele. He's transformed it into a truly elegant establishment, now famous for the excellence of its cuisine.

As a result, the Bird & Bottle has become even more popular for that most sacred of weekend activities, Sunday brunch. Today, it's necessary to call manager Faye Thorpe at least a week before your country jaunt.

Reservations assure you an enchanting afternoon, easily compensating for any loss of spontaneity. Just ask Dorothy Hamill, James Caan, Sally Field, and Bob Hope; even they had to do a little planning in advance to experience the $15.95 prix-fixe brunch at the Bird & Bottle.

There are two seatings, noon and 2:00 P.M., and a menu that covers all bases—a choice of nine appetizers running the gamut from fruit cup to mussels in sour cream and dill, complemented by a salad and followed by any one of twelve entrees. Not being big egg fans, we tend to skip the Benedict and omelets and head straight for the real food. We especially like the chicken livers sautéed with mushrooms and garlic in a port wine sauce, served on a bed of rice.

Should you arrive a bit early, while away the minutes in the aptly named Drinking Room, a cozy spot with low-beamed ceiling, roaring fire, and large bay window overlooking the lovely grounds. The main dining room is equally delightful, lined with period wallpapers, hung with old botanical prints and copper sconces. Here, too, the crackling logs in the large fireplace that dominates the room often take the chill off an autumn or winter afternoon.

Despite its popularity, brunch is not the only food story at the Bird & Bottle. Chefs Robert Carpino and Loren Centrello cook a mean dinner too. The roasted pheasant deglazed with Madeira, truffled pâté, and demi-glace at $39.50 is a special treat. And the brace of chefs are whizzes at dessert too. There's always a large selection of homemade pastries, cakes, and soufflés made fresh daily. The chocolate soufflé with *crème à l'anglaise* is every bit as good as it sounds.

The best news is that you can experience dinner and brunch (lunch on Saturday as well) by spending the weekend at the inn. Right now, there are two double rooms and a one-bedroom suite, as well as a separate one-bedroom cottage available for overnight guests. But the irrepressible Ira has plans for eighteenth-century-style additions to the Bird & Bottle. Meanwhile, any of the current accommodations are delightful, if hard to come by, requiring reservations about eight weeks in advance.

The Warren Room boasts another of the inn's seven fireplaces and a comfy four-poster. The $185 rate for two includes breakfast and dinner, more than making up for the bathroom across the hall. The suite and cottage go for $215, with the same deal on breakfast and dinner. The Robinson Suite is particularly charming, up the stairs and down an appropriately creaking hallway. Its sitting room, with the two wingback chairs facing the fireplace, invites you to curl up with a glass of port after dinner. There's a wonderful private terrace for breakfast or for stargazing before answering the beckoning call of the canopied bed.

No, George Washington did not sleep at the Bird & Bottle, but he did dine here at Warren's Tavern. You should too, and you can one-up America's most omnipresent guest by sleeping here as well.   🍒

Le Château

Route 35 at Junction 123   (914) 533-6631
South Salem, NY 10590

We knew we'd stumbled on a genuinely civilized place, when we drove up the long dogwood-lined driveway of Le Château. It seems a world away, but it's only fifty-five miles outside of Manhattan, a short distance from the Connecticut line.

Overlooking the Hudson River Valley, high on a stately hillside, Le Château is set on thirty-two acres of some of the most glorious gardens in the state, the restaurant occupying a grand mock-Tudor mansion built in 1907 by J. P. Morgan as a gift for his friend and former minister, Dr. William S. Rainsford.

Morgan was meticulous about the construction of this remarkable twenty-room mansion, employing one hundred Japanese laborers to execute the intricate stone and brick work. Today the mansion, originally named Savin Rock, would be all but impossible to build in terms of the financial investment and craftsmanship required.

Dr. Rainsford, the retired rector of St. George's Episcopal Church in New York City, lived at Savin Rock until his death in the 1920s. His tenancy was followed by that of Colonel Frederick Sansome, who lived there until the 1960s. For most of the next decade, the house stood uninhabited, until it was bought by Yves and Denise Lozach. They worked on its restoration for over two years before opening Le Château Restaurant in 1973 with Yves as chef. In 1980, the Lozachs sold the restaurant and estate to its present hosts, their daughter and son-in-law, Monique and Joseph Jaffre.

Le Château retains the graciously elegant ambience of the original estate, with its grand staircases and massive stone fireplaces. The lovely high-ceilinged rooms are paneled in hand-hewn chestnut, cherry, and oak. Huge chestnut beams are visible throughout the mansion.

The dining rooms open onto expansive patios and the exquisite gardens overlooking the valley. A small lake is discernible through the woods beyond, and you can often catch a glimpse of the wildlife that call the estate home—deer, fox, pheasants, quail, ducks, and Canadian geese. There's a lot to be said for calling well enough in advance to secure a window table.

As its name suggests, Le Château's culinary orientation is French, with chef Albert Bouchard at the helm. Lunch and dinner are served daily except Monday, when the restaurant is closed.

We like to visit for an early Saturday or Sunday evening dinner, at the end of a day of antiquing in the country. Dinner is served from 6:00 P.M. both nights, so you can have a leisurely meal and still get back to the city at a reasonable hour.

Leisurely is the key word here. The service is courteous and efficient, but Le Château is dedicated to serious dining, each dish prepared only after it's ordered. We like either the marinated duck breast with walnut dressing on a bed of lettuce for $9.50 or the baked oysters in a spinach, curry, and mousseline sauce for $9.75 as first courses. Both the $20.50 sliced roast veal with fresh mushrooms, pearl onions, and sweet red peppers and the sweetbreads in a tarragon Armagnac sauce have proved to be excellent main courses. The desserts are exceptional—there's always a soufflé of the day for two, which we heartily recommend.

There's no need to dress for lunch here, but at dinner gentlemen will be more comfortable in a jacket. One final tip—try to book one of Giovanni's tables. He's been here for eleven years and offers excellent counsel on the menu. He'll make sure your Le Château experience is *vaut le voyage.*   ❦

Tappan Hill Restaurant

81 Highland Avenue   (914) 631-3030
Tarrytown, NY 10591

For years the Tappan Hill offered more than the ubiquitous complimentary cocktail with Sunday brunch—its bonus was a spectacular view. Only 45 minutes from Manhattan, poised high above the Hudson River and overlooking the Tappan Zee Bridge, the restaurant occupies a 1915-vintage stone mansion, which in turn sits on the site of a farmhouse once owned by Mark Twain. Typical of the grand manses built along the Hudson by the most fashionable families of the late eighteenth through early nineteenth centuries, the house is very grand, designed to impress.

You enter through an immense foyer, often graced by a roaring fire in the baronial fireplace. The sweeping white staircase looks headed for heaven, but leads only to two small rooms reserved for private parties. The real drama is in the dining room, through the foyer at the back of the house. Formerly the terrace, it has been glass-enclosed to take advantage of that wonderful view. Despite the somewhat pedestrian decor of the room, there were few better places to enjoy a $16.95 brunch (including the "gratis" cocktail). That's all changed now since caterer Abigail Kirsch (often heralded as Glorious Foods' biggest competition on the big-time party circuit) bought the place—the view is still unforgettable, but the decor has benefitted from a face-lift that has kept Tappan Hill closed for a year and there's no longer a Sunday brunch. Indeed, there's no longer any regular Sunday meals here. While the restaurant is open for lunch and dinner on the weekdays, the weekends are devoted to private functions.

Of course, we knew Abigail was a great chef, now we're convinced she's a pretty savvy businesswoman too. You see Tappan Hill has always lent itself well to special occasions, but the potential had never been fully realized. Tappan Hill counted on its popularity as a dining spot for high-powered Westchester County executives from corporations like IBM, Pepsico, Hitachi, General Food and Texaco. Under Abigail's regime, Tappan Hill is THE perfect place to throw a memorable fête. The food has improved considerably (you already know about view) and the physical plant has been set-up to deal with any number of festive configurations. Here you can indulge in the kind of decadence the builders of the Tappan Hill estate would most certainly have understood and appreciated.   ❦

CHAPTER FOUR

A Sudden Yen for . . .

*Something for every taste, every mood,
every moment*

*J*ust about any whim can be satisfied at virtually anytime in New York. From Carnegie Hill to Cobble Hill, there's some place that will provide nearly anything for any occasion, be it for one or a thousand—for a price, of course. The price can be pretty steep. But how do you put a price on that perfect pâté, those fabulous flowers, the consummate caterer, the ennobling entertainer?

A little bedtime snack and a bouquet to cheer you up after a hard day up and down the Avenue? A little soirée for 800 in the Temple of Dendur? New York's got something for every taste, every mood, every moment. There's no need, ever, to do it yourself in New York. Certainly there are untold numbers of restaurants, but you don't have to be consigned to a fate of always eating out. There are purveyors of fine prepared foods that can be carted to hotel or home for an evening's repast. Or you can have your meals delivered. Or you can throw up your hands altogether, sit back, and let a capable caterer along with the new breed of florist called "party designer" plan your evening's entertainment.

This most entertaining of cities is set up better than any other *for* entertaining—for pampering yourself, those business associates you want to impress, *and* the friends whose company you want to enjoy. The variety is endless, the means to satisfy a sudden yen boundless. So jump into that bottomless pit of opportunities to spoil yourself and others, for a new idea, a new twist, a new dent in that thousand a day...before lunch.

PURVEYORS OF FINE FOODS

Dean & DeLuca

560 Broadway   (212) 431-1691
at Prince
New York, NY 10012

Like the Statue of Liberty, Dean & DeLuca should be on everyone's list to visit, at least once. Chances are, though, you'll want to go back again and again. If you're into food, you can't help but be seduced by this most epicurean of gourmet food stores. The displays are like jewelry—beautiful and tempting; the prices are like jewelry, too—some costume, some precious.

In the precious category, we found a fabulous smoked Mediterranean swordfish at $40 a pound. As for costume, there was an exceptional serrano-style ham for $14 a pound, just one of twelve different types. Dean & DeLuca's own $15-a-pound country pâté is perfect for hors d'oeuvres. Their cob-smoked bacon at $6 a pound makes breakfast a feast.

Pasta? These folks know a lot about it—in all possible colors and configurations—squid-ink-black linguini, green spinach fettuccini, and red tomato linguini or fettuccini, with at least ten more varieties to choose from. Breads? The fantastic display with twenty or so different kinds dominates the middle of the store. Whether you're thinking picnic or formal dinner party, you'll find just the right loaf. We especially like the Russian health at $3.40, but it's hard to pass up the sourdough rye at $5. As for the baguettes, we've been known to grab one and munch as we shop!

If cooking is not your forte, but your palate demands good food, head for the prepared goodies, truly a feast for the eye. There is a tremendous selection of appetizers, entrées, vegetables, and salads worthy of your best entertaining efforts, or a solitary treat.

Wild and wondrous condiments line shelf after shelf—all sorts of jams, honeys, mustards, oils, and vinegars, including every flavor recipe from *Gourmet* or *The Silver Palate Cookbook* has ever thrown at you.

A candy counter caters to the sweet tooth, and dried fruits and nuts encased in enormous jars satisfy the health enthusiast. And, oh, by the way, there is a case full of staples like milk, eggs, and butter, lest you forget this is a real market.

Baked goods are well represented, particularly by the scrumptious Russian spiced coffee cake with nuts, raisins, and sour cream, which serves twelve to fifteen and sells for $25. But the cheese department is truly outstanding with over 250 different kinds—from a single creamy brie at $7 a pound to a rare Corsican sheep-milk cheese covered in rosemary at $17.

When you enter Dean & DeLuca, you are surrounded by breathtaking arrays of fresh fruits and vegetables, along with huge baskets of onions and potatoes. You're tempted, indeed almost dared, to fondle each and every one of them, so we suggest you head straight to the back of the store and slowly work your way forward in a civilized manner. Let the classical music soothe you into a state of making sensible choices— otherwise you'll walk out of here with all sorts of things that look too good to pass up. Dean & DeLuca is a temple of impulse buying. You really shouldn't enter without a list. We can't tell you how many fascinating but totally useless gadgets we've bought from their extensive housewares department.

As you might assume, Saturdays here are a madhouse, with upwardly mobile types and more than a smattering of notables from all over the city wandering through. Fortunately, Dean & DeLuca is open from 8:00 A.M. to 8:00 P.M. Monday through Saturday and from 9:00 A.M. to 7:00 P.M. on Sundays. We highly recommend visiting during the middle of the week, unless you're more interested in people-watching than in shopping.   ❧

Fraser Morris

931 Madison Avenue   (212) 288-2727
at 74th Street
New York, NY 10021

1264 Third Avenue   (212) 288-7716
at 73rd Street
New York, NY 10021

Love to eat, but hate to cook? Fraser Morris may become your favorite
haunt. Owner Eric Rosenthal sends scouts all over the world looking for
exciting delicacies that will dazzle you. Whether it's a new offering for
the bakery department or something in prepared foods, Eric spares no
expense and expects you will do the same to sample his finds.

Much to our chagrin, we learned just how much Eric thinks the market will bear to indulge in gourmet goodies. Great salesman that he is, he
convinced us that we just had to try his latest discovery—Dallmayr, re-
putedly the richest coffee in the world. He seduced us with a whiff of its
full-flavored, alluring aroma and assurances that it has no bitter after-
taste, irritants, or acids. Suitably impressed, we asked for a pound and
then tried to maintain our composure when the cash register rang up
$21! We were just too embarrassed not to take it.

Occasionally outrageous prices aside, Fraser Morris can be a godsend,
particularly during the holiday season—Thanksgiving, Chanukah,
Christmas, New Year's. Should you find yourself throwing a little get-
together or in need of the perfect hostess gift, Fraser Morris will fill the
bill. They'll deliver everything for your holiday dinner, including reheat-
ing instructions, and even arrange for help to serve it. As for that gift,
who wouldn't be thrilled with some of their excellent Scottish salmon,
sliced paper-thin, or a selection of their exotic condiments?

If Eric isn't around when you require some gourmet guidance, ask for
Peter, the assistant manager. He'll put together anything you need—from
a picnic basket for the polo game to a romantic posttheater dinner for
two. Whatever your heart's desire—roast capon, orange-glazed Cornish
game hens, poached Norwegian salmon, or a little roast pheasant,
perhaps—Peter will make sure they're impeccably prepared and garnished. After all, he regularly satisfies perfectionists like Cicely Tyson,
Woody Allen, and Carly Simon.

We suspect their sweet tooths are particularly attracted to Fraser Morris. The assortment of minitarts always reminds us of an (edible) Old Master still life, and at Christmas the *Bûche de Noël* is a wonder to behold. Even baked apples and poached pears reach new heights in taste and appearance here.

Fraser Morris even titillates the appetite with vegetables. Made fresh every morning, they glisten invitingly—emerald green broccoli, pearllike little white onions, glossy glazed carrots, and delicate *haricot verts*.

Be you gourmet or gourmand, Fraser Morris can accommodate your penchant for fine food. 🍒

Manhattan Fruitier

210 East 6th Street　　　　　　　　　　　　(212) 260-2280
between Second and Third Avenues
New York, NY 10003

Jehv Gold used to be a lawyer. Partner Lee Grimsbo was the produce manager of Dean & DeLuca. Both yearned to own a small specialty business catering to the carriage trade. Fate intervened in the form of Jehv's sister, who introduced them. Together, they concocted a singular, whimsical business based on exploiting the decorative and delectable potential of fruit.

Their gimmick is erecting exquisite, stylized gift baskets and centerpieces, like still lifes by the Old Masters. So colorful, so inventive, so intriguing, the baskets, in particular, have become the gift currently in vogue with many a Condé Nast editor. Other visually artistic types like Oscar de la Renta and Adrienne Vittadini find them equally appealing.

The East 6th Street location is a workshop dedicated to filling telephone orders, but you can drop by to have a word or two with Jehv or Lee; we highly recommend it. It's a real treat to perch on one of their bar stools and chat with these two laid-back individuals while they construct their wondrous creations. You're surrounded by the beauty of glorious fruit and soothed by the sound of classical music, punctuated by the purring of the house cat, Kato.

Prices start at $50 and go up to about $200, depending on the exotic quotient of the fruit used. The world is Manhattan Fruitier's supplier—apple pears from Asia, blood oranges from Sicily, finger bananas from Ecuador. They're even connected to small growers with just a few trees devoted to the most special strains, like the Esopus Spitzenburg apple, Thomas Jefferson's favorite.

You have the option of picking up your fruit fantasy or having it delivered for a $10 charge in Manhattan. Delivery further afield can also be arranged, but not too far. In the interests of freshness, Jehv and Lee stick to a radius where they can "hand deliver"—they don't ship.

To complement the fruit in the baskets, they often include tasty tidbits like Biscotti biscuits imported from San Francisco, chocolates handmade locally by Lawrence Burdick, or New York cheddar cheese sticks by John Macy. All encourage breaking into and nibbling on the arrangement, which otherwise seems just too pretty, just too perfect to eat.

Give Manhattan Fruitier at least a day's notice on your order. In turn, they will provide you with an ornamental, edible item which, once consumed, will leave behind an indelible impression.   🍒

Murray's Sturgeon

2429 Broadway   (212) 724-2650
between 89th and 90th Streets
New York, NY 10024

Talk about specialty shops! This may be one of the most specialized; it is certainly one of the best. For the most part, people line up in this long, narrow space for just two edibles—sturgeon and salmon (although the delicious homemade salads shouldn't be ignored). We think they also get a kick out of owner Harold Berliner—he wields a mean fish knife. And as popular as Murray's is, Harold just about never stops slicing, any thickness you want.

The sturgeon, which comes from Canada, costs $39 a pound. The salmon is imported from Norway, but smoked in New York, and priced at $36 a pound.

Murray's customers come in weekly for their smoked-fish fix. They're so addicted, when they're out of town, many have it shipped overnight by UPS. Sensibly, Murray's doesn't add a markup for shipping. You just pay the UPS charges.

So who's keeping Murray's so busy that they're open every day, except Monday, from 8:00 A.M. to 7:00 P.M. ('til eight o'clock on Saturday evenings)? Just about everyone who ever enjoyed bagels, lox, and cream cheese for brunch—like Tony Randall, Linda Lavin, and Robert Duvall. Henry Winkler regularly has fish shipped to him in Los Angeles. Apparently, even in L.A., there's no place quite as special and specialized as Murray's!   ❦

Orwasher's

308 East 78th Street   (212) 288-6569
between 1st and 2nd
New York, NY 10021

An East Side fixture since 1916, Orwasher's does bread and does it better than anyone else. Every roll, muffin, and loaf of bread is made from scratch on the premises, right below the tiny storefront, in the same brick ovens built by Abraham Orwasher seventy-three years ago.

Two generations later, grandson and namesake, Abraham, still insists that absolutely no artificial flavors or preservatives are used. Abraham refuses to make bread any way but the old-fashioned way. He won't allow the conditioners used by most bakeries to make dough rise faster, or even the mechanical equivalent of speeding the process with steam boxes. At Orwasher's, the dough rises naturally, at its own pace, in time-honored wooden boxes.

Certainly it would be a lot easier to employ modern methods and mixes, but that would never suit the palates of the likes of Gene Shalit and Itzhak Perlman, who count on Orwasher's for their daily dose of bread. On Saturdays you might run into Henny Youngman here. Leonard Bernstein can't do without Orwasher's, though the maestro has no time for the lines that assemble Monday through Saturday from 7:00 A.M. to 7:00 P.M. So he sends over his butler.

Given its 10021 location, "the best zip code" in New York, all the importance attached to making everything by scratch, and its upscale clientele, you might think Orwasher's prices would be high. Wrong! Basic rolls run 40 cents apiece, a loaf of bread $2.50 a pound. Then there are rye breads for $1.50 a pound, cinnamon raisin at $2.25. Muffins— blueberry, bran (with or without raisins), corn, banana, walnut, and the ubiquitous oat bran—range in price from 65 cents to $1.20 each.

Of course, you can spend more (but only in cash, since no checks or charge cards are accepted). Have Orwasher's make a loaf for a special occasion—a heart for Valentine's Day, a cornucopia for Thanksgiving, or a wreath for Christmas.

Off-the-rack or custom-designed, Orwasher's bread is quite simply first-rate. And you really don't have to stand in line to sample it. Orwasher's products pop up at all the best places in Manhattan—from Gracie Mansion to the University Club, from Bloomingdale's to Balducci's, everywhere that quality and value are truly appreciated.　❦

William Poll

1051 Lexington Avenue　　　　　　　　　　　　(212) 288-0501
at 75th Street
New York, NY 10021

Rumor has it that William Poll's Nova is sliced so thin that you can read *The New York Times* through it. But then, what would you expect from an establishment that's been practicing the fine art of salmon slicing since 1921? Self-proclaimed "first in gourmet luxuries and catering," William Poll's is still in the capable hands of the founding family. Stanley Poll is the third-generation owner.

He's the one Jackie O. calls to fill her orders. He takes care of Christie Brinkley, Cheryl Tiegs, and Lauren Bacall when they stop by. A famous Palm Beach hostess turns to Stanley every time she plans a dinner party. After preparing everything, he packages it beautifully and sends it off with a courier on the first plane to West Palm the morning of her party.

A tad extravagant? Perhaps, but William Poll's legions are very loyal folk who don't count their pennies, but do count on the unwavering quality of the food. Many are particularly fond of Stanley's dear little finger sandwiches that show up at all those chic teas. The wonderful hors d'oeuvres are another draw. Most are frozen, so you can stock up at home for that impromptu party, then just pop them in the microwave. A tray (about twelve to fourteen pieces) of such bite-size appetizers as papillons—flaky strudel filled with goodies like chicken and chestnuts, spinach, cheese, or mushroom and bacon—costs $12 to $15.

William Poll's dips are also great to keep on hand. The sun-dried tomato with olive oil, sour cream, and secret seasonings is sensational. The eggplant in olive oil and wine vinegar is another good choice, as is the smoked turkey with sour cream, mustard, and spices. Our favorite is called Fromage—a mixture of several French cheeses, laced with brandy, dill, olive oil, and assorted spices. All the dips range from $6 to $10 for a half-pound container, and, according to Stanley, each will serve as many as eight for cocktails.

If you prefer to entertain on a more lavish scale, spoil your guests with William Poll's rich, velvety foie gras imported from Perigord and Strasbourg. Depending upon the current state of the dollar, it costs about $120 for a ten-ounce block and yields an unforgettable taste sensation.

William Poll's also features a wide variety of entrees—from stuffed cabbage to chicken pot pie—sold by the serving for $14. Then there are the whole smoked hams and turkeys. Salads? The list seems to go on forever. Stanley estimates they sell at least 100 pounds of chicken salad alone every day!

Desserts run the gamut from chocolate chip cookies to baklava. And don't forget that William Poll stocks virtually every packaged gourmet condiment imaginable. Anything prepared or sold here can be delivered anywhere in Manhattan for a $20 minimum.

But if you really want to treat yourself to the essence of William Poll's long-standing popularity with the rich and famous, order one of Stanley's beluga caviar sandwiches for $125. Served on white bread without a trace of sour cream, egg, or onion, it is a purist's delight. Stanley won't say exactly how much caviar is carefully placed (so as not to break the eggs) on that plain old white bread. "Enough," he laughs, "that you certainly won't go hungry." ❦

Word of Mouth

1012 Lexington Avenue	(212) 734-9483
at 72nd Street	
New York, NY 10021	

Kitchens just aren't what they used to be. A professional cook is, unfortunately, no longer standard equipment. Still, you can pretend there is a wizard in your home if you avail yourself of the services of Word of Mouth. With fifty-some entrees, an equal number of pastas, more than a hundred salads and nearly a hundred desserts to choose from, this place gives a whole new meaning to the term *takeout*. You even have to adjust the way you order. Nothing is sold by the piece or the item; everything is by the pound. Basically, a pound feeds one person piggishly, two people moderately.

Owner/chef Christi Finch splits her time between overseeing the kitchen, which is in full view of all her customers, and experimenting with delicious new recipes. So even regulars find it virtually impossible to work their way through the menu. There are always new dishes to be tried and savored. Christi follows the seasons to ensure the freshest ingredients—chicken corn chowder is a special summer treat. And she takes holidays into consideration too. Traditional delights show up at Rosh Hashanah, Thanksgiving, Chanukah, Christmas, St. Patrick's Day, and the Fourth of July.

We know of one chic lady who, despite the fact that her husband is in the restaurant business, relied upon Word of Mouth for sustenance throughout her pregnancies and the early years of raising her family.

While you wouldn't know it by the number of limos lined up outside, Word of Mouth does deliver, between 10:00 A.M. and 6:00 P.M., with a $10 delivery charge. That tends to keep people from having lunch for two delivered, which is exactly Christi's purpose. She's after bigger game—a luncheon for the working committee of your favorite charity, for instance. And you can take all the credit for being a virtuoso in the kitchen for a lot less than it would cost to keep a cook. Entrées start at about $8 a pound, salads range from $6.50 to $15 for some of the exotic seafood varieties. Divide that $20 delivery charge by twelve guests and it becomes downright negligible!

If it still rankles, take heart in the fact that Christi's staff will help you into a taxi with your order. So with Word of Mouth at your disposal, there is no excuse for not entertaining right in your own home.   ❦

Zabar's

2245 Broadway   (212) 787-2000
at 80th Street
New York, NY 10024

There's just no other place like it. Zabar's is a real trip, an overwhelming assault to the senses—the aroma of fine coffees and cheeses, the sight of food and housewares covering every square inch of floor and ceiling space, and the sound of hordes of crazed people shouting "Here!" as their long-awaited number at the smoked fish or prepared-foods counter is called.

On Saturdays and Sundays a visit is likely to leave you black and blue. New Yorkers are mighty aggressive shoppers and those are the days they come from all over to shop Zabar's. They come for the amazing variety—the breads (up to 60 kinds), the cheeses (possibly 500), the coffees (over 30,000 pounds sold each week), the wall of cured and smoked meats, the feast of prepared foods, the stacks of condiments, the "mezzanine" sporting every kitchen utensil known to man. Oh, yes, and the prices are terrific, as in bargain!

In fact, the pre-Christmas caviar price war between Zabar's and Macy's is an eagerly anticipated annual event. Neither establishment gives any quarter, both lose money, but get lots of publicity and lots of traffic in the process. We think no one gets more of a kick out of it than Stanley and Saul Zabar's affable partner, Murray Klein—his eyes light up at the very thought of the yearly fray.

Actually, Murray gets pretty excited about everything here. No wonder—all those cash registers lining the front of the store never stop ringing, Monday through Friday from 8:00 A.M. to 7:30 P.M., 'til midnight on Saturday, 6:00 P.M. on Sunday. No one walks out of Zabar's without buying something, be it a 40-cent French bean cutter or a $1,200, four-pound tin of caviar. Just in case you do escape without a single purchase, you can satisfy your Zabar's cravings via mail order. Their catalog, chock-full of gadgets and goodies, circulates to over 600,000 Zabar's fans around the world.

Despite the obvious emphasis on numbers and diversity, Zabar's is no slouch when it comes to quality. The smoked salmon is flown in daily. The coffee is roasted on the premises. Zabar's truly represents exceptional value and consequently has become a beloved institution. Rumors of a sale to David Leiderman of David's Cookies fame prompted a line of customers at the "cash only" checkout line to chant spontaneously, "Don't sell!" One shopper told a *New York Times* reporter that "the entire West Side is having a nervous breakdown over this."

Zabar's dates from 1934, when founder Louis Zabar rented a fish counter in a grocery two doors down from the current location. The business grew to a four-store empire, which sons Stanley, Saul, and Eli later consolidated into the one and only Zabar's. In 1964, Eli was bought out (eventually heading east to establish E.A.T. on Madison Avenue), and Murray Klein, who began his career as a delivery boy at Zabar's, was brought in as partner to tap his marketing creativity—witness the caviar war and his battle with Cuisinart. In 1975, Murray was selling their then-revolutionary food processor for $135, while department stores were charging $180. Murray was selling a lot of food processors, getting a lot of publicity, and making competitors very angry. Bowing to pressure, Cuisinart cut off the supply. Murray retaliated by suing, generating still more publicity. The suit was settled out of court.

As testimony to Zabar's stature, consider the fact that when Murray donated a dinner for twenty catered by Zabar's to a City Meals on Wheels benefit auction, it sold for $10,000—or $500 a person! Then there's the transplanted New York woman, now a Chicago matron, who couldn't imagine her son's bar mitzvah done without platters from Zabar's. No problem—Murray sent out everything she needed by courier. For years, *New York Times* managing editor Abe Rosenthal and metropolitan editor Arthur Gelb, en route to Albany for the annual legislative correspondents' dinner and show, would stop in and load up with brown bags full of Zabar's specialties. After the performance and late into the night, the likes of Nelson Rockefeller and John Lindsay would feast on the *Times* and Zabar's.

Indeed, documentation as to the wonders of Zabar's are endless. Leonard Bernstein has been quoted in the catalog describing the store's whitefish as "a symphony of delicacy and succulence." And how appropriate that the great chronicler of the tales of New York, Woody Allen, uses Zabar's to cater meals for his cast and crew when filming. He's joined in his admiration for this greatest of the city's food emporiums (not a market like Dean & DeLuca or Balducci's—no fruits or vegetables) by Neil Simon, Lauren Bacall, and Zubin Mehta.

They all know it's ridiculous to have to fight their way through the crowds and wait in endless lines to be served, only to wait in more endless lines to check out. But oddly enough, at Zabar's it's all part of the fun and part of the folklore.

There are some vestiges of civilization in this endearing madhouse. We appreciate the fact that if hunger strikes, you can have them make you a sandwich and retire to their little café next door for some of the best cappuccino or espresso in town. There you can sit quietly, amusing yourself by drawing pictures in the sawdust on the floor with your toes and pondering your next purchase. Ah, bliss!   ❦

Zito's Bread

259 Bleecker Street   (212) 929-6139
between Sixth and Seventh Avenues
New York, NY 10014

We've all tittered self-consciously at the double entendre phrase "a bun in the oven." Somehow the vulgar overtones evaporate when it's applied to Josephine Zito, who gave birth to son Julius in the back room of the bakery she and her husband, Anthony, founded in 1924! Having interrupted the family business with his debut, Julius has devoted his life to it, as have his three brothers, Vincent, Charles, and Jimmy, and sister

Frances. Julius's son Anthony also works here, representing the third generation of Zitos dedicated to the fine art of baking—lots of baking.

The original brick ovens, still fueled by coal as they were when they were built, are full twenty-four hours a day with Zito's preservative-free products. The result is mouth-wateringly fresh breads that keep this tiny shop crowded with patrons seven days a week. Of course, the neighborhood has long relied on Zito's; rumor has it that Charles Zito has been forced over the years to transfer his flirtatious attentions from generation to generation, from mother to daughter, even to granddaughter. But Zito's domain stretches far beyond the Village. They supply decidedly uptown restaurants like Tavern on the Green and Elaine's. And some of the world's most famous descendants of Italian heritage beat a path to Zito's door—Lee Iacocca stops by on weekends when he's in town, and we hear Robert DeNiro is addicted. Ol' Blue Eyes, Frank Sinatra himself, has his Zito's bread delivered to him at the Waldorf Towers, while Mayor Koch picks up his own. Yes, we know he's not really Italian, but hizzoner has, at one time or another, claimed faithful allegiance to every ethnic group.

A loaf of Zito's delicious white bread costs $1.10, 20 cents for a roll. Whole wheat comes as loaf, baguette, or roll—$1.15, 95 cents, and 20 cents, respectively. They also make a wonderful Sicilian bread, which resembles your basic white variety, but the dough is worked longer (by hand, of course) to give it a thicker crust. Dusted with sesame seeds, it comes in several shapes, sizes, and price, from 95 cents to $1.50.

Zito's is open Monday through Saturday from 6:00 A.M. to 6:00 P.M., Sundays from 6:00 A.M. to 1:00 P.M. But if you plan to shop on Sunday, make plans to get here early—they're usually sold out by noon.   🍎

CATERERS

Glorious Foods

172 East 75th   (212) 628-2320
New York, NY 10021

There are those who believe an affair without Glorious Foods is not worthy of being considered a party. So many, in fact, have come to this religion, that the firm grossed close to $11 million last year, and founding partner Sean Driscoll finds his biggest challenge is making sure Mrs. X isn't served the same food night afer night at a series of different events. The enormity of the problem is evident when you consider that on any given night during "the season" Glorious Foods might be handling as many as seven parties. Their sixteen chefs, directed by Jean Claude Nedelec (Sean's partner since 1984), are under constant pressure to come up with innovative menus that live up to Glorious' well-deserved reputation for excellence.

Many of the East Coast's most memorable events have counted on that reputation. Glorious Foods catered Caroline Kennedy's wedding in Hyannisport. They were responsible for one of the presidential dinners at the Bush inaugural in Washington, and it was Glorious that produced the Statue of Liberty's centennial dinner on Liberty Island in New York harbor. Financier and philanthropist G. Bernard Cantor and his beautiful wife, Iris, chose Glorious for their dinner saluting the debut of the world-renowned Degas show at the Metropolitan Museum of Art. And Blaine Trump charged them with feeding 900 guests at the American Ballet gala, by all accounts one of the most perfectly orchestrated benefits in recent history. True to form, Glorious took a cue from the evening's theme, Swan Lake, and produced a stunning dessert—white chocolate swans, filled with strawberry ice cream and swimming on lakes of raspberry sauce napped with *crème à l'anglaise*.

As large as the company has become, employing an army of well-trained waiters (150 full-time and 500 part-time) and fifteen administrators in addition to those sixteen chefs, it had humble beginnings. It all started in Sean's kitchen, where he and then roommate and future partner, Christopher Idone, began cooking for private dinner parties. Word quickly spread about their imaginative food. Before long they were in business for good—at least Sean was. The partnership dissolved in 1980, when Christopher left to pursue a writing career.

Meanwhile the firm has continued to grow. At this point, chairmen of major events are advised to engage Glorious's services six to nine months in advance. Smaller affairs should be booked at least eight weeks ahead. Still, as with all things in life, there are no hard and fast rules. Don't be shy about calling Glorious at the last minute—the date just might be open. And if you're one of the many faithful, Sean will make every effort to accommodate you.

Of course, there are tremendous demands on his time. Don't be put off if you're assigned to one of Sean's executive staff to plan your party—

Philippe Maleval, Jay Jolly, Stephen Baroni, Don McCoy, or Kevin Ryan. They're as talented and resourceful as Sean, having been with him for years. Tap their expertise when it comes to flowers, music, and decorations—they won't steer you wrong.

A glorious Glorious dinner will hit your budget at the $150-to-$250-a-head level, more like $50 to $75 for cocktails and tidbits. Bear in mind that the price includes what amounts to an assurance of the social acceptability of your soirée—particularly important, even crucial, for those aspiring to climb society's treacherous ladder. But don't start that climb between December 23 and January 8. There is rest for the weary, if they work for Sean Driscoll. At the height of holiday party frenzy, he closes Glorious's doors. He can well afford to! ❦

Great Performances

125 Crosby Street   Personnel (212) 925-9090
New York, NY 10012   Catering (212) 219-2800

We all know who to call when it comes to ghostbusting, but who're you going to call when you need help—help in the kitchen, in the dining room, at the bar? Perhaps you're having a few friends in for a little cocktail, nothing elaborate. A call to Fraser Morris or William Poll takes care of the hors d'ouevres, but what about passing them? You can't pass and tend bar at the same time. Call Great Performances. They'll take care of everything.

While Great Performances is now a full service catering company, it made its 1979 debut as a party personnel service. And, while we have attended some perfectly marvelous affairs catered by the company, it is still their provision of very attractive, most accommodating, and extremely professional temporary staff that we count on.

Liz Newmark founded Great Performances in her living room in 1979 with a $1,700 investment. At first she focused only on securing waitressing jobs for women in the visual and performing arts who needed to supplement their incomes. Through regular workshops, Liz taught them how to serve, present, and garnish food, tend bar, and how to maintain their composure in the midst of the chaos that is often the backstage of a party. In less than a year, business was booming. Ten years later she has a staff of over 500 and an enviable client list, including AT&T, Coca Cola, American Express, Callaghan & Co., Macy's, the New York Stock Exchange, and Seagram's.

For an agency fee of $25 for the first person and $15 per person thereafter, Great Performances will send over as many of their well-trained staff (those workshops Liz started a decade ago continue to be mandatory) as you need. Outline the occasion for them and they'll even define your staffing requirements for you. There's a five-hour minimum per person at $15 an hour.

Since most of the Great Performances staff really are performers, they are to a man, or woman, good-looking and well-groomed. They always show up with clean, pressed uniforms—tuxedos for the men, white blouse, black vest, and skirt for the women. They also come equipped with their party kits, useful items like corkscrews, sharp little knives, and peelers. Most importantly they arrive with smiles on their faces, which seem sincere and never diminish under the most trying circumstances. And, boy have we tried them. There was the time we kept running out of ice; worse, the elevator was broken. Kevin, the bartender for the evening, didn't once balk at climbing six flights loaded down with ice. He had to do it three times.

So who are you going to call, when you need to put on staff for the day, afternoon, evening—Great Performances, that's who. 🍎

Remember Basil

11 Old Fulton Street	(212) 753-3955
Brooklyn Heights, NY 11201	(718) 858-3000

Dounia Rathbone remembers and honors her illustrious grandfather, the great actor Basil Rathbone, every time she lays out one of her theatrical culinary spreads. Dounia and the catering firm she owns with husband, Donald Beckwith, are known for deliciously imaginative food and dramatic presentation, themed to embellish special occasions like *The New York Times's* Fourth of July celebration of the Statue of Liberty's birthday. Often called upon to operate under somewhat difficult circumstances, Remember Basil produced a patriotic feast for 300 aboard a party boat, sans galley, as it cruised New York harbor amidst the international flotilla of Tall Ships.

Dounia says she uses food to create or match an environment. She feels every party should make a statement. Clients like Mary Tyler Moore, Pete Rozelle, and Hubert de Givenchy agree. When super model Dianne DeWitt recently married, Remember Basil put together a memorable reception saluting her Texas roots. Guests were greeted by Western-clad fiddlers making foot-stomping music. Dinner-jacketed waiters carrying silver trays offered thirst-quenching beverages— champagne in elegant flutes and bottles of Lone Star beer. Lavish buffets of Tex-Mex treats, including chili, guacamole, and fajitas titillated the tastebuds. People are still talking about the sensational oyster shooters— succulent mollusks topped with salsa and served in a shot glass.

Once you become a Remember Basil regular, Donald, as manager and event producer, will arrange for just about anything—within reason, he laughs. He even considers dinner or breakfast for two reasonable, but he's not crazy about it. Generally speaking, Remember Basil takes on dinner parties for 50 to 2,000 and cocktails for *at least* 100. As a first-time client, you should be thinking in those terms or seek services else-where. Typically, a cocktail reception runs about $35 to $40 a person. For dinner, plan on a minimum of $110 apiece.

Call for an appointment to discuss your function with either Dounia or Donald. They're capable of last-minute miracles, but if you're planning a party for October through the first of the year, book two to three months ahead of time. If there's a wedding in your future, call the minute you set the date.

For a while you could have the pleasure of attending a Remember Basil affair, by attending a performance of *Tamara* at the Seventh Regi-ment Armory on Park Avenue. To make some sense of the convoluted soap opera plot, the novel play requires each member of the audience to adopt one of the cast and spend the rest of the evening chasing after him or her through the cavernous set approximating an Italian villa. The strenuous evening is broken by a 45-minute intermezzo during which Remember Basil served a necessarily hearty and very tasty buffet, criti-cally acclaimed as one of the highlights of the evening. But at some point the producers realized they had a kitchen and a staff. Some economies could be realized by producing the meal in-house. But the association with the play had given Dounia the opportunity to strut her stuff nightly before an appreciative audience. And what stuff it was—roast filet of beef with green peppercorn sauce, curried chicken salad sweetened by raisins and apples, Italian green beans tossed with red pepper and almonds, and a pasta primavera laced with snow peas, mushrooms, tomatoes, and pesto. As if that weren't enough, there was a tossed green salad and an artfully displayed assortment of crudités.

High drama and an opportunity to orchestrate a statement-making party eight times a week—Dounia was truly in her element here. No doubt grandfather Basil would have enthusiastically approved. ❦

Susan Holland & Company, Inc.

142 Fifth Avenue   (212) 807-8892
New York, NY 10011

Susan Holland says the greatest measure of the success of a catered affair is the degree to which it reflects the host's personal style. A former painter and sculptor, Susan believes that creating a memorable meal should be like creating a work of art, composed of a variety of elements—food, flowers, music, decor, ambience—all filtered through the host's sensibilities.

Admittedly, Susan counts on her clients having pretty sophisticated sensibilities. She's not interested in putting together casual backyard barbecues, though she certainly will for regular clients like Ann-Margret and Peter Allen. Re-creating the French Riviera at a beachfront home on Fire Island or concocting a winter wonderland evoking the spirit of the *Nutcracker Suite* is more her style.

A less dramatic, but equally impressive, dinner party can be staged in your home. For ten, it will cost at least $1,500, including two waiters and two people in the kitchen. Consider it an investment in your memory banks. After all, a party is like a flight of fancy, one special moment caught in time that exists only for you and your guests.

Just imagine—assorted passed hors d'oeuvres like stuffed Michigan morels, Scottish salmon with scrambled eggs and tarragon served in corn cups, and parmesan pastry leaves with carpaccio of veal. They might be followed by a first course of quail and veal quenelles in a nest of pasta, sitting on wilted baby spinach and laced with fresh tomato beurre blanc. For the second course, Susan could whip up a charred filet of beef with red pepper blini, garnished with fresh chive cream and sautéed baby vegetables. Following European tradition, Susan saves the salad for the third course, then a Napoleon with lemon curd, golden raspberries, and ginger might serve as the finale.

Interested in hosting a less formal affair? For about $45 per person, Susan will supply the food, staff, and rentals for a cocktail party. Such a soirée might include delicacies like Peking duck, lump crab with currants and chives in barquettes, and phyllo triangles with broccoli rabe, sweet sausage, and thyme.

Don't be afraid to confront Susan with a difficult assignment, like catering a corporate fête at the Bronx Zoo. Her favorite affairs are those that present the greatest creative challenges and logistical obstacles. In our experience, Susan always rises to the occasion with wit, style, and perfectly marvelous food.   🍂

Sylvia Weinstock Cakes

273 Church Street   (212) 925-6698
New York, NY 10013

Who says that being an exemplary housewife is not good training for a career outside the home? Certainly not Sylvia Weinstock. She took her talent for baking and turned it into a booming business.

It all started when she found herself with some extra time on her hands during weekend trips to her family's ski house on Hunter Mountain. While her husband and kids were off skiing, Sylvia entertained herself by baking. As her repertoire and skill grew, she began baking for local restaurants. Recognizing her own potential, she forsook her part-time career as elementary school teacher and apprenticed to various pastry and dessert chefs in the city's finest restaurants.

In 1980, when Sylvia was finally ready to go out on her own, she quickly assembled a client list that included such institutions of culinary excellence as the Pierre, the Carlyle, and the Metropolitan Club.

Sylvia's cakes are instantly identifiable by their flawlessly delicate floral decoration—sugar peonies, tulips, roses, and daffodils that look as though they'd been plucked from the garden. Someone once even mistook a Weinstock cake for the centerpiece!

But her expertise stretches well beyond flowers. Sylvia takes great pride in being able to re-create just about anything in edible form.

One gentleman, seeking a clever way to surprise his ladylove with a diamond ring, sought Sylvia's advice. She designed a shopping bag, complete with tissue, coyly disguising the contents. It was all edible, of course, down to the bouquet of flowers, which, when removed from the bag, yielded the ring.

Sylvia's creations titillate the tastebuds as well as the eye. And, oh, those tastes—so many and in every combination imaginable. All of Sylvia's cakes are made to order, so you can have absolutely anything your little heart desires as long as you are prepared to spend at least $300.

Plenty of people are—Barbara Walters, Susan Gutfreund, Mercedes Bass, Donald Newhouse, Anna Murdoch, Adrien Arpel, and virtually any bride worth her salt. In fact, there is one school of thought that holds a wedding just isn't legal if it doesn't include a Sylvia Weinstock cake. Certainly, Laura Steinberg subscribed to that theory when she married Jonathan Tisch. Her eight-tiered Grand Marnier and apricot cake, decorated with "flowers" matching those on the tables, took six hours to assemble at its place of honor in the Metropolitan Museum. It stood eight feet tall, fed 400 guests, and reportedly cost over $15,000. However, Sylvia will neither confirm nor deny that report. She is the very soul of discretion, a quality very much appreciated by her already overexposed clientele.

What may not be so appreciated is her very downtown location. We suspect, in fact, it's about as far below 57th Street as many of her patrons have ever ventured. But venture they do. Sylvia insists on it, just as she insists on an appointment. Talk to Sylvia about the kind of party you are planning and she will help you select colors, even the appropriate flowers. Of course, the cake will perfectly reflect the spirit of the occasion.

Even with a staff of seven, Sylvia often produces as few as twenty cakes a week—each is so elaborate and time-consuming. Moreover, timing is crucial, as they are prepared only a day before your event to ensure freshness. So once you have determined a date for a special occasion, be sure to book Sylvia first. And don't worry if it is slated for out of town. Sylvia routinely has cakes delivered by driver to Washington, Boston, and territory in between.

Planning a wedding further afield? Sylvia will hand-carry all the components of the cake on a plane and assemble them at your site. Granted, she'll charge you for airfare, hotel, and expenses, but consider the alternative—the shocking notion of a wedding not sanctioned by a Sylvia Weinstock cake. 🍃

FLORISTS

Philip Baloun Designs

340 West 55th Street   (212) 307-1675
between 8th and 9th Avenues
New York, NY 10019

There may be no greater testimony to Philip Baloun's talents than all those mentions in Suzy's column about his "unique," "glorious," "extraordinary," "spectacular," "dazzling," and "memorable" decorations. After all, Suzy has been chronicling the world's great parties for more years than her official picture indicates, and is not easily impressed. But Philip's parties have a theatrical quality that excites even the most jaded on the social circuit. You see, this boy from Chicago hit town 12 years ago with aspirations of becoming a big-time director. Few fill their dreams so spectacularly. He's made the big time with clients like Laura Pomerantz, Carrol Petrie, Carolyne Roehm, the Metropolitan Opera, Chanel, and the New York Philharmonic, and he's certainly a director—though his stage is more often a ballroom in a hotel or a tent stretched over a plaza than a Broadway theater.

In the tranquil environment of his magnificent apartment filled with Oriental urns and screens, Philip creates memories—a lavish wedding like the Bass-Kellogg nuptials or an inaugural ball. For the Bush inauguration, Philip was turned loose on the Washington Hilton's vast Exhibition Center, transforming its 45,000 square feet into a glittering party palace for 8,000. He camouflaged the space's forest of support columns with beautifully draped translucent fabric lit from behind by tens of thousands of tiny shimmering lights. Huge urns filled with massive displays of red, white, and blue flowers added to the opulence. For Mercedes Kellogg's dream wedding to Sid Bass, he created a breathtaking orangerie in the Terrace Room of The Plaza. Philip beautifully and cleverly divided the space into three separate areas for the ceremony, cocktails, and luncheon with stunning 12-foot topiary trees, arches, and trellises laced with garlands.

The cost for such superb extravagance? Philip's much too discreet to be specific. But "average" budgets for charity affairs run from $10,000 to $25,000, while for private functions they might easily run up to $100,000. By the same token, for a modest-sized dinner at home, they might just as easily hover in the more comfortable $1,200 to $3,500 neighborhood. Remember, Philip is a planner of parties, not just a decorator of them. And a very detail-oriented planner at that. He's concerned with every visual element, "from the colors of the plates, to how the napkins are folded, to when the candles will be lit." While Philip's certainly capable of last-minute miracles, it's not unusual for him to spend six months planning an event.

It shows. Take the Venetian palazzo he created out of a tent in Lincoln Center's Damrosch Park for the New York Philharmonic's 1988 masked ball gala. Ten-foot faux marble columns supported six thousand yards of gold taffeta that festooned the ceiling. A towering white and gold triumphal arch dominated the center of the room, while stupendous glass chandeliers cast a festive glow across the gold damask-covered tables adorned with three-foot-tall Venetian vases spilling over with masses of white peonies and orchids. This event is held only once every two or three years, so Philip has lots of time to plan for the next, but what a challenge topping this one.

And the source of Philip's inspiration? For the Philharmonic party it came from a period drawing of a Venetian masked ball he found in a book. He has a lot of those. But it could come from anywhere, even the hostess. In fact, especially the hostess. He's a stickler for making sure a party's atmosphere is a mirror reflection of the hostess's taste and style. While he's a star in his own right, he's not in the business of foisting his personality on your party—although you probably wouldn't mind since he's a good-looking charmer. Self-deprecating too. He claims not to be a peer of his high profile clients, and in fact ruefully maintains that he's not in a league where "I can afford to go to my $1,000-a-plate dinners." This, despite the fact that he puts together some 200 soirées annually and grosses $2 million or so.   🌱

Renny

159 East 64th Street   (212) 288-7000
between Lexington and Third Ave.
New York, NY 10021

Renny, Renny, Bo-Benny, Banana-Fana-Fo-Fenny, Me-Mi-Mo Menny, Renny! Apologies to Dionne Warwick, but we couldn't resist. You hear the name so often, always alone. This master of the floral arts does have a last name (Reynolds), but no one seems to have used it since he first burst on the scene with his heavenly design of Bill Blass's penthouse terrace in 1974. Ever since, Renny has been on the tip of a lot of tongues when it comes to decorative flora, flowering, and otherwise.

While his dramatically romantic 1880s mansion serves as both home and shop, where you can pop in for a bountiful bouquet as long as you've got the $45 minimum, Renny is not just a florist. He prefers to be considered a party designer. And indeed, one room in the house is reserved as sort of a staging ground, where his ideas for an event's look come to life. When he's ready to present his plans, he makes it easy for even the most unimaginative clients to visualize them by arranging the room with his envisioned decor.

It may be that veterans of world-class entertaining like Brooke Astor and Anne Bass don't need this particular service, but they do need Renny. Indeed, they wouldn't dream of having a party without him, whether it's one of Anne's chic little dinners at home for 24 or one of her charity functions for hundreds. When Anne chaired the France Dance, Renny turned the National Academy of Design into an eighteenth century French château.

Corporations depend on Renny too. For Compaq Computers he transformed the Manhattan Center into a space-age fantasy as the backdrop for a presentation of their latest computing innovations. Fantasy is Renny's specialty. A party in the outdoor courtyard of the Modern Museum of Art prompted him to create umbrellas out of vines for the tables and to hang fishbowls with candles from the wisteria. He decorated each of the tables in a different pastel theme, coordinating tablecloths, napkins, candles, and china.

He'll create tiny bits of fantasy for your more private parties in the form of a glorious centerpiece or other decorative touches for about $500. And while one of his extravaganzas, like a dinner dance for 2,000 at the armory, might cost upwards of $70,000, he can work wonders on considerably less. Once when Hanae Mori took over the old Hubert's on 22nd Street for a dinner party in honor of Anna Moffo, he perked up the rather austere restaurant with swags of white flowers weaving through a sea of votive candles on the windowsills. Garlands of white orchids decorated the lengths of the four tables set for ten, punctuated by the tallest tapered candles known to man. The effect was shimmering, understated grandeur for less than $2,000.

Renny, himself, is a delight to work with. There's nothing pretentious about this man despite a client roster that includes Calvin and Kelly

Klein, Diana Ross, Jim and Linda Robinson, Oscar de la Renta, Gianni and Mirella Agnnelli, and Lillian and Edmund Safra. Claudia Perelman absolutely adores Renny as does husband Ron ever since Claudia overwhelmed him with Renny's work. For Valentine's Day she had Renny sneak into Ron's office and cover every square inch of it in red flowers— *Revlon* red of course.

When you get a sudden yen for one of his lovely orchid plants (a specialty) or refined arrangements, and Renny's not available, ask for Pat McCoy, or Ric Bauman. They've been with him a long time and each is a marvelous purveyor of the Renny magic.

Robert Isabell, Inc.

89 Jane Street   (212) 645-7767
New York, NY 10014

Calling Robert Isabell a florist is like describing Michelangelo as a painter. Truly, Robert is a creator of environments—environments that play host to many of the city's most lavish parties. None is more elaborate than the spectacular Steinberg/Tisch wedding, which is rumored to have cost corporate raider Saul Steinberg millions. *W* speculated that the flower bill alone (read *Robert's bill*) ran into the hundreds of thousands.

In 24 hours, Robert transformed the Metropolitan Museum of Art with 15,000 tulips imported from France, countless Casablanca lilies, innumerable sweetpeas, and myriad lilies of the valley. Garlands swagged across walls draped with softly glowing white muslin (cleverly lit from behind). At least that's what the gushing (and impressed) press reports claimed. Robert is decidedly circumspect about what he really did, and his lips are absolutely sealed about what it cost. You see, the Steinbergs are one of his best and favorite clients. The divine, but by all reports down-to-earth, Gayfryd gives him interesting and lavish assignments, like the recent bash for husband Saul's 50th birthday.

Robert transformed the Steinbergs' beach house on Long Island into an ocean front Versailles with hundreds of flickering lights in terra-cotta pots, identical twins impersonating twins in the swimming pool, and dancers and banner wavers in period costumes. To celebrate Saul's status as a collector of "Old Masters," Robert decorated the tent stretched over the tennis court to resemble a seventeenth-century Flemish eating-and-drinking house. The walls were hung with photographic reproductions of Saul's art collection, while tableaux featuring posed actors recreated some of the world's greatest paintings—perhaps some of Saul's future acquisitions?

Perhaps a tad much for your taste? Keep in mind that Robert adjusts his style to his clients. He's a master at reflecting his clients' personality in the decor of their parties. He can grasp your most outrageous fantasy and produce it visually.

Although he will put together a single arrangement and charge a minimum of $100, that's not his interest or his forte. He'd much rather create and execute a design theme for your next dinner party. It'll probably cost $1,000 to $3,000, but it's likely Robert will custom-design the linens. He'll definitely produce a dramatically beautiful setting for a memorable meal.

There'll be flowers, of course, in exquisite color combinations that complement the decor of the room. Some will be arranged in pieces from his fabulous collection of containers—perhaps an eighteenth-century English porcelain or something contemporary in glass or silver designed by Richard Meier. Candles might take the form of dozens of twinkling votives or long, slender tapers set in dazzling candelabras. And in addition to the centerpieces, he'll do arrangements for the entrance hall, living room, and even the powder room.

When Caroline Kennedy got married, Jackie enlisted Robert's services. When he does dinners for Georgio Armani, the look is contemporary, sleek, and simple. All of Bergdorf's special events benefit from his exceptional touch, and the too-chic-for-words Royalton Hotel relies on Robert's creations to lend a little warmth to its public spaces.

Like Jackie, his clients are secure, sophisticated women, who often dare to do the unexpected. They want to add a touch of the theatrical to their parties, and they know that with Robert in charge they'll get rave reviews. They also tend to be married to very rich men. 🍏

Stamens & Pistils

875 Third Avenue   (212) 593-1888
at 53rd Street
New York, NY 10022

With its track lighting dramatically illuminating the striking arrangements, Stamens & Pistils more closely resembles a gallery than a floral shop. Upon closer inspection, it becomes clear that there's nothing run-of-the-mill about this establishment. Few of the flowers and greens are familiar. Most have an exotic, almost alien quality, not to mention unpronounceable names—heliconia, phaleonopsis, and protea.

There's a reason for all this. Owner Asa Ige is from Hawaii's most beautiful island, Maui; that's where he gets most of his blossoms and foliage. Furthermore, he studied to be a graphic artist, which explains his unusual, almost architectural, approach to floral arrangements. Each is different, a one-of-a-kind work of art—no FTD formula orchestrations here.

Asa's artistry has attracted an impressive clientele of diplomats, show-business celebrities, and others who appreciate the uncommon. He's a little uncomfortable about name-dropping, but with enough encouragement, he can be persuaded to utter "David Letterman" or talk about deliveries to Katherine Hepburn and Elizabeth Taylor. Then there are all those glossy magazines that have featured his work—*Architectural Digest, Interior Design, House & Garden,* and *Smithsonian.*

Stamens & Pistils' minimum order is $40, although prices can escalate into the hundreds; $70 tends to be the average. For about $110, Asa will "dress" one of his spectacular dendrobium nobile orchids with decorative stakes and imaginative foliage treatments. It's a bargain, when you consider it will last at least a month, probably two.

Asa also makes house calls. He'll design a plant and flower plan for your home, execute it, and even maintain it. He makes boat calls too, regularly supplying flowers for Joan Kroc's yacht, *Impromptu.*

If Asa isn't in, any of his affable staff of ten will do, but try for Elsie. She's Asa's very proud mom and his best promoter. If you're not already convinced of the extent of Asa's talent, Elsie will finish the job. ❧

CHAPTER FIVE

Shopping

If it's not here, it doesn't exist

*I*f you can't find it in New York, it probably doesn't exist. No matter that it could have a very large price, it may be very hard to find (though not with this volume in hand), and it's perhaps one of a kind. New Yorkers are a persistent, if demanding, breed, and what they demand is the very best of just about everything. You can count on some store to satisfy them.

For the "shop-'til-you-drop" school, one has only to start at Fifth Avenue and Central Park South, work your way down to, say 42d Street, around to Madison, then head north as far as your stubby little legs will carry you. You'll find everything, and we mean everything, you'd find on Rodeo Drive or Michigan Avenue, the Avenue Montaigne or the Faubourg, the Vias Condotti or Montenapoleone, the Ginza area in Tokyo.

For the most discriminating "when-the-going-gets-tough-the-tough-go-shopping" school of both sexes, there are the unique custom tailors, that out-of-the-way boutique for neckties-to-order, the home-accessories shops that'll fill a studio in Kips Bay or a forty-room cottage in Newport.

It's not surprising that the city that's become the world capital of everything from cuisine to finance to the arts has also become the world's shopping bazaar. And in true bazaar fashion there is room for some judicious bargaining here and there. Don't try it at Tiffany's (they invented the unassailable price tag) or at any of the larger stores. But at some of the smaller ones, especially those featuring big-ticket items like jewelry and furs, there may be some room for negotiation. Approach the subject with caution, backed up by resolve.

Time was when there were little groceries and dry cleaners along Madison, when Carnegie Hill was a neighborhood. Park Avenue matrons could actually shop for their food and run their more mundane errands right in their own backyard, rather than ordering in, or out. No longer. Today, Pratesi jostles with Porthault, Baccarat with Lalique, Lauren with St. Laurent. That wonderful little custom hi-fi shop at 70th and Madison, where we bought our first stereos, has given way to Yves and his couture.

Neighborhood shops have been replaced by a staggering array of boutiques laying claim to internationally known names. That's why you'll need this book, to sort out the best from the merely mediocre, and at least a thousand a day before lunch.

FOR MEN

Arthur Gluck, Chemisiers

37 West 57th Street   (212) 755-8165
between 5th and 6th
Room 403
New York, NY 10019

For thirty years, since long before gentlemen "dressed for success," Arthur Gluck's has been doing just that—dressing gentlemen with that smooth, expensively tailored look that gives anyone wearing one of his shirts a little edge at the bargaining table. We've no doubt that the perfectly comfortable fit of Arthur's shirts has helped get, and keep, such power moguls as Lou Wassermann, Lee Iacocca, and Henry Kissinger where they are today.

Arthur operates on the theory that shirts are a very personal matter, magnifying the individual's appearance and personality. So he spends a great deal of time with new clients, discussing personal preferences. He presents fabrics in all conceivable colors and patterns from his vast inventory—bolts and bolts of the finest imported cottons, broadcloths, and silks. He gives advice about the all-important collar spread. For oval faces, he suggests a narrow spread; he likes to widen it for round faces.

Careful measurements define neck size, the slope of the shoulder, and posture. A pattern is created that will ensure a flat, wrinkle-free front and just the right amount of collar and cuff showing under the jacket.

With all this time and attention, it's not surprising Arthur sets a first-timer's minimum order of eight shirts. Two fittings will usually be required, and it takes eight to ten weeks for the order to be completed. Prices start at $175 and go up from there. A tuxedo shirt may run $250 to $300.

Once past the hurdle of the initial order, there is no minimum, but Arthur says most of his clients buy sixteen to twenty shirts a year. No wonder so many—clients and shirts—turn up on the world's "best-dressed" lists!

If you're concerned about the proper care and feeding of these precious shirts, you should know that Arthur maintains his own laundry service. Prices start at $7 for a "basic" shirt, and range upwards, depending on fabric and style. Silk shirts should go to a good dry cleaner, but if they lose a button, call Arthur. He'll send a replacement right over! 🦋

Beau Brummel

410 Columbus Avenue between 79th and 80th Streets New York, NY 10023	(212) 874-6262
421 West Broadway at Spring and Prince New York, NY 10012	(212) 219-2666
1113 Madison Avenue between 83rd and 84th Streets New York, NY 10021	(212) 737-4200

In 1958, it occurred to Sol Laxer that what Forest Hills in Queens needed was a men's store combining the quality and variety found in Manhattan with a convenient neighborhood location. Twenty-five years later, he decided what Manhattan really needed was a store like the one he owned in Queens, catering to a neighborhood and dedicated to high-fashion quality. Given the success of Beau Brummel's first foray into the city's store wars on the Upper West Side, he was right.

Since opening in 1983, the small shop, elegantly turned out in wood and brass, has been a smashing success. In fact, the Beau Brummel formula of locating in a trendy neighborhood, where its target twenty-five to forty-year-old customer lurks, has worked so well that two more locations were justified—and we understand more are on the way.

The stores cultivate a calm, serene atmosphere, enlivened by fun, jazzy music, and the complimentary serving of assorted libations. The salespeople are all young, impeccably groomed, and very informed about their primarily Italian collection. Indeed, Italian fashion is considered Beau Brummel's specialty, though French, Japanese, and German lines are represented too. In fact, there's always an exciting mix of merchandise, thanks to Sol's partner, Avram Goldman, who began his career twenty-two years ago as a stock boy at the Forest Hills store. Avram understands his young, mostly professional clientele and provides them with the latest fashion trends, tempered by good taste.

Suits featuring a wide-shoulder, narrow-hip silhouette sell from $695 to $1,500. Shirts go for $55 to $265. Jackets range from $400 to $900. And sweaters average about $350. Beau Brummel is definitely for the man who appreciates the finer things in life, no matter how old he is, as long as he can afford it. Have you noticed how smart Regis Philbin has been looking on his nationally syndicated television show? Thank Beau Brummel.

Service has been the firm's trademark since its earliest Forest Hills days. There was a time when they could guarantee same-day alterations, but no longer; they're simply too busy and good tailors are too difficult to find. Still, you can generally count on less than a week, and they will make every effort to schedule fittings at your convenience. They'll open early, stay late, or send the tailor to your home or office. In any case, alterations are, of course, free.

Sol's son Marc acts as manager at the Soho West Broadway location. His store is, so far, the largest, and in deference to the neighborhood carries slightly more avant-garde clothing than the others. So stop by if you're feeling especially bold. Otherwise, any of the Manhattan locations will suit, with high fashion and a high level of personal service.

Bijan

699 Fifth Avenue   (212) 758-7500
between 54th and 55th Streets
New York, NY 10022

Since he first burst on the scene in 1976 with his Beverly Hills "By Appointment Only" men's boutique, Bijan Pakzad has become one of that elite set of public figures who can be identified by first name only—à la Liz, Cher, Frank, Dustin. He has also taken the fine art of excess to new heights.

Consider his white marble palazzo of a showroom on Fifth Avenue. It took two years and $10 million before it could suit Bijan's extravagant tastes. When it opened in 1983, one journalist estimated, "The brass and glass stairway leading to the designer's office cost nearly as much as the whole building did seventy-three years ago." He wasn't even calculating the expense of the incredible Baccarat chandelier illuminating that grand winding staircase.

As at its Rodeo Drive predecessor, shopping at the store is by appointment. Naturally, the door is locked. However, the white-gloved doorman presiding over it will admit you after you've announced that you either have an appointment or intend to purchase one of Bijan's fragrances.

Once inside the palatial establishment, feast your eyes on the priceless antiques, including an enormous Greek vase and remarkable marble tables. Presentation is everything—haberdashery is presented like jewels in Moroccan leather cases stored in closets lined with scarlet silk. Clothes are arranged in color-coordinated groupings in lacquered wardrobes. Bijan's is a studied, rarified atmosphere designed for the privacy and comfort of a very special clientele—King Hussein of Jordan, King Juan Carlos of Spain, Ronald Reagan, Walter Annenberg, Roger Moore, Teddy Kennedy, Frank Sinatra, Julio Iglesias, and Jack Lemmon among them.

The store often seems almost empty. This should not be cause for concern about the state of Bijan's business. Given the $3,000 suits, $2,200 sports jackets, $750 slacks, and $175 ties, it's easy for a single customer to drop a substantial sum in one sitting. G. Dale Murray, of Murray Industries, once figured he spends $25,000 during each of his visits. Bijan claims that's not uncommon. Then he tells the story of the head of a royal Middle Eastern family who once sent his 727 to pick up

Bijan, a fitter, several tailors, and sixty-five crates of clothes. Before the first stitch was ordered, the tab was $250,000!

Bijan's clients are men secure enough to express their individual style, rarely seduced by the trendy or merely fashionable. They appreciate Bijan's elegant approach to dressing, his commitment to excellence, and his own personal designs for everything they might need, from jewelry to socks to briefcases. As Bijan says, he exists "for men of power who expect the best, and recognize the care and attention required to create and choose the best."

They also have to have the resources to pay astronomical prices for what is, after all, ready-to-wear—Bijan's clothes are off-the-rack, albeit a very high quality rack, and the store's expert tailoring will make them seem as if they've been made expressly for you.

Having made $100 million from his first store and become an international celebrity with flashy promotions featuring his dark good looks and exuberant smile, Bijan broke new ground when he introduced the first perfume for men in 1982. He packaged it in a limited-edition, six-ounce, Baccarat crystal bottle and smashed pricing barriers by selling it for $1,500. Now $3,000 collectors' items, the original bottles can be refilled. Today a one-and-a-quarter ounce black crystal bottle of what remains the only concentrated perfume for men is available for a mere $250.

In 1987, Bijan launched a fragrance for women dedicated "to people of taste for whom affordability and availability are important." So the toilet water version of this subtle, sexy scent retails for $55 and is carried by national outlets like Saks Fifth Avenue and Neiman Marcus.

We suspect that Bijan is really most attached to the perfume. At $300 an ounce, after all, it's much more his style!   🍂

Brooks Brothers

346 Madison Avenue   (212) 682-8800
at 44th Street
New York, NY 10017

Of course, you know Brooks Brothers put the "tradition" in traditional men's clothing, but did you know it is the oldest retail men's store in the U.S.? Not only that, Brooks Brothers was probably the first company to manufacture and sell ready-made men's clothing. No wonder the word *venerable* comes to mind with this most conservative of stores.

The company and the traditions it stands for have withstood the test of time with flying colors. Today, as it has for generations, Brooks Brothers outfits men in quietly classic clothes that project an unassailable image of good judgment and practical taste. As it has for generations, Brooks Brothers is still fitting the Establishment with its uniforms. Indeed there are many scions of America's oldest families who have never known another clothing shop—from their first knickers to their first blazer to their first pinstripe.

President Bush has been a client for years, as have been a number of his Republican predecessors. Gerald Ford chose to wear a Brooks Brothers morning coat and ascot for his historic meeting with the late Emperor Hirohito of Japan. On what turned out to be a considerably less happy, but more historic occasion, Abraham Lincoln wore a Brooks Brothers suit to Ford's theater to see a play starring John Wilkes Booth. Abe Rosenthal of *The New York Times* began shopping for his suits off the rack. As he moved up the editorial ladder, he moved from ready-made to custom. Fittingly, Brooks Brothers is strolling distance from such pantheons of the establishment as the *Times*, the Century Club and the *New Yorker*, the Harvard, Yale, and Princeton Clubs, and, of course, the New York Yacht Club.

It's true that the store's signature soft-shouldered, three-button suit hasn't changed much since it was first designed just toward the end of the last century. In fact, it's not only true, it's the whole point! It's a little like the club tie. Those who are truly members of the Brooks Brothers Establishment can still recognize each other by the oddly placed buttonhole square in the lower half of the lapel. This suit was considered novel when it first appeared and it still is—but it's only one of a number of innovations the store has notched in its all-leather belts down through the years. It was, for instance, Brooks Brothers that introduced the deerstalker to the U.S., as well as the Shetland wool sweater, and the first wash-and-wear shirt. Furthermore, the camel-hair polo coat is attributed to the store, as are Indian cotton madras clothing and lightweight summer suiting. Its soft slippers and supple leather shoes are all from the best British booters.

Most notably, John E. Brooks, grandson of founder Henry Sands Brooks, invented that staple of the businessman's wardrobe, the buttondown shirt, as the result of a trip to England in 1910. While watching a polo match, he noticed the collars on the players' shirts were anchored by buttons to keep them from flapping in the wind. Upon his return to

New York he suggested Brooks Brother make such a sport shirt, which slowly evolved into a dress shirt and the company's best-selling item. In a tribute to the ample girth of most captains of industry and government, it's never given in to tapering, and its tent-like style hangs in tenaciously. Button-down and otherwise, Brooks Brothers shirts sell for $45 and $65. They are displayed in such a way as to make it easy and comfortable to make your choices about collars and patterns. Complementary ties run the price gamut of $27 to $40.

As for suits, we recommend the Own Make selections, tailored and produced by Brooks Brothers' own manufacturing facilities. Top of the line, they sell from $400 to $750. There's also the 346 suit, made by contractors to Brooks Brothers' specifications. And there's always the custom-tailoring option—their salespeople have been here for decades. They know their merchandise and they know the general profile of their customer. Discuss your needs with them and trust their judgment to know what's best.

They'll outfit you very correctly, sportswear to black tie. Indeed, a young gentlemen's purchase of a Brooks Brothers tuxedo is considered a rite of passage in some circles. Prices range from $495 to $595, not including all the paraphernalia that goes with it, which of course the store carries, right down to the proper shoes and socks. As for the latter, with black tie a Brooks Brothers salesperson will lobby for a nonribbed, over-the-calf sock.

Secure in its refined gentility, the store's subdued wool paneling and lithographs of old New York City make you feel confident and secure. Alas, the store has made one concession to modern marketing; Brooks Brothers Telemarketing often has selections even the store's venerable and accommodating salesmen can't produce—the frustrations of progress! Still, there's a comforting aura of aristocracy about the store's trademark known as the "Golden Fleece." Adopted as Brooks Brothers' own in the 1850s, it's a modified version of the insignia used by the famous order of knighthood known as the Golden Fleece. Today, it appears in their advertisements, on their packaging, on certain merchandise, and in the decor. It's quite enchanting—and somehow a reminder that this is one store in which you can be absolutely sure you won't be taken, or fleeced!

Cristofaro-Reddy, Ltd.

119 West 57th Street   (212) PL7-7240
Room 818
New York, NY 10019

What do you get when you cross an Italian perfectionist and an Indian charmer? In this case, you get a perfectly tailored custom-made suit. Italian Cristofaro is the designer and pattern-maker. He oversees the six tailors and two seamstresses, while Indian-born Uma Reddy is in charge of quality control and sales—sales to exacting clients like Dr. Norman Orentreich, the Metropolitan Opera's Bruce Crawford, and theater impresario Jimmy Neiderlander. They value the flattering fit and classic cut, made stylish with just a dash of flair.

Cristofaro-Reddy uses nothing but the finest woven fabrics from England. Suit prices start at $2,250, though cashmere can run to $3,600. For sports jackets, plan on $1,500 to $1,800, and slacks range from $425 to $600. One of their last-half-a-lifetime overcoats runs about $2,400.

Clients earn "regular" status by ordering an average of four to six suits a season. Each takes about four or five weeks and requires two fittings. New clients, of course, need to be measured and should figure on at least six weeks before hanging a new suit in the closet, as they'll need three fittings.

Uma keeps a file on each client's purchases, with swatches. He knows exactly what they need, because he knows what they already have in their wardrobe. So he welcomes last year's suit, in need of a few alterations due to gain (or loss) of weight, like an old friend. Of course, there's never any charge for such services. Cristofaro and Uma are even so fond of their handiwork that they happily encourage clients to bring in their suits for pressing. It's done by hand here—so much better for the shape of the suit than the machines and steamers the neighborhood cleaner uses. They just want to make sure nothing happens to embarrass you—or them—when you're wearing a Cristofaro-Reddy. After all, their names are on the pocket, not yours! 🌿

Davide Cenci

801 Madison Avenue	(212) 628-5910
between 67th and 68th Streets	(212) 628-5911
New York, NY 10021	

Even if you're a habitué of the original Davide Cenci, which opened in 1926 in Rome, isn't it comforting to know that you can now find the same unique combination of classic style and Italian flair right here on Madison Avenue?

David Cenci, grandson of Davide, runs the New York store and caters to American tastes, particularly the current passion for sweaters. Indeed, much of the first floor is devoted to the enormous selection—bin after mahogany bin lined with a glorious array, all theatrically lit so their colors and textures virtually leap off the shelves. Most are from Italy. The Cenci family has scoured their native land for resources and have identified several fine manufacturers who knit designs exclusively for them. Scottish products are also represented, but they are in the very distinct minority.

Lightweight summer sweaters, perfect for cool mountain evenings or midnight walks on the beach, sell for $175 to $400. Warmer winter weights range from $225 to $1,700. Naturally, our favorite was of the four-figure variety, but then it is a reversible eight-ply cashmere cardigan, solid on one side, patterned on the other.

There's row upon row of dress and sport shirts to match with the sweaters, all of Italian origin and very much a part of the Cenci tradition. It seems Davide Cenci began his career in Rome as a custom-shirtmaker. At his grandson's establishment, you can get a sense of what launched Davide Cenci's international reputation by purchasing one of the firm's ever-so-elegant hand-finished shirts—$180 and up. Their handsome standard line of shirts starts at about $95.

The second floor houses suits and other tailored clothing. They all have that sleek Italian cut, with enough panache to satisfy the more daring, yet classic enough to suit conservative tastes just slightly to the left of Brooks Brothers. The top-of-the-line, hand-worked suits run from $1,250 to $1,450. A more pedestrian, but still dashing, group sells for closer to $900.

David and his young, congenial staff are very adept at pleasing their clients. They keep extensive files on each, so they can guide the building of a coordinated, practical Davide Cenci wardrobe. This is truly a gentleman's haberdashery, where he can buy everything from socks and underwear to suits. And David takes great pains to ensure that his gentlemen are looking their very best. When a new batch of sweaters or shirts arrives, he'll call those whose cards reveal they might be in need of a fashion boost.

Of course, once you've become a part of the extended Cenci family in New York, you're automatically embraced by the Roman contingent. David's dad, Paolo, and uncle, Germano, hold court there. Just behind the Italian Parliament, their store is much larger, so you can expand your Cenci collection a bit. But if an Italian sojourn is not in your immediate future, don't be dismayed or feel cheated. The Cenci selection on Madison is even better suited to American tastes, extensive enough to satisfy all but the most extreme shopping habits. 🍎

Maurizio—Custom Tailors

18 East 53rd Street   (212) 759-3230
between Fifth and Madison
5th Floor
New York, NY 10022

Tony Maurizio, a tall, slim, perpetually tanned native New Yorker, is the very image of the elegant men he's been dressing to such perfection since 1947. Tony is the reason Henry Kissinger, Alan King, Steve Lawrence, and Nelson Rockefeller, Jr., always look so well groomed. They made their way to his beautiful, clublike, wood-paneled showroom years ago and would never dream of going anywhere else.

Tony's suits cost $2,500 and up. Naturally, they are made of the world's finest fabrics, English wools and Italian silks. They are constructed by hand. And each of Tony's nine tailors has been with him more than twenty-three years.

Custom tailoring is a marathon, with an initial visit to choose fabrics and take measurements, at least two more fittings, and five to seven weeks of waiting for the finished garment. But it's worth every bit of it. Remember the old saying that clothes make the man? The fact is, you look different in a custom-made suit; you stand taller, walk straighter, feel better, secure in the knowledge that all those inevitable flaws in your profile are cleverly disguised by custom tailoring. Everything is considered, everything muted—the slight paunch, the less than perfect posture, even the bowed legs.

Whether it's a cashmere sport jacket for $2,200 or a tux (price depending on the cut and fabric), Tony pays a lot of attention to your neck measurement. He maintains that the most important part of a jacket is the way it hugs the neck, which crucially affects the balance. If the neck doesn't fit properly the rest never will.

Fit, of course, is the name of Tony's game—from $800 silk slacks to $3,000 topcoats. In fact, Tony became so renowned for the extraordinary fit of his clothes that the wives of his customers began clamoring for his services. So now he will outfit very special ladies with blazers for $2,200, skirts for $650, and his trademark pleated trousers with cuffs and three-quarter-inch self-belt for $700.

Whether you're a gentlemen or a lady, owning a suit (or pantsuit) from Tony Maurizio is a sign of good taste and an indication that you have most definitely arrived.   ❦

Paul Stuart

Madison Avenue at 45th Street	(212) 682-0320
New York, NY 10017	(800) 678-8278

Sociologists claim it's human nature to resist change. That all-too-human discomfort with innovation may have a lot to do with the ongoing popularity of Paul Stuart. Nothing much has changed here since Ralph Ostrove opened the store fifty-two years ago. It occupies the same site, the Ostrove family still runs it, and Paul Stuart remains a bastion of good taste in gentlemen's (and ladies') furnishings.

Walking onto any one of the three selling floors is a little like slipping into an old, comfortable shoe; a feeling of well-being envelops. Things can be counted on here—things like quality, since everything is made exclusively for Paul Stuart, selection, and service.

We know any number of nattily attired men who swear by the custom-shirt department. They lionize Nageb Kalid, who's held sway here for fifteen years. His department features traditional style, with just the right touch of flair in shirts that range from $68 to $125. There's a four-shirt minimum order and a lead time of four to six weeks. For the more daring or creative types, Nageb provides the tools for designing their own shirts—a wide variety of collars, cuffs, and fabrics to mix and match. Unsure which style or color monogram? Nageb knows. Which stripe is appropriate with your hair color? Nageb knows. A dart in the back or a spread to the color? Nageb knows.

Appropriately, just across the aisle, the tie department provides an enormous selection of the perfect accessory for the perfect Paul Stuart shirt. From silk paisleys to knits, from neat prints to stripes, not to mention the ubiquitous club, the ties are constructed to form an always-fashionable three-and-a-quarter-inch column and cost between $35 and $75.

Jewelry, socks, underwear, and an extraordinary array of sweaters complete the first level's complement of exceptional merchandise. And they have such a sensible system—one salesperson can help you throughout your tour of the floor. When it's time to go upstairs to investigate the suit situation, he'll guide you and introduce you to your next escort. Our favorite first-floor fellas are Louis Agront, Dan Greenberg, and Alfred Goldstein.

The oversized, rather grand wooden staircase leads past a mezzanine reserved for women's sportswear and business attire, to the second floor devoted to suits, sport coats, trousers, and overcoats. The natural-shoulder look sets the standard. "Off-the-rack" suits sell from $600 to $1,400. Custom-made, like those of Paul Newman, Frank Sinatra, and a whole pack of Wall Streeters, cost between $1,000 and $2,000, depending on design and fabric.

Frank Lombardo will lead you through the three fittings and six-to-eight-week wait for a suit made expressly for you. If you're hard-pressed to find the time to run over to Paul Stuart for all those fittings that ensure tailoring perfection, he'll even arrange to have a fitter visit your hotel, home, or office.

If you've no time, or patience, for shopping altogether, consider the expert services of Paul Stuart's personal shopper, Maureen McCormack. She can assemble an outfit—suit, suspenders, shirt, tie—or an entire wardrobe and dispatch it wherever you are, or wherever you're going. She'll even keep track of important birthdays and anniversaries, select the proper gift, and have it delivered in time for the celebration.

Prefer to do your own shopping from your own turf? Paul Stuart's beautifully produced catalog will come in handy. Distributed twice a year, mid-March and mid-September, its mailing list bears witness to the store's sophisticated international clientele—Japan, France, England, Saudi Arabia, Switzerland, Hong Kong, Italy, Venezuela, Colombia, and more are represented in droves. To join the ranks, just call Paul Stuart's toll-free 800 number. There's a one-time $2 sign-up charge, but the catalog is free thereafter.

House charge accounts are available. They're especially useful for some of Paul Stuart's more luxurious items, like the absolutely divine navy blue cashmere topcoat, with hand-stitched lapels and collars, lined in Chinese weasel. Naturally, at $4,300, the lining is removable.

For a dose of sheerly frivolous pleasure, guaranteed to lend a little Fred Astaire debonair dash to even the most conservative investment banker, pick up a $115 black walking stick topped with a sterling silver crown.

So if you subscribe to the theory of clothes making the man, make sure Paul Stuart makes your clothes. You'll be assured of presenting an image of affluence, success, and impeccable taste.   🍒

Sivone—Maker of Custom Ties

45 West 57th Street   (212) 371-4540
between 5th and 6th
3rd Floor
New York, NY 10019

It may be difficult, but don't let the hideous red and black carpet prejudice you against this intriguing establishment. Feast your eyes, instead, on the gorgeous selection of silks that adorns Ivonne Finelli's walls. She's been making custom ties for twenty-two years for an elite clientele who do their very best to keep her all to themselves. Her name and that of the shop are quietly whispered to a chosen few in boardrooms all over the country, East to West Coast, Wall Street to Hollywood, Saul Steinberg to Paul Anka.

In an age of instantly recognizable $100 ties worn to convey status on any old Tom, Dick, or Harry, the real movers and shakers are wearing Ivonne's distinctive $50 handmade numbers. During her annual buying trips to Italy, Ivonne takes only enough of any one silk to make about a dozen ties. So none of her clients, who hail from all over the globe, are likely to see themselves coming and going.

Each tie is made by her staff of Italian seamstresses in a workroom in the back of the shop and takes about two weeks. They use a very light wool interlining to give the ties body and shape—they never shrink. The silk outside lining always matches the predominant color of the tie. And speaking of matching, Ivonne will make handkerchiefs to go with any tie for about $16 each.

The tie width currently in vogue is three and a half inches. Should you not be a slave to fashion, Ivonne will go narrower or wider, whatever you prefer. As accommodating as she is, she has no minimum order.

To start your custom tie wardrobe, just bring in swatches from your favorite suits and shirts. Ivonne keeps a file on them, as well as your measurements and knotting preferences; proper length is determined by how you intend to knot the tie. For instance, the popular Windsor requires an inch and a half more fabric than most alternatives.

However you choose to tie your cravats, you'll be glad you ignored the carpet and placed yourself in Ivonne's capable hands. You're bound to become an addict, and at these prices why not knot to your heart's content?   ❦

William Fioravanti, Inc.—Custom Tailors for Men

45 West 57th Street   (212) 355-1540
between 5th and 6th
4th Floor
New York, NY 10019

You've arrived. You're the Chairman of the Board. You're the President, the CEO. Once there, your first call should be to William Fioravanti— though if truth be told, a call earlier in your career might help hasten the climb up the corporate ladder. He is, after all, at the top of that same ladder, when it comes to custom tailors for men. Of course, William works only by appointment. He deals with only one customer at a time in his ever-so-refined wood-paneled showroom where, for a quarter century, he's been dressing some of the world's most powerful men.

The Fioravanti look is fitted with a broad shoulder (the better to bear all those burdens?), and executed in soft, sensuous fabrics with mostly British origins. Yes, the lining silks are Italian—and exquisite. But the premier fabric in the Fioravanti stable is worsted spun cashmere. A two-piece cashmere suit will run about $3,250; regular worsted wool suits are more like $2,950. Slacks hover in the $750 neighborhood, while sport coats start at $2,350. As for topcoats, the price depends on the fabric. Whether it's camel or cashmere, it could cost you $3,850 to $4,250. A raincoat to complete your Fioravanti wardrobe will set you back $2,850, but you'll look so elegant on even the dreariest days.

Being outfitted by William requires a little advance planning. For one thing, no matter how large your first order may be, he'll cut only one piece and work with it until you're happy and he's happy. Then, and only then, will he proceed with the rest. And getting to that happy phase is a lengthy process, because William is so meticulous about creating the absolutely perfect fit.

It starts with a first visit, when William spends a lot of time chatting with you about your life-style, so he can get a handle on the kind of clothes you should have. He bases his recommendations upon the nature of your business, the number of homes you maintain, the amount you travel, the places you go. Once you and he have come to an agreement on your needs, he works with you to pick the appropriate fabrics. Finally, he sets about taking your measurements, which may take half an hour or so. He's very precise and the measurements are very detailed. Brother Anthony is meticulous in making sure the pattern is perfect. You won't see William or daughter Raquel, who's been taking good care of clients here for ten years, 'til at least three months later, when you come in for the first fitting. The second fitting takes place two to three weeks later, the final one about a week after that. We're talking a minimum of four months. If you need clothing for fall, see William by June, as Ronald Perelman and Steve Wynn do. Like them, you'll know all the time and effort is justified the first time you put on a Fioravanti suit. The fit is fantastic—the shoulders straight, the back flawless, the lines clear and uncluttered.

He can do the same for ladies, perhaps in deference to his daughter and his wife, Olga, who also works with him. But he doesn't do it often. It's a matter of talking Raquel into it and then relying on her to convince her father. When they do decide to honor a special request from the fairer sex, they produce very tailored, very ladylike suits for about $3,000. We beg for the $795 slacks. And we're negotiating a couple of drop-dead cashmere coats with them.

We want everyone to know we've arrived too. Fashions by Fioravanti make such a success statement, because they don't just clothe a body, they adorn it.   ❦

FOR WOMEN

Adolfo

36 East 57th Street	(212) MU8-4410, 4411
between Park and Madison	(212) MU8-4519
4th Floor	
New York, NY 10022	

If you love the Chanel look à la Coco, not Karl, you're bound to adore Adolfo. With sparkling eyes and devastating charm, he remains the master, with a stranglehold on the crowd that wears their Adolfos like badges of honor. His is a recognizable look, particularly when it's worn by Nancy Reagan, Harriet Deutsch, Betsy Bloomingdale, or Claudette Colbert. All these California girls come East to visit his sumptuous, all-white, by-appointment-only salon. And what a lot of appointments he has with ladies clamoring for his exclusive made-to-order designs—Adolfo has three phone lines that never stop ringing.

The popularity is justified. His classic, signature three-piece suits go everywhere, all day and all night. In an Adolfo, you're correctly dressed for any occasion. Indeed, with the automatic fashion insurance they carry, the $2,000-and-up price tags become very palatable indeed.

Actually, Adolfo rather coyly describes his prices as being "elastic"—especially appropriate where his evening clothes are concerned. You see, in addition to the extravagant ballgowns he delights in designing season after season, Adolfo believes in separates for evening. He feels it gives a woman so much flexible chic—a beaded jacket can be worn for one occasion over black evening pajamas, for another with a short skirt to make a memorable dinner suit. The elastic prices start in the same $2,000 neighborhood as the suits, and rise to considerably pricier heights. When Adolfo shows his collection at the Plaza, the ladies who lunch turn out in force, and mental notes are made about who is seated where. The secret to a good assignment is the cultivation of Elizabeth Bixon, who's been with Adolfo since his earliest days as a milliner. She has an uncanny knack for remembering each and every client, their measurements and purchases. She'll recommend just the accessory to perk up your last Adolfo indulgence, no matter how long ago you bought it.

You should also know that gaining the approval of Victoria III can also help you win the seating war. Victoria III is Adolfo's diminutive black pug, who sits regally on one of the little gold ballroom chairs in the salon and surveys the scene with a permanently bemused expression on her flat little face.

If you're having trouble getting through on one of his three lines, and your time in New York is short, you might stake out La Grenouille or 21. Adolfo frequents both. Ever-gracious, he really is one of the world's more accessible designers and is sure to take pity on your plight. Otherwise, you can check out your local Saks, where a few pieces from his current collection are always in residence. Saks will order your choice in the proper size from the salon. Or you can wait for his seasonal trunk shows, when he or one of his associates shows up with the entire collection. Then it's almost as if you did get through on that dratted phone in the first place!   ❦

Chanel

5 East 57th Street   (212) 355-5050
between Fifth and Madison
New York, NY 10022

Sometimes in a world of quilted handbags, little black dresses, gobs of chains and pearls, cardigan suits, white collars and cuffs, blazers and black-tipped sling-back shoes, it's hard to believe that the woman who first introduced them, first popularized them, is no longer with us.

Coco Chanel, or just Chanel: the name is so often invoked when fashion mavens speak of true style and elegance. She revolutionized the way women dressed in the 20s, liberating them from long skirts and constricting styles. Today, her signature is more prevalent than ever, thanks to the inspired interpretation of Karl Lagerfeld (whose designs for other labels are far superior to his own). The number of Chanel copies in every price range is testimony enough to the continued importance of the house that Coco built.

If you'll settle for nothing less than the real thing, then head for this glamorous store with its full range of Chanel products. It may not be quite as large as its Rue Cambon parent in Paris, but it's every bit as chic—all done up in beige, black, and cream, with gleaming mirror, brass, and chrome as accents. You find yourself hesitating at the bottom of the baby-grand staircase, looking up just in case you might catch Coco's ghost about to descend.

The cosmetic center near the entrance carries all the Chanel products that you can find at other counters, plus a few items exclusive to Chanel boutiques—Bois Noir men's fragrances at $50 for 4.2 ounces of eau de toilette and the $30 eye-lift gel, which reduces puffiness and lines.

Beyond the cosmetics you'll find men's ties for $65 and a marvelous selection of silk scarves. The classic 36 × 36 goes for $160, even more for the 56 × 56 versions, which make great beach or pool cover-ups. The $360 over-sized wool challis lends a special Chanel touch to what otherwise might be an ordinary suit or dress. And speaking of accessorizing with Chanel, who can resist some of the classic costume jewelry first made fashionable by Chanel. A basic go-anywhere gold-and-pearl clip runs about $115. Glitzier and larger evening earrings go for closer to $585. To decorate your waist, day or evening, collect the archetypal "C" chain belt, which varies slightly every season, but always sports the hallmark Chanel medallion. It's priced from $500 to $700, depending on the thickness of the links and the length, defined as how many times it can wrap around.

A great new addition to the accessory collection is a dear little purse that hangs from a leather belt and is just right for essentials like lipstick and keys. Alone, it sells for $350. The belt to attach might run as high as $555.

Upstairs are the clothes that exemplify Coco's fashion edicts— "Nothing goes out of style more quickly than a fashion, while elegance is for all time." "A dress that is not comfortable is a failure. To be elegant is to wear clothes that permit you to move easily, gracefully, comfortably." "A woman can often be over-dressed, never over-elegant."

In Chanel, you'll never be over-dressed or over-elegant, but you will pay a not inconsiderable sum for such self-confidence. Two-piece suits start at $2,100, and prices can go as high as $14,000 for a truly glamorous evening gown. Chic little day dresses fall into the $1,600 to $3,000 category. For evening, a classic black satin might cost about $2,000, but we can never resist the slightly more elaborate concoctions with just the right amount of beading for closer to $3,000.

The shoes and bags that have become so much a part of the landscape are here too. And here, you can be sure they're the real McCoy (or real Chanel). A basic black pump with the hallmark stitched toes runs about $380. An elegant little silk evening slipper with a tiny sparkling sequined bow or some jet beading falls into the $400 to $550 range and complements most any ensemble. Then there's *the* bag complete with quilted leather and gold chain threaded in leather. They come in all shapes, sizes, and colors with a similar variety of inventive closures. But start with the time-honored black shoulder version for $870. You might also think about the ultimate in carry-on bags, a crocodile shoulder style large enough for weekend travel for $8,200. For *long* weekends, though, you might be better off with the Chanel duffle at $900 and perhaps a well-constructed cosmetic case for $470.

This is the principal store of Chanel's eight free-standing U.S. boutiques. As such it can draw from the stock of any of the others. If colors or sizes available here don't quite suit, manager Brigitte Gorrand or her assistant Bay Wellington will conduct an all-out search. They'll also make sure your packages are delivered, while expert repairs are made on any (perish the thought) defective merchandise. And if you're in desperate need of something Chanel, but just can't find the time to stop by, call Bay and she'll send it over. She's used to such requests from sophisticated international clientele, including a fair number of French, Germans, and Japanese. Each of those languages, by the way, is spoken in the store and all of the multilingual staff carry beepers. If you can't seem to find your favorite salesperson, ask and she'll be instantly summoned.

Who exactly are Chanel clients? It's almost easier to say who *isn't* wearing a piece or two of Chanel. Now, with the recent introduction to the Chanel jewelry collection of four new diamond watches (very much the real thing) starting at $5,400, the ranks of Chanel devotees are bound to swell even further.   ❦

Fendi

720 Fifth Avenue	(212) 767-0100
at 56th Street	(212) 489-0061
New York, NY 10022	

Fendi—in the U.S. the fabled name was most often associated with furs and fragrance, until last fall when those five fabulous sisters opened their U.S. flagship store: A 20,000 square-foot, three-floor Roman palazzo, showcasing everything that is Fendi—$8 body lotions to $15 leather pocket agendas to $200,000 sable coats.

Rumor and retailing common sense has it that this is just the beginning of the Fendi conquest of America. Naturally, though, New York had to be first, never mind that it meant ending the long and successful relationship with Bergdorf Goodman, once the only place in the city you could get those fantastic Fendi furs.

And what they've done to that space! Roman arches, columns, marble floors, and parchment-covered walls transport you to another time and place. The superb lighting bestows a lustrous jewellike quality on every piece of merchandise. That same lighting caressing the beautiful grain of light wood with dramatic black accents lends a certain serenity to the store, which makes shopping very pleasurable indeed. What's more, the specially recruited and trained staff doles out genuinely warm Italian hospitality. Their goal is to make clients feel welcome and valued, not intimidated. The lovely, spacious dressing rooms and the presence of the sisters themselves (on a rotating basis) add to your sense of *dolce vita*.

The main floor houses the Fendi fragrances, men's and women's shoes running the gamut from classic to high fashion styles, and a vast assortment of small leather goods—including limited edition handbags that were formerly available only in Rome. The ground floor is devoted to men, who even have their own label here—Fendi Uomo. Predictably, it's a senuously luxurious line, heavy on the cashmere. Indeed, we can imagine few things more decadent than the cashmere/cotton blend jogging suits. If jogging (or lounging) is not your style, there's plenty of clothes and equipment for other sporting activities here as well—from tennis (shorts-to-racquets-to-balls) to steeple-chasing right down to saddles and horse brushes.

But despite the temptations of the other floors, we tend to make a bee-line for the second floor, home to women's clothes and the fur salon. Here many Americans are getting their first look at the handiwork of a third generation of Fendis—Fendissime, created by the Fendi sisters' daughters and nieces, Maria Teresa, Sylvia, and Fredica. It's a complete line of clothes, furs, and accessories designed for the young and the young at heart. And, of course, it is here that you will find the Fendi ready-to-wear, the result of a most successful collaboration with Karl Lagerfeld that dates from 1965. He consistantly does the Fendis proud, and indeed helped put them on the international fashion map with the creation of the famous double F logo.

And then there are the furs—those, oh, so fabulous furs, the result of years of experimentation and research lead by Paola Fendi. She and her team of craftsmen have changed the nature of fur from a precious but stiff material into one that is light, soft and above all easy to wear. They have done so by developing new tanning and dying methods and innovative ways to cut and construct fur. While we're generally overwhelmed by the wondrous selection of their work here, we have been known to zero in on the exquisite cashmere scarves and shawls trimmed in fur—about $1,000 and $4,000 respectively. The shearlings, made surprisingly light by a special process, and the fur-lined raincoats (both available for men and women) have also captured our attention.

The Fendis' approach is to create an aura of enticing, sophisticated femininity (or masculinity) in all they design. There is an elegant, witty, even humorous quality to their creations. After all, these are the girls who dared to make fur fun, dramatic, and surprising. The same qualities infuse everything bearing their distinctive trademark, from jewelry, watches, and handbags to luggage, stockings, and evening wear.

The likes of Georgette Mosbacher and Nan Kempner get a kick out of the Fendi style, as you will too—especially when you're ordering that custom-made fur throw for your yacht. Or was that meant to be a surprise for Donald and Ivana? Never mind, you can get them a special little something for their helicopter. At Fendi the possibilities for custom-made items, especially in fur, are boundless.   ❦

Givenchy

954 Madison Avenue   (212) 772-1040
at 75th Street
New York, NY 10021

There was a time when it seemed every woman in the whole world wanted to look like Audrey Hepburn (many of us still do!). Doubtless, one of the reasons was that she always looked so incredibly elegant, yet girlish and coquettish, partly due to her on- and off-camera wardrobe by Hubert de Givenchy. Was she his muse? Perhaps. But one thing is certain—it is all but impossible today to think of one without evoking images of the other.

So naturally, Audrey pops into your mind as you cross the refined and graceful threshold of Givenchy's boutique. Here he offers his myriad ready-to-wear clothes and accessories. The boutique's merchandise covers the whole gamut—day to evening wear, suits to sports separates, cocktail dresses to ballgowns. There are coats and raincoats to cover the suits, capes to shelter bare shoulders exposed by evening clothes, and shoes, gloves, and jewelry to set off everything. And sunglasses, there are even sunglasses.... Ah, Audrey! And then, of course, what would you expect from the only freestanding Givenchy boutique in all of the good old USA?

The divinely chic and sophisticated Yuta Powell presides over this empire, where timeless suits start at $1,500. You can't touch an evening gown for less than $2,500, but then who wants to? We're most fond of Monsieur de Givenchy's versatile cashmere capes, with their generous ruffles that are so flattering to the face. He remains the master of classic clothes with a sense of humor and a touch of fantasy.

He also remains very much involved with his business. You might catch sight of his tall, elegant presence here. Givenchy directly oversees the operation of the boutique, often making the trip from his native Paris to check things out.

Should you decide to indulge in a complete Givenchy makeover, call Yuta or Veronica (who's been here for ages and knows everything there is to know about the extensive choices). They'll set up an appointment to put you together—head to toe. Naturally, it's quite an investment, but you know that Givenchy's women count on him to design timeless clothes. He doesn't disappoint; you'll be wearing your new wardrobe for years, never feeling dated.

Timing-wise, we've found the best time to shop for fall is during the months of July and August. Look for spring clothes in the dead of winter. What else is there to do in January and February? Once you become a regular, you can get even further ahead in your planning by ordering from the photographs Yuta always brings back from the Paris shows. She'll call the minute she returns. Let's see now, that means you can deal with fall in March and spring in October!

Whichever schedule you follow, the boutique's excellent fitters will have ample time to adjust your new duds to perfection. They're so good, they can even improve considerably on nature, hiding a nasty little figure problem or two.

There are a lot of big names in the fashion business, but very few class acts, very few who understand and respect their clientele. Hubert de Givenchy is a notable exception. He knows they expect the best and he delivers.

Helene Arpels

470 Park Avenue   (212) 753-1581
between 57th and 58th Streets
New York, NY 10022

The perky green-and-white striped awnings beckon. They summon you
to wander into the small, pale blue salon of the tall, slender Madame Helene Arpels, designer of the city's most comfortable, chic, and pricy
shoes.

Her absolutely smashing footwear is now complemented by a few select pieces—clothes, handbags, and accessories. She has an exquisite
black silk/satin belt, delicately decorated by black jet beading, which
sells for $400. It'll spruce up that old reliable standby little black dress.
For further drama, you can cover it with a soft gray panne velvet cape.
Gold threads run through the velvet, and it is trimmed with a small gold
lamé pleated ruffle—drop-dead glamour for $2,200. Then there's the
butter-soft three-quarter leather and suede jacket with a small band of
black fox at the collar and a detachable hood. It turns ordinary slacks
and sweater into a couture costume for $3,400.

But enough of this. It's still the shoes that are the real draw at Helene
Arpels. And what extraordinary shoes they are. She has a pair of lizard
pumps dotted with a few hand-sewn rhinestones, tri-colored in platinum,
silver, and pewter for $1,800. Perhaps a pair of alligators would be just
the thing for that dear little Givenchy dinner suit—light and delicate in a
dramatic combination of brown, rust, and black at $2,500.

Well, maybe you don't need quite so much gator. You can soften the
look and the price with the purchase of a shoe crafted in alligator and
suede for around $1,700. For evening, the hand-embroidered silk slip-
pers can be either high- or low-heeled. They come in a rainbow of conventional colors, or can be colored to match an uncommon shade for
$1,800. Special orders take about four weeks.

At these prices, you'll be pleased to know Helene provides an extra
pair of heels, so you can actually wear these puppies on the streets of
New York with impunity. The first grate that seizes your heel will not be
cause for any ill-considered suicide.

Of course, the heel issue evaporates when it comes to Helene's luxurious suede loafers, the ultimate in comfort and a favorite with clients for
the last thirty-five years. They come in any color or skin you might want,
with a broad price range—leather and suede for $350, lizard for $850,

ostrich for $1,350. The ultimate—in crocodile these casual little loafers will cost $2,500.

Naturally one does not wear Helene Arpels shoes in inclement weather. One does, however, don her signature rain boots, which also happen to be the least expensive item in the store. Rubber-soled patent leather, they're trimmed in red, black, or taupe leather. Devotees tend to have a pair of each.

Helene's fans hail from all over the world. Hers is a very personal business. She showers clients with attention and embraces them with her philosophy that life is beautiful, especially if it includes some of her beautiful things. Eternally elegant clients like Nancy Reagan, Gloria Vanderbilt, Barbara Taylor Bradford, and Betsy Bloomingdale wholeheartedly endorse that hypothesis.

But we think you're not a true believer until you order one of Helene's caftans. All hand-beaded, each takes two years to make, once Helene has designed it. The price—not a penny less than $13,500. Only those seeking the most beautiful of lives need apply.   ❦

Henri Bendel

712 Fifth Avenue   (212) 247-1100
between 55th and 56th
New York, NY 10022

With its recent move to Fifth Avenue, it's become a dead heat between Henri Bendel and its arch-rival Bergdorf Goodman for the best traveled store in town. Bendel's journey began in 1896, when Henri Bendel set up a little hat shop on East Ninth Street. His clientele appreciated his personal service (he made a point of learning each customer's name) and attention to detail. As his business prospered, he added perfumes, then custom-made clothes to his inventory. Soon he was in the market for a larger location, and in 1912 opened the first store on what was then the residential 57th Street. Situated literally in the backyard of families with names like Vanderbilt and Whitney, Henry Bendel began to cater to the crème de la crème of New York society.

Bendel's reputation as a store for the carriage trade developed over the years to near epic proportions. The introduction in 1957 of the innovative "Street of Shops," a series of individual boutiques on the main floor, created a sensation. As designers' names became household words, Bendel's was in the vanguard of securing exclusive arrangements with some of the world's top couturiers, and the store elevated window dressing to an art form. Fashionable New Yorkers made it a point to study Bendel's windows to find out what was new and exciting. Bendel's was the most special of specialty stores, always the dependable source for something intriguingly unique.

Then came the merger and acquisition mania of the 80s. Even Henri Bendel succumbed, ending up as the crown jewel in retailing wizard Leslie Wexner's empire—The Limited. Despite Wexner's vision for continuing Bendel's prosperous growth on a national level, there were nay-sayers who claimed his mass market sensibilities were not equipped to deal with the Bendel's mystique, that he was incapable of understanding the Bendel's client. Whether or not they were right is a moot point, because Wexner wisely hired the dynamically charming Mark Shulman as president and CEO of Henry Bendel. He seems to have a handle on the specialness of Bendel. Under his leadership, Henri Bendel New York has truly become a flagship, moving into space four times larger than its former location. Now, three fabulous new Bendel's are set to open in Chicago, Boston, and Columbus.

Lots of what was familiar at the former 57th Street site has been transferred to the new setting, while some old Bendel's traditions that for a while had been lost in the shuffle have reemerged. The elegant Bendel's brown-and-white-striped shopping bags continue to be a souvenir of your visit. Elevator operators in their crisply elegant and appropriately brown uniforms still whisk you between the four floors. Rome, the doorman, continues to usher clients in or out of cabs and limos with equal aplomb. Upstairs, Mark Shulman is systematically rebuilding Bendel's stable of designer exclusives. And the European "Street of Shops" theme has been reintroduced throughout the store.

Despite the profusion of French stone and Italian marble, entering the foyer of the new Henri Bendel's is like entering a private home—which is exactly the idea. Mark says his fashion-savvy, sophisticated international clientele likes to shop in an intimate environment. They appreciate the store's division into a series of seemingly self-contained little shops, rather than departments. Henry Bendel is a prime example of the old axiom of the sum of the parts being greater than the whole.

The main floor houses an exceptional sweater shop, featuring goodies Mark has collected from all over the world, as well as the always-popular Sentiments Boutique—everything warm and wonderful for the home.

Here you'll find Frank MacIntosh's terrific table-top accessories and Bebe Winkler's lavish collection of luxurious linens.

Further along you'll run across Bendel's Beauty Checkers, home to the wonderfully reliable mascara Amy Green came up with, still selling for only $5. There's also a group of luminously moist lipsticks at $12 each. In addition, Bendel's is the exclusive U.S. purveyor of the Canadian Mac cosmetics and skin-care products. The range of colors, developed for Mac by internationally acclaimed makeup artist Frank Toscan, is enormous. The featured treatment line is Valmont, hailing from Switzerland and composed of all natural ingredients.

A grand staircase beckons you to the second floor. Of course, the elevator is also an option, but the stairway provides a great bird's-eye view. You might spot Barbra Streisand, Cher, Teri Garr, Kelly McGillis, or Linda Gray from your perch. Then again, you might not. Sensitive to his celebrity clientele's desire for privacy, Mark has been known to whisk them up to his office where an assistant presents them with the store's treasures. In fact, Mark is a diligent practitioner of the Henri Bendel legacy of beyond-the-call-of-duty personal service. Special Bendel's customers know they can depend on Mark to open early or stay late to accommodate crowded schedules or a last-minute trip. He assigns a personal shopper to guide them through the store and puts a fitter on call. During regular business hours, Mark's been known to offer office-away-from-office service for many a busy lady desperate to make a few quick phone calls in comfortable isolation. Actually, they don't really have to bother Mark (we suspect they just want an excuse to chat with him) since all the dressing rooms in the couture area have telephones!

Another Bendel's tradition that Mark has embraced is the semiannual opportunity to design your own cashmere sweater. Every June and October, cashmere connoisseurs from all over the world descend upon the store to create the sweater of their dreams. Stephanie Powers recently ordered two, intricately beaded in a pattern of her design. Naturally, prices vary depending on the style and amount of handwork required, but you can count on a six-to-eight-week wait. If you can't make it to New York during the designated months, send a photograph or sketch along with instruction. Bendel's will, of course, accommodate you.

Should you be more secure relying on the creative genius of others, check out Mark's newest fashion finds. We're just crazy about the sportswear of New Yorker Ethan Cohen. A former apprentice to Givenchy,

Ethan has a fresh new viewpoint executed in exciting silhouettes and unusual fabrications. His jackets sell for $300 to $600—slacks from $150 to $275. Kermit Smith, now designing women's clothes, is another label at Bendel's. His is a line of very casual sportswear called Krunch, nothing even approaching serious, but great weekend wear. Jackets run about $300, slacks and skirts in the $100 to $200 neighborhood.

So, as far as we're concerned, the legendary Bendel's mystique seems to be very much intact. And Mark is determined to keep it that way, bent on maintaining Bendel's fashion leadership. We want everyone to subscribe to his theory that if Bendel's says it's right, it has to be right. No doubt, Henri Bendel would approve. 🍎

J. S. Suárez

26 West 54th Street   (212) 315-5614
between 5th and 6th
New York, NY 10019

These days it's so embarrassing to be seen in public sans sack screaming Chanel, Hermès, or Bottega Veneta slung over your shoulder. It's equally embarrassing to explain their price to husbands, lovers, mothers (especially mothers) who think a purse is meant to be utilitarian, not an indication of your economic and social standing.

There is a solution, a compromise between fashion sense and common sense, provided by José Suárez. At J. S. Suárez you can purchase that status bag, minus the status label, at half the price. And with the exception of Hermès, it really is the same item, having been produced by the same manufacturer responsible for the authentically labeled version.

As for the Hermès look-alikes, they're definitely copies, but who can tell? The classic Kelly bag with the shoulder strap in leather, ostrich, lizard, or crocodile is only $379. A larger version sells for $399. The "Hermès" trim bag is about $290.

The "Chanels" run from $149 to $400. Did we say half the price? Try a third!

We also found some exquisite generic bags fashioned in luxurious ostrich. From the smallest clutch to the largest tote, they run $600 to $3,000. Elsewhere, you couldn't touch any one of them for less than $1,500.

José won't reveal the names of any of his customers and neither will his daughter Ramona, who's usually here as well. They know their business is built on illusion. Their customers would be horrified to be identified as such. After all, the whole point is to convince the world that the Chanel on their shoulder is the real McCoy.   ❦

Jacomo, Inc.

25 East 61st Street   (212) 832-9038
between Madison and Park
New York, NY 10021

This is another of those intriguing, tiny, very specialized boutiques that seem to thrive in New York. Jacomo, located in the same inviting little space since opening in 1960, is owned by Jimmy Kaplan. It sells nothing but exquisite handmade bags—some new, some old, and all constructed on extraordinarily beautiful frames from all over the globe.

Jimmy travels the world looking for unusual, often antique, frames. He draws inspiration from them and designs his bags to set them off to their best advantage, always using the finest, most supple skins available. They last a lifetime and confer a degree of authority, plus a great deal of style, on those who carry them.

Evening bag prices range from about $600 to $4,500. At the lower end you might find a whip snakeskin purse with an Art Deco frame. For $4,500 you could own a black crocodile beauty attached to an Art Nouveau brass frame from Austria, encrusted with semiprecious stones. A cognac-colored ostrich bag with a Bakelite frame selling for $1,850 also caught our eyes.

Indeed, frames made of Bakelite, a form of lucite very popular in the twenties and thirties, are a bit of a specialty with Jimmy. Handpainted, except for the very rare clear ones, they are very much a collector's item. Bags built on Bakelite start at $1,500 and quickly climb the price ladder.

Jimmy also has a knack for finding museum-quality vintage bags, from the first third of the century. He restores these treasures to mint condition and offers them to those who appreciate their value, while not flinching at the price. We were tempted by a matte coffee-colored crocodile dinner bag on an Italian sterling silver frame etched with tiny cherubs for $3,250.

Jacomo's directress, the warm and welcoming Hilda, knows the origins of all the vintage bags, as well as that of all the frames that structure Jimmy's creations. If you don't see anything that really captures your imagination, she or manager Heidener will help you sort through the tremendous selection of frames and the equally imposing inventory of skins. Jimmy, who lives and works in Cannes, will then design a bag to combine the two to perfection. Of course, if you fancy yourself a designer, he will gracefully accept your guidance.

Whether it's your design or Jimmy's, you'll never be satisfied elsewhere. Each Jacomo bag is absolutely unique and so enchanting. Once you become the proud owner of one, you'll want another, then another. Many people, like Lauren Bacall and Carol Bayer Sager collect them. How clever they are to accumulate an item as practical as it is beautiful.

La Lingerie

792 Madison Avenue   (212) 772-9797
at 67th Street
New York, NY 10021

You'll find whatever milady desires, or whatever turns her fella on, in this tiny shop jam-packed with intimate apparel. From flirtatious bras and teddies to glamorous nightgowns and robes, manager Diane Tucker can help you assemble a seductive wardrobe meant for your (or his) eyes only.

Despite its name, not all the merchandise qualifies as underwear or nightclothes. There are those eye-popping bikinis by La Perla, the Italian firm specializing in hot colors and hotter shapes, starting at $85. One of the $750 silk nightshirts could serve as a beach cover-up, but they're a little tailored for our taste. The tantalizing silk-ribbed bodice Jean Harlowesque nightgown at $1,600 is more our style. There's a $750 robe to go with it and dear mules by Jacques Levine at $65 a pair to complete this most decadent of lounging ensembles.

For the bride, La Lingerie is sheer heaven—all those coquettish bras and panties for her trousseau. The beautiful beaded lingerie cases make for perfect honeymoon packing. We found one truly extraordinary one, more like a work of art than a particularly practical item, for $215.

With the help of La Lingerie, you can certainly subscribe to the theory that it's what's inside that counts.

Martha

475 Park Avenue	(212) 753-1511
at 58th Street	(212) 826-8855
and Trump Tower	
New York, NY 10022	

This is the kind of store to which you either are born or aspire. The first assures your warm welcome at this chandeliered and mirrored temple of high fashion. You'll inherit one of the savvy sales ladies, who already knows about you from your mother. In fact, she agonized with her through those difficult formative years of yours and now stands ready to guide you unerringly through fashion's firmament—from your $30,000 Pat Kerr wedding gown to the $12,000 Galanos for your debut as a charity event chairlady. The word *lady* is key. As Bill Blass once declared, Martha is a shop for "a lady, and we use the word correctly."

So if you weren't born to Martha, you're in the position of somehow proving your ladyship before you are embraced by the staff. Make your first trip to Martha in the company of a friend, who's known as a regular client, someone like Cece Guest, Barbara Walters, Ivana Trump, Judith Leiber, Barbara Davis, Diana Ross. If you're not personally acquainted with any of these ladies, flip through your Roladex until you come across names like Astor, duPont, Phipps, or Vanderbilt, all suitably well-heeled families that have been part of the Martha faithful since Martha Phillips opened her first store in 1934. It was the height of the depression, but she was convinced that no matter what the price, "if it was beautiful, I could sell it." She did and has been selling beautiful clothes ever since, so successfully that now there are four Martha shops, all at very good addresses—Park Avenue and Trump Tower in New York, Worth Avenue in Palm Beach, and the prestigious Bal Harbor mall outside of Miami.

Should locating a Martha regular prove unfeasible, as Martha's daughter and president of the firm Lynn Manulis says, "we sell to one tenth of one percent of the population," go armed with a well-rehearsed tale of a fabulous event you're in town to attend. Tell them your friend (drop a good name) assured you that the store would have absolutely the perfect thing to wear. It's not that they're really unfriendly here, it's just that they need to know that you somehow belong in a store where the average customer easily spends $2,000 plus per visit. The sales ladies' time is very valuable indeed at Martha. They simply can't be bothered with casual browsers.

And indeed, there's not much available to be casually browsed. Most of the stock is hidden away in storerooms, where it is carefully tended. Each piece is separately encased in its own plastic bag and aired, pressed and re-bagged on a regular basis. Thus it hangs, waiting to be presented to a likely purchaser in one of the plushly carpeted fitting rooms, so large that they rival the size of many a New Yorker's studio apartment.

Now if it sounds like you have to go to a lot of trouble to gain a welcomed admittance to a store, which is ostensibly public; it is—but it's worth it. The selection of gorgeous clothes is awesome. You'll see, touch, and try on some of the world's most exquisite and expensive fashions. Furthermore, they won't waste your time. Providing you're the lady we know you are, you'll be shown clothes you can truly appreciate and that make you look sensational. *Miss* Martha and *Miss* Lynn (you can't even imagine anyone calling either of these elegantly coiffed, dressed, and jeweled ladies anything else) know their clients and those that should be their clients. They understand their lifestyle and select merchandise accordingly, buying in depth from their favorite designers.

Because of the expense of such well-chosen merchandise, Martha has a reputation as being a store for matrons. Note that the reputation stems from the fact that it is often only matrons who can afford to shop here. It's definitely not a reflection on the style of the clothes featured. This is, after all, the store that discovered and introduced to America such designers as Valentino, Carolina Herrera, Mary McFadden, Andre Laug, Mila Schon, Laura Biagiotti, Zandra Rhodes, and David and Elizabeth Emanuel. Martha, now well into her eighties but still going strong, and Lynn are always on the look-out for new talent and have an uncanny ability to zero in on the very best. Lynn, particularly, is fearless in her enthusiasm for risking Martha's reputation and resources on talented unknowns, whose success is then guaranteed by virtue of having been discovered and promoted by Martha.

Indeed, in an ongoing effort to expand their clientele and to attract a younger audience, the Trump Tower store concentrates on younger more avant-garde designers like Thierry Mugler, Claude Montana, and Gian Franco Ferre. Because of its location, it also draws a touristy crowd, many of whom don't really belong but don't have enough sense to know it (the bane of all the Trump Tower emporiums). Still, some outstanding new customers have emerged from the unwashed hordes, so the staff here is a little warmer toward unknowns. You might consider making this the site of your first assault on Mt. Martha.

Alternatively, you might visit the latest jewel in the Martha empire—Martha International, right next door to the Park Avenue store. Miss Lynn's brainchild, it represents a new direction for Martha. While sticking to the store's signature guns of quality and fashion authority, Martha International is positioned to appeal to younger career women not yet able to afford most Martha offerings. It is as Miss Lynn once told one of us, "a store for girls like you, dear."

Calling in a few chits, Miss Lynn has persuaded some of the world's great designers to produce capsule collections exclusively for this new store. She asked for and got versatile, superbly styled clothes that go all day and well into the night, selling for prices ranging from a couple hundred dollars to a couple thousand—or a lot less than the Martha. Actually, you might consider Martha International a store with training wheels, preparing you for the big-time next door.   ❦

Maud Frizon

49 East 57th Street   (212) 980-1460
between Madison and Park
New York, NY 10022

Black granite, mirror, and natural wood form the dramatic scenery of this enchanted land of shoes that are spectacularly presented on black marble tables. Take a load off and sink into one of the extremely comfortable black leather chairs and let any of manager Carl Grimm's helpful staff cater to your shoe fantasies—or fetishes.

Since Maud designs over 700 shoes for each of her two collections annually, it's likely something will appeal to your sense of shoe style. If not, Maud would be the first to tell you to look elsewhere. She believes shoes are a very personal thing; they should be a reflection, and extension, of the wearer's personality. If you're of a feminine, romantic frame of mind and have a sense of humor, Maud's shoes with their distinctive look are for you. Whether it's the curve of the heel or the flounce on the side, every pair announces it was designed by the ever-creative Maud. A basic black pump is never all that basic from Maud Frizon, nor should it be at $300 and up...and up!

At any given time, all 700 styles may not be available at the store. But if they don't have that pair you saw in *Mirabella,* Carl will get it for you. He'll even arrange to have it made in a special color or with a different heel if you want. Just be prepared to wait ten days to two weeks for a custom order and to add twenty percent to the cost.

Fortunately, the dear little pair of alligator flats we wanted were in stock—for $800. We also like her suede boots in a broad range of colors for $600 to $700. Then there's the playful pair that comes up over the knee and sells for at least $1,000, depending upon whether you want it in suede, leather, lizard, or crocodile. And who could resist the satin evening slippers inspired by the legendary Folies Bergère dancer, Mistinguett, encrusted with pearls, rhinestones, and feathers for about $600. No wonder Bianca Jagger, Régine, Shirlee Fonda, and the sisters-in-law Trump have such a tough time making their choices.

Their lives are further complicated by the prolific Maud's line of pantyhouse and stockings, designed to go with her shoes and ranging from $18 to $65 a pair. We like the sexy black lace Ecstasy pattern for $65, topped by a pretty lace brief. Her silky stockings at $45 come in a wide variety of colors and feature Maud's logo right at the top, just exactly where you're meant to attach a barely-there garter. Remember, Maud is French, even though all her factories are in Italy.

If you want to take your Maud Frizon coordination one step further, her store can outfit you with her versatile collection of bags in all shapes, colors, and sizes, as well as Maud Frizon luggage. The bags tend to sell for $300 to $2,000, while the luggage goes for $900 to $2,000 per piece. Of course it's all handmade leather, so you might consider saving it for trips on the Concorde or MGM Grand Air, when it's sure to be handled with tender loving care.

Speaking of which, you can even shoe the precious little feet of your children in Maud Frizon at $180 a pair. The store carries shoes for little ones of both sexes, starting at age three. Danielle Steel loves to pamper her children with them. And when Mrs. Bruce Willis, aka Demi Moore, was pregnant, she got terribly excited about the notion of her child wearing Maud Frizon. In fact she was so carried away that Carl had to speak to her very sternly about the merits of, at least, waiting till the baby was born to buy out the store!

If there's a teenager in your life, you might want to take a look at Maud's latest venture, a lower-priced shoe collection—$250 to $400—called Maud Frizon Club. At those prices the thought of an active sixteen-year-old tearing through them in a couple of months isn't quite so horrifying. In fact, we know one or two women of substance who have invented an imaginary teen for whom they *claim* to purchase shoes. No dummies, they get that distinctive Maud Frizon cachet for hundreds less than the cost of the signature line. 🐦

Montenapoleone

789 Madison Avenue   (212) 535-2660
at 67th Street
New York, NY 10021

Maria Scotto, the managing director of this sleek little shop, knows exactly what makes a woman feel deliciously female. A fine practitioner of the Italian woman's art of appearing both sexy and sophisticated, Maria maintains that one's appearance is predicated on a sense of inner well-being. She feels Montenapoleone's merchandise is just the ticket to give you that sense of being special.

We couldn't agree more, and neither could Barbara Walters, Charlotte Ford, or Mercedes Bass, who frequent the store for its exclusive selection of intimate apparel, bathing suits, cover-ups, and resort clothes. Nothing sold here is available anywhere else in the U.S.

The first floor is all lingerie, most of it Hollywood glamorous. We found a wonderful two-piece red silk charmeuse pajama set for $300. If red is just a little too racy for you, it comes in a variety of other colors too! For serious lounging, there's a sensuous cashmere gown at $900. And the sandman will gallop to your bedside to ensure your night's sleep, if you're swathed in one of their bias-cut silk charmeuse nightgowns. Figure-flattering to within an inch of your life, they start at $90 and go up to $700.

Upstairs, you'll find the resort wear. With so many of her clients traveling so often to the world's most exciting sunny climes, Maria keeps her resort collection fresh and dazzling twelve months a year. The evening ensembles are a particular joy—it's usually so difficult to find something dressy and chic, yet casual enough for poolside cocktails. Once found, don't be disappointed if the size or color isn't quite right. Maria will place a special order for you, but it may take up to six weeks. Basic alterations are handled on the premises, usually within twenty-four hours and delivered right to your hotel or home.

Montenapoleone also offers a delightful range of gifts and accessories—small tasseled silk tissue holders for $15, lingerie bags at $45, comfy terry slippers for $45. The silk camisoles at $50 lend a feminine allure to that all-business suit.

Treat yourself, or someone else, to unadulterated feminine indulgence
at Montenapoleone.   ❧

Sock Express

265 Columbus Avenue	(212) 769-3610
between 72nd and 73rd streets	
New York, NY 10023	

Socks, socks, and more socks—jeweled socks, animal socks, socks that
play music, and even plain-old sweat socks. That's almost what this cute
little store is all about—almost, but not quite. As the Rockette line of
gorgeous gams in the window indicates, Sock Express deals with more
leg territory than just the ankle. There are leggings, thigh-hi's, pantyhose, and garterhose as well.

While Sock Express carries a number of name brands, like Calvin
Klein, E.G Smith, and Bill Blass, the big story is their own label, Barton
G., in honor of owner and designer Barton G. Weiss. Barton's show business background is evident in his flamboyant, fun, sexy, and occasionally
outrageous designs. The black cotton lycra thigh-hi topped with a
gauntletlike faux-leopard cuff is a prime example at $28. Wearing these,
people will notice your coming and going.

Barton considers hosiery a fashion accessory that can make, break,
and totally change the look of any outfit. Once you visit Sock Express,
you'll probably agree. Take the cotton lycra footless black tights, heavily
and colorfully jeweled with large polished stones for $38. They glamor-
ize any little black dress for evening and can make a little skirt and
sweater ensemble a formal affair. We also like the black thigh-his with
the line of prim brass buttons up the back at $15. Very Chanel!

As for socks, there's lots—many carrying a Celeste Stein or Barton G.
hangtag. These are the really precious ones decorated with all sort of
wonderful, whimsical "things" that give each pair a theme. We can't wait
for the next sock-hop to wear "Hollywood"—white anklets with turned-
down cuffs sporting rhinestone encrusted sunglasses. They're a hoot for
$14. Celeste, who hails from Galveston, Texas, and now designs exclu-
sively for Barton, even goes so far as to reinvent the classic denim jacket,
also available at this sock store that is so much more than socks. Hers
are canvases for her wildly imaginative designs in stones, studs, crystals,
pins, paint, and patches. They range in price from about $200 to $1,800
dollars.

You'll also notice items here that border on lingerie, pretty sexy lingerie at that. The one-piece combination of black lace garter belt and stockings is a knockout, practical (virtually run-proof) and comfortable, too, for $40. We've been dispensing the white-lace version to brides, to give them a naughty-but nice feeling while they're at the altar, not to mention a treat for the groom later on!

We've discovered that a new pair of cute socks or alluring legwear is the '90s equivalent of the '50s solution to the blahs—going out and buying a new hat. And these days a much cheaper solution at that! It perks you up, lifts your spirits, makes you feel like a whole new woman. Go on, give it a shot. What have you got to lose?   ❧

Sylvia Pines—Uniquities

1102 Lexington Avenue   (212) 744-5141
at 77th Street
New York, NY 10021

While there's no telling what treasure you might unearth in this small shop delightfully cluttered with Victorian, Art Nouveau, and Art Deco goodies, be sure to concentrate on plowing through the amazing collection of unique and antique purses. Remember mother's intricately beaded evening bag? Sylvia's got hundreds, from $55 to $500. She's also amassed a huge selection of French Deco purses glittering with marcasite. Starting at about $475, some go for as much as $2,000.

In the eight years Sylvia Pines has been cramming her tiny space with intriguing tchatchkies like lovely antique-looking glasses and charming silver picture frames, she has developed a special affinity for beautiful day and evening purses of a certain age. She even has a bag hospital of sorts. If cleaning out the attic of the family manse yields a purse or two in need of repair, Sylvia can probably handle it. She'll either fix it herself or send it to one of her excellent sources for refurbishing.

Sylvia's penchant for purses is contagious. As regular browsers, we became addicted. . .and collectors. Besides being unique fashion accessories, they make very respectable objets d'art suitable for strategic display—a Uniquitous addition to any decorating scheme.   ❧

Victoria di Nardo Fine Millinery

68 Thompson Street   (212) 334-9615
between Spring Street and Broome
New York, NY 10012

This teeny tiny shop is a real treasure. It's teeming with the most disarmingly enchanting hats, all designed by Victoria di Nardo. Whether you want a casual beret in linen, wool, or velvet, or a bridal headpiece and veil, it's here—or Victoria will make it for you. She creates hats for all seasons, all occasions.

The lightweight slouch hats run about $220, in velvet, silk, organza, or jersey. Victoria's shapes change seasonally, but she works with you to find a shape that flatters your face.

She always has some sort of variation on the derby for about $145, but it's her flirtatious cocktail chapeaus that are the real showstoppers. Victoria outdoes herself with these seductive little confections that run $200 to $400. Each makes a statement, and you most definitely make an entrance wearing one.

In fact, any of Victoria's hats assure that you'll be noticed. Molly Ringwald, Mia Farrow, Phoebe Cates, and Deborah Winger count on them, even if they might be noticed on their own merits. Or maybe they're trying to hide under the hats. If so, the device isn't very successful—these hats are just too good-looking to ignore.

Custom-designed hats take about ten days to two weeks, a little longer for wedding gear, which tends to fall in the $350 to $500 range. Remember, each piece is entirely made by hand right here on Thompson Street. Victoria is a very rare breed indeed, a real old-fashioned milliner.

So it's not surprising she works good old-fashioned long hours. The shop is open Tuesday through Friday, 11:00 A.M. to 7:00 P.M. Weekend hours are noon to 6:00 P.M. both days, except during the summer when she doesn't bother to open at all on Sunday. And she's never open on Mondays.

If Victoria's not in, be sure to ask for her assistant, Kelly Christy. Her second opinion is as good as Victoria's and ever so necessary when it comes to the purchase of hats. We can't conceive of buying a hat without asking someone how it looks. Can you?   ❦

Walter Steiger

739 Madison Avenue   (212) 570-1212
between 64th and 65th Streets
New York, NY 10021

Monday through Saturday, 10:00 A.M. to 6:00 P.M., is the time to shop for soft, sensuous shoes at Walter Steiger. The petite store reflects the luxurious quality of its shoes; sumptuous black leather couches line the gray-carpeted walls. A burgundy lacquered ceiling surveys the rather seductive scene.

Amy Fleischmann is a fountain of shoe knowledge and can direct you to the perfect pair, all designed in Paris by Walter Steiger, crafted in his manufacturing facilities in Italy. He's known for his signature curved heel, but recently has been showing a new cone shape, which we think is terrific.

In any case, Walter Steiger has the best walking shoe in New York, with its one-and-a-half-inch stacked heel that defies destruction. It comes in every color in the rainbow (and then some) for $275. If you want it in lizard or another non-cow skin, it'll cost closer to $400. If crocodile's your choice, you'll have to talk to Amy about the price; like gold, it tends to fluctuate with the market.

The Walter Steiger version of the classic Dorsay pump, cutout on both sides, is available in myriad materials, suitable for a complete day-to-evening shoe wardrobe—from a sturdy leather rendition with the traditional wooden heel to a dainty all-silk moiré number for evening. Prices start at $275 and go up, way up, depending on style and fabric. With clients like Madeline Kahn and Shirley MacLaine, you can be sure that Walter Steiger has employed some of the world's most fabulously extravagant fabrics and skins to execute his popular styles.

While his shoes are available at many fine stores throughout the country, this is the only freestanding Walter Steiger boutique. New York is the one place that you'll find the whole collection, which explains why so many elegant out-of-town ladies drop off their luggage at the nearby Mayfair Regent or Plaza Athénée, then make a beeline for the store. They just can't wait to see what they've been missing.   ❧

Ungaro

803 Madison Avenue   (212) 249-4090
between 67th and 68th Streets
New York, NY 10021

No one, but no one, designs sexy feminine clothes like Emanuel Ungaro.
He is truly the master of the seductive fit, using every trick in the book
to accentuate and define the female body. Ungaro claims to love women.
It shows in his designs.

Considered the master of prints, his silks, especially made for him in
Milan, are extraordinary—for their sophisticated floral patterns and their
bright, radiating colors. But they're not for everyone. We suspect Ungaro
counts few wallflowers among his clientele. Rather, his women are secure, self-confident types, who enjoy making entrances in his statement-
making clothes.

Of course, these days there are plenty of women who fit the Ungaro
profile—women like Marisa Berenson, Morgan Fairchild, Oprah Winfrey, and Joanna Carson. Some even make a habit of collecting his designs, happily and comfortably wearing them for years, secure in the
knowledge that, for them, the feminine approach to dressing is always in
style.

His Madison Avenue boutique, part of what has become a $450 mil-
lion fashion empire, is always busy with browsers and buyers alike.
Charming manager Amy Stein oversees the action, dispensing advice
when asked, but never offering it unsolicited. She knows her clients are
contemporary, decisive women who know what they want. In this case
they want Ungaro's tailored no-nonsense but nonetheless provocative
suits, which start at about $1,600. The wide shoulders and other ele-
ments of the fit do wonders for slimming the waist and hips. His signature dress silhouette with lots of draping or shirring through the bodice is
even more form flattering. Almost liquid in the way they undulate along
womanly curves, they're definitely not for everyone from a figure point of
view. Usually constructed in his famous silk prints, they seldom constitute business attire but are dynamite for ladies' luncheons and cocktails
for $2,000 or thereabouts.

As for evening clothes, think grand, glorious, and about $3,500. Of
course, there's also sportswear by Ungaro—slacks for $500 to $900,
sweaters starting at $600. They bear his distinctive style, but for our

money you're better off sticking with the suits, dresses, and evening gowns since that's where he really excels.

We do, however, have one exception to that edict. Try his Diva perfume at $200 an ounce. Dedicated to the great (and very public) love of his life, French actress Anouk Aimée, it's romantic, seductive, and daring. But then what else would you expect from one of the very few designers whose clothes inspire passion, both literally and figuratively?!

FURS

Alixandre

150 West 30th Street   (212) 736-5550
between 6th and 7th
New York, NY 10001

Alixandre's is a number you should remember, because it's the key to an experience you won't forget. The terra cotta–colored walls and the marble entry welcome you into a lush yet refined showroom carpeted in a deep forest green—a most civilized environment in which to purchase a new fur coat from the Schulman family.

They've been in the fur trade for over seventy-five years. The second generation—brothers Edwin, Stanley, and Jerome—are in charge, backed up by a third generation, Edwin's son Lawrence and Stanley's son Brett. The boys take care of the clients, while their fathers keep tabs on the family's reputation for excellent quality and craftsmanship.

Master artisans, the Schulman brothers leave the designing to virtuosos Valentino and Calvin Klein. The designers sketch their ideas for the collections and work with the Schulmans to perfect the style in muslin, before turning over the execution in fur to the experts.

Valentino's collection is produced in conjunction with his couture operations. Ever the couturier, the master tailor, his eye for detail and proportion is extraordinary, and his furs reflect those qualities. His directional three-quarter golden sable coat is versatility personified at $50,000. It looks smashing over casual slacks or a formal gown. He does the same body in black Russian broadtail for $23,000—simple, elegant, and genteel.

A natural wild mink done skin on skin with a stylish full sweep might run $25,000. It's a bargain, when you consider the $350,000 price tag on a natural Russian lynx. Using only the belly portion of the skin, this coat is almost pure white and light as a feather. Less spectacular, but far more practical for stormy weather, are Valentino's urbane raincoats. One lined with sheared nutria and trimmed in mink sells for $4,900. Trimmed in sable, it's $7,000.

As you might expect, Calvin Klein's collection is sportswear-oriented, providing a dramatic contrast to Valentino's couture look. Klein's fashion takes a minimalist approach. His lines are very simple, very clear. Our favorite Calvin Klein fur is a pea coat done in natural lunaraine mink. It's easily thrown over any outfit—chic, timeless, and classic, it's only $11,500. Another classic is the sheared mink balmacaan coat with ragland sleeve and notched collar with a soft, easy back for $15,000. As for sable, Klein uses one of the noblest varieties, the natural wild Barguzine from Russia, for a full-length coat with generously wide sweep and broad shoulder for $140,000.

The best time to review the Alixandre collections is about the second or third week in May, during the traditional fur shows for the new fall season. That's when Alixandre's limited, very exclusive clientele are solicited. So if you get an invitation, consider yourself special and join the ranks of Jane Seymour, Marlo Thomas, and Cathy Lee Crosby. Typical Alixandre clients, they are glamorous and knowledgeable about fashion without being contrived. Their greatest interest in fur is quality. And at Alixandre, they know they'll get it. As Lawrence Schulman says proudly, "we're concerned about producing the finest." Indeed, their commitment to quality so impressed Carolyne Roehm that she just signed her first fur-licensing agreement with Alixandre. And we all know that Mrs. Henry Kravis demands the very best.   🐾

Dennis Basso Couture

352 Seventh Avenue   (212) 564-9560
between 29th and 30th Streets
9th Floor
New York, NY 10001

No matter how many you've bought in the past, no matter how knowledgeable you think you are, when it comes to investing in furs you are at the mercy of the furrier. It's like buying fine jewelry or soliciting the advice of a doctor or lawyer—somehow you feel you're at a disadvantage. Enter Dennis Basso, with the immediate bond of trust he establishes, his exuberant warmth, his obvious enthusiasm for his craft.

At thirty-five, in business barely six years, he has built an enviable reputation as furrier to the jet set. He claims his success with that discerning crowd is due to the fact that he is one of its members and thus understands how to satisfy their needs. Judging by the number of times his name or picture appears in the society pages, his claim is credible, though with all that cavorting, we wonder where he finds time to design his flamboyant hundred-piece collections!

But design them he does and for the likes of Barbara Walters, Ivana Trump, Jaclyn Smith, Neil Sedaka, Joanna Carson, and that chronicler of the rich and famous himself, Robin Leach. In addition to patronizing their "pal," they are attracted to the excellent quality of fur Dennis uses and to the fashionable flair he confers upon his creations. Dennis believes that a fur has to work with a woman's (or man's) wardrobe. So he follows the fashion pages faithfully. According to him, "a fur is only good if you use it. Wearing a fur only for special occasions is a philosophy lost in the forties."

If your idea of a versatile coat is a simple mink, Dennis can oblige you with a little something in the $6,000 to $10,000 range. But Dennis Basso Couture is best represented by Dennis's more creative designs, like a wild mink coat, with a full body and a flounce at the knee, where the skins are worked on the diagonal. With a turned-back cuff and a stand-up cross-cut collar, it costs about $9,500.

Then there's a fisher coat done in polo style with a low-notch collar, kick pleat, and belted back for $25,000. For fun and a mere $5,500, you might like the seven-eighth double-breasted jacket in sheared muskrat with Persian lamb capelet and turned-back cuffs.

For serious money, $60,000 to $100,000, try luxuriating in the ultimate fur—natural Russian sable. And if none of the styles quite suits your fancy, Dennis will design a piece to your most demanding specifications.

Whatever your inclination, fashion fur or classic, be sure to call first. Dennis Basso Couture is open Monday through Friday, but only by appointment.

Galanos Furs
Yarmuth-Dion, Inc.

345 Seventh Avenue

(212) 563-4611, 4612

between 29th and 30th Streets
New York, NY 10018

We're going to go out on a limb here and state unequivocally that we think Jimmy Galanos is this country's best designer. Consequently, we think anything he's associated with is destined to be special, including his furs produced by Yarmuth-Dion—actually, especially his furs. It's a winning combination—Galanos designs executed by master furrier Peter Dion, who's been in the business for just over forty years and associated with Jimmy for the last eight.

At Yarmuth-Dion, the Galanos touch extends to the showroom, designed by Jimmy. With its marble floors, mirrored walls, and black lacquer tables, it reeks of classy style. It's the sort of place where Jimmy's fans like Nancy Reagan, Iris Cantor, Elaine Goldsmith and Diana Ross feel comfortably at home as they select their investment-quality furs.

The value starts with the skins, absolutely the best. Peter travels to Russia three times a year to handpick gorgeous sable, broadtail, and lynx skins. The difference his efforts make is readily apparent when you get a gander at the spectacular Galanos cocktail suit made of very fine, very flat Russian broadtail. The skirt is topped by a short jacket accented by hand-beaded embroidery. We've never seen anything like it—it's a $30,000 knockout.

But not the only one. We saw a glorious three-quarter-length broadtail jacket with a tucked and shirred sleeve that is another showstopper at $18,000. Our confusion about what we really liked best was compounded when we discovered the *full-length* broadtail coat with the natural Barguzine sable collar for $40,000.

Our indecision, not to mention our respect for Jimmy's talent and Peter's craftmanship, increased tenfold when we were presented with an incredible Black Onyx seven-eighths swing jacket with a tuxedo collar. All the pelts are worked horizontally. It looks like velvet, feels like silk, and sells for $18,000. By the way, Black Onyx is a very special strain of mink, exclusive to Peter Dion. They are fed a steady diet of calf's liver, which makes the pelts shinier, silkier, and smoother. A street-length classic in Black Onyx—raglan shoulder with a horizontal and narrow shawl collar—will set you back $22,000.

And then the ultimate—Jimmy's $125,000 natural Russian sable coat with a stand-up yoked collar and a full swing. "Breathtaking" doesn't do this coat justice. No wonder Jimmy's furs are sold only in such exclusive stores as Bergdorf Goodman, Saks Fifth Avenue, and I. Magnin.

In addition to the Galanos furs, Peter is responsible for the Yarmuth-Dion line, a bit trendier than Jimmy's. They're made, Peter freely admits, of skins that are not quite as fine as those used for Galanos. Still, Peter selects them himself for labels that read I. Magnin, Saks, and Nordstroms, so you know they're good. And a client can always request superior quality skins on a special order.

His line includes a great-looking street-length Blackglama mink coat for $12,500. He also works a lot with fox—Golden Island, Silver, and Cross. Beautiful skins that shed very little (remember, the better the skins, the less they shed), they make timeless yet exciting coats that sell for about $8,000.

The Yarmuth-Dion line comes in all sizes up to twenty. But to wrap up in a Galanos fur, a lady has to be in the six to twelve size range. Whatever the size, though, a fur should be stored during the summer and Peter is happy to accommodate. If Peter's not available, ask for Harriet Dion. Soft-spoken and gracious, Harriet is the person to call for a private appointment and to cajole into an invitation to the annual June show.

She'll also direct you to a wonderful resource if you want a hat to go with your new coat—Lenore Marshall at 235 West 29th Street. Take your coat over and work with Lenore to decide on a style that will complement it and you. Then she'll call Peter to order the number of matching skins she needs. *Et voilà!* You'll be warm and glamorous from hem to head. ❧

J. Mendel

691 Fifth Avenue   (212) 546-0240
between 54th and 55th
New York, NY 10022

There's another reason to visit Elizabeth Arden besides the pursuit of beauty—the J. Mendel Fur salon on the second floor. Presided over by Gilles Mendel, scion of a family that's been in the trade for five generations, it's a fur salon with a difference.

Certainly they're in the business of selling furs, beautiful coats and jackets designed by Gilles, who has a knack for working fur like fabric, draping it, plaiting it, creating designs and mosaics. He's also a designer who delights in mix and match combos—like cashmere and fur. We love the tobacco colored cashmere trenchcoat with wild mink notched collar and cuffs at $4,500. For all-out flirtatious glamor the hip-length green/gray cashmere swing cape, belted at the waist and trimmed with sheared muskrat, is tough to beat. Somehow it's both casual and elegant for $3,800, just as good with jeans as with evening pajamas.

As for all-fur furs, J. Mendel's are exceptional, benefitting from the familial collaboration between Gilles and his father, who oversees the family's European operations. Working out of his Paris atelier, Jacques Mendel is one of the continent's most respected furriers. Together, combining the wisdom of experience and the excitement of youth, the master furrier and the designer create works of art in fur like the trapeze swing coat of the finest Barguzine Russian sable with shawl collar and large turned-backed cuffs. The skins are assembled on the diagonal, forming a pattern that can best be described by likening it to a beautifully burnished parquet floor—a $90,000 masterpiece. Less dramatic, but even more fun, is the sheared mink pea jacket accented with a double row of glowing brass buttons. Available in navy, red, or black it sells for $12,000.

What really sets J. Mendel apart is the firm's interest in reworking furs. Of course, most furriers will lengthen or shorten a hem, add a cuff, or alter a collar. But we don't know of any other that will take a coat apart, adding, subtracting, or rearranging skins to dramatically redefine its whole look. Gilles calls it metamorphosis and he's a master at it with an international reputation.

Mrs. Alan Bond, the wife of the Australian corporate raider, heard about his work from a friend. Without ever having met him or having visited any of the J. Mendel salons, she sent her chinchilla coat to Gilles in New York. The accompanying note explained that while it was virtually brand new, she thought it had a somewhat dated look—it wasn't as bold or as dramatic as she would like. She had taken it to a number of furriers in Australia, but none would touch it. They didn't want to take the responsibility. Could or would Gilles do anything with it?

Used to such requests and stimulated by the challenges they present, Gilles was delighted to accommodate her. After inspecting the coat and noting the superior skins used in its construction, Gilles sketched several solutions to Mrs. Bond's problem. He sent her choices for the front and back of the coat, along with estimates of the cost to purchase matching skins and the labor involved in the metamorphosis of the coat. Thrilled with Gilles' suggestions she selected a version that would add considerably to the volume of the coat, both front and back, and involve the addition of a yoke on the back. As a result, Mrs. Bond now has a coat she delights in wearing, one that is now even more valuable than it was when she first sent it to Gilles.

Naturally, work of such magnitude does not come cheap, and not everyone has a fabulous chinchilla to work with in the first place. But for relatively modest sums, Gilles can take your mother's old dried out Persian lamb coat or dog-eared mink jacket that's been taking up room in the closet and do wonders with it. The lamb could wind up as the luxurious accent trim to a new cashmere coat made just for you, while the mink could be the lining, collar, and cuffs of an excitingly stylish leather blouson jacket. It's up to your budget and Gilles' imagination.

Intrigued with the notion, but no plans to visit New York any time soon (even though you're reading this book)? Do what Mrs. Bond did. Send Gilles the fur you want reworked. He'll do for you just what he did for her—in fact he does it all the time. He'll send you sketches and estimates. And, of course, you can always call to discuss them.

Should you opt to stop by (after all you might get some ideas from pouring through Gilles' current collections), don't fret if Gilles isn't in. Speak to Julio, who's as knowledgeable as he is handsome. Though he's not a designer, he's been in the business longer than you might imagine by looking at him. He can give you some idea of what's possible and what isn't. Trust your coat to him. He'll make sure Gilles gets it, and you'll be reviewing sketches in no time at all. ❧

Laurence Kaye Furs

345 Seventh Avenue   (212) 695-8340
between 29th and 30th Streets
21st Floor
New York, NY 10001

The soft gray tones of Laurence Kaye's showroom set the stage for two remarkable, yet wildly different, collections of furs—the sophisticated, elegantly refined designs of French couturier Hubert de Givenchy and the sporty fur-and-fabric potpourri creations by American designer Kip

Kirkendall. Both designers take a hands-on approach to their collections, personally working with third-generation furriers Sy Schreibman and Paul Raphael, the owners of Laurence Kaye.

Givenchy's adherence to the principles of classic taste is apparent in his black-dyed karakul lamb jacket. Beautifully proportioned, it is semi-fitted with a blouse-like sleeve—great with slacks, skirt, or dinner dress for $3,950. In the versatile jacket category, we also liked the natural wild mink, fingertip-length version, buttoned down the front and selling for $7,500.

For more formal looks, there's a marvelous seven-eighths coat with all the natural heather lunaraine mink pelts worked diagonally. Longer in the back than the front and sporting a luxurious full sweep, it'll cost you about $10,000. For exquisite Russian sables, you're talking around $75,000, and if Russian lynx is your fantasy fur, plan on spending something in the low six-figure neighborhood.

Kip Kirkendall's innovative designs, which she describes as "living furs," provide a dramatic contrast to Givenchy's sublime creations. Kip's work is anything but subtle or traditional. Her furs demand attention; they are self-conscious showstoppers, veritable stews of fur and fabric, festooned with stones or beads. She combines fur with handwoven fabrics, with leathers, cashmere, or mohair. She's been known to lace a coat with silver bullion thread or stud it with Venetian glass beads, raw Colombian emeralds, or Austrian crystals. Kip's look is totally her own—fashion forward, yet reminiscent of thirties glamour.

Indeed, we think some of her work can be classified as wearable art, like the $2,000 reversible hip-length lamb jacket accented by antique buttons and trimmed with an intricately stenciled suede. Then there's the full-length shirred fox in sapphire blue with a very pretty and unusual gathered sleeve for about $5,500. Typical of Kip, it's worked to look as much like fabric as fur.

But our favorite is the seven-eighth broadtail and mahogany mink coat beaded with onyx, topaz, and garnets. Despite the stones, the coat isn't too flashy for daytime use. She uses the jewels to accessorize the fur, like a great-looking pair of earrings. Fashioned as an expansive swing coat with a drop shoulder and a very soft sleeve, it sells for $6,000.

Janet Kaye is the person to discuss either collection. She'll make an appointment for you at the showrooms or tell you where you can find the furs in your hometown. On the West Coast, look for Givenchy at I. Magnin or Montaldos. In Philadelphia you'll find his furs at Nan Duskin, and in Palm Beach at Sara Fredericks. As for Kip's designs, check out

Neiman Marcus and Saks Fifth Avenue. And ask about her outrageously extravagant fur blankets from $2,000 to $12,000. ❧

FOR MEN AND WOMEN

Barneys New York

106 Seventh Avenue	(212) 929-9000
at 17th Street	
New York, NY 10011	

Barneys New York may be the official title, but for 65 years it's been just plain "Barney's" to New Yorkers who enthusiastically embrace its unique formula of diversity, value, quality, and service. Now, the self-described "largest specialty store in the world" (as opposed, we suppose, to Macys, the world's largest department store) is poised to conquer the nation. The first three Barneys New York stores outside Manhattan opened in the Fall of 1989, and the strategy calls for as many as 30 nationwide by the mid '90s, ambitious plans for an organization that until 1988 had essentially one location. But then what would you expect from the enterprising Pressman family, who have parlayed a $500 investment into a $100 million-plus business?

It all started in 1923, when at his wife's suggestion, Barney Pressman pawned her engagement ring for $500 to cover the cost of renting a space on lower Seventh Avenue and stocking his first 40 suits. He quickly established a reputation for providing quality clothing and service, despite a discount pricing policy. Today, the shop that Barney built houses an inventory of more than 30,000 suits and employs over 1,000 people, including 150 in-house tailors. And it is decidedly no longer discount oriented.

Under the leadership of Barney's son Fred, his wife, Phyllis, their two daughters and two sons, along with the boys' wives (we did say it was a family business), Barneys has moved into the ranks of the upscale—skirmishing with Bergdorfs and Saks over designer exclusives, while developing a somewhat avant-garde or cutting-edge attitude. In the process it has expanded its dedication to men's clothing and furnishings to include boys' wear, gifts, silver, china, antiques, jewelry, and women's clothes and accessories. And in fact, in 1986, Barneys transformed six turn-of-the-century brownstones adjacent to the men's store into a

70,000-square-foot store for women. The entire physical plant of Barneys New York, now and forever the flagship of the soon-to-be national chain, has become a staggering 170,000 square feet—some specialty store!

Inspired by the Parisian department stores of the early 1900s, the women's emporium is classic yet modern. A sky-lit atrium with a sweeping marble stairway forms the nucleus of the interior. Each floor encircling the staircase reflects the character of its merchandise in an elegantly intimate setting. And each of the six floors benefits from the natural light provided by the brownstones' original windows, as well as Art Deco and Wiener Werkstaette pieces along with custom fixtures crafted in Europe.

There are a number of new departments in the women's areas— lingerie, cosmetics, and two floors devoted to clothing for the professional woman. (Interestingly enough, the entire wardrobe for the hit film *Working Girl* was purchased here, and Diane Keaton's clothes for *Baby Boom* hailed from Barneys.) But, you don't have to carry proof of your "ladies-who-lunch" status to venture to the upper floors sporting names like Beene, Valentino, Montana, Lagerfeld, Mugler, and Edelstein. But healthy bank balances or unlimited credit are helpful. Prices are indeed special, creeping into five figures in some instances. On the other hand, the "professional" clothes, some 50 percent of which are exclusive to Barneys, are as well-priced as they are diverse—Anne Klein II, Mary Ann Restivo, Ralph Lauren, Calvin Klein, Albert Nippon, Ronaldo Shamask, Christian Dior, Byblos, and Charlotte Neuville to name just a few.

Professional or not, you can take advantage of the personal shopping expertise of the divine Louise Maniscalco. If you're more of a do-it-yourselfer, you'll do it better here than in most stores with such a large selection. The salespeople can travel with you, gathering merchandise along the way for you to try on all at once. In fact they're so accommodating that once you're in the dressing room, they'll send down for the proper shoes for each outfit if you desire.

If you're a bargain hunter but not trouper enough to endure the indignities of most operations regularly offering that elusive commodity, head for Barneys CO/OP. It's a complete store, part of the total complex just past the women's regions, featuring the best in contemporary clothing for women—cosmetics, shoes, accessories, and activewear, as well as sportswear from the likes of Basco, Kenzo, Yohji Yamamoto, Norma Kamali, and Matsuda. Prices stay under the $500 level here, but the collections are just as tightly edited as they are in the rest of the store. Barneys knows its female customer—women like Christie Brinkley, Cher, and Sigourney Weaver—whether they're in the market for $25 leggings from Barton G. or a $9,000 Victor Edelstein evening gown.

Of course, Barneys is equally well acquainted with its male clientele. After all, they built the business in the first place (as the world's largest *men's* store, Barneys had nothing to do with women until it added a *department* in 1976). Originally dependent upon American manufacturers' close-outs, Barneys expanded its purchasing horizons, not to mention pricing policy, and in 1968 became the first men's store to feature European designers. Five floors were designated "international" encompassing the city's most complete selection of designer men's fashion.

In 1976, Barneys introduced the designs of Giorgio Armani to America, demonstrating its on-going commitment to discovering and developing new, innovative talent. Today, that policy means Barneys carries $450 sportcoats by Byblos, $250 sweaters by Romeo Gigli, and $1,000 suits by Comme des Garçons. For more traditional tastes, much of the second floor is filled with clothing of the reliable British variety—suits, double and single breasted, by Gieves & Hawkes and Oxford. The bespoken suitings of H. Huntsman & Sons and Kilgour, French & Stanley are also represented.

Made-to-measure shirts in the $80 to $140 range are just one example of the American furnishings that occupy the main floor. Rainwear, outerwear, and the boys' department fill the lower level, as well as Le Café serving breakfast, lunch, tea, dinner, and Sunday brunch. While we wouldn't necessarily make a special trip just to dine here, the charming garden setting does provide a pleasant respite from the rigors of shopping. And the kitchen serves food far superior to that of most *department* stores—we can't think of a single specialty store kitchen to compare with it!   ❦

Bergdorf Goodman

754 Fifth Avenue   (212) 753-7300
between 57th and 58th
New York, NY 10019

It's difficult to fathom these days, but only a few years ago Bergdorf Goodman was in trouble. Smart money was betting that the stately store was as much an anachronism as the carriage trade it had served so well since 1901. Smarter money, that of the Carter Hawley Hale Stores, thought otherwise and purchased the store from founder Edwin Goodman's heirs in 1972. The retail giant brought in a new management team and committed $15 million to a facelift. The store's newly plush interior, with its rediscovered sweeping Central Park vistas from long-hidden windows, was nice. But it was the management team that would make the difference for Bergdorf's and set the tone for its current domination of fashion excitement in New York.

In 1975, Carter Hawley Hale chairman Philip Hawley hired Ira Neimark for his new Bergdorf's team. He in turn brought Dawn Mello into the fold. And for a good long run they were chairman and president respectively. Together they transformed the once haughty Bergdorf's—the private preserve of New York's wealthiest women seeking safe, conservative designs—into a store dedicated to presenting the newest fashion trends to a clientele that includes the ladies who work as well as those who lunch. With its commitment to providing featured designers with generous space, attention and exposure, adoption by Bergdorf's is every fledgling designer's dream.

As fashion director (until she recently jumped ship to work her magic at Gucci), Dawn demonstrated infallible taste reminiscent of Edwin Goodman who built Bergdorf's reputation for excellence. Edwin entered the field of women's tailoring in 1899 at the age of 23 as an apprentice in the firm of Bergdorf and Voight. When Mr. Voight died two years later, Edwin became a partner in the new firm of Bergdorf Goodman. Buoyed by Edwin's flair for fashion and his insistence on impeccable workmanship, the firm's business flourished, enabling him to buy out Mr. Bergdorf upon his retirement. Under Edwin's sole leadership, business continued to grow, with the city's leading socialites becoming frequent visitors to the store's sumptuous West 32nd Street quarters, which resembled those of the great couture houses of Paris.

By 1914, Edwin was in need of more space for Bergdorf Goodman. He moved the store to 616 Fifth Avenue, where the entrance to the Rockefeller Center Gardens is located today. But another move to even larger quarters was still to come. When Edwin heard the great Vanderbilt mansion on the corner of Fifth and 58th was to be razed, he determined that its site overlooking the beautiful fountain of the Pulitzer Plaza and Central Park beyond was perfect for Bergdorf's future and final home. The building now occupied by the store was completed in 1928.

Actually, there is one more move ahead for Bergdorf's, or more accurately for a portion of it—the men's departments are about to become The Men's Store, across the street in the former FAO Schwartz location. Scheduled for a Fall 1990 opening, you can bet Bergdorf's new annex will be gunning for Barneys. As it is, men are far from second-class citizens. The 57th Street entrance is one they can call their own, as it spills into the men's sportswear area featuring Perry Ellis, Valentino, and marvelous sweaters by Joseph Aboud.

Furnishings and suits are on the second floor—Turnbull and Asser for shirts, Charvet for ties. Predictably with Bergdorf's fashion-forward attitude, suits seem to be heavy on the Italians, lots of Armani and Ferrer. To Boot offers a small shoe boutique, and Sentimento has an outstanding collection of antique cufflinks. Still, space-wise, men have somewhat of a step-child status at Bergdorf's. But the new store, with its three selling floors, is about to change all that—there'll be more room for more designers to be better represented.

Meanwhile, women will continue to take advantage of Bergdorf's philosophy of showing complete, though carefully edited, collections, rather than just a few pieces here and there. A number of the best American and European designers have entire boutiques within the store—Calvin Klein, Donna Karan, Geoffrey Beene, Ralph Lauren, Galanos, and Carolyne Roehm represent the Americans. From across the Atlantic, Bergdorf's features St. Laurent, Chanel, Ungaro, Ferre, Armani, Valentino, Krizia, Gaultier, and Montana. But there's nothing carved in stone about the list. Ira Neimark claims, "It is not so much what we have as it is what we don't carry, because of what Dawn Mello won't let in the store." A mediocre to bad collection or two and a formerly favored designer can find him or herself out of Bergdorf's good graces. St. Laurent and Montana have only recently been reestablished within the store.

While fashion is the driving force at Bergdorf's, it's not just clothing fashion. The seventh floor presents an eclectic host of fashionable treasures for the home. There's an antique shop supplied by its parent emporium from Kentshire, England. The best of Frette and Pratesi line the shelves of the linen department. Exquisite crystal and china sparkle here too, casting pretty patterns on the selection of contemporary gifts. And the Etro shop invites you to browse through its lovely collection of Italian stationery and desk accessories covered in beautiful fabrics.

Café Vienna beckons as well for lunch, tea, or a light snack. But the more popular meeting and eating spot seems to be Pasta and Cheese two floors below on five. The name says most of it, but don't discount the truly superior salads and be prepared to wait in the perennial line.

Of course, though shopping at Bergdorf's is considerably more civilized than at some stores, you still might want to take advantage of the personal shopping service offered by Mary Kavanagh and her staff. They work by appointment and will either gather merchandise for your review or guide you through the store. But, once you've ensconced yourself as a regular client, you can call Mary with a description of your needs and she'll have an appropriate selection of merchandise sent to your hotel, office, or home.

As talented as Mary is, we never use her service when we're in the market for accessories here. It's just too much fun strolling through the spectacular array on the main floor—you find whole collections of bags, belts, scarves, and jewelry from the likes of Paloma Picasso, Chanel, and Donna Karan. Here too you find some of Bergdorf's famous exclusives. The stylish designs of Frances Patiky Stein are found nowhere else in New York. Every time you spot the ubiquitous Chanel bag, you're seeking another example of her work as she's been the design genius behind that house's accessories for years—she launched her own label two years ago.

The unique jewelry of Barry Kieselstein-Cord is another exclusive knock-out here. His stunning signature muted gold pieces have a vaguely medieval yet distinctly contemporary look. Barry has a flair for setting precious and semi-precious stones to their best advantage, and his sterling belt buckles have become intrinsic to any truly chic wardrobe. As you consider how your credit cards will react to the attempted purchase of the gold necklace of large rectangular links studded with emeralds, you might run into Barry's much photographed wife, muse, and business partner, Cece.

But she's only one of the rich, famous, and beautiful you might find yourself standing next to at Bergdorf's. Candice Bergen strolls over from her Central Park South aerie. Cher stops in as do Anne Bass, Anne Johnson, and Nan Kempner. And Sarah Brightman spent almost as much time here as she did at the theater during her star turn in husband Andrew Lloyd Webber's *Phantom of the Opera*.

Obviously, it's not difficult to spend a fortune here and many happily do so. But Bergdorf's can be enjoyed without spending a dime. Consider it an exhibit of much of the best the world has to offer, displayed in luxurious surroundings. Wandering through Bergdorf's can be an educational, and free, experience. 🐛

Billy Martin Western Classics

812 Madison Avenue   (212) 861-3100
at 68th Street
New York, NY 10021

Boots? You say you want boots? Well, just drag those poor tired ol' dogs of yours to Billy Martin's to perk 'em up with the best selection of Western boots this side of Texas. Actually, it may be better than anything they have in any one place in Texas; Billy Martin commissions special designs from bootmakers all over the Lone Star State.

Sophisticated and stylish yet decidedly Western, the boots here are anything but prosaic. The same goes for the clientele—Bruce Springsteen, Linda Gray, Elizabeth Taylor, and Goldie Hawn come here to satisfy their cowboy fantasies. General manager Larry DeGray works with them to pick just the right heel, the perfect toe. He will also arrange for a custom-made number if perchance there is nothing here that quite suits.

But that's most unlikely. This down-home store is chock-full of boots in every fabrication you can possibly envision—from calfskin for about $195 to alligator or lizard at $2,500, and everything in between. Have a hankering for ostrich skin, or hippo, or elephant? Billy Martin has it, along with an appropriately Western assortment of belts and belt buckles. The sterling silver buckles made by artists hailing from Santa Fe are particularly striking.

Whether riding your favorite horse, dancing at your favorite club, or making a fashion statement is your goal, Billy Martin has the boot of your dreams. 🐛

Bloomingdale's

1000 Third Avenue   (212) 705-2000
New York, NY 10022

Self-proclaimed as the most famous store in the world, Bloomingdale's is that and more—much more. In fact, it's ten floors and one city square block of more. And all of it is a far cry, literally and figuratively, from the tiny "Bloomingdale's Hoop Skirt and Ladies' Notion Shop" that brothers

Joseph and Lyman opened in the late 1860s. But almost from the beginning, the brothers Bloomingdale demonstrated a daring retailing style incorporating constant change that would become the Bloomingdale's trademark.

Their first store took advantage of the rage for the hoop skirt ignited by Empress Eugenie. As that craze faded, they opened the East Side Bazaar, offering a wide variety of ladies fashion—a bold move in an era of very specialized shops. In the 1880s, as the popularity for bicycling made the fashionable bustle impractical, the Bloomingdale boys were among the first to recognize the fact and adapt their styles accordingly. And by 1886, they changed the face of retailing forever, opening their new store at 59th and Third. Always the pioneer, Bloomingdale's stood alone on the muddy field punctuated by tenements and railroad tracks that was then the Upper East Side—all other stores were below 34th Street. But Joseph and Lyman attracted shoppers—brought by their use of the latest technology, plate glass and cast iron, to create large open spaces brightened by natural light and filled with a vast array of merchandise. They were enticed by innovative window displays, themed rather than crammed with a potpourri of products that was the custom of the day. Joseph and Lyman supported their windows' themes with special promotions inside the store—the forerunner of today's famous country and state promotions.

Business was good, very good. And Bloomingdale's embarked on an expansion program. By 1929, it had acquired the entire block it occupies today. But it was the 60s and 70s that really put Bloomingdale's on the world map. The country themes and other promotions were so lavish, so exciting that there was an air of theatricality about the store. It became "Bloomies," a destination, a place to go, a Saturday afternoon diversion, an adventure—so much more than just a store. Indeed, rumor had it that Bloomingdale's was New York's second biggest tourist attraction after the Statue of Liberty. The store was always mobbed.

It still is, and frankly we find it a little overwhelming. All those people with all those accents (foreign and otherwise) and all that attitude. The only way to cope is to retreat periodically to one of Bloomingdale's five restaurants to get away from the maddening crowds. Our favorite is the sixth floor's Le Train Bleu, evoking the tranquil, romantic atmosphere of a 19th-century dining car. On Saturdays, the restaurant serves an elegant champagne brunch starting at 11 A.M. A full luncheon menu and cocktails are available from noon every day, except Sunday when Le Train Bleu is closed. Afternoons, from 3:30 to 5:00 P.M., you can pop in for a light snack, and supper is served until 7:30 P.M. on Mondays and Thursdays when the store is open until 9:00 P.M.

For more casual dining there's 40 Carats, featuring food on the self-consciously healthy side—creative salads, vegetable casseroles, and frozen yogurt. Then there's the Showtime Café on the seventh floor, with its cafeteria style, albeit rather elegant, service. As if all that weren't enough, Bloomingdale's boasts an Espresso Bar, a continental-style coffee and wine bar that also sells delicious muffins and croissants fresh from the store's bakeries. The Tasting Bar, with its selection of inventive soups, salads, and sandwiches, completes the Bloomie's dining scene, but not the food story here.

There's a whole food department, which puts many so-called gourmet stores to shame. The collection of delicacies, both foreign and domestic, is huge—106 different coffees alone are available, along with innumerable vinegars and oils laced with every conceivable flavor. Bloomies-made baked goods and candies abound as do freshly prepared entrées that require only the warming touch of the microwave to captivate the palate. Like every other department, it is an embarrassment of riches.

Indeed, we find the only way to shop the store sensibly is to let someone else do it for us. When we're in the market for a couple of wedding gifts, a powder room overhaul, or a getaway weekend wardrobe we head straight for the fourth floor and At Your Service. Director June Selig and manager Ivy Booksin oversee a platoon of personal shoppers, dedicated to ferreting out just what you're looking for, even if you're not quite sure what it is. They'll cover the whole store from housewares to furs, selecting appropriate items along the way. Then they'll set you up in a spacious dressing room where you can review the loot in leisurely privacy. Sip some coffee or tea while you sort through it all—enjoy a light lunch while you're at it. Indeed, spend the whole day.

For truly special Bloomies' assignments, however, we've come to rely on Hope Golden at Hope's Corner. She accomplishes personal shopping miracles, like getting the buttons changed on the otherwise divine Ungaro suit or accessorizing to perfection that stunning Oscar de la Renta gown. Call her directly at extension 3375.

Gentlemen, don't despair, Bloomingdale's is also equipped to handle your needs with At His Service. Run by Frank Levandoski, this department does it all—from putting together a wardrobe for a young buck about to take Wall Street by storm to keeping track of special occasions for an older buck's wife or girlfriend (or both). Frank keeps extensive files on birthdays and anniversaries. One call to him at extension 3030 and Frank will make sure the right gift in the right size will go to the right person to celebrate the right occasion.

Our final tip for coping with the Bloomingdale's experience is to check into the Estée Lauder spa. You can take a mini-vacation here by indulging in the Day of Beauty—5½ hours of pampering for $175, including manicure, pedicure, body massage, facial, makeup lesson, and application, not to mention lunch. Even if you don't have that kind of time, you can take advantage of this oasis of calm in a sea of madness by dashing in for any one of those services.

In all fairness, though, we should note that rah-rah days of retailing are over. Under the continually inspired stewardship of Chairman Marvin Traub, Bloomingdale's has taken up the banner of the late eighties—it is, these days, a kinder, gentler store with a renewed concern for the customer, and service. So the sales staff numbers almost 2,000 and the store has been reconfigured to make shopping easier, more comfortable. Each fashion floor offers accessories that complement its merchandise. Consequently, if you're buying a Chanel suit on the 4th Floor you can be secure in the knowledge that just the right shoes, handbags, hats, scarves, and jewelry (Chanel and otherwise) are within only a stone's toss away.

So Bloomingdale's continues to adapt, to evolve just as it has for over a century. The store that discovered Ralph Lauren, Perry Ellis, and Norma Kamali continues to seek up-and-coming designers. It's brought Sonia Rykiel, Kenzo, and Fendi ready-to-wear to America, and Bloomingdale's continues to shop the world for incredible variety. You can spend as little as $1.25 on a muffin (lemon, zucchini, pumpkin, cinnamon, apple, blueberry, or even chocolate) or untold sums on fine jewelry. And the whole scene, driven as it is by Marvin Traub's self-described "daredevil approach to merchandising, display and advertising," continues to titillate even those whom you might expect to be somewhat jaded—the likes of Jackie Onassis, Liza Minnelli, Diana Ross, Isabella Rossellini, even Queen Elizabeth. They have all been intrigued by the institution that is Bloomingdale's.

Bottega Veneta

635 Madison Avenue   (212) 371-5511
between 59th and 60th Streets
New York, NY 10022

It's so refreshing—an upscale European emporium of leather goods and accessories that doesn't believe in splashing its initials all over the merchandise. Bottega Veneta feels your own initials, if you are so inclined, will suffice as testimony to your good taste and the size of your bank account.

They've built their twenty-five-year-old business around connoisseurs of quality, subtlety, and elegance. Born in Northern Italy, the company began with handbags, briefcases, and luggage. Bowing to retailing trends, they've expanded to large, luminous, exotically printed scarves, a selection of unusually good-looking ties, classic mix-and-match sportswear separates for men and women, and in the head-to-toe mode, shoes too.

As a further sign of the times, they've even branched out from their leather roots in the handbag and luggage arena with a new line—vinyl and leather called Marco Polo. A large soft-sided thirty-nine-inch suitcase costs about $600. If you want to make a real statement while traveling, go for the massive $6,000 steamer trunk. Should you suffer a serious reversal in your fortunes, you can always live in it!

Their latest line of all-leather luggage is made of dark brown calfskin and starts at about $800. More practical than you might imagine, it's a great complement to the Bottega Veneta trademark, woven leather handbags. You've seen it a thousand times (and probably spent some time surreptitiously searching for some identifying initials); the pencil-thin strips of lambskin are intricately interlaced to assume the look of a basket weave. The bags are all made by hand in the company's factory in Vicenza and are priced from $300 to over $1,000. Bottega Veneta also makes divine crocodile, lizard, and ostrich bags, with prices that are best described as "on request"!

The New York store is the company's flagship and the largest of the seventeen outlets in the U.S., Europe, and the Far East. The entire collection is showcased here. However, even in this light and airy space, not everything can be displayed. So if you see something that strikes your fancy, but the color doesn't quite suit, be sure to ask. Manager Alberto Cassola will find it for you, either from stock or from one of the other stores.

If he's busy working with regulars like Harrison Ford, Donald Sutherland, Bette Midler, Steve Martin, Diana Ross, or Glenn Close, look for Nina Kleinschmidt or Kimberly Formato. They're just as knowledgeable as Peggy and are whizzes, too, at putting together that very special order.

🍒

Burberry's

9 East 57th Street　　　　　　　　　　　(212) 371-5010
between 5th and Madison　　　　　　　　(800) 284-8480
New York, NY 10022

Okay, so you probably figured some guy named Burberry invented the raincoat favored by yuppies and other dressed-for-success types. But we bet you had no idea that Thomas Burberry was, even more importantly, the inventor of waterproof clothing. Born and bred in mid-19th century rural England, he noticed that shepherds' gear seemed to keep them comfortable in the region's often wet weather. Upon closer inspection, he realized the close weave kept the moisture out.

Armed with this knowledge and his natural bent for improvement, he set about experimenting with the weave using other fabrics, especially cotton. The result was his invention of gabardine—a waterproof fabric that is cool and comfortable because air passes through it. Burberry's coats made of gabardine were a vast improvement over their chief rival, the hot, rubber-lined mackintosh. By 1888, Burberry had developed a loyal clientele, many of whom were avid sportsmen like himself. He was advertising hunting and fishing garments as well as clothing "suitable for India and the Colonies." He also sold tennis, golf, and archery wear.

In 1899, with the help of his two sons, he moved the business to London and began to wholesale his wares to retailers throughout England. Still, for the longest time, there was no real name for his best-selling coat, which Burberry simply described as a "slip-on." It was left to King Edward VII to name the garment. He would say, "Get me my Burberry" when he wanted his favorite coat. The appellation caught on throughout his kingdom and, eventually, the world.

But it wasn't until World War I that Burberry created his signature piece—the trenchcoat. At the onset of the war, Burberry designed a new variation of his gabardine coat and proposed it as part of an officer's formal uniform. It was especially produced to deal with the conditions of trench warfare. Today, as the trademark of such stars as Alan Ladd and

Humphrey Bogart, it has become a universally recognized symbol of adventure, drama, and intrigue.

Despite America's love affair with the trenchcoat, Burberry, a public company since 1920, didn't stake out any U.S. territory until 1978, when Barry Goldsmith opened the New York store. While there are now 12 others across the country, the New York store remains the largest, with four floors of selling space.

The first floor of this little bit of country house Britain, so lovingly tended by Barry, houses men's furnishings—shirts, ties, and sweaters. The shirts have that distinctive Burberry point of view, particularly those with wide, bold stripes and white collar and cuffs for $60. As for the ties, they're in a class by themselves. Burberry's buyers head for Como, Italy, home of the world's finest silks, to secure exclusive patterns. Prices of silk ties range from $35 to $80, depending on the weight of the fabric.

The best of Burberry's sweaters are, of course, cashmere. And you can be sure they are made of the best quality cashmere. Barry goes to the Scottish mills to personally select the colors, shapes, and styles. Prices start at about $325 for a basic V-neck, and run up to around $450 for an argyle pattern.

On the second floor you'll find the classic raincoats, as well as suits. You'll also probably find store manager Michael Bishop. Like his boss Barry, he is British and a Burberry veteran. He's also one of the most customer-oriented retailers we've ever met, another Burberry trademark. Worldwide the company's staff is invariably charming, good-looking, and impeccably dressed. Even royals like Charles, Diana, Andy, and Fergie seek their advice when it comes to Burberry specialties, like the practicality of a detachable lining in a raincoat. Depending upon the state of the lining and the style, the coats sell from $320 to $995.

Have something dressier in mind? How about an elegant cashmere topcoat—$1,500 for the single breasted style, $1,650 for the double breasted. It comes in black, navy, gray, and vicuna, but Barry and Michael tell us navy is by far the most popular. They also say that men are wearing more dressy coats these days, which explains why they have difficulty keeping the $895 wool coats with velvet collars in stock. Top it off with a white silk scarf for $145 and you're set for a black-tie evening. For the blackest-tied of formal affairs, you might want the ultimate scarf—silk on one side, cashmere on the other, for $225.

The third and fourth floors are dedicated to ladies, and given these tailored, time-honored clothes we do mean *ladies*. A stylish houndstooth suit runs about $670—an accompanying silk blouse is priced in the $350 neighborhood. The extensive collection of Lady Burberry sweaters features styles in cotton wool and cashmere, with prices starting at $50 and going up to about $800.

Ladies' trench and top coats come in a multitude of colors and designs. Still some generalizations can be made. They're cut fuller these days to go over suits, and they're longer in length. All in all while fashionably styled, they are more practical than they've ever been. The tan trench raincoat remains a favorite at $895. But we prefer the long, sleek look of the Chesterfield for $695.

There's something so civilized about Burberrys—the store, the clothes, above all, the clientele. Perhaps Lionel Barber of the *Financial Times* described the Burberrys mystique best when he reported that the people at the Bush Inaugural "arrived in their furs and Burberrys." ❦

Charivari

18 West 57th Street   (212) 333-4040
between Fifth and Sixth
New York, NY 10022

Few enterprises have a flagship store and several branches all in one city. But then no one would ever accuse Selma Weiser of being conventional. Quite the contrary, the robust red-haired dynamo has made a retailing phenomenon out of being decidedly unconventional from merchandise to merchandising, decor to advertising.

With more chutzpah than resources, Selma opened her first store on Upper Broadway in 1967. She chose the name Charivari because, in old French, it means "uproar." She hoped to create one by concentrating on the cutting edge of fashion, on new young designers. She succeeded, having introduced Issey Miyake in '74, Yoji Yamamoto in '83, and a host of others in between. Designer of the moment Marc Jacobs, now wearing the Perry Ellis mantle, "practically grew up with us" and enjoyed protégé status at Charivari. Fueled by Selma's eye for innovation tempered by quality and a strategy of stocking a strong core of updated but basically conservative and versatile merchandise, Charivari has grown into a six-store mini-empire, with plans for further expansion on the drawing board.

Charivari enthusiasts like Barbra Streisand, Carly Simon, Rod Stewart, Kelly McGillis, Steve Guttenberg, Mia Farrow, Christopher

Reeves, Diane Keaton, Robert Wagner (and daughter Katie), and Diana Ross know that each store has a distinct character, merchandised for a specific clientele with a neighborhood orientation—the two stores on Upper Broadway, one for women, one for men, may not have the same offerings as the 57th Street flagship, which, because of location, caters to a more eclectic audience. By the same token, the West 72nd Street store is not a duplicate of any other. A West 79th Street location is devoted to sportswear, and the Workshop on Columbus features new untested designers who Selma, daughter Barbara, and son Jon have discovered on their travels. Buying is a family affair, with one rule of thumb, according to Selma—"nothing that is dumb."

The 57th Street store is the largest and most dramatic with its soaring foyer and stunning staircase. There's an oriental economy to the decor which allows the clothing to double as the principal decoration. Indeed, it has won several design prizes for its creator, Japanese architect Yojeda.

There's an exhilarating quality about the atmosphere intensified by the upbeat music and the enthusiasm of the young, singularly attractive staff (mostly actors and Fashion Institute of Technology students). Divided into levels opening on to the foyer, the store is one of areas. Downstairs, you'll find the Workshop featuring clothes for both men and women by designers known and unknown—including Dries Van Noten, Vivianne Westwood, Matsuda, and Hugo Boss. It's a place for mixing and matching with prices that start at about $200.

The entrance level boasts a Byblos boutique, while the mezzanine is for women interested in the work of designers like Gaultier, Montana, Genny, and Gigli. And you can get very interested indeed as large portions of their respective collections are represented, day through evening wear. What's not in stock you can see on Sony video monitors that constantly play tapes of the collections' original presentations in Paris, Milan, New York, London, or Tokyo. Here prices can range from $1,200 for a Romeo Gigli suit to $2,000 or so for a Giorgio Sant Angelo cocktail dress.

Charivari also carries a terrific selection of accessories, including uniquely theatrical jewelry that the Weisers buy from sources all over the world. But the piece we liked best was of a homegrown variety. A collaboration between Barbara Weiser and Eric Beamon, it's a chandelierlike collar of a necklace consisting of twenty-five strings of gold-painted crystals and sells for $750.

Upstairs you'll find an example of Jon Weiser's creativity, the extensive men's department, his baby since 1971. Spacious, light, and airy, it showcases, from sweaters to suits, the designs of Mugler, Montana, Versace, Gaultier, Yamamoto, and Comme des Garçons. We found a black, sinfully soft, cashmere turtleneck by Issey Miyake for a friend who wears it everywhere. One of the best $350 investments we ever made, the sweater with its easy fit represents that updated, yet conservative, core of merchandise at Charivari.

Despite its size—over 6,000 square feet—and diversity of merchandise with prices starting at a little over $100 and peaking at about $5,000, the store makes a cohesive fashion statement. It flows and in the process upholds Charivari's fashion forward, somewhat avant-garde and definitely daring image—an image that is also effectively reinforced by very distinctive advertising.

Created by Kirsch, Baum & Baum, the black-and-white ads in publications like *Vanity Fair* are arresting enough to make you stop flipping pages. One recently depicted a woman in a striking, oversized brocade coat resplendently trimmed in fringe. Dangling high above the harbor, with Manhattan spread out beneath her, she is rather tenuously connected by one hand to the top of the Statue of Liberty. The headline reads, simply and succinctly, "Charivari. On the edge." That, we believe, just about says it all. 🐛

Emporio Armani

110 Fifth Avenue   (212) 727-3240
at 16th Street
New York, NY 10011

There's never been any doubt about Giorgio Armani's design genius. His development of the Emporio Armani concept, essentially lower priced, more accessible, proved his business acumen as well. With the 1981 opening of the first Emporio right across the street from his Milan headquarters, Armani firmly established his worldwide fashion empire by expanding his audience. Originally, "for kids who can't afford Armani" and stocked with fast, faddy goods often made out of remnants swept up from the atelier floor, Emporio Armani has evolved into a purveyor of a vast array of fashion (dressy clothes and sportswear), accessories, even goodies for the home. The common thread is a distinctly sleek Armani look with a mass appeal in design and price.

This handsome Fifth Avenue branch of what has become a chain of 150 boutiques is the first in the U.S. Designed to incorporate many of the building's original Stanford White touches, the 15-foot-wide red brick window bays and chestnut wood floors, the store also displays some amusing touches—wood sculptures of bras, panties, and ties, along with an air conditioning unit shaped like the Emporio's eagle logo, spreading its wings across the ceiling. There's a very spirited, young-at-heart atmosphere about the decor and the merchandise, reinforced by the up-beat music, that is drawing hordes to this new Armani outpost.

You enter into the accessories area—eyewear to jewelry to luggage and everything in between. We were taken with the canvas getaway tote for $200. Their soaps, in sets of three for $21, make the perfect gift for your weekend host. The natural notepaper pads with pigskin covers are another terrific choice at $33.

The men's department stretches along the right side of the store, from front to back. Suits range from $650 to $800 and Armani's signature loosely cut sports jackets are available from $350 to $575. For more casual dressing, there's a large selection of comfortable sweatsuits in a variety of colors and patterns.

Jeans for men and women occupy their own significant space here. We love the classic five-pocket, straight-cut style for $115, with either button or zipper fly. It's always available, but there's a new jeans collection designed every season, so you can choose a more fashionable model—a pleated fatigue version perhaps at $150 for men and about $130 for women. Jackets, matching and otherwise, range from $250 to $300. And there's a line of T-shirts and stone washed cotton tops to complete your Armani jeans look.

Or almost complete it. To be thoroughly Armani, dive into the rather spectacular collection of underwear for men and women. From dull to daring, it's all here, along with bathing suits and a great line of coordinated robes and towels.

In outerwear for women, there are slacks ranging from $175 to $250 and jackets at about $500. We particularly like the bright colored numbers in silk and crepe, from $450 to $550. Day or evening, they're perfect—teamed with a black blouse and trousers.

In fact, about the only thing we don't like about Emporio Armani is the decision making—there's just too much to choose from. But then we're in good company. Manager David Johnson tells us that even such seemingly self-assured types as Debbie Gibson, Mary Tyler Moore,

Marlo Thomas, Stockard Channing, Mike Tyson, and Tom Cruise have been known to founder a bit when faced with all the store has to offer.

E. Vogel—Custom Boots to Measure

19 Howard Street   (212) 925-2460
at Broadway and Lafayette
New York, NY 10013

Right smack in the middle of Chinatown sits a little shop left over from another time and place. For four generations, since 1859, E. Vogel has been making boots, specializing in those meant for riding, English-style. The smell of leather fills the tiny showroom, where you're likely to meet some member of the Vogel family; brothers John and Harold Vogel now own the company. John's son Dean is general manager, and nephew Jack Lynch is involved as well.

They make and sell over 3,000 custom shoes and riding boots a year. Shoes cost $480 for the first pair, $430 for the second. Boots range from $395 to $735 and slide into the stirrups of the U.S. equestrian team and most foreign riding teams—and of Cliff Robertson, Sigourney Weaver, Sly Stallone, Tatum O'Neal, Bo Derek, and Jackie Onassis too.

Vogel boots make them all look very smart atop their mounts. Remember, it's the rider's boot that tends to be at eye level for those left on the ground. So from a vanity standpoint, properly shod feet are just as important to the rider as they are to the horse.

For showing, dressage, and eventing, Vogel recommends French calf leather because of its lightweight softness, suppleness, and fine grain. Perhaps most importantly, it "shines up beautifully." It seems domestic leathers, while more rugged and long-wearing, aren't quite as pretty; they're better suited to polo, fox hunting, and cross-country hacking.

Of course, all of Vogel's boots and shoes are made right here. The leather is cut on the first floor. It's taken up the creaky stairway to the third, where the uppers are sewn together. The second floor reeks with the smell of glue; that's where the soles are cemented to the uppers, rather than sewn. Dean Vogel maintains that gluing yields the strongest possible shoe.

Once measurements have been taken, there's a twelve-to-sixteen-week wait for the finished product. Remember, Vogel's boots and shoes are "bench made," a careful, time-consuming combination of handwork augmented by some machine operations.

But it's worth the wait and the work. Vogel's boots and shoes are the product of good old-fashioned American craftsmanship and enterprise. It's almost your patriotic duty to buy them. As Dean says, "There aren't many of us left."   🦃

Gianni Versace

816 Madison Avenue   (212) 744-5572
at 68th Street
New York, NY 10021

Versace's clothes are sleek, hot, and sexy—and so is this, his flagship boutique in the U.S. The man whose designs gave the Don Johnson look to Don Johnson has created a dark gray granite, marble, and steel fortress dominated by a breathtaking skylight. And it all houses the most complete selection of Versace clothes and accessories for men and women in the country.

His sophisticated, fashion-forward prêt-à-porter carries price tags that spell *made to order* for many other designers. His signature silhouette for men—broad-shouldered, tailored jacket over always-pleated and very full trousers—runs $1,300 to $2,000 for a suit. Those distinctive one-button sport jackets in delicious pastels can be had from $950 to $1,500. Slacks sell for $285 to $600. Shoes, socks, belts, and even ties (there's no rule that says Versace's jackets have to be worn with T-shirts) are available in a broad range of prices, though it would be difficult to categorize any as modest.

For women, the look tends to be extravagantly, exuberantly sexy—and expensive. Suits range in price from $1,800 to $3,000, blouses from $600 to $2,000. For evening, there's nothing for less than $2,000, and several elaborately embroidered numbers approach the $12,000 mark.

As for what Versace calls couture for both sexes (read *more* expensive prêt-à-porter executed in better fabrics and benefiting from handwork finishing), expect to pay a minimum of $3,000 per piece. Made to order, it takes seven to ten weeks and may make you feel closer to Versace disciples like Phil Collins, Rod Stewart, Diandra Douglas, Candice Bergen, and Elizabeth Taylor.

In the "if you have to ask how much it costs, you can't afford it" category, there's his new Atelier line. These are absolutely one-of-a-kind outfits designed and made exclusively for those who dare to venture into this rarified territory beyond couture. It means flying to Milan to be measured by Versace's specially trained team; it also means joining the ranks of Cher, Jane Fonda, and Elton John, who have already done so.

The delightful Afrodita Badescu is the person to call if you have any special requests, if you need something sent over on approval, or if you want to stop by before or after hours. Don't be hesitant or shy about it. With a clientele like this, she's heard it all! ❦

Giorgio Armani

815 Madison Avenue   (212) 988-9191
at 68th Street
New York, NY 10021

It's fitting that a former art gallery houses what was, before the advent of Emporio Armani, Giorgio Armani's flagship in the U.S. Armani's designs are, after all, works of art. Indeed, they are displayed as they might be in a gallery—each design occupying its own space, hung facing outwards instead of sideways, with nothing in the rather spartan decor to distract the eye from its beauty. Waxed black steel forms square frames around the clothes, while soft museum-quality light bathes them. Actually, since this store features the upper end of Armani men's and women's wear, while the Emporio is aimed more toward a mass market, we still prefer to consider this *the* Armani store in town.

It's certainly more intimate than its downtown sister store, one third the size in fact. The 3,000 square feet are equally divided on three floors. The first houses women's clothes, accessories, fragrances, and shoes. Manager Paula Faulk is the lady to see about which of Armani's masterfully tailored looks suits you best. His jackets are really fantastic, starting at about $1,500. Simply cut in fabrics that move with the body, they are a particular favorite with Lee Radziwell. And who can blame her, even if they do look best with blouses for just under $750 and trousers in the $800 range?!

Armani's evening wear follows the seductive look of his daytime outfits, but is translated into even softer dressing, ever softer fabrics. Plan on spending about $3,000 for an evening gown and $1,600 for a cocktail dress. Needless to say, we were drawn to something a wee bit more extravagant—an exquisitely handbeaded jacket of $8,000. Truly a couture piece, it was finished beautifully on the inside. You could almost consider it reversible, thereby helping to justify its cost, not to mention the $1,200 for the matching skirt.

Keith Scott oversees the second and third floors devoted to men's wear—clothes with a full complement of furnishings, accessories, shoes, and leathergoods. Men who appreciate a highly styled yet Italian look, fully cut and decidedly un-conservative clothes, haunt these floors. Often from the theater or the arts, they tend to be some of the more successful inhabitants of those worlds. They don't bat an eyelash at sports jackets starting at $1,200 or trousers at $400. Suits are around $1,600, while shirts hover in the $200 to $300 range.

There's a subtle richness about Armani's designs, which is reflected in this store where you can indulge in a total Armani look. We think the Emporio is fun, but this is fashion.   ❦

Gucci

685 Fifth Avenue (Main Store)   (212) 826-2600
at 54th Street
689 Fifth Avenue (Shoe Store)
at 54th Street
New York, NY 10022

It all started in 1906, when Guccio Gucci began tooling the finest leather saddles money could buy. It almost ended a few years ago, when Guccio's son, Dr. Aldo Gucci, ran afoul of the law over a little matter of several million dollars in tax fraud. Now that unpleasantness is behind Gucci. The government is satisfied and a new consortium is in charge, bent on reinstating Gucci's reputation for unparalleled quality and service. The results are quite evident in the New York store; the selection of bags, suitcases, leather accessories, shoes, scarves, clothes, jewelry, and decorative home items befits a world-class organization. And the staff assembled by store managers Stephanie Gail and Petervandermark is knowledgeable and helpful. The attitude problem that beleaguered Gucci for so long—snobbish salespeople who made you feel as if they were doing you a favor even speaking to you—has been banished.

Customer service is now the byword. Maurizio Gucci (Aldo's nephew and worldwide chairman) has seen to that. He instituted a training program for the entire sales staff, which assures that they are familiar with their merchandise and stresses the importance of customer satisfaction.

The classic Gucci loafer, as well as an extensive collection of other stylish shoes for men and women in leather and other fine natural materials, occupies a space on the northeast corner of 54th and Fifth; the rest of what Gucci has to offer is housed on four floors on the southeast corner.

The first floor boasts small leather goods and handbags, some made of precious skins like crocodile and ostrich for equally precious prices. You're encompassed by that rich aroma reminiscent of the leather interior of a brand-new Jaguar. Should it become a bit too rich, head for the perfume counter. Gucci 3 is for the ladies at $120 for a half ounce. For the gents, Gucci makes Nobile, four ounces at $50.

Watches are a big draw at Gucci. Sometimes you literally have to line up to purchase their bracelet watch. Gold-plated, it comes with twelve interchangeable bezels in different colors to coordinate with any outfit and sells for $195.

Of course, you don't need us to tell you about Gucci's scarves and shawls; they're legendary with their spectacular, colorful, and instantly recognizable signature prints. Prices start at $185.

The clublike atmosphere of the second floor flatters the merchandise—men's Gucci-designed and Italian-made clothes, from sportswear to suits. Women are catered to on the third floor. Again, there is a complete collection, active wear to cocktail dresses.

The fourth floor houses the gift department with crystal, silver, and china. You'll also find Gucci's splendid luggage here—a set suitable for jet-set living runs about $2,000.

It seems as if there's a little something for everyone at Gucci, much of it acting as testimony to the shopper's good taste with the identifying stamp of the Gucci stripes, logo, or crest. All those "Gucci-isms" are internationally recognized and respected, which explains the store's popularity with the United Nations set. When the UN is in session, Gucci is awash with foreign dignitaries and their families, but they're not the only status-conscious shoppers here. You're just as likely to run into Bill Cosby, Frank and/or Kathie Lee Gifford, Whitney Houston, or Carly Simon.

They all come for their Gucci fix and a dose of the warm Italian hospitality that is once again extended by the house that saddles built. ❦

Hermès

11 East 57th Street   (212) 751-3181
between Fifth and Madison
New York, NY 10022

When Thierry Hermès first opened a harness shop in the Paris of 1837, we wonder if he ever imagined that the firm bearing his name would one day dress not only horses but royalty and that it would be the producer of *the* status accessory for men. Doubtful. For one thing, he never could have conceived of the World War I carnage that decimated the horse population of France. He could never have dreamed the residential Champs-Elysées filled with beautiful horse-drawn carriages sporting Hermès trappings could be transformed into a commercial thoroughfare ruled by a whole new mode of transportation—the motorcar.

Fortunately for Hermès, his grandson Emilo-Maurice was not thrown by these events, which could have proved devastating to the firm. Quite the contrary, he was inspired to set a new direction for the company. Using the material he knew best, leather, he turned Hermès on to the path it has traveled ever since, making handbags, luggage, wallets, and attaché cases for the carriage trade. For the first time, the Hermès signature saddle stitch—visible top-stitching accomplished by two needles—lent a handsome decorative touch to accessories. While Emile-Maurice had changed the course of Hermès' future, indeed assured that it would have a future, he adhered to the basic tenet of the company, which remains the same today: "Leather, sport, and the tradition of refined elegance."

Motivated by the worlds of sport and travel, the Hermès collection expanded over the years to include watches, jewelry, clothes, and designs for the home. The first leather agenda appeared in 1930, the first scarf in 1937, and the first ties in 1954.

After a false start (the first Hermès store in the U.S. was felled by the market crash of 1929), and 30 years of a limited American presence maintained by boutiques in stores like Lord & Taylor, Bonwit Teller, Neiman Marcus, I. Magnin, and Bergdorf Goodman, Hermès firmly established its U.S. base in 1983 with the opening of this exquisite 57th Street shop. Here Hermès flourishes with the full range of its exclusive patterns. Designed by architect Rena Dumas (who also happens to be the wife of the current chairman of the company, Jean-Louis Dumas Hermès), the interior has a richly understated, classic look reminiscent of the Faubourg shop in Paris—cherrywood display cases, handcrafted brass trim, Hermès' hallmark "grecques" lighting, and the ex-libris inlaid in brass in the floor. The walls are decorated with artworks from the famous Hermès Museum collection (something else the family can thank Emile-Maurice for) interspersed with photographs of famous clients—a Princess Grace clutching her "Kelly" bag in one hand, and a young Caroline by the other; Ingrid Bergman carrying her twin babies and wearing a "Collier de Chien" belt; and Queen Elizabeth, her royal coif covered by a Hermès scarf.

The first floor houses the fragrance counter, home to the delightful Hermès scents—Caleche, Amazon, and Parfum d'Hermès. For men, they have Belle Ami and Equipage, but we think Eau de Hermès suits everyone, a truly unisex fragrance. You can pick up a handblown crystal flacon of it for $500. Further along is the area devoted to Hermès' famous colorfully printed silk scarves, which, like the tie counter upstairs, is always crowded. Sometimes, when a tour bus of Japanese tourists descends on the store, the scarf counter looks like the object of a shark feeding frenzy. Indeed, Hermès scarves at $175 each are to women what Hermès ties are to men—an internationally recognized status symbol. We've never quite gotten over the time we spotted a young lady using one for a sling. How chic.

Leather goods are displayed throughout the store, from the "in" gift of the moment (a $60 case for "post it" notes)— to the famous $2,000 Kelly handbag, and beyond, way beyond. If you want the Kelly bag in ostrich, it'll cost about $6,000—$8,000 for one in crocodile. And 25-year-Hermès veteran Claude Gandrille stands by to repair or re-condition any of your purchases. He knows just about all there is to know about leather and what can be done with it. Claude will give counsel on any special custom order you might have in mind. He's even been known to put together the leather interior of a private plane and fashion a crocodile bicycle seat.

The ties hold court on the second floor. Even at $85 each, gentlemen scoop them up by the dozen, and often pick up matching pocket squares while they're at it. Ties, however, are not the only men's story here. There's a whole ready-to-wear department complete with suits, sports jackets, dress shirts, and sport shirts, sweaters, bathrobes, pajamas, and underwear. We think the silk pajamas, $800 to $900, are sensational, but generally we find Hermès accessories more exciting than the clothes. Ditto for the women's ready-to-wear on the first floor, unless you're an equestrian.

If you're into horses, this is definitely the place to be outfitted with their complete line of riding clothing, jodhpurs to raincoats. In fact, you can purchase just about everything you need here except the horse—the saddle, all the tack, crop, whip, saddle, and glycerine soap. No boots, though.

The home designs are another highlight here. What could be more soft and snugly than a cashmere blanket trimmed in leather for about $1,800. But it's the beach towels that are truly spectacular, as well they should be for $500. They look like paintings, since they benefit from the same printing process used on the scarves. The colors of the intricate patterns are incredibly bright and true. Their lavishly large size, 60 × 72, makes quite a statement on any beach.

From horse blankets to beach blankets, Hermès stands for unparalled luxury, craftsmanship, and quality. If you don't believe us, just read their *World of Hermès* publication, a beautifully produced, brilliantly conceived piece of marketing propaganda. It's bound to convince you.   🍂

Leggiadro

700 Madison Avenue   (212) 753-5050
between 62nd and 63rd
New York, NY 10021

You've bought the perfect dress and the most divine little pair of pumps, but there is something missing, something in-between, which is needed to truly complete the ensemble—leggings. No longer just stockings, to-day's legwear is an important fashion accessory, and comes in a mind-boggling assortment of colors and fabrics.

Leggiadro offers a vast selection of stockings, pantyhose, tights, and socks in virtually every configuration imaginable from all parts of the globe. More importantly, the store offers the personal service and ency-clopedic knowledge of owner Ann Ross. She opened Leggiadro four years ago because she recognized the need in New York for a leg-coverings store with an eclectic inventory, realistic prices, and a view of leggings as fashion.

Ann knows how leggings can make or break an outfit. Open and friendly, she will work with you to find the perfect complement to any style. As you begin to become a regular, Ann establishes a record of your likes and dislikes, what you've bought, and what you haven't yet tried.

When you are in the market for basics, Ann might suggest a pair of El-beo pantyhose for $8.00. A German product, they are sheer, yet strong and dependable. They come in umpteen colors, none of which are blotchy, and they don't sag. Far from basic, Elbeo also makes pantyhose for those glittering evenings—black and silver sparkles are electroplated onto them. Is that sterling silver? They sell for $60!

Looking for some adventure in the way of daywear? Check out the Missonis made of cotton and lycra in exciting patterns at $75. Then there's the classic $20 Missoni fishnet.

The Wolford tights and stockings from Austria make a fashion state-ment in unusual cotton and wool patterns. Wolford makes perfectly smashing evening stockings too. They're classic, but with a little bit of pizzazz. Some in lace sell for about $40 a pair.

This is not a place where men should fear to tread. Not only do beau-tiful leggings make a sexy gift for that special someone, but men can shop for themselves as well. Ann carries a substantial array of men's socks, ranging in price from $18 to $40, and from the conservative—England's Pantegerella—to the outrageous—the wild patterns in high colors from Italy's Missoni. For the ultimate in luxurious comfort, there is Royce's American-made cashmere sock at $25.

There's just no comparison; Leggiadro is the ultimate in legwear. And if that weren't enough to make it irresistible, Ann Ross makes it such a pleasurable place to shop. ❦

Macy's

151 West 34th Street   (212) 695-4400
at Broadway
New York, NY 10001

They say there's no place like Macy's. It's our guess that suits the NCAA just fine—another nationally televised Thanksgiving-Day parades would wreck havoc with all those lucrative television contracts. Since 1924, Macy's has presented a seasonal gift of monumental proportions to the city, and, since 1948 via TV, to the nation. It's the annual Macy's Thanksgiving-Day parade. Over 2,000 Macy's employees and their fam-ilies are joined by a dozen or more marching bands and numerous themed floats sprinkled with celebrities. But for most spectators, all 57 million or so of them, it's the giant balloons that *are* Macy's Thanksgiv-ing. At least a couple of million line up along Central Park West and

Broadway to watch it live, while another 55 million view from the comfort of their homes.

Frankly, we usually opt for the latter. But we have been known to bestir ourselves the night before to witness a part of the annual pageantry that isn't televised—the annual ritual of inflating Snoopy, Superman, and all their balloon pals. "Inflation Eve," as it's known to parade mavens, begins every year at about 6:00 P.M. on 77th Street, between Central Park West and Columbus, adjacent to the American Museum of Natural History. "Oohs" and "Ahs," punctuated by cheers of applause, fill the crisp evening air as the assembled crowd marvels at the spectacle of the balloons being brought magically to life. If you're in town, join the fun. This is truly a cheap (absolutely free) thrill.

Visiting the store responsible for this annual pageant is a thrill too, though it's likely to be none too cheap. With the exception of major appliances, cars, airplanes, and yachts, there's not much you might want or need that the "world's largest store" doesn't have. Rising nine stories, not counting a balcony and cellar level, and occupying an entire city block, Macy's is, according to its brochure, "part theatre, part welcoming forum that reflects your lifestyle needs." We can't argue there. Nor can we come up with an answer for the brochure's rhetorical question, "Where else can you find a financial planning seminar, cooking lesson, a fashion shoe, a complete beauty make-over, an interview with your favorite author and Santa Claus—all under one roof?"

In addition to such special events and appearances that keep Macy's hopping, you can dine at any of five restaurants, book a trip at the American Express Travel counter, mail a letter at the post office, fill a prescription at the old-fashioned apothecary shop, have your hair done at the Glemby Hair Salon, get your jewelry appraised, and have your film developed. If you have any time left, you might even want to check out the merchandise, a daunting task indeed—there's just so much of it.

Macy's even has a solution to that "problem" in the petite form of Linda Lee who runs the "Macy's by Appointment" service. From the perfect gift, to a complete wardrobe, just give her and her staff of consultants a budget and let them do the work. Of course, it's easier if a girl's got unlimited funds for a new look. They can just pick out a little Armani this, a little Montana that. But Linda and company are equally adept at working with $500, assembling the wardrobe equivalent of soup to nuts, shoes to lingerie to business suit to cocktail dress. They might even throw in a fabulous new fragrance to top it all off. Gentlemen, don't fret.

It may cost you a tad more than $500, but they can do the same for you—no matter who you are or where you come from. Seven languages are spoken at Macy's, so somebody's bound to speak yours. After all, there's one universal language called "shop."

Shopped for clothes till you've dropped, or drooped? (Even sorting through all the duds Linda collects can be exhausting.) Dreaming of relaxing at home, only to have the vision dashed by memories of shredding towels and sheets? Stop by the sixth floor and wonder at the selection of bath and bed linens, along with every conceivable accessory. They carry all the designer towels and sheets, lots of Lauren and beaucoup de Buatto (as in Mario, the first of New York's celebrity decorators to successfully license his name), along with the more moderately priced Macy's private label. Upstairs on the ninth floor, you can buy a bed to go with your new sheets as well as furniture for every other room in your home. From classic to contemporary styles, the entire floor is devoted to the enormous array.

If it's your kitchen that needs a bit of sprucing up, head down, all the way down to the basement, otherwise known as The Cellar. Inaugurated in 1976, it has been a major attraction ever since, stocked with much of the world's finest housewares and gourmet delicacies. Here you'll find everything from the latest in garlic presses (and there have been some major improvements) to the most impressive of espresso machines. Foodwise, The Cellar runs the gamut too. There are the ingredients for a fabulous feast in the fresh meats of Ottomanelli and calorie calculated spa dishes. The Gourmet Gazelle features great smoked fish and caviar. (Buy it when Macy's is locked in its annual pricing war with Zabar's!) Then there are the cheeses, the coffees, the condiments, pastas, the baked goods, the candy, the everything necessary for a dynamite dinner soirée—including a department called Take Note, where you can have the invitations printed and addressed, even arrange for their hand delivery.

For a lift out of the dog days of summer or dreary mid-winter, visit the year-round Christmas Shop with ornaments starting at $3.50. Equally sparkling and inspiring is the extensive crystal, china, and silver department on the eighth floor. Of course, it boasts Waterford, Orrefors, Lenox, Royal Doulton, Rosenthal, and Spode. So you can spend a lot. But you can also spend a little—like $70 for a boxed 20-piece set of good-looking stoneware.

Likewise for kids, the Littlest Shop carries a full line of imported children's clothes and accoutrements. You can spend hundreds on a lace trimmed christening gown, thousands on a full layette. But in other areas dedicated to children you can find a christening gown for $36 and play clothes starting at $12. Edward S. Finkelstein, chairman of R.H. Macy & Company, is very protective of the Macy's tradition of offering alternatives and value.

This tradition dates from the store's 1858 founding by a Quaker, Rowland H. Macy. As his 20-foot-wide dry goods store on Sixth Avenue near 14th Street prospered, he became "Captain," trading on the fact that he had spent four years of his youth plying the coast of his native New England on a whaler. A souvenir from those days, a red star tattooed on his arm, became Macy's symbol.

From modest beginnings—first day's sales were $11.06—the store grew into a New York fixture, strong enough to survive Rowland's death in 1877, and two successive mediocre management partnerships. The Strauss family, involved since 1874, took complete charge in 1896 and set Macy's firmly on the road to retailing greatness. It was Isidor and Nathan Straus who engineered the risky but wildly successful move uptown to Herald Square in 1902—a move that catapulted the store solidly into the 20th Century.

We wonder if the "Captain" could ever have imagined his Macy's as site of the annex to the Metropolitan Museum of Art Gift Shop or home to an Antique and Estate Gallery. Certainly, the assortment of electronics—from telephones to TVs to computerized date books—on the fifth floor would have baffled him. Still, like most men, he could have lost himself here. And certainly he would approve of the extremely knowledgeable staff. You can rely on them to tell you what technology will operate in which part of the world. No more purchasing a nifty little gadget in the U.S., only to discover it won't work at your hunting lodge in Scotland.

And speaking of traveling, there are loads of useful guides in the eighth floor book department, this one among them. You'll also find a good selection of children's books and current bestsellers, along with all those glossy numbers meant to decorate your coffee table.

So who's braving the acre of Art Deco that is the main floor with its sentries poised to spritz you with the latest fashion fragrance? Here we can be both general and specific. Generally speaking, Macy's is for the busiest among us, who appreciate one-stop shopping. Should we name a name or two, the list would include Busy Persons Cher, Christie Brinkley, and Kathleen Turner. Maybe it should include you too! ❦

Mathias—Boot Makers
Custom Made Ladies' & Gentlemen's Shoes

20 East 69th Street   (212) 737-3984
between Madison and 5th
New York, NY 10021

The name on the bright yellow awning says Mathias, but the talent behind the name rests squarely in the experienced hands of Hungarian-born Imre Nemeth, who's been making shoes for fifty-two years. He made his first pair when he was fifteen. In 1956, he emigrated to the U.S. and has been in his present location, right across the street from the Westbury Hotel, for the last twenty-seven years.

Superb European craftsmanship and decades of experience are evident in every handmade pair of Mathias shoes and boots. Perfection is Imre's goal and he delivers. Of course, at an average price of about $800, he should! Women's shoes start at $600. Men's and ladies' boots range from $800 to $1,200 in calf or suede. Alligator, lizard, ostrich, or any other more unusual leather is liable to cost more.

The sheer beauty of Mathias shoes, inside as well as out, and the custom fit attract a loyal clientele including Frank Sinatra, Marlo Thomas, Jack Lord, and Paul Newman. Imre has carefully measured each of their feet to make a wooden last, upon which he constructs their shoes, just as he will for you. But it takes a while. Imre, with the help of an eighty-six-year-old Armenian named Edward Tchorlin, makes only about six pairs a week. And fashioning the initial last can take as long as two months.

Once that's done, however, it serves as a permanent record of your feet's requirements. You can simply call Imre to order any style shoe you want, either one of his models or a design you've seen elsewhere. He can duplicate any look, while immeasurably improving the quality of any "store-bought" product. Mathias shoes still look great long after the natural life of any other pair you might own. Once they do start showing some age, Imre will be happy to give them a tune-up.

Actually you should probably consider stocking up on Mathias shoes. After all, Imre's getting on in years and he's got an octogenarian coworker. Neither of his children is interested in the business and they just don't make shoemakers like they used to. So Imre may, one day, be forced to give up the trade he has practiced for so long.   ❦

Polo/Ralph Lauren

867 Madison Avenue   (212) 606-2100
at 72nd Street
New York, NY 10021

Have you ever walked into someone's home and coveted everything in sight? Our guess is you'll feel that way when you walk into this crown jewel of Ralph Lauren's 125-Polo-store empire. And make no mistake, you will feel like you are walking into a home, albeit in a *very* grand one, done to within an inch of its life, which is exactly the way Ralph wanted it. He spent five years searching for the perfect location to showcase the Ralph Lauren lifestyle. He finally settled on the landmark Rhinelander Mansion, built in 1895 to resemble a French chateau of the Loire Valley. Then he spent 18 months restoring the mansion's architectural integrity and designing the interior to properly present his creations, all of his creations—from clothing and accessories to home furnishings—in their natural habitats. It's doubtful this old house ever looked this good, this opulent in its heyday!

You really do want to move right in, which is exactly what manager Charles Fagan did. He lives on the fifth floor, which must be like being king of a mountain of treasures—from silver-lidded antique perfume bottles to one-of-a-kind sterling charm bracelets starting at $375.

There's the Cashmere Bar on the first floor, a plethora of sensual riches if ever there was one, including a double-breasted sweater for $750. Others go for as much as $1,200, but you can pick up a classic crewneck for $395.

The small collection of men's shoes is nothing short of exquisite, so beautiful they even draw sighs of envy from women. Now, while we're thinking leather, check out Ralph's line of hard leather luggage. It took him four years to get it right. Presumably it was worth the wait. The luggage is certainly lovely, and heavy, and totally impractical unless you charter your own jet to carry it. At $1,250 for a train case and $2,100 for a trunk, it's either that or have plastic slip covers made for it (but don't tell Ralph, he doesn't like reminders of his Bronx beginnings).

It's no secret that the Polo knit T-shirts are terrific, not to mention part of the upwardly mobile uniform. The weathered mesh variety runs

$47.50. In sea-island cotton, they're $185 and both versions come in every color imaginable. Close by you'll find cotton and silk ties for $30 to $60. Oxford cloth shirts are only $52.50, but pale in comparison to the sea-island cotton versions at $145. They look so chic under one of Ralph's silk robes for $600, or better yet, a cashmere lounger for $1,500. And what true gentleman's wardrobe would be complete without a $345 umbrella with a crocodile handle? It really hurts when you lose that one.

An imposing wood paneled stairway leads to the second floor, home to boy's and men's wear along with a magnificent Waterford chandelier. You can impose the Ralph Lauren lifestyle on a youngster as young as four years old here. For older boys, trousers run from $90 to $400. Seersucker sports jackets can be had for as little as $265. Cashmere jackets go for as much as $900. Suits fall into the $700 to $1,500 range, with two labels that differentiate the look. The Polo I features a natural shoulder and boxy fit, while the Morgan models are a bit more constructed with a padded shoulder and tapered waist.

The men's fitting room was once the mansion's music room and remains a hospitable place. In the morning you can enjoy coffee and croissants while an expert tailor works on you. Later in the day, you might get a light lunch or a glass of wine.

Ladies' clothes, from business suits to active wear, are on the third floor. For the woman who works, suitable skirts, blazers, blouses, sweaters, trousers, and suits occupy a large price range, from $125 to $2,500. You'll also find clothing for active and spectator sports—a little tennis outfit for playing at Wimbledon, as well as a little something to wear while sitting in the Royal Box.

There's also a terrific selection of weekend wear—lots of western style jeans for around $60, with matching jackets for $90 and change. In addition to denim, Ralph does great work in suede and buckskin. We found a fabulous hand-painted buckskin jacket for $2,000.

Ralph's home collection occupies the fourth level. Twice a year the whole floor is redone, in only five days. It's so complete, so cozy, and so inviting that you feel as if all you need is a toothbrush to settle in. Everything is for sale. Lately, the bounty has been compounded by the addition of the Polo Country Store, all very folksy and old-fashioned, sort of Ralph's vision of the American past—possibly more fantasy than reality. But from folk art to moccasins it's all very attractive, if you like that sort of thing.

Polo/Ralph Lauren, more than a store, is a way of life embraced by an eclectic group of celebrity regulars like Tom Selleck, Bruce Springsteen, Pat Buckley, and Demi Moore. We did say eclectic—Ralph's concept of the American dream is shared by a large and interesting cross-section of this and several other countries, which explains his annual $3 billion in sales!   ❦

Saks Fifth Avenue

611 Fifth Avenue   (212) PL3-4000
between 49th and 50th
New York, NY 10022

Unlike its four "Big Brother" (Barneys, Bendel's, Bergdorf's, and Bloomingdale's) competitors, Saks started out to be exactly what it is—a large, up-scale, high-fashion specialty store. It was the dream store of Horace Saks and Bernard Gimbel, both of whom operated independent retail stores on 34th Street at Herald Square in the early 1900s. The union of the financial clout of these two retailing families allowed Horace and Bernard to purchase a site on upper Fifth Avenue and realize their vision of a store synonymous with fashionable, gracious living. Saks Fifth Avenue opened for business September 15, 1924.

While the name said "Saks," the driving force that would make the store a legend was named Gimbel. With the untimely death of Horace Saks in 1926, his assistant (and Bernard's cousin) Adam Gimbel stepped into the SFA presidency. From the beginning, he displayed a unique flair for a business in which he had relatively little experience—he was only 30 when he assumed his exalted role. To attract greater numbers of affluent customers, he first remodeled the brand-new store in the sophisticated Art Moderne style he had admired at the Paris Exhibition of 1925. He felt Saks should have the appearance of a sumptuous home, stocked with elegant, exciting merchandise. So he hired buyers to scour the earth for the finest goods money could buy, concentrating on suppliers who would guarantee exclusivity to Saks.

The tone Adam set for the store has endured through the decades, including its acquisition by holding company giant Batus Inc., and the recently completed expansion of the original store that increased its selling space by 30 percent. The enlargement was accomplished by the addition of a 36-floor retail and office complex built in partnership with the Swiss Bank Corporation. The first 10 floors have been skillfully blended into the existing structure by using a handsome walnut paneled escalator atrium to function as a transitional area between the two buildings. The remaining upper floors of the tower house the U.S. headquarters of the Swiss Bank.

The expansion has particularly benefitted gentlemen seeking Sak's impeccable brand of good taste. Always heeding Adam Gimbel's policy of providing men with the same level of quality and service it offers women, Saks has now doubled the space to do it. Dress furnishings are the focal point of the additional square footage on the main floor, while men's sportswear, formerly scattered across the first and sixth floors, has virtually taken over the expanded fourth floor. And extra room on the sixth floor accommodates an enlarged collection of traditional, European, and private label men's clothing. The highlight here is a New Edward Sexton shop, his first in the U.S., and patterned after his elegant, Savile Row emporium in London. It includes his off-the-rack collection of suits and sports jackets ($1,200 to $1,500), shirts ($175), and ties ($60 to $95). In addition, custom tailoring services are available, offering a selection from over 1,000 different fabrics and two- or three-piece suit styles, single or double-breasted. Fashioned in Sexton's London workshops, made-to-order suit and jacket prices vary, depending on the fabrication and style. But the wait is a dependable eight to ten weeks.

Of course, women haven't been given short shrift in the remodeling of Saks. The impressive collection of accessories has been made even more awesome—Saks carries the largest collection of Donna Karan hosiery in the city, as well as the largest selection of Judith Leiber's exquisite evening bags. One gentleman recently bought seven Judith Leiber minaudières, some with prices approaching $2,000, for his wife who collects them. Apparently she was appropriately grateful, beacuse he returned shortly thereafter for three more.

The new third floor extension has enabled the further development of Saks' couture business, with an emphasis on evening wear from the likes of Giorgio Armani, Yves St. Laurent, Ungaro, and Adolfo. The dramatically luxurious furs of Revillon have new larger quarters here overlooking Fifth Avenue and Rockefeller Plaza. And the bridal department, possibly the city's best, has been expanded to fill much of the remaining space. It features European and American designers of bridal wear, as well as custom-made gowns by Monica Hickey. Her beautifully romantic handiwork starts at about $4,000 per dress and demands at least a three-month lead time.

Of course, the expansion has benefitted nonfashion areas, too. One long-awaited addition to Saks's customer services is a café-style restaurant—two levels facing Fifth Avenue with fantastic views of Rockefeller Center and St. Patrick's Cathedral. The elegant, subdued decor is rich with wood, marble, and slate, providing a serene respite from the rigors of shopping.

The new state-of-the-art salon and spa is an alternative retreat. Services for men and women, including hair styling, facials, and manicures are performed by expert practitioners in an architecturally dramatic marble and slate setting. Adding amenities like food service, monogrammed robes and towels, and phones at each chair probably gives them the right to call it a "spa."

But if you're determined to do nothing but shop at Saks, consider joining the Fifth Avenue Club. There's no membership fee for this club (one of the few in this city that can boast such a claim!) and it furnishes personal shopping services and more. The club's Ambassador Service is truly unique in that it reaches far beyond Saks's walls—not only will the staff of the Ambassador desk on the main floor assist you with matters relating to the store, but they will make restaurant reservations, arrange for theater tickets, and recommend hotel accommodations. Saks is the only store we know of with such first-class concierge service. Take advantage of it by calling (212) 940-4141 or -4143.

All in all we imagine that Adam Gimbel would be pretty pleased with the current state of Saks—its enlarged digs and expanded service. With $300 million invested, and all the hoopla, it might even impress this impresario of the department store. And that's without mentioning the never-ending search for new, exciting, and exclusive merchandise that began when Adam himself was traveling the globe. Chairman and CEO Melvin Jacobs and President Burton Tansky are always on the lookout for goods worthy of a Saks label. And we do mean they are personally on the prowl. Not long ago in Paris, during the madness that is the semiannual presentation of the ready-to-wear collections, we had the opportunity to watch Mel and Burt in action. They kept a killer schedule, in the front row at nearly every show, and still found time to do some extracurricular scouting. Marilyn Evins, well respected as a big PR gun, hounded them about visiting a couple of French manufacturers she was courting—one the producer of extraordinarily beautiful and expensive embroidered linens, the other a maker of mouth-watering chocolates.

Despite their impossible itineraries, Mel and Burt found the time to checkout Marilyn's would-be clients.

If there was any possibility they'd be special enough for Saks, it was a possibility neither gentleman could resist. ❦

Susan Bennis/Warren Edwards

440 Park Avenue	(212) 755-4197
at 56th Street	(800) 634-9884
New York, NY 10022	

Remember Cher's red silk pumps in *Moonstruck?* They were classic Susan Bennis/Warren Edwards—extravagantly beautiful and maybe just a teeny bit naughty. They're the kind of shoes that turn people into collectors. We don't know if Imelda Marcos ever darkened the door of this perfectly laid-out shoe showcase, but we do know that fanciers of fantasy footwear like Diana Ross, Marvin Davis, Patty Raynes, Robert Redford, Ann Getty, Paul Simon, and John Travolta are regulars.

They come for the unique designs, the quality, and the attentive, personalized service. Susan Bennis and Warren Edward are a true creative team. They do everything together, from the fashion-forward designing of men's and women's shoes and directing production, to creating the catalog that serves a worldwide clientele.

All their shoes are handmade in limited editions—no style numbers here. Each design bears a name, and they're only available at this store or through the catalog. Some 200 steps go into each pair, which goes a long way toward explaining the prices—a simple summer sandal can be $295, while more substantial shoes start at $375. There are plenty of pairs priced closer to $1,000 and boots start at $675, rising to about $5,500 for an alligator pair.

The collection is always a work in progress, but don't despair if your favorite design is no longer in stock. Records of each customer's purchases are kept. A brief description will point the salesperson to the exact shoe you want. It can then be custom-ordered from the Italian factories, assuming you're willing to wait six to eight weeks.

Staff members like Walter Sommer and Karen Robbins take special pains to familiarize themselves with the latest clothing fashions. So if you've done some serious damage at any of the area's designer boutiques, a call to them describing your purchases is enough to guarantee you the perfect footwear companions. They'll send them right over for you to try on.

With a firm foothold on the upper end of the designer shoe market in New York, Susan and Warren are venturing into a new and more popularly priced arena. A new line has been launched called Pret, starting at about $225. Still handmade, they will be less detailed than their more expensive counterparts, making them perfect for simpler, more sporty outfits.   ❦

Tender Buttons

143 East 62nd Street   (212) 758-7004
between Lexington and 3rd
New York, NY 10021

Tender Buttons—it's a curious name for a curious though absolutely enchanting shop dedicated to guess what. The brainchild of Diane Epstein and Millicent Safro, it's the only place we know of where you're sure to find just what you're looking for—the perfect button(s). Whether you need a little touch for that classy new blazer, or to jazz up a tired old jacket, you'll find it here.

The selection is enormous. Ask David Gibilie or Melissa Zexter to help you wade through it. They'll show you everything from the extraordinary collection of late-nineteenth-century enameled buttons from $40 to $200 apiece, to a marvelous medley from the 1930s. They run $40 to $45 each. Many make terrific earrings or cuff links, and Tender Buttons provides conversion service at $35 for either. Earrings can be made with clips or with posts for pierced ears.

Actually the decorative possibilities of all these beautiful buttons are limitless, which probably explains why designers like Romeo Gilly and Patrick Kelly (the king of buttons) spend so much time here. Other creative types are also inspired by Tender Buttons—Ali McGraw, Michael J. Fox, and Judy Peabody.

If it's difficult for you to visualize buttons as anything but buttons, check out the assortment of antique cuff links and studs. We found a sensational pair of black onyx and diamond links in 18-carat gold for $2,100. We also liked several sets of English enamels in sterling for around $250.

But back to basics—and to buttons. The store offers the ultimate in decadence—a 14-carat solid-gold blazer button set. Available by special order, it takes five or six weeks for delivery and the price—well, it tends to fluctuate with that of gold. Suffice to say, it will be considerably more than the $250 charge for a very attractive set dating from the late 1800s.

We're still not sure about the tender part of the name, unless it's meant as a verb. After all, the store certainly does tender buttons.   🍒

T. O. Dey

9 East 38th Street   (212) 683-6300
between Madison and 5th
New York, NY 10016

No part of the human body seems to work so hard and be so neglected as the foot. After all, have you ever even considered the amount of punishment a foot takes every day? Don't you just take your feet for granted, until they rebel and cause you discomfort, even excruciating pain?

Tom Bifulco and brother Gino imagine that's the case. Indeed, they count on it—their business depends on it. Since 1926 their company, T. O. Dey, has treated feet with tender loving care, by custom-making shoes specially designed to correct painful problems. As Tom is fond of saying, doctors often tell people, "Look, you don't need an operation—just go get some custom-made shoes." More often than not, by following doctors' advice, they'll wind up at T. O. Dey.

Tom and Geo didn't found the company (neither did their father, who ran it for twenty-six years before turning it over to the boys), but they have perfected the technique that allows their twenty-four cobblers to construct corrective footwear that conceals all the modifications inside the shoes. On the outside, they appear to be simply beautifully, currently styled loafers, pumps, or boots. Whatever your fashion fancy, they can make it—or copy it—while assuring you carefree feet.

It's quite a process they've developed, starting with a pedegraph—an ink impression of the feet in a weight-bearing position. The graph reveals their secrets as to where they may be absorbing too much weight, or not enough. Then measurements are taken and both feet are completely encased in plaster of Paris. Just before they dry, the casts are cut in half so the feet can be removed. Subsequently, the halves are reassembled to form two negative casts. Positive ones are made by filling the negatives with liquid plaster. Once the plaster sets, the negative casts are removed, leaving behind exact models of both feet.

Using the model and the information from the graph, T. O. Dey's master craftsmen literally mold shoes for each foot that can camouflage any peculiarity, even deformity. Most ready-made shoes are manufactured on standard blocks with identical right and left feet, despite the fact that many people's right and left are markedly different.

At T. O. Dey's, no two rights and lefts are exactly alike. In fact, each customer's initial casts are kept as a permanent record, allowing reorder by phone or mail. Just choose the style, color, and leather and an absolutely perfect pair of shoes will be yours.

There's always an eight-to-ten-week waiting period, and the first pair costs at least $650. Additional pairs run more in the $500 neighborhood, but can cost as much as $1,500 to $2,500 if special leathers are requested—skins like ostrich, crocodile, alligator, stingray, or snake.

Given the company's celebrity-studded client roster, we imagine there are plenty of those exotic shoes walking around. After all, Kiss's Gene Simmons is a devotee, as are Prince, Mike Tyson, and Betsy Johnson. Tony Randall and Hugh Downs head up a large group representing more conservative taste.

They'd probably be horrified by the notion of Tom and Geo's most novel service. For $350, the Bifulco boys will make shoes for a (very) pampered pup! The practice began with a cocker named Tassels, whose paws had become irritated from walking on salty New York sidewalks.

What's the old adage about dogs and their masters looking alike? If they frequent T. O. Dey's, it's entirely possible their feet can be identically clad, at the very least! 🐛

Yves St. Laurent Femme

855 Madison Avenue   (212) 988-3821
between 70th and 71st
New York, NY 10021

Yves St. Laurent Homme

859 Madison Avenue   (212) 517-7400
at 71st
New York, NY 10021

Yves St. Laurent—YSL; YSL—Yves St. Laurent. Let's face it, that's all we really need to say about the man who is to fashion what Elvis was (is?) to rock'n'roll—The King. In fact, he's so imperial that he's gone public. His is the first fashion house to have shares traded on the Bourse, the French stock exchange.

Even before he made this latest fortune, he had invested a considerable sum in the recent revamping of his 21-year-old U.S. flagship store on Madison. It is now just as elegantly modern and sleek as is his clothes, with black the predominant color. No wonder. It's St. Laurent's favorite. And he makes it anything but basic, especially when it comes to his classic "Le Smoking" pants suits—so understated, so mannishly-tailored, yet utterly feminine, and oh so comfortable.

Besides a reminder of St. Laurent's passion, the black serves as dramatic backdrop to the clothes. They almost leap off the walls and look very accessible, inviting you to browse, to touch, to feel. They seem to beg to be tried on, and St. Laurent has wisely provided some of the city's largest dressing rooms for that very purpose. Once you've slipped into one of his jackets and admired yourself as you privately pirouette in front of the generous mirrors, you're hooked. His jackets and slacks fit to the proverbial T.

While he may prefer black, St. Laurent is a superb colorist, reveling in unusual combinations that work brilliantly together despite their decidedly non-complementary nature. Indeed, a few seasons with YSL will develop your eye for color, giving you new courage on the mix-and-match front. You'll find yourself expanding the horizons of last year's suit by topping the skirt with a new jacket in a richly contrasting hue, or jazzing it up with a blouse in a hot, luminous color.

The price palette is almost as broad as the color. Blouses range from $125 for a T-shirt to $1,200 for a silk evening blouse. Slacks start at about $300 for a cotton pair and wander up to the $1,800 neighborhood for the tuxedo variety. And while you can pick up a little cotton suit for $1,100, an elaborate brocade evening suit can cost you $5,000.

Saint Laurent's jackets and coats, which we absolutely adore, can be had for $1,000 to $3,000. The ante is upped as high as $7,000 for his fabulous fur-lined raincoats. Their straight, no-nonsense lines make them ever-so-versatile—great and yet elegantly appropriate for formal evenings.

Manager Mary Kate Moulton epitomizes the St. Laurent client—contemporary, chic, and sophisticated, just like fellow foot soldiers in the YSL legions—Liza Minnelli, Blaine Trump, Diandra Douglas. And if you're not exactly an Anna Wintour (another St. Laurent devotee, not to mention editor-in-chief of *Vogue*) when it comes to fashion, take comfort in and make use of Mary Kate's sense of style. She'll help you make all the right purchasing decisions and keep a permanent record of them so she can help you add sensibly to your YSL wardrobe in the future. Should she be unavailable when you stop in, don't fret. All her very knowledgeable salespeople keep these records in an environment where service is the byword. Alterations are done on the premises by three talented seamstresses—no charge, of course, to make that new dress fit perfectly. There's only a minimal fee to alter a piece from a previous collection.

All the all-important accessories are available to complete any outfit. From handbags, hats, shoes, gloves, and belts to umbrellas, costume jewelry, even bathing suits. Any will brighten your day considerably for relatively little in the way of cash—a drop-dead belt for $60, perhaps a pair of flirtatious earrings starting at $50. But if you're in need of a real lift, visit makeup artist Louis Philippe in his little *domaine* filled with the complete line of YSL cosmetics. Louis will do your makeup and send you out into the world a new woman.

If the world is more (or less) than you care to face with your new countenance, mosey on over to the men's YSL store next door for some world class trolling. (Gentlemen take note, it's a two-way street here.) The YSL man tends to be every bit as classy as his female counterpart. He's a successful type who wants a European look to his wardrobe, without totally abandoning classic traditions. He loves luxury, savors the feel of superior cloth, and revels in interesting design. He's somebody like John Kennedy, Jr., David Bowie, or Paul Simon—none of whom have any trouble plunking down $800 to $1,500 for a suit.

Blazers run from $600 to $1,200 and feature a broad shoulder that is a YSL trademark where jackets are concerned. Slacks fall into the $175 to $300 neighborhood, while sweaters range from $200 to $500. All of the YSL collection for men is courtesy of Bernard Sanz, formerly of Hermès. Of course, he gets some guidance from St. Laurent himself who is ever so fussy about any item that bears his name. So rest assured that between the Yves St. Laurent label and Bernard's Hermès experience, YSL for men spells yummy color, superb materials, luscious design. ❧

FOR THE HOME

Asprey & Company, Ltd.

725 Fifth Avenue   (212) 688-1811
Trump Tower   FAX (212) 826-3746
New York, NY 10022

Founded in London in 1781 by William Asprey, Asprey & Company has long been *the* source for cultivated gift-givers seeking the elegantly unusual. Fortunately, the Asprey Group has elected to open an outpost of priceless chic on this side of the Atlantic in Trump Tower, whose overwhelming pink marble and brass, alas, clash with the understated opulence of this special preserve.

Mercifully, one does not have to deal with the visual assault and the chaotic masses of the tower to enter Asprey. You can walk in right off Fifth Avenue, where there is a friendly doorman to greet you. He ushers you into this fantasyland with appropriate pomp and circumstance. Once inside, it may be all you can do to restrain yourself from leaping like a delighted child from one area to the next. Your eye might first be caught by the enchanting collection of hand-carved animals, boxes, and frames in semiprecious stones. There's also a superb selection of items crafted in ivory, such as a dresser set for women, priced at $2,000.

If your fancy leans toward antique porcelain or silver, there are whole departments devoted to these costly collectibles. They are staffed by erudite and helpful people, like Elaine Werner, an authority on eighteenth-century Viennese porcelain. There's also an antique jewelry department headed by Marilyn Meyers, and even a bridal registry.

While browsing, your imagination might be captured by the sterling silver hard hat, the quintessential gift for the real estate magnate in your life. It's a mere $12,000 and comes in a beautiful leather presentation case. Not surprisingly, Asprey stocks only one at a time. Should it have been sold, and you just can't live without it, not to worry. They will make one up for you in their London workshop, but it will take three months or so—all hand-made, don't you know.

Even more unusual is the antique Russian travel bidet. Made in 1885 for Princess Xenia Feodorovna, daughter of Alexander III and sister of the unfortunate Czar Nicholas II, it is a kidney-shaped sterling silver contraption sitting on a four-legged wooden box. At $25,000, we think it would make a magnificent cooler for a bottle of vintage Dom Perignon or two.

Obviously, this is a one-of-a-kind item, but once gone it will be replaced by another equally fascinating and novel piece. Robin Raw, president of the store, dispatches people to all parts of the globe, looking for the world's most original treasures.

No visit to Asprey is complete without stopping by Kathleen O'Brien's book department, home to rare first editions and reprints. She also offers the extraordinary service of binding your masterpiece in fine hand-tooled leathers. Asprey maintains two binderies in London. Custom bindings start at about $400, including your choice of endpapers. The book department also conducts searches for the titles and authors missing from their library.

One of Asprey's most intriguing items is available only between Thanksgiving and Christmas. It involves the British tradition of crackers, those brightly colored paper cylinders that when pulled, break open with a loud crack and reveal a wonderful little gift. They have an incredible selection of festive crackers and gifts to fill them—a champagne stopper for $40, a sterling silver key ring for $145, an 18-carat gold collar pin at $190, or a little enamel box at $95.

It's a delightful tradition to adopt and the best part is that it will keep you coming back to Asprey & Company year after year.   🍃

Baccarat

625 Madison Avenue	(212) 826-4100
between 58th and 59th Streets	FAX (212) 826-5043
New York, NY 10022	

Before *Baccarat* became internationally synonymous with exquisite crystal, it was the name of a tiny village in the midst of then heavily forested northeastern France. In 1764, the village was part of the domain of a certain Bishop of Metz, by the name of Monseigneur de Montmorency-Laval. Troubled by the burg's unemployment problem, he devised a clever solution. The good Monseigneur petitioned King Louis XV to grant him the authority to establish a woodburning glassworks. He reasoned that it would put the area's resources to good use, as well as provide work for Baccarat's unemployed woodcutters.

We figure the king was less concerned about the plight of the woodcutters than he was about the fact that, at the time, France did not produce any art glass. Large quantities of francs were leaving the country to import Bohemian decorative glass. The Bishop of Metz's proposal was a way to stem the ebbing tide of funds that were sorely needed in France to deal with the recovery from the crippling Seven Years War.

Whatever arguments swayed the king, he granted the request on October 16, 1764, thereby creating a company that has (so far) survived three revolutions, four invasions, and the patronage of czars, kings, popes, and presidents. Originally a producer of rather simple glass, Baccarat had evolved by 1817 into the creator of elegant full-lead crystal that is still its hallmark today. Each Baccarat piece is meticulously made by hand—lots of hands; a goblet may be handled by fifty people during the course of its production. The result is nothing short of perfection—no specks, no ripples, nothing but the luminous sparkle of light dancing on crystal.

The New York store is designed to show off the artistry of Baccarat with dark charcoal gray museumlike display cabinets and superb lighting. Light caresses crystal everywhere you look—from the majestic Imperial Eagle priced at $31,625 to a $52 wine goblet.

Manager R. Glen Wilmoth delights in the sense of wonder that overcomes so many clients as they cross the threshold. He says youngsters seeking their first "good" glasses are particularly struck by the beauty of the crystal. Glen enjoys guiding them through the patterns and uses of the various sizes.

Of course, you don't need the "Crystal 101" course—Glen might skip the more mundane and take you straight to the Ballee pattern. Glasses start at $2,400, and you'll be glad to know there is plenty of stock.

Feeling royal, but not quite that royal? Check out Capri. It was Princess Grace's choice for her stemware and starts at $52 apiece. Not what you had in mind? Take a look at Perfection, a timeless design created in 1886. It was Coco Chanel's favorite, an opinion apparently shared by many of her countrymen; in 1933 the wine growers of Bordeaux named Perfection the perfect glass for toasting.

Aware of the fact that glassware can look a tad lonely on a table all by itself, the store does sell china and flatware too. Somehow, displayed as it is in the back of the store, it seems an afterthought. Crystal—elegant, pure, gleaming crystal—is really what Baccarat is all about. ❦

Christofle

680 Madison Avenue   (212) 308-9390
at 62nd Street
New York, NY 10021

Have you ever been to an embassy dinner and wondered about the origins of the breathtakingly beautiful silver? We know you've sailed on the Trump Princess or flown on Henry Kravis' private plane, where you've taken a surreptitious look at the trademark on the blade of your knife. Or maybe it was the Kluge yacht, the *Virginian?* At any rate, all of these private retreats of the very rich are outfitted with Christofle silver. On the *Virginian*, the Christofle collection is particularly extensive—from plate to sterling.

Considered the premier French silversmith since 1830, Christofle continues to pursue its motto of "one quality: the best." Christofle created the exclusive silverware used by King Louis-Philippe, the Emperor Napoleon II, and the Imperial Court. Known for its timeless, sophisticated designs, the firm's New York base reflects its reputation. Elegant and chic, the sleek wood cabinets gleam with Christofle's complete line of sterling, silverplate, goldplate, and stainless steel flatware, as well as table accessories and gift items.

Manager Helga Calvo knows her silver and can guide you in your selection. If you're after silverplate, she'll tell you why you've come to the right place. Christofle revolutionized the whole industry in 1842, when it bought the patent rights to the new process of applying precious silver and gold onto metal by electroplating. They might also show you Christofle's latest technological coup—*les cloisonnés lague de chine.* As executed in the Talisman pattern, $325 for a five-piece place setting, it combines silver and either natural sienna or black Chinese lacquer. Christofle has rediscovered the ancient cloisonné technique, entwining luxuriant arcades of shiny lacquer with delicate silver threads.

More conventional sterling patterns featuring Christofle's signature attention to design detail—each fillet, each bead, each flourish is hand-finished—range from $175 to $325 per place setting. The simple, pure form of the Albi pattern is vintage Christofle with its delicate ridge as the only decoration at $175. More elaborate is the Aria with its fluted handles gathered at top and bottom by bands plated with 24 carat gold. As with any Christofle plating, it is dishwasher safe, and the standard five pieces sell for $325.

As you would expect, Christofle has a bridal registry, but with a French twist. Rather than sending the gifts selected by relatives and friends, they send a card. So after the honeymoon, the bride can sort through the cards to weed out the duplicates or items she no longer wants. Christofle will send all the final selections at one time—so much easier than lugging the gifts destined for exchange.

Christofle likes to call its products *French Couture Pour La Table.* We can't argue—a table set with Christofle is the most fashionable we can imagine.   ❧

D. Porthault & Co.

18 East 69th Street   (212) 688-1660
between Madison and 5th
New York, NY 10021

They have become such a part and parcel of our lives, it is difficult to imagine that in 1925, when Madelaine Porthault first designed prints for her family's linen business, they were considered a radical notion. Inspired by the Impressionists, the lush florals that she silk-screened onto Porthault sheets were to have a lasting impact on the world's tastes in home furnishings.

Today the firm's colorful products can be found in over 200 locations in 24 countries and the business has expanded to include table linens, towels and bathwear, lingerie, children's clothes, porcelain, accessories, and home fragrances. In New York, Porthault occupies a landmark townhouse just off Madison Avenue that shows off their merchandise to its best advantage. A series of rooms has been created to display it in the kinds of settings that might be found in a private home. You'll know just where to put that breakfast set in Porthault-patterned Limoges for $290 and the matching tea cart that will add another $570 to the cost.

No matter how tempting the other products, concentrate on the linens and towels—that is where Porthault made its name for exceptional quality and setting new trends. After all, it was Porthault that first introduced scalloped borders, lace borders, piped toweling, printed toweling, and the coordinated look of matching bed linens and towels.

All the sheets are one hundred percent cotton, woven in the firm's factories in France. There are over 200 patterns to choose from, but remember that bottom sheets do not come fitted as a matter of course.

However, you can order a fitted bottom sheet for no extra charge—just a little extra time. It will take about three weeks.

Our favorite design is called C126. Lavishly embroidered, a queen-size set with two pillowcases will set you back $2,800. With her taste for expensive luxury, it's no wonder that the Duchess of Windsor (our own dear Wallis Simpson) would only sleep on Porthault sheets. She traveled with several sets, as she just couldn't count on every household she visited to be up to her exacting standards.

We understand that Malcolm Forbes, Jackie Onassis, Charlotte Ford, both Mesdames Bass, Nan Kempner, Estée Lauder, and Pat Buckley share her fondness for Porthault, but fortunately not her obsession.

You should know that the Porthault family still runs the company and that they offer special services to their discerning clientele. Their designers will work with you and/or your interior decorator to create motifs best suited to your decor.

Perhaps Marc Porthault, the president, who is also Madelaine's son and inheritor of her extraordinary talents, sums it up best when he says, "Porthault is a luxury business. We are a guarantor of French quality and taste." ❧

Ffolio

33 East 68th Street   (212) 879-0675
between Madison and Park
New York, NY 10021

Since 1970, Muriel Glaser has been filling a unique niche—stationer to the city's elite. Distinctive invitations are a specialty; wedding, birthday, barbecue, or black tie, Muriel makes sure they are stylish.

There are no rules. If there were, Muriel would make a point of breaking them. As she says, life's traditions are in constant flux, why should stationery remain unchanged? Let your imagination run free with a custom-designed invitation, just as Cheryl Tiegs, Susan Newhouse, Candice Bergen, and Marlo Thomas do.

Express yourself in writing paper for business correspondence or just billets-doux. Muriel helps choose your personal and unique typeface and color to make you feel good dashing off a congratulatory note or writing that long-overdue thank you.

Muriel thinks that brightly colored notecards and envelopes brighten people's day. We agree. Why not indulge your WASP fantasies with gloriously pink notecards, enveloped in bright green with name and address in dramatic type? One hundred cards and envelopes go for as little as $150. Add $80 to $100 for special complementary envelope linings.

For longer musings, Muriel prefers bordered papers—one or two bright colors on white paper. There is a wide selection of border patterns, and the paper and color choices are myriad, not to mention the prices.

Certainly, everyone can find something here to truly reflect his or her personality, just as Margaret Truman and other letter writers of note have done for years.

This charming store, chock-full of stationery in every conceivable color, size, and shape, is also a treasure trove of paper-related gifts—desk accessories for $15 and up, any one making the perfect hostess gift. Ffolio's photo albums, some bound in leather, others in unusual fabrics, all filled with acid-free paper, make a more substantial present in the $40 to $125 range.

Ffolio—we think the extra *f* stands for *fantastic!*   ❦

Fortunoff

681 Fifth Avenue   (212) 758-6660
at 54th Street
New York, NY 10022

Fortunoff, the self-styled "Source," has come a long way from its origins as a little neighborhood housewares store—as far as Brooklyn is from Fifth Avenue. Founded in 1922 by Max and Clara Fortunoff, the company remains a family-run operation with four locations, which most New Yorkers can recite, having been exposed for years to extensive, even aggressive, advertising.

Not that we're complaining. Fortunoff does have a lot to crow about. The Fifth Avenue flagship store opened in 1979 as a veritable four-story testimony to the good life reflected in contemporary jewelry, estate pieces, watches, fine china, porcelain, and silver—lots and lots of silver, with managing director Bea Borower overseeing it all.

It's silver where Fortunoff truly stands out as a resource. Just ask Jerry Blumert, the resident expert. Ask him anything imaginable about silver and he'll have an answer—it will even be accurate! Silver devotees like Dustin Hoffman, Joan Rivers, Christie Brinkley, and Robert Duvall depend on his advice when they browse for that treasured collectible or for the perfect gift. The third-floor collection of antique sterling Georgian, Sheffield, Victorian, and Tiffany silver is mind-boggling. Arrayed with the enormous selection of modern silver, it's almost overwhelming.

Absolutely overwhelming is the range of flatware—plate, gold-plated, and stainless, not to mention sterling—the largest assortment available anywhere in the world, with over 500 patterns to choose from.

In the spirit of one-stop shopping, you can also pick up crystal and china to accompany the silver. Not surprisingly, the bridal service department is one of the best in the city.

Jewelry is also very important at Fortunoff's. The first floor, always bustling with activity, glitters with its displays of rings, bracelets, necklaces, and brooches. Many pieces are designed exclusively for Fortunoff and carry price tags that always strike us as more than reasonable. Due to the stores' tremendous volume, Fortunoff tends to offer a lot of glitz for the buck.

Moreover, Fortunoff sticks by its glitz. Everything sold can also be repaired or restored in the second floor service department. With three watchmakers, three hand engravers, two machine engravers, and two polishers, you can have any Fortunoff purchase serviced here for a lifetime.

Still, the most intriguing thing about Fortunoff is its sheer breadth of merchandise, artfully displayed in a 20,000-square-foot arena—from a $25 silver-plate frame to a 30-carat flawless diamond for $100,000, there's something for almost anyone at The Source. 🍎

Frette

799 Madison Avenue   (212) 988-5221
between 67th and 68th Streets
New York, NY 10021

Since 1860 Frette has been making the things that household dreams are made of—beautiful sheets, table linens, towels, blankets, and even lingerie. The traditional supplier to European royal families, deluxe hotels, international embassies, and indeed the altar of St. Peter's in Rome, the Italian company has had this outpost on Madison Avenue since 1981.

Recently redone to look like an elegant townhome, it is a warm and inviting place. After all, there's a working fireplace, and antique paintings decorate some walls. Others are covered by Frette-made tapestries dating from the turn of the century. The lingerie department resembles the most seductive of boudoirs.

While Porthault is renowned for prints and Pratesi for embroideries, jacquards are Frette's great claim to fame. Though jacquards present the effect of a print, the decorative elements are actually woven. Frette mastered the technique in the 1880s with the introduction of sophisticated state-of-the-art machinery and has devoted much of its energy to refining its patterns and designs ever since. Pastels are a specialty, but the color spectrum runs from boldest red to trendiest jet black. Furthermore, if none of their colors really matches your scheme, they'll customize just the right dye for you.

Using only the finest Egyptian cottons, Belgian linens, and Italian silks, sheet sets—top, bottom, and two shams—sell from $750 to $3,700. We're very fond of a pattern called Leonardesco Novecento, fashioned after a ceiling in the Palazzo Sforzefco in Milan. Even at $800 for a king-size set, the pattern is so popular that Frette had a loom specially computerized to weave it.

So what do you get for $3,700? Nothing less than pure sensuous silk, ornamented by hand-embroidery and complete with a recommended laundry service—none other than Berkley Sutton on York Avenue. Their services are expensive, but then you can't trust these silken treasures to just anyone!

Just ask Rita Miccoli, Frette's U.S. coordinator. She takes care of their home-consulting department. Rita will work with you to coordinate everything Frette can supply for your home, be it bedroom, powder room, or exceptional linens designed exclusively for that very special occasion. Rita worked with Ivana Trump on the restoration of the Plaza Hotel. Now all the hotel's sheets, towels, even the luscious terry robe in each bathroom, are Frette. We suppose, if you're interested in outfitting your home in Frette, you could take a test drive by spending a night at the Plaza!

People like Joan Collins and Oprah Winfrey count on Rita to make their tables the most hospitable in the neighborhood. Place mats start at $65. Hand-embroidered beauties go for as much as $250 apiece, including matching napkin, while tablecloths range from $250 to $3,000. But are Frette's custom-design capabilities what most interest the likes of Joan and Oprah? You, too, can have your own design, your own logo or family crest embroidered on your table linens. Rita will work out the price with you. Ask about machine-embroidery as opposed to hand, if you want to save a few dollars, and be prepared to wait eight to twelve weeks for delivery.

They can also pick up the patterns in your wallpaper or in the fabrics of your furniture. Whatever your taste in design, Frette, and Rita, can work with it.

Looking for the perfect bed set for the world's greatest bachelor pad? Look no longer—it's Frette's Oriente, a black silk jacquard. It's dramatic, alluring, and oh, so inviting. It's yours for $3,400. The quilt will cost you another $2,200, but it's worth every lira for all those nights of *siogni d'oro*—sweet dreams, of course. 🍒

The H. Lexington Collection

907 Madison Avenue   (212) 570-0060
between 72nd and 73rd Streets
New York, NY 10021

Debbie Hecht wanted to create what she calls a lifestyle boutique—a place to find all those unnecessary little accessories that add to the beauty of your home and to the quality of your life. There may not be a single thing in her store you (or anyone else for that matter) really *needs*, but there's sure to be plenty you want.

The H. Lexington Collection is the sort of place you go to browse for sheer enjoyment. Of course, since there are so many irresistible items in this intimate, clubby boutique, browsing quickly turns into serious shopping, especially if you're in the market for a gift or two. We've very pleasantly surprised a couple of friends with a lovely oak and brass English board game for about $60—something neither would ever have dreamed of buying for themselves. They still don't know how to play it, but it makes a very pretty conversation piece. We've also found Debbie's selection of dried flower arrangements to be a terrific source of inspiration, gift-wise. Beautiful and long-lasting, they range in price from $45 to $400.

Debbie believes in the gracious touch—the custom of taking tea, for instance. She can put together a basket dedicated to that civilized tradition that is guaranteed to motivate even non-Anglophiles to practice the ritual—small boxes of herb teas at $2.50 each, a $7 tin of genuine English biscuits, an assortment of small jars of Oxbridge jams for $7, and a $17.95 book entitled *Proper Tea*.

We'd be tempted to add the ever-so-serviceable silver-plated toast rack for about $20. Not a *de rigueur* tea accoutrement, it does seem, nevertheless, very properly British, *and* it works so well as a napkin or letter holder. If the latter strikes you as the best use, you'll probably love Debbie's wonderful group of desk accessories, including letter openers and magnifying glasses in "never needs polishing" gold-plated brass with *faux* ivory handles intricately carved with a medieval motif. They're $38 and $58 respectively.

For just $20, the H. Lexington Collection has the perfect gift for a loved one, be it from mother to daughter, husband to wife, friend to friend. In fact, it's called a Love Book and it's filled with charmingly sentimental poetry, each page scented with a light, captivating fragrance. Equally appropriate a present for a special someone is the large, warm, and woolly Scottish tartan travel rug. Made of mohair, it's available in light and heavy weights for $125 to $175. Debbie even carries *The Tartan Book* for $5.95, so you can study the history of your clan or the one that claims the tartan you chose.

If all of this doesn't tempt you, H. Lexington's unique collection of cards certainly will. All imported, mostly from England, they make your greetings stand out from those of the masses—no Hallmarks here—and sell for about $2 each.

From attention-getting $2 greeting cards to a handsome $1,000 partners' desk, something at H. Lexington Collection is bound to appeal to your sense of a life lived in style.   ❧

Lalique

680 Madison Avenue   (212) 355-6550
between 61st and 62nd Streets
New York, NY 10022

These days, every dawn seems to brighten on the announcement of a new, often celebrity-associated fragrance, each more seductively named and lavishly packaged than the last. We wonder how René Lalique would have felt about the consequences of what he and his friend Roger Coty wrought on the world in 1907.

It all started when Coty asked Lalique, then internationally renowned as a designer of exquisite jewelry, to fashion a label for a perfume he intended to launch. Having reached what seemed to be the pinnacle of his career at the tender age of forty, Lalique was ripe for an exciting new challenge. He decided Coty's fragrance deserved something more distinctive than a label. He began experimenting with glass and produced a sumptuous bottle to encase the scent.

That bottle not only signaled Lalique's new career as a glassmaker, it revolutionized the perfume industry and paved the way for the current big-bucks fragrance sweepstakes. Prior to this innovation, perfume had been sold only in perfumeries where customers brought their own bottles to be filled from large glass storage containers. The Lalique-Coty collaboration enabled people to purchase perfume at countless outlets and positioned the bottle itself as a vitally important part of any particular perfume's mystique.

Lalique's expertise and creativity as a glassmaker blossomed as the demand for his bottles and other decorative objects grew. By 1933 his glassware collection consisted of over 1,500 items, and he had applied his imagination to fountains, furniture, doors, chandeliers, and entire buildings.

Upon René's death in 1945, his son Marc assumed responsibility for design and production. It was Marc who transformed Lalique glass into crystal and who virtually patented the use of an acid-etched finish to enhance decorative elements. Marc's daughter—René's granddaughter—Marie-Claude carries on the Lalique tradition of designing richly decorated glassware, working in René's studio and overseeing the production in the Alsace factory he opened in 1921.

The Madison Avenue shop dedicated to her family's legacy is tiny, but oh, so sophisticatedly gray—gray carpeting, gray leather banquettes, gray suede walls. The interior was designed and built in Paris. Shipped to New York in large containers, it was reassembled and installed here two years ago as the first store in the U.S. entirely dedicated to the fine art of Lalique.

Stemware starts at about $65 per piece and goes up to $140. Decanters range from $245 to $800. For collectors, there's quite a selection of the 2,000 items currently made by the company, from a $125 perfume bottle to the fabulous $2,200 vase called Bacchantes with its graceful, luminous nude figures.

Serious collectors should sign on to the two-year waiting list for the horse-head sculpture that sells for $12,500. You see, only fifteen are made each year. Manager Alexandra Murkowska will be happy to estimate when you can expect yours.

Quite spectacular and precious is the truly awe-inspriring Lalique chandelier in the center of the store. It's called Champs-Elysées. Frankly, it took us a long time to screw up our courage to ask Alexandra about its price. At only $7,750 we'll put it on our wish list. Maybe we could arrange for a waiting list for it too.

Pratesi

829 Madison Avenue   (212) 288-2315
at 69th Street
New York, NY 10021

From the outside, it's a pretty nondescript-looking store. There's something about the configuration of the windows on this corner location that reminds us of an old five-and-dime—that is, until you take a good long look at the display. Then there's no question that you're gazing at some of the most beautifully lavish, yet understatedly elegant, sheets and towels imaginable.

The ground floor at Pratesi is done in subtle tones of gray, dramatically accented by black, to show off the incredible selection of embroidered towels. All the toweling is made of Egyptian cotton, but the design and production is done in Pistoia, Italy. It's all very thick, very luxurious, and costs from $110 to $190 per bath towel, depending upon the elaborate quotient of the embroidery.

The sheets are instantly recognizable as Pratesi with their fine three-line stitch and chain-pattern embroideries. Others have tried to copy the look but are stymied by the subtle delicacy that has been the Pratesi trademark for four generations, transforming an ordinary bedroom into a captivating boudoir. King-size sheet sets (top, fitted bottom, and two shams) start at $890 for cotton and can go to $4,000 for silk. If you want to special order a color, add thirty percent.

If you want to ensure truly sweet dreams, treat yourself to a cashmere blanket. The cashmere is Chinese, only the best of course, but it is woven in Italy. In king size, it will be $2,600 worth of warmth—and cool. Cashmere is a great natural insulator.

Some families choose to launch their children into an appreciation of the finer things in life very early with Baby Pratesi. A complete bassinet costs $2,500. For the crib, Baby Pratesi sheet sets are $200.

If you're into more the sublime than the ridiculous, check out the Pratesi gift selections—men's and women's handkerchiefs for $20, cocktail napkins for $9 to $18 apiece. We were entranced by the traveling cosmetic and jewelry cases in the pretty flowered Vivaio pattern. Machine washable, they run from $30 to $70.

Senior vice president Adelaide Goitien is a delight, and is always there to help you pick the perfect Pratesi bed and bath wardrobe to pamper and please you.   🌑

Puiforcat

811 Madison Avenue	(212) 734-3838
at 68th Street	FAX (212) 734-3165
New York, NY 10021	

Until December 1988, it was difficult to find examples of Puiforcat's mastery of the art of silver craftsmanship in the U.S. The occasional piece or pattern was available only in a few select shops. Eliane Scali rectified the unfortunate situation when she opened this small store dedicated to the artistry and tradition of Puiforcat.

As manager Eva Merritt will tell you, it is a tradition that can be traced to 1820 and to Paris, where Emile Puiforcat established a silversmith dynasty in the Marais district. Originally a workshop devoted to the mass production of industrial silverwork—serving dishes and hollowware—the house's shift toward the creation of luxury pieces sold directly to a wealthy clientele began a century later under Louis-Victor Puiforcat. He moved the operation "uptown" to the Boulevard Haussmann, where it remains today. He also began to amass a monumental collection of the most exceptional silver designs ever produced.

Much of that collection now belongs to the Louvre, though about a hundred pieces remain with the Société Puiforcat. In any case, the firm retains exclusive rights to the entire collection, allowing it to reproduce a staggering 180 flatware patterns and 10,000 hollowware designs.

Puiforcat silver continues to be made entirely by hand—each piece individually crafted, each destined to become an heirloom.

Five-piece place settings like the popular Cannes or Annecy are about $1,250. They are representative of the inspired work of Jean Puiforcat, who was the unchallenged master of Art Deco–style silver. He designed the silver for that ill-fated floating temple of Art Deco, the *Normandie*. (She caught fire while docked in New York and sank, courtesy of the New York Fire Department, causing irreparable damage to Franco-

American relations.) Fortunately, the pattern named (what else?) the Normandie endures.

You get a sense of Louis-Victor's unparalleled collection and the quality of Puiforcat's current craftsmanship in the stylized reproduction of a sterling tea set originally commissioned by an eighteenth-century King of Portugal. With ivory handles, it's priced at $263,000. If they're out of stock, don't worry. It takes only six months for them to make another.

In more contemporary vein, there's a spectacular Empire soup tureen for $31,105, as well as Puiforcat's concession to modern economics—silver plate. They've translated three of their patterns into plate, which sell for about $200 per place setting. True to form, while it is not made by hand, the quality is exceptional—heavily coated with forty microns of silver that will last at least a lifetime. And it is hand-finished.

Jewelry is another relatively new addition to the Puiforcat repertoire. Crafted in sterling silver with vermeil trim and studded with semiprecious stones, the cuff links, earrings, and bracelets are translations of Jean Puiforcat's dinner and hollowware designs. They are priced from about $800 to $5,000.

Puiforcat—it is to silver what haute couture is to fashion—the hallmark. 🌣

Schweitzer Linens

457 Columbus Avenue   (212) 799-9629
between 81st and 82nd Streets
New York, NY 10024

1053 Lexington Avenue   (212) 570-0236
at 75th Street
New York, NY 10021

1132 Madison Avenue   (212) 249-8361
at 84th Street
New York, NY 10028

First opened by Sandy Schweitzer some twenty years ago, this ultimate of linen stores has enjoyed considerable expansion in recent years. The second location opened on Columbus Avenue in 1982, a third on Lexington in 1989. Schweitzer Linens has a guileless formula for success—a large and complete inventory, mattress pads to place mats, featuring well-priced quality items.

Schweitzer is quite simply the most complete, upscale linen store in the city. It stands out in a market otherwise dominated by specialty boutiques dedicated to one label, usually French or Italian, and department stores committed to domestic brands. But here, be it French, Italian, Belgian, German, Chinese, or domestic, you can find a healthy selection. Florals, stripes, bold patterns, and embroideries, from cotton sheets to damask tablecloths—they have it all.

You can adopt the look of Porthault, Pratesi, Frette, or your own mix-and-match motif. Schweitzer carries the best, but the prices are lower than you might expect. King-size sheets run from $375 to $600 for a set including two standard shams, usually with button closures.

Schweitzer's big on terry too—American terry, which the family swears is the best. Accordingly, they carry a terrific assortment of towels, terry bathrobes too. While it would seem they already feature every color you could possibly envision, if nothing quite matches your color scheme, bring in some sample swatches or paint chips. Schweitzer will custom-color terry merchandise to match. It will take six to eight weeks, but there's no additional charge.

The inventory here changes frequently, so you might consider taking a cue from Princess Yasmin Aga Khan, Yoko Ono, Anthony Quinn, and Liza Minnelli and stop by on a regular basis to see what's what.   ❦

Steuben

715 Fifth Avenue	(212) 752-1441
at 56th Street	(800) 223-1234
New York, NY 10022	

A bona fide American art form, Steuben glass has been chosen by every president of the United States as a gift of state since 1947, when Harry Truman started the tradition by presenting Princess Elizabeth with the Sidney Waugh–designed Merry-Go-Round Bowl upon the occasion of her marriage to Prince Philip. Appropriately enough, President and Mrs. Reagan gave Steuben's Crusaders Bowl to Lady Diana when she married Prince Charles.

Lucky her! Steuben, a part of the Corning Glass works since 1918, makes some of the finest clear lead crystal in the world. Its works are represented in important museum collections in a number of countries, and are prized for the excellence of their design and purity of form. Steuben is the only major glassmaker that never uses acid polishing. Instead, the company employs a time-consuming hand-finishing technique that gives Steuben crystal its legendary brilliance. Furthermore, there are no seconds at Steuben. Every piece is thoroughly inspected at various stages of production—about one quarter are rejected in this rigorous process and destroyed.

The firm's Fifth Avenue shop boasts the world's most complete collection of present-day Steuben. Its window displays are always arresting, thanks to the talented Mark Tamayo. The store itself is dramatic and compelling, designed to show off Steuben's sculptural, ornamental, and functional glass to its luminescent best.

Head for the museumlike back room dedicated to special exhibitions of their engraved and sculptural works, each in its own locked, spotlit case. Prices start in the $1,675 range for a piece descriptively entitled *Triangles Two.* Or perhaps a $55,000 sculpture by avant-garde artist Peter Alridge is more your style.

Whatever your style, whatever style Steuben you seek, Mary Minstrell is the person to see. She knows absolutely everything there is to know about Steuben, as well she should—she's been here for twenty-five years. Mary will show you the precious collection of animals, known as "hand coolers." The name comes from nineteenth-century etiquette, which dictated that well-bred ladies carry a piece of glass in their palms when attending dances to keep them from sweating—excuse us, we mean perspiring. At any rate, these tiny charmers start at about $120 for a palm-sized, soothingly smooth owl, or a two-and-a-half-inch-wide curled-up cat.

We also adore the snail, the first animal Steuben's artists ever created, for $165. Only three and a quarter inches long, the little creature is a delightful representation of the fluidity of crystal, as is the graceful bouquet vase. Decorative as it is practical, shaped to encourage blooms to cascade over its sides, the base sells for $240. A larger version goes for $360.

Should you wish to commemorate a very special occasion with a totally unique piece, talk to Clifford R. Palmer, who arranges all commissions. He will discuss your original concept and then coordinate with Steuben's designers to translate it into a crystal work of art. There's a

$25,000 minimum and up to a year's wait once the order is placed. And there can be a substantial wait before Steuben can even accept the order.

For more urgent occasions, you can always have certain pieces engraved with a meaningful inscription. Andrea Berta is in charge of those services, which generally take six to eight weeks, depending on the time of year. The closer you get to Christmas, the longer the wait. The popularity of Steuben glass as gifts is, after all, not the private preserve of presidents.   ❦

CHAPTER SIX

Jewelry . . .

Baubles, bangles, and big bucks

*I*f we start with Breakfast at Tiffany's, where will we ever find ourselves by lunchtime? Destitute, no doubt, if we're doing a thousand a day before lunch.

While the oil sheikhs may still buy some of their baubles in Geneva or Zurich, where they keep their money, the real place to find the world-class sparklers is right here in Old New York. Whether you're going for the high style of the great Fifth Avenue houses (native or transplanted)— Winston, Cartier, Bulgari, Buccellati, not to mention Tiffany—or the downscale chic of the 47th Street Chasidim, you don't have far to look.

But designing-your-own is taking its place alongside these pillars of the jewelry establishment. The small custom-houses with original craftsmen and impeccable taste may well become the Winstons of tomorrow. Their locations may be on Fifth or Madison, but their styles are decidedly nonconformist. And they're making a noticeable impact on fashion and style, not to mention jewelry boxes and wallets.

Whatever the origin, though, New York is truly lighting up these days—and all that glitters may not be gold. While all those crime stories about New York haven't discouraged the glitter at the society soirées, they have given a big boost to some of the city's most celebrated costume jewelers. Their work may look real, but costs less—so much so that your thousand will go a long way to outfitting you in fabulous fakes.

Buccellati

Jewelry	(212) 308-5533
725 Fifth Avenue	
between 56th and 57th Streets	
New York, NY 10022	

Silver	(212) 308-2900
46 East 57th Street	
New York, NY 10022	

Buccellati. The name caresses the tongue—the jewelry and silver bearing that name seduce the eye.

A family enterprise founded at the turn of the century, the House of Buccellati draws upon a traditional art of gold- and silversmithing that dates back to the eighteenth century. Now run in America by the founder's namesake and grandson, Mario Buccellati II, the company maintains its reputation for innovative creations and excellent workmanship with all design and production still originating in Milan by Buccellati-trained craftsmen.

The company's presence in New York is twofold—a jewelry store in Trump Tower and a space devoted to silver in the Buccellati Building on 57th Street.

The frenzy of the Trump Tower seems a universe away once you step into the refined world of Buccellati, into a store designed to evoke the interior of a jewel box—plus fabric-covered walls and a hand-painted ceiling depicting lush foliage. Here you can marvel at the Buccellati signature pieces that employ a jewelry technique pioneered by the firm—texture engraving. Using special tools, lines are engraved in the metal, creating beautiful patterns. They capture and reflect light in a unique way, with the metal adopting a lustrous jewel-like appearance. The result is breathtaking, like the intricately patterned yellow and white gold cuff-bracelet with 140 diamonds totaling 9.11 carats and priced at $128,000. There's a distinctive delicacy about Buccellati designs, whether they take the form of an elaborate $81,500 yellow and white gold necklace with nine oval rubellites, forty-two sapphires, and fifty-six diamonds or a sweet $1,750 yellow, white, and rose gold pin fashioned as a thistle and laced with silver.

Manager Robert Philipson is a fountain of knowledge about jewelry, Buccellati and otherwise. If none of his one-of-a-kind pieces quite suits, rest assured that something can be designed especially for you, to your specifications.

A visit to the silver store is equally intriguing. The two levels are connected by a dramatic curved staircase. At the base, cradled in the curve, rests a magnificent silver centerpiece. It is cast as a mythological sea setting with Neptune as the central character, and playful mermaids, seahorses, and children surrounding him. The tray, balanced on ten supports, encases a mirror that gives the illusion of a reflecting pool. The centerpiece took three years to complete and is priced at $750,000.

The first floor houses the Buccellati collection of flatware—twenty-two patterns with prices ranging from $600 to $1,600 for a five-piece place setting. We're partial to Milano at $610. It's contemporary, yet timeless, and graced with classical elements like beading, a combination typical of the Buccellati style in silver and in jewelry. As one family member says, "We have been influenced by Italian Classical and Baroque jewelry and even more by eighteenth-century French and Italian art. We use elements from each to create contemporary style, but we reject practically no influence—be it architecture or even a sunset. After all, some things are universally beautiful. And we are not afraid to incorporate anything in the design and execution of our pieces."

A little of the Italian classic meets contemporary influence in our favorite Buccellati gift item—the $390 champagne opener. Executed in what Buccellati calls Old Italian, it is elaborately beautiful and eminently practical. It not only makes popping the cork a mere twist of the wrist, it even sports a device to cut the wire.

Buccellati—the beauty of the name does the product proud.

Bulgari

730 Fifth Avenue   (212) 315-9000
at 57th Street
New York, NY 10022

The name is Greek but the home base of this jewelry dynasty is Rome, where the shop that Sotirio Bulgari opened near the Spanish Steps with sons Giorgio and Constantino in 1905 was once described by Andy Warhol as the city's "most important museum of contemporary art." Since 1977, New York has had such a minimuseum tucked away in a corner of The Pierre. But the growing demand for Bulgari's lifestyle jewelry, which works as well with jeans as it does with evening gowns, has prompted the current generation of Bulgari brothers, Paolo, Gianni, and Nicola to expand their Manhattan base with this brand new store on Fifth Avenue.

Designed by Piero Sartogo, it's essentially an enlarged version of the gem of a boutique in The Pierre—lots of glass, mirror, chrome, and brass skillfully combined to produce a luxuriously rich, surprisingly warm environment. It's the kind of place that encourages you to come in, relax, and relish the opportunity to fondle beautiful jewelry. The divinely debonair Nicola, who's often on the floor, encourages you to pick up the pieces, hold them up to the light, and put them on. He maintains that "fine jewels are to be enjoyed and experienced."

In the process of experiencing Bulgari you'll notice certain traits that serve as the firm's signature. The firm emphasizes the use of colored stones and tends to use yellow gold for settings rather than white gold or platinum. They also have an interesting habit of intermingling gold with steel and other seemingly incongruous materials. And the cabochon cut—rounded and polished rather than faceted—first adopted by Bulgari in the '30s, revolutionized the look of serious jewelry as did their innovative use of semiprecious stones like tourmalines, rubellite, topazes, periodots, amethysts, coral, and turquoise.

The broad range of materials and the Bulgari penchant for the constant evolution of their designs allows for prices that run a very wide gamut, several hundred dollars to well over a million. It's likely that whatever your budget you can find something that suits it. The inventory of their handcrafted jewelry is large and varied, with prices and styles for the young, as well as the not-so-young.

We were taken with an 18-carat gold necklace, its heavy carved links accented by steel balls. Resting solidly at the base of the neck, its substantial, elegant look breezes through day into evening at $13,000. More formal, and more expensive, is the six-millimeter pearl necklace laced with amethyst rondelles set in gold for $25,000 and the stunning $59,000 gold and diamond collar—large, gold, heart-shaped links alternating with oversized links of pavé diamonds set in geometric patterns. For truly important evenings there's a pair of killer earrings of pavé diamonds alternating with baguettes and surrounding two good sized marquis cut diamonds—$98,000. The 7.66-carat, flawless oval diamond surrounded by 28 baguette emeralds weighing 4.23 carats makes a perfectly complementary ring for $235,000.

For everyday Bulgari wear, there's a never-ending stream of new styles of modestly priced bracelets, gold and steel woven to embrace aquamarines, pink tourmelines, or amethysts and running about $9,000. They're the sort of pieces you can put on and never take off, as is the new Anfiteatro watch, available for men as well as women. Introduced in December 1988, it is already a status symbol classic with its recessed Roman numeraled dial, gold beveled case curved to nestle on the wrist, and brown crocodile leather strap. For men, the watch is priced at $4,200—$3,900 for women.

Typical of Bulgari, it's just as finely finished on the inside as it is on the out, just as beautifully detailed. Indeed, most Bulgari pieces could be considered reversible if it were possible to physically turn them inside out. Knowing Bulgari, they're probably working on it. As Nicola says, "design, design, design. It's everything." ❦

Cartier

653 Fifth Ave. at 52nd Street   (212) 753-0111
New York, NY 10022

Cartier established its beachhead in America in the best Manhattan tradition. In 1917, Pierre Cartier, grandson of the firm's founder, traded a couple of strings of beads for a five-story Fifth Avenue mansion, now designated a historical landmark by the city of New York, and still Cartier's home. Of course, even in the early years of the century, the double strand pearl necklace Pierre Cartier handed over to Mrs. Morton Plant in exchange for her palacelike home was worth considerably more than the legendary $24 value of the beads used to purchase the isle of Manhattan—$1,200,000 to be precise. Even translated into today's dollars, it would seem that Pierre had as fine an eye for real estate as he did for jewelry.

But it was really his older brother Louis who was responsible for catapulting the family business that began in a small Paris workshop in 1847 into the firm that Edward VII of England proclaimed, "if they have become the Jewelers of Kings, it is because they are the King of Jewelers." Louis was the first jeweler to work with platinum. He was the first to fashion transformable diadems—crowns and tiaras that could double as necklaces or other ornaments. Today that may not sound like a stunning innovation, but in an era when the coronation of Edward VII generated orders for 102 royally jeweled headpieces, the notion of being able to wear one's crown on occasions other than those of state was both novel and intriguing.

Louis also put Cartier on the map for timepieces. He was determined to restore the great clock-making traditions that had been lost toward the end of the 18th century. The clocks and watches made under his supervision competed with each other for their beauty, originality, and technical perfection. The best known example of all three qualities is the Cartier tank watch, designed as a tribute to the American Expeditionary Forces and presented in 1918 to General Pershing and several of his officers. Louis's inspiration for the now classic design had been a World War I combat tank he'd seen the year before.

The other Cartier hallmark initiated by Louis is the animal styles so beloved by the Duchess of Windsor. The recent sale of her jewels has revived the popularity of Cartier's "Great Cats." If you want to jump on the bandwagon, may we suggest the breathtaking double tiger necklace? The tigers, dazzlingly rendered in pave canary diamonds and striped with onyx, crouch on a gold collar encrusted with diamonds. So intricate (the tigers' heads move, their emerald eyes never missing a trick), it took two years to create. It is a one-of-a-kind piece priced at $675,000. Should it have been sold by the time you stop in, you can always console yourself with a $4,000 trinket, the charming 18-carat-gold panther pin with its bright emerald eyes and pert onyx nose.

Or you might consult with salon manager Jill King about another of the fabulously jeweled cats, like the platinum and diamond panther brooch with sapphire spots. Indeed, you have to speak to someone about them as the prices are only available upon request. But don't be intimidated by the prospect. The whole staff under Jill's gentle direction is a delight. Each is an expert, dedicated to quality and service—Walter Kroehnert, for example, the watchmaker who's been here for 53 years. If there's anything he doesn't know about watches we'll eat ours! Then there's the legendary Cartier service department run by Anne Holbach. They can reload your pen, redesign Aunt Tillie's ugly old brooch, or open the jammed lock on your leather attaché case. Theirs is complete service dispensed with warmth and humor.

George Raymond oversees the stationery department. It was another of Louis's innovations to develop and carry accessories complementary to precious gems—like original creations in enamel, silver, and crystal, fancy leather goods and distinguished stationery. Certainly, George and his lovely selection of writing papers, cards, invitations, and announcements must be just what Louis had in mind. George is one of the country's foremost experts on protocol, so you can be sure of the social acceptability of anything you order from him.

But the person truly synonymous with Cartier in New York is the firm's U.S. Chairman of the Board, Ralph Destino. Tall, lean, and elegantly handsome, Ralph is an accessible, hands-on executive, always happy to make sure that all your Cartier needs are attended to. He's just as concerned about your satisfaction as he is Elizabeth Taylor's or Elton John's or Lionel Ritchie's. Whether you're in the market for the $5,000 Tank Americaine watch, the latest version of the celebrated classic, or the price-available-on-request white and yellow pave diamond tiger watch that doubles as an entrance-making bracelet, Ralph wants you to enjoy your Cartier experience.

We always do. It's just a pleasure to wander through the plush store, ogling all the goodies. And we've discovered a terrific and inexpensive souvenir of our Cartier visits—the divine Panthere de Cartier perfume. For only $200 you get an ounce of wonderful scent in an exquisite refillable flacon that admirably represents Cartier's distinctly elegant, always tasteful art.   ❦

Ciner Fashion Jewelers

20 West 37th Street   (212) 947-3770
between Fifth and Sixth
New York, NY 10018

Now here's a label to look for—not at their wholesale-only showroom, but at Bergdorf's, Ciro's on Fifth, and Jolie Gabor's on Madison. Ciner makes the most amazing costume jewelry, absolutely indistinguishable from the very real and very expensive thing. In fact, director of sales Jacqueline Rogers takes great pride in the knowledge that "at every Hollywood function, every Washington ball, every East Coast gala, you will see many prominent stars and socialites wearing incredible 'Ciner Designs' that have the look of Winston, Bulgari, Van Cleef, etc."

There's a good reason Ciner jewelry looks so real. The firm, founded by Emanuel Ciner in 1892, operated as a manufacturer of fine jewelry until the 1930s, when the family recognized a growing market for beautiful bargains. They entered the business of fabulous *fauxs* by applying to their manufacturing the same techniques they had employed to make the more precious variety. Two generations later, Emanuel's granddaugher Pat and her husband, David Hill, are still insisting that every stone is hand-set, every pearl hand-strung and-knotted. Furthermore, each piece is finished with an 18-carat-gold-plated process that withstands the test of time. We know women who inherited their mothers' Ciner jewelry—it looks just as good and is just as fashionable as the day it was purchased decades ago.

We adore Ciner's black enamel frog, complete with gold bumps and emerald cabochon eyes for approximately $180, depending on the retailer. There's a pavé version closer to $220. Other brooches are multijeweled with large cabochon or pearl center stones and sell for about $325. At around $1,300, Ciner's gold and rhinestone collar is a knockout, particularly with a strapless dress or gown.

By our calculation, you could put together a world-class Ciner jewelry collection for less than $10,000. And we guarantee that only you and your bank account would know the difference. Your friends would have to attack you with a loupe, and even then it's doubtful they'd know what to look for. We've graciously accepted any number of compliments on our Ciner pieces from some of Winston's and Bulgari's best clients, while commiserating with them over the cost of insurance and the security risks associated with wearing such serious jewels!

You don't have to wait for your next trip to New York to start that collection, either. Ciner jewelry is sold at fine stores nationwide. Just call Jacqueline and ask her where you can find it in your area—or ask that friend of yours who has been a little coy about the origins of the awesome diamond necklace she's been wearing lately.   ❦

Gorevic & Gorevic

635 Madison Avenue   (212) 832-9000
at 59th Street
New York, NY 10022

Gorevic & Gorevic—it sounds like a family business. And it is. The Gorevics have been at it for seventy-five years; they're into the third generation of specialists in antique and estate jewelry, objets d'art, Russian and Viennese enamels, antique silver, nineteenth-century French animal sculptures, and of all things, American carousel horses. They also pride themselves on their selection of contemporary Italian designer jewelry. Diversification is a Gorevic byword and clearly sets their firm apart from any other jewelry in the city.

It all started nearly a century ago when Ferdinand Gorevic left his native Russia for Czechoslovakia, where he opened an antique store. In fear of the Nazi takeover in 1940, he set sail for New York where he opened the precursor of the current establishment. Eventually, his son Charles and his grandson Roger joined him in the business.

Today, it is Roger and his wife, Cali, who are most in evidence in the store, though Charles makes regular appearances. In fact, you can count on a Gorevic being on duty Monday through Saturday, 10:00 A.M. to 6:00 P.M.

Shopping, even browsing, here draws you into the family. Roger and Cali are more interested in developing a regular clientele, in making new friends, than in just making a sale. For them, it's not a proper transaction unless they feel they can expect to see the buyer again. To help ensure the comfort of their clients, whom they treat more like guests, Roger and Cali even take pains to accommodate youngsters who might have tagged along. A desk in the back is stocked with crayons and paper. The resulting works of art are proudly displayed in a gallery devoted exclusively to the children.

But make no mistake, while friendly and unassuming, Gorevic & Gorevic is the site of very serious merchandise, serious even when it tickles your fancy with a cherished memory. The carousel horses strike an emotional chord in most people. Exquisitely hand-carved and hand-painted, they once inhabited the thousands of carousels that brought joy to millions across the country. Today, only 183 operating merry-go-rounds remain. Is it any wonder that Gorevic & Gorevic's relics command $25,000 apiece?

Charming as they are, the horses are a bit on the large side. Smaller and certainly more versatile is an extraordinary Deco diamond necklace. The pendant can be worked into several configurations—an opera-length diamond chain, two bracelets, or a choker—five pieces of jewelry with a total weight of 33 1/2 carats for only $75,000!

If, at those prices, nonwearable art is more your style, you might be interested in the delightful little cherub astride a goat. Perfect as a desk ornament, it's silver gilt, circa 1580. The goat has diamonds for eyes, hooves of real horn, and the head comes off to reveal that this little statue doubles as a decanter—at $30,000.

Should silver be your heart's desire, you will fall in love with Gorevic & Gorevic. They have an exceptional collection, ranging from the sublime to the ridiculous—from the classic lines of an eighteenth-century English bone marrow scoop for $300 to a modern British rendition of a silver champagne fountain, complete with electric pump encased in its wooden base, for a staggering $250,000!

And remember, whether your budget calls for a $450 gold charm by Italian designer Pomellato or that amazing fountain, you will be subject to the added value of becoming a member of the Gorevics' extended family. 🍀

Harry Winston

718 Fifth Avenue   (212) 245-2000
at 56th Street
New York, NY 10019

"Talk to me, Harry Winston, tell me all about it!" demanded Marilyn Monroe while declaring "Diamonds Are a Girl's Best Friend." No dumb blond, she knew whereof she spoke; Harry Winston the entrepreneur was known as the King of Diamonds, and the jewelry empire he founded remains the purveyor of the world's most fabulous stones.

Don't let the massive gates, the locked door, the black-clad receptionist intimidate you. Harry Winston really is a warm and welcoming place, once you state your business. Of course, it helps to look as if you have the wherewithal to deal with their *very important* jewelry—like the Burmese ruby and diamond necklace set in platinum for $1.8 million. Or perhaps that other necklace, sparkling with 120 carats of D-flawless diamonds, all pear shaped, and priced at $7 million, is more your style.

The receptionist is not nearly so forbidding as her clothing suggests. She has to wear black. It's a tradition. Harry, a great showman, knew how well black sets off stones—no vibrant colors to compete with his precious gems. Still, once you pass muster, you are almost instantly enveloped in a serene cocoon of gray—gray carpet so lush you can be forgiven if your steps falter, gray silk-covered walls, luxuriously draped gray curtains.

This is the Main Salon, more museum than store. Nothing—not the beautifully understated Empire desks, the touch of gilt here, the mirror there—nothing detracts from the breathtaking flights of fancy in the cases embedded in the walls. The sense of a museum is appropriate. Many of the major pieces on display at the Smithsonian's Hall of Gems claim some association with Harry Winston—cut by, designed by, donated by. You've heard of the Smithsonian's pride, the Hope Diamond? You guessed it, a little gift from Harry.

The debonair Peter Kairis is in charge of Harry Winston's New York treasure trove. As sales manager, he will lend you the benefit of his considerable experience to find or commission the bauble destined to announce to the world that you have arrived.

If you're not quite ready for a museum-quality piece, you can trot across the street to the Petit Salon in the Trump Tower. There you can choose from a less serious collection—adorable gold taxi whistles encrusted with a glittering array of precious stones in the $4,500 to $6,000 range or a lovely group of pavé diamond earrings for $5,000 to $6,000.

As part of what Winston considers their "boutique line," the Petit Salon carries the new Ultimate Timepiece Collection—watches doubling as decorative jewelry. Made to order, to mirror the client's individual taste and to his or her wrist measurement, the watches can be constructed in any combination of gold, platinum, and jewels. It takes about six months and the cost runs $15,000 to $150,000. Mercifully, and in keeping with Winston's philosophy of watches being jewelry, there is no identifying logo splashed across the face of these timepieces, although an HW is discreetly tucked away in the invisible clasp.

Be it square-cut or pear-shaped, an 11 1/2-carat $800,000 emerald set in platinum, framed by pear-shaped and round diamonds from the imposing Main Salon or a $1,500 pair of sapphire cuff links from its jewel-box-like offspring, you can count on Winston's classic, elegant design and exquisite workmanship. Each piece is fashioned on the premises in the fascinating workrooms upstairs.

Indeed, there's much more to Winston than meets the eye—much more than the awe-inspiring finished jewelry. There's an incredible story here, a history sprinkled with people and gems sporting impressive titles—it's the stuff legends are made of. Winston vice president Laurence Krashes has chronicled it all in *Harry Winston—The Ultimate Jeweler,* the ultimate coffee-table book full of beautiful pictures of Winston's rare jewels of the world. At $100, anyone can take home this little bit of Winston.

And you know you are shopping in very good company as a Winston client, but we can't tell you exactly who, because Winston won't tell us—protecting the identity of their definitely rich and often very famous clients is another Winston tradition.

Helen Woodhull, Inc.

743 Fifth Avenue   (212) 826-1212
between 57th and 58th
New York, NY 10022

Helen Woodhull's is a world apart, literally and figuratively. Her cozy
gem of a salon sits eight stories above Fifth Avenue. You have to know it's
there—there's no glitzy window display at street level to tempt you inside. Once you step out of the tiny elevator, barely big enough for you
and the attendant, you enter a lovely, comforting environment, which, it
seems, just happens to showcase some very beautiful and quite distinctive jewelry.

The term "salon" is truly appropriate here. You feel like moving into
the space that Helen carefully restored to some of its early twentieth
century glamor (the building had been built originally to house elegant
bachelor quarters). Exquisitely carved wood mantels once again grace
the two fireplaces. Stately Chippendale chairs are everywhere, a plush
sofa invites you to sit and relax, while the pretty little silver tray on the
buffet, always supporting (depending upon the time of day) a tea service
or a decanter of sherry, indicates the hospitality that awaits.

Helen breezes in with her four-star smile and earth mother manner,
resplendent in a double strand of luminescent pearls. She loves pearls,
as you can see from a quick study of the cases housing some particularly
fine indications of an oyster's discontent. We had a passion for the dazzling earrings consisting of two large Burmese pearls dangling from a cap
of diamonds attached to a rosette of diamonds and pearls, until she recently sold them for $18,000. We may have to "settle" for the statement-
making pair of mobe pearls surrounded by an 18-carat setting of stylized
leaves accented by rubellite tourmalines for only $3,500.

Pearls are only one hallmark of the Helen Woodhull style, which has
been valued by connoisseurs since she first started designing jewelry in
the '60s. She's known as a pioneer for her revival of Egyptian, Greek,
Roman, Medieval, and Renaissance motifs, executing them with long-
neglected jewelry-making techniques like granulation, beading, the use
of bezel settings, and cabochon stones. Her distinctive leogryph pin is
her signature, typical of the delight and whimsy captured by many of her
designs. Part lion, part bird, the pin is crafted in 18-carat gold, shimmering with almost two carats of full-cut diamonds on the wings and base. It
costs $7,500 and sells regularly to a loyal clientele that have been col-

lecting Helen's work for years—Joanna Gleason, Anne Reinking, Kathleen Turner, Stephanie Zimbalist, Christine Hearst, and Sale and Robert Johnson.

Often they come up just to visit. It's such fun to sit and chat with the effervescent Helen, sipping some tea (or sherry) while she shows you her latest treasure. There's always something new to talk about, something new to take out of its case to try on and in such an incredible range of prices. A simple gold ring with a classical impression may sell for as little as $280, while a stunning 6.6-carat oval sapphire and diamond ring may fetch closer to $40,000.

But not all that glimmers here is gold, not all of Helen's treasures are jewelry. Tucked behind the salon, down a narrow corridor is Helen's gallery—home to an alternating series of permanent collections. Typically, it is a fascinating, somewhat eccentric assemblage—abstract paintings by 90-year-old Edna Gluck, antique embroideries mounted and framed as affordable art (about $700 and up), and an extraordinary selection of Medieval and Renaissance miniature paintings. Owning a gallery was a life-long dream of Helen's, one that her recent move from Madison Avenue to her Fifth Avenue aerie made possible. Though intimate, bordering on miniscule, it's rapidly gaining a reputation among collectors. When Helen mounted her first show of the miniature paintings, originally the illustrations of ancient manuscripts, it was the most important exhibition of such works in New York in more than 30 years, and valued at several million dollars.

So stopping by Helen Woodhull is a thrice enchanting experience—you get a chummy chat with Helen, as well as a chance to play with her wearable art and look at her hanging treasures. ❦

Kenneth Jay Lane

725 Fifth Avenue   (212) 751-6166
Trump Tower
New York, NY 10022

The story goes that one day Richard Burton walked into the connubial bedroom to find the bed strewn with astonishing baubles. "Priceless" necklaces, bracelets, and rings covered virtually every square inch. He flew into one of his famous larger-than-life rages, certain that the divine Elizabeth had gone on a shopping rampage at Harry Winston or some other store where one can drop millions. It took all of La Taylor's considerable feminine wiles to calm him down enough to listen to her explanation that it was only Kenny Lane's costume jewelry.

Only is perhaps a bit of an understatement. Ever since Kenneth became convinced that fake jewelry could be just as beautiful as the real thing and created his first rhinestone-encrusted bangles in 1963, he has been responsible for any number of raised eyebrows and catty comments about where *she* might have gotten *that!* Since he works like a fine jeweler, devising his designs in wax, or by carving or twisting the metals, it can be extremely difficult to identify Kenneth Jay Lane pieces as imitations.

Take his fantastic diamond and ruby choker. It'll set you back only $375, but it'll definitely set minds wondering and tongues wagging. The "diamonds" are so bright, the "rubies" so richly colored—Ken has many of the "stones" he uses made exclusively for him, to his very exacting specifications.

Of course, due to her refreshing candor, we all know about the fabulous fakeness of Barbara Bush's famous pearls (the three-strand choker runs about $150), but who would imagine that such glamour pusses as Joan Collins and Gina Lollabrigida might opt for anything less than real? Even the Princess of Wales and the Duchess of York (Di and Fergie to Kenneth, one of the world's most sought-after escorts) have been known to revel in his opulent jewelry.

So what's stopping you from enjoying that incredibly delicious feeling only exquisite jewelry can bestow? No matter how much of the real stuff you have in the vault, another trinket or two can't hurt. What about a terrific-looking brooch—a charming diamond bow trimmed in gold. At $87.50 it's the perfect finishing touch for that little St. Laurent cocktail suit. There's also a black enamel, gold, and diamond choker—an indispensable accessory in any woman's wardrobe for $185.

Still, the pièce de résistance of the collection is Kenneth's signature multicolored stone belt—a knockout, priced at $825. Self-consciously and deliberately counterfeit, it's fun and flirty. It also comes in an all-rhinestone version, at the same price, for real evening sparkle.

Vice president Michele Doolan is the person to see at the Trump Tower boutique. She'll assemble a versatile jewelry ensemble for you. Since it's from Kenneth Jay Lane, you'll know it's fake, but it's also definitely fabulous. 🍂

Marina B.

809 Madison Avenue   (212) 288-9708
between 67th and 68th Streets
New York, NY 10021

There's something familiar about Marina B.'s creations—something about the heavy settings, the massive stones, the use of cabochons and pavé motifs that reminds you of a very distinctive style of jewelry design. Once you realize the *B.* is short for *Bulgari*, it all becomes quite clear.

When Marina Bulgari left the family business to strike out on her own, she had to agree not to use her last name in connection with her new independent enterprise. She may have lost a few letters, but she gained a rather singular period and the freedom to create what *Connoisseur* has described as some of "the most extraordinary pieces of jewelry seen in this century."

In New York, she displays her work in a sleek jewel box of a store furnished in black lacquer and brown suede. Simple cabinets lined in white silk are theatrically lit to set off the jewels inside. It's a quiet, discreet place conducive to discussions about major purchases.

If you're interested in trying something on, you'll be ushered to the rear of the store and seated in private. There you will be dazzled by leather tray after tray of Marina's opulent but startlingly modern jewelry. She has taken the traditional art she learned from her father, the great jeweler Constantine Bulgari, and revolutionized it with the use of twentieth-century technology.

What makes Marina B.'s creations so instantly recognizable? Simply the way it fits—a quality not usually associated with jewelry. She likes it to conform to the body; her chokers and bracelets fit like clothes because she's devised a tiny spring implanted in each piece that enables it to cling comfortably to the neck or wrist.

We like the look and the fit of the Onda I (Marina often names her pieces after friends or the person for whom the prototype was fashioned). With diamonds set in 18-carat gold, the Onda I sells for $15,000. More elaborate and perhaps more representative of Marina B. is the choker with the ionized black finish on an 18-carat yellow gold base. Five different patterns in diamonds dance along the surface—over 10 carats in all. We didn't catch the choker's name, but we do know it costs $28,000.

In addition to her frequent use of "black" gold, Marina has another signature—a heart shape, minus the indentation. One spectacular use is the Caty reversible earring. A tiny hinge makes it possible to flip the casings around the large central pear-shaped sapphire. So the earrings can be worn with onyx surrounds, pavé diamond, or one of each—day into night, night into day. What flexibility!

Perhaps it's such a combination of practicality and exquisite extravagance that draws fans like William Paley, Diana Vreeland, and Princess Yasmin Aga Khan. We're sure the personal rapport Marina establishes with many of her clients is another attraction. She works with them to alter pieces to suit their tastes and to create designs based on their ideas. If you have something in mind, be sure to check her schedule, as she is in town only about four times a year.

In the meantime, treat yourself to a serious look at the magical, unrestrained, even playful jewelry that is Marina B.'s.   ❦

Matthew C. Hoffman

777 Madison Avenue   (212) 439-9107
New York, NY 10022

It's a long way from a mobile home to Madison Avenue, but it's a journey Matthew Hoffman knows all about. He's done it with a jewelry business born and bred in Ann Arbor, Michigan, and now comfortably ensconced in Chicago and New York, with plans to open in Los Angeles too.

At 15 Matthew made his first silver ring. Inspired by his fascination with the sculptural beauty of rocks and other works of nature, it was most unusual. Still, his mother had no trouble selling it at the local mall. Flush with success, Matthew started buying up friends' class rings and melting them down, refashioning them into his own distinctive, almost architectural, and decidedly contemporary pieces. As he developed his style, his hobby became his livelihood and he became involved in a love affair with stones, particularly colored gems, that has never abated. Matthew's work enhances the natural beauty of precious and semi-precious stones—his settings accentuate the look and cut of the stone, rather than vice versa.

His salon in New York is just as uniquely dramatic as the work it showcases. Tiny, lined in matte-finished steel vault like display cases, there's something about it reminiscent of Captain Nemo's underwater home. It has what must be the only leather floor on Madison Avenue.

We were knocked out by the Bern Munsteiner-cut aquamarines. Matthew often collaborates with this world-famous gem cutter as his one-of-a-kind stones are perfect complements to his one-of-a-kind settings. Munsteiner's stones are not merely faceted, but carved to become designed works of art in themselves. The boldly cut, juggernaut-looking aquamarines are featured in a matching set—necklace, ring, earrings, totaling 70 carats of the Caribbean-sea-blue stone and 5½ carats of brilliant white full-cut diamonds. You can have all three for $66,000. Individually the 18-carat-gold necklace with the 42-carat aquamarine and 2½ carats of bezel-set diamonds sells for $42,000. The ring and earrings sell for $11,000 each, both sport 14 carats of aquamarines in 18-carat gold, but the earrings are further enhanced by the other 3 carats of diamonds.

Drawn to the mystique of the Munsteiner stones, we also liked a collar of 18-carat-gold links, featuring a 36-carat ametrine (half ameythst, half citrine) in the center, accented by diamonds, for $36,000.

If you like unique, statement-making jewelry, it's hard to imagine that something here wouldn't strike your fancy—it's certainly struck Kathleen Turner, Liza Minnelli, and Joanna Gleason. But if not, explain your problem to Matthew—he won't take offense. Instead, he'll encourage you to share your jewelry fantasies with him and come up with a way of combining his style with your taste or needs. Matthew will refine the concept and sketch a design for your approval. Then he and his staff of twenty-five jewelers will make the piece just for you, never to be duplicated. Price wise, the sky's the limit depending on the kind and size of stones involved. A three-week wait is customary, however.   🍒

Neptune Gem & Pearl

18 East 48th Street   (212) 838-0402
between 5th and Madison
New York, NY 10017

Pearls are Fred Richter's passion and have been for the last thirty years. He knows all there is to know about them and is always eager to share the wealth. Fred waxes poetic about pearls—all pearls, from the world's most common cultured variety to natural freshwater pearls to rare south-sea beauties. He's as enthusiastic about a $5000 strand of 10-millimeter cultured pearls from Japan as he is about an extremely fine $250,000 string of precious 15-millimeter south seas from Australia or Tahiti.

Fred makes sure that you understand exactly what you're buying and how to take care of it. As jewelry goes, pearls are rather fragile; there's a whole list of dos and don'ts that Fred carefully outlines.

Despite his personal passion, Fred's inventory does include other gems, though they all tend to be suitable for stringing—like ruby, emerald, and sapphire beads. Maybe Fred just has a thing for round. He's got a huge selection of semiprecious beads too—jades and tourmalines in every color in the rainbow, as well as lapis, onyx, and malachite. He strings them in every conceivable combination, then twists and turns them into fascinating shapes and adds the pièce de résistence in the form of a spectacular clasp. They're absolutely superb and terribly sophisticated.

Be forewarned, you have to make an appointment, but it's worth the effort. If Fred is out, ask for Sidi. She's warm and just as well versed in things stringable as Fred. And if you run across a pearl or bead necklace in a magazine that you just have to have, bring in the picture and have Fred make it for you. Chances are he made the original in the first place!

Norman Landsberg

66 West 47th Street   (212) 586-7422
between Fifth and Sixth
New York, NY 10036

Everyone's most outlandish jewelry fantasy can become a reality at this small counter manned for the last thirty years by Norman Landsberg. A veteran of the industry for some forty-one years, Norman has developed an outstanding business based on quality merchandise at very competitive prices. The arrival of his two good-looking and extremely knowledgeable sons, Jonathan and Jeffrey, indicates that we can all look forward to the Landsberg touch for at least another generation.

It's a good thing too. While other counters in this crowded arcade are often deserted, there's always action at the Landsbergs'. Their business has been built solely on referral; relationships with their clients are all-important. As Jeffrey says, "You may have to wait in line here in Landsberg, but then no one here is going to give you a line. The clients know they can depend on our reputation for quality and value—that's why they come back." That reputation is truly comforting in an era of almost daily reports of jewelry scams.

What a relief to know that the bargain here that borders on being too good to be true is true indeed. You see, Landsberg's young designer, Tina Gartenberg, is a treasure. Not only are her own creations divine, but she can duplicate anything you've fancied elsewhere. Remember those popular Tiffany "kiss" earrings that sell for a small fortune? They're only $375 here. Or perhaps a Bulgari-style gold and diamond bracelet is the object of your desire. Uptown, the price tag reads five figures. At Norman Landsberg it costs about $3,000. Indeed, if a jewelry ad catches your eye while flipping through *W* or *Town & Country*, tear it out and bring it in. Tina will sketch and price it for your approval. Once given the okay, they'll fashion a wax mold and cast the piece. Voilà—an exact replica for considerably less than the advertised price.

Please, let's keep this just between us—Norman Landsberg is a real find, one we don't want to share with just anyone.

Runsdorf, Inc.

45 West 47th Street   (212) 575-1919
New York, NY 10036

Lee Runsdorf, who runs this little gem of a place, has been in the jewelry business for forty-six years. His family was involved in the trade for four generations before him, and now his daughter Elise, a graduate gemologist, represents the sixth. To compound the family's association with jewelry, Lee's Belgian-born wife, Lucette, hails from a long line of diamond merchants. Her family has been supplying his family with glorious diamonds for ages.

Today Runsdorf's business encompasses estate jewelry and closeouts from other manufacturers, as well as their own designs, and operates on both a retail and wholesale level. While many of the other merchants in the diamond district were trained by this family, the Runsdorf's business still stands a cut above the rest.

It has a lot to do with the broad scope of their merchandise and their sources. The pieces here are distinctive, starting with unusually detailed gold bracelets for $300. We found a spectacular pair of David Webb earrings for $30,000 and a wonderful Van Cleef Art Deco diamond watch for $25,000, not to mention Schlumberger diamond clip earrings for $4,000. At these prices, they probably cost less here than they did from Webb, Van Cleef, and Schlumberger in the first place!

If you can't deal with the concept of "previously owned," you can enter virgin jewelry territory with a piece made by Lee just for you. He showed us an amazing necklace he had just finished for a client—round diamonds with a total weight of 50 carats and a price of $60,000. Of course, Lee insists on issuing a certificate stating the size and quality of all stones and backed by the Gemologist Institute of America. None of those famous shady 47th Street deals here.

Lee will also search the world over for whatever you have in mind. He recently fulfilled a client's commission with the purchase of a flawless 7.56-carat, $250,000, emerald-cut diamond from Sotheby's in Geneva. He wouldn't tell us who it's for, but we do know that many of his clients appear regularly in the nation's social columns. They come from across the country to take advantage of Runsdorf's extraordinary selection and prices. Many have grandfathers who bought from Lee's grandfather; frequenting Runsdorf tends to be a family tradition. After all, it's one of the oldest established American wholesale and retail jewelry businesses in New York. Why not put a little something from Runsdorf on your family tree?

Tiffany & Co.

Fifth Avenue at 57th Street   (212) 755-8000
New York, NY 10022

When you visit this cavernous (by jewelry store standards) emporium, with aisles and elevators swarming with people (3,000 on a slow day, 25,000 on a Christmas season Saturday), it's difficult to believe that when Tiffany & Co. (then Tiffany and Young) opened in lower Manhattan on September 18, 1837, the first day's sales came to a grand total of $4.98. Today, despite the broad range of merchandise and prices, there's not a single item you can take home in one of their signature robin's egg blue bags or boxes for that amount.

Charles Tiffany and John Young didn't start out to establish a world-class, let alone world-famous, jewelry store. Rather theirs was a shop full of stationery and "fancy goods"—fashion and home accessories that had nothing whatsoever to do with jewelry. A couple of years later, a line of paste was introduced, but it wasn't until the mid-1840s that the real thing was offered—diamonds, not paste.

Indeed Tiffany's association with fine gemstones was largely a quirk of fate. It just so happened that in 1848 John Young's annual European buying trip coincided with the final downfall of the French monarchy. By the time he reached Paris, the city was in chaos, overflowing with aristocrats long on jewels but short on cash and desperate to flee the country. With the glut of diamonds on the market, prices dropped dramatically, and John, knowing that partner Charles would enthusiastically approve, took full advantage of the situation, acquiring, among other treasures, a substantial share of the French crown jewels.

Having already experienced the benefits of publicity (his then novel policy of putting a non-negotiable price tag on every item in the store had made headlines nationwide), Charles leaked the story of Tiffany's priceless acquisitions to the press and the store's identity as a purveyor of fine jewelry was assured. It was reinforced by the development of the six-pronged Tiffany setting that revolutionized the manner of mounting gems—formerly settings had covered all but the top of the stone. And the Tiffany legend became indelible with the 1877 purchase of the "Tiffany Diamond," a 287.42 carat yellow diamond. Even after being cut to 128 carats it remains the world's largest flawless canary diamond, and a proudly displayed symbol of the Tiffany mystique.

Of course, it's not for sale, but if your taste runs to large yellow diamonds, check out the necklace with the 107 carat canary center stone surrounded by pear and marquis shaped white diamonds. It does have a non-negotiable price tag—$7,000,000. And while you can still pick up a piece of crystal or Tiffany's famous silver for considerably less, there are many more items like the necklace in the store's inventory than there were during the darkest period of Tiffany's history, 1979 to 1984, when Avon was in charge.

Charles Tiffany was the first and last Tiffany to preside over the store. Since his demise, it has operated under a succession of owners and managements, none more successful than the current stewardship of William Chaney. Under his direction, the store walks the fine line of appearing exclusive with showpieces like an $800,000 pear-shaped diamond ring and a $250,000 18-inch string of iridescent Tahitian black pearls, while not intimidating its large middle class clientele, who count on Tiffany's for their wedding invitations and classic single strands of cultured pearls, a Tiffany specialty. Avon, on the other hand, had stepped way over the line to appeal to the masses with a preponderance of $7 wine glasses and garden variety engagement rings, displaying very little truly serious jewelry. Tiffany's was, for a while, a place not to have breakfast, or anything else as far as we were concerned.

But all that has changed now, and Tiffany's is once again a worthy destination for anyone trying to unload a thousand dollars a day (before lunch). One reason to stop by is to ogle the work of Paloma Picasso, their newest exclusive designer. Her bold, statement-making jewelry, in sterling as well as gold with exotically colored stones like rubellite or citrine, sells for $60 to $70,000, a typically Tiffany's range. As a designer who's work is only found here, she follows in the footsteps of such luminaries as Angela Cummings (before she defected to Bergdorf Goodman) and Elsa Peretti. Indeed, Elsa remains a popular attraction here—her counter is always crowded, often by the Japanese who seem particularly drawn to her fluid designs that are so very close to nature. You'll recall that Elsa is credited with spurring the development of sterling silver jewelry design and was heralded for her innovative "diamonds-by-the-yard" design—diamonds set in 18-carat-gold chains.

After the main floor filled with cases of precious jewels, our favorite floor at Tiffany's is the second. It's the home of the silver for which we have a particular weakness, as do many other connoisseurs ever since Tiffany started winning international prizes for its designs over 100 years ago. In 1867 the firm was the first American silvermaker ever to be awarded a prize by a foreign jury at the Paris Exposition. The rich and intricate English King flatware pattern, first introduced in 1885, has developed a worldwide following. And now, courtesy of Tiffany, 150 place settings of it grace Blair House, the recently renovated official guest quarters of the White House—quite a donation at $480 each.

The other main attractions on the second floor are the spectacular table settings—by far the highlight of the store's otherwise somewhat pedestrian decor. Changed every six weeks (and also adorning the third's china and crystal department), they're always the creation of artists, fashion designers, socialites, interior decorators—persons of note and taste. They're usually worth a visit.

You can see one of Tiffany's most famous sights without even setting foot in the store—its five windows along Fifth Avenue and 57th Street. Since 1955, Gene Moore has been amusing New Yorkers with his titillating displays. With his ability to reflect prominent issues of the day while complementing exquisite pieces of jewelry, it's impossible to walk by his windows without taking a peek. Once during a city transit strike he decorated the windows with roller skates, pogo sticks, and a unicycle. A water shortage prompted his featuring a fountain merrily splashing gin. And every Easter he creates a new set of windows using eggs in some shape or form—one year he even scrambled them!   🐛

Van Cleef & Arpels

744 Fifth Avenue   (212) 644-9500
at 57th Street
New York, NY 10022

One of the most revered names in jewelry is the result of the union between a Dutch diamond cutter and the French daughter of a dealer in precious stones. Alfred Van Cleef left Amsterdam for the brighter lights of Paris where he ran into the Arpels family. Alfred married the daughter and went into partnership with the three sons, opening a jewelry salon on the Place Vendôme in 1906. The original salon remains in the same prestigious location, while the business is still family owned and operated. Jacques Arpels is in charge in Europe. His son Phillipe presides here, with branches in Palm Beach and Beverly Hills.

The creative use of rubies, sapphires, and emeralds is the Van Cleef & Arpels hallmark. Their designs have a distinctive delicacy. Stones are shown in soft, feminine forms like the diamond clip made in the 1940s called Lady Dragonfly. Made of diamonds set in platinum, "she" most closely resembles a truly twinkling Tinkerbell with exquisite rose-cut diamonds in her delicate wings. The clip is not for sale and has become somewhat of a Van Cleef mascot. Renamed the Spirit of Beauty, three new smaller versions have been fashioned to celebrate the firm's 50th anniversary in the U.S.—they opened in New York in 1939. Each is destined to be sold at silent auction in the three U.S. cities with Van Cleef stores and the proceeds donated to charity. Phillipe feels it's important to "express our appreciation, to give something back to the communities in which we have experienced our success."

Much of the success is due to Van Cleef's 1936 perfection of the "invisible setting." It is exactly what its name suggests, a setting constructed so that none of it, not a single prong, is visible to the naked eye. When you see a flower clip, its petals invisibly set with rubies or sapphires, each cut and fit with such precision that the surface has a velvety look and the setting is completely hidden, you can be sure it's the work of Van Cleef & Arpels. Indeed, impeccable, flexible settings are a Van Cleef signature. Imagine a necklace of alternating oval- and emerald-cut emeralds surrounded by round diamonds set in platinum. Not too difficult, but just try to figure how they could make it so that you could wear it as: 1) a double row of emeralds in the front with diamonds continuing in the back; 2) a single row of emeralds all the way around; or 3) a single row of emeralds in the front with diamonds in the back with the shorter row detached and worn as a bracelet. "Upwards of a million dollars," it was snapped up shortly after we marveled at its practicality. But not to worry; typical of Van Cleef artistry, there's bound to be something similar to it, but not exactly like it—each piece is copyrighted and numbered.

The good news is that at Van Cleef, you can work your way up to such important pieces and still savor the renowned quality and workmanship. Their boutique on the main floor of Bergdorf Goodman, right next door, features items from $1,500 to $20,000. Ask for Nancy. She's a delight and seems to really enjoy helping novices navigate the jewelry roadmap. If you can't quite afford a sable coat yet, why not get a sable brooch? A representation of the entire animal done in black enamel with a ruby eye and pavé diamond throat and tail, it's only $11,000.

Back in the main salon, one of the most interesting pieces is the braid of round diamonds set in 18 carat gold, each braid defined by a band of caliber cut rubies. It's quite extraordinary at $280,000. Our favorite salesman William Lorenzo told us we'd be pleased to know that there are matching earclips. Our other favorite is the necklace featuring a collection of brilliantly white oval diamonds with a total weight of 66 carats. They're surrounded by pairs of marquis shaped diamonds with a total weight of 34 carats. So now we're talking a 100-carat necklace with a price tag of $1,363,000, yet for all that it is surprisingly delicate, even subtle. But then, what else would you expect from Van Cleef & Arpels?

CHAPTER SEVEN

Art and Antiques

Pleasure vs. Treasure

*I*f the great chefs are beating a path to New York's door from the
world's culinary capitals, it shouldn't be a big surprise that the great
dealers (and buyers) are on their way too. In fact, most of them are already here. New York has staked out the rarefied territory long occupied
by London and Paris in world-class art and antiques. And not surprisingly, it has added a few touches of its own.

Sotheby's and Christie's may have their roots in England, but they're
lining their pockets in New York. Go take a gander; you never know
what they'll be selling next—estate jewelry to Impressionist paintings to
Dorothy's ruby-red slippers from the *Wizard of Oz*—but the auction
houses represent just the tip of the iceberg. From the posh Upper East
Side to the frontiers of SoHo and beyond, the city's awash in shops and
galleries loaded with treasures from centuries past and present. Think of
Manhattan as a repository of some of the world's greatest riches, yours
for the taking if you have the taste, and the purse to match the appetite.

Not that money's really necessary to enjoy one of the great revolving
shows in the world; up, down, and all around the town, there's enough
new and different or old and original to fill a dozen world-class museums.
And while some dealers have, shall we say, a certain attitude, most are
better than the chattiest tour guide. They'll take you through their
collections with the pride of possessors, not to mention the avarice of
salesmen.

There are even bargains to be found, though fewer in art than in antiques. Indeed, art is so hot that many galleries steer clear of quoting prices unless you're on the premises, checkbook in hand. From the tiniest hole-in-the-wall gallery in SoHo to the toniest on Madison Avenue, they know what they've got and they know they can get their price.

But the antiques market is taking off too. If you want to buy top quality at top dollar stay at the top of the town and call on Didier Aaron, Bernard Steinitz, Israel Sack or any of the folks in the highfalutin but somehow disappointing Place des Antiquaires. If, however, you want a shot at a real find and have fun too, head downtown to where some of these uptown folks unearth a lot of their merchandise.

Whether they're uptown or downtown, however, discretion is the name of the game in this high-stakes world of buying and selling. Both the art and the antiques people are downright skittish when it comes to any discussion of clientele.

They're equally protective of their own reputations, which is good news for you. Dealers stand behind their merchandise, its authenticity, and its value. This concern is your guarantee—whether you've purchased a $40,000 Regency table or a $1 million Jasper Johns, it's the real thing. They're all here—and more. Food and fashion, furnishings and fun, art and antiques—if you can get it anywhere, you can get it here, for a thousand dollars (at the very least) before lunch.   🐚

A La Vieille Russie

781 Fifth Avenue   (212) 752-1727
at 59th Street
New York, NY 10022

Admittedly, it takes a little chutzpah to darken these particular revolving doors. The objets d'art in the windows are so obviously exquisite treasures. The rose-colored interior looks so unabashedly rich, as befits a store noted for delicately crated artifacts and opulently gilded icons. But Paul Schaffer, his brother, Peter, and their mother, Ray, are the epitome of warm hospitality in this little bit of old Russia.

Their store, founded by Ray and her late husband, Alexander, in the forties, is a collector's paradise. In fact, the collector's collector, Malcolm Forbes, regularly drops by to see what he doesn't own—yet. It was here that he purchased some eighty percent of his fabulous collection of Fabergé eggs, which is now the world's largest. Fortunately, so far,

Malcolm's left behind plenty of other beauties from the Fabergé workshops—delightful egg trees, elegant snuffboxes, and lovely picture frames. Indeed, A La Vieille Russie has become known as the country's premier purveyor of the priceless works of the nineteenth-century jeweler. Some have gone so far as to describe it as "the house of Fabergé" in America.

But Paul Schaffer notes that his selection of Russian treasures is far broader and more eclectic, as suited to those seeking interesting gifts as it is to world-class collectors. Prices start as low as $50, but escalate rapidly. An eighteenth-century royal porcelain box belonging to Augustus the Strong might fetch $60,000. But then there's a dainty porcelain cup and saucer, probably from the last days of Czar Nicholas II's reign—an original gift or the base of a new collection for $250.

If boxes are more your cup of tea, A La Vieille Russie has the most collectible bunch of boxes you've ever seen—all small but ever-so-practical gems. Some are gold, some enameled, others jeweled. They start in the $3,000 to $5,000 range, but it'll cost more like $9,000 to $12,000 for a truly fine example in gold, of this, the world's most collected item.

Jewelry is also important here. Indeed, theirs is one of the largest inventories of vintage and antique jewelry, some dating back to the 1630s. We were intrigued by a glamorous pair of emerald, ruby, and pearl earrings for $1,950. But it's so hard to decide—there are so many pieces, each chosen more for the beauty of its design rather than for age or value. The Schaffers feel that jewelry, more than anything else, should be truly wearable to be enjoyed. Hear! Hear!

A grand wooden staircase leads to the second level, where the brilliant gold icons that once decorated Russian Orthodox churches are housed. Prized for their rarity and intrinsic value, virtually every important icon now in the hands of wealthy collectors has, at one time or another, passed through this store.

Another room, overlooking Central Park, resembles the interior of a Russian palace with its heavy, ornate furniture and gilt-framed paintings of Russian nobility. Now here's a tip for the would-be collector—the Schaffers say that turn-of-the-century Russian paintings are just beginning to hit their stride in the marketplace. Today, prices start around $10,000, but may be poised to take off into the six-figure stratosphere.

A La Vieille Russie allows you a seductive glimpse at another place and many other times. It's a treat to the eye and a threat to the checkbook.   🍃

André Emmerich Gallery

41 East 57th Street   (212) 752-0124
5th and 6th Floors
New York, NY 10022

André Emmerich has been in the art business for more than a quarter of a century, and represents some of the great modern painters and sculptors of our time. He's firmly ensconced in the Fuller Building, the preeminent 57th Street address for art. If you've got a million or so burning a hole in your pocket, stop by to see some fine examples of Hans Hofman, Californian Sam Francis, or Helen Frankenthaler, who was recently honored at the nearby Museum of Modern Art with a retrospective.

André's pretty happy these days—with good reason. David Hockney has been with him forever and his prices are skyrocketing with a new auction record set in May 1989. Even better, Hockney, fresh from a traveling retrospective and set design for Wagner operas, is producing lots of new work. His lithographs now go for as much as $300,000 and more. But we're rather taken with the so-called Home Made series of prints produced on Xerox machines and selling for $6,000 to $12,000.

Hockney aside, don't miss the back rooms of this gallery with the huge, dripped canvases of Morris Louis, Al Held's bright abstractions, and lots of other fabulous work lined up against the walls. Of course, André is still offering some of the finest pre-Columbian artifacts and antiquities known to man. In fact, he's written two books on the subject, and for a few hundred thousand you can begin your collection by taking home several urns, figurines, and pieces of statuary. We once found some delightful golden frogs for $5,000—André tells us they're now worth triple that amount. Ask André to direct you in assembling your collection. He'll tell you what to buy and what books to read in order to learn about your new hobby. After all, this really is his all-consuming and none-too-secret passion, which the gallery allows André to pursue with a vengeance.   🍃

Berry-Hill Galleries

11 East 70th Street   (212) 744-2300
New York, NY 10021

Directly behind the Frick is another palace dedicated to art—the new home of the Berry-Hill Galleries. A little over a year ago, cousins James and Fred Hill abandoned what had been the seat of the family business for over thirty years on Fifth Avenue just across the street from Bergdorf's to move into these spacious new quarters carved from several floors of a double-width townhouse. As with Hirschl & Adler just down the street, this is a "must" stop for American masterpieces—with a decided emphasis on the eighteenth, nineteenth, and twentieth centuries.

If you're a history buff, you might covet one of Gilbert Stuart's several portraits of the father of our country. This particular likeness of George Washington once belonged to James Madison. Now it can be yours, for $2.5 million. Or perhaps you would prefer something a trifle less stern—like a Maurice Pendergast watercolor called *Revere Beach* for $1,250,000.

The gallery seems to flaunt more marble than the Vatican. In actual fact, thanks to architect John Sullivan's research, it owes its highly polished stone to the same Tennessee quarry that supplied the marble adorning the East Wing of the National Gallery of Art in Washington, D.C. But we're talking art here, and besides the great works by Fitzhugh Lane, Edward Hopper, and the hard-to-find Georgia O'Keeffe, Berry-Hill has just opened a department of contemporary art—no stars yet, but give them time. They're also working on a sculpture garden featuring turn-of-the-century American statuary.

Every time we visit this gallery, we want to set up housekeeping. It has such a homey feel, in a majestic sort of way, from the proprietor's wood-paneled office to the curved marble stairway leading to the lovely outdoor garden. Maybe that's really the best way to view paintings—as they would look in the home, assuming your home looks like a palace. 🌑

Bruce Gimelson

305 East 24th Street   (212) 889-4273
New York, NY 10016

One of the best-kept secrets in New York is the private apartment/office of Bruce Gimelson, a dealer in rare books and manuscripts. Among the paper- and book-laden shelves and table tops, you can find great historical, political, and literary documents—works from George Washington to Lewis Carroll.

Bruce also hosts a show on cable television called "What's It Worth?" where he appraises art and antiques. Viewers are invited to call the station and describe an item, which Bruce then defines as trash or treasure. He also has a personal and private clientele, recently appraising Walter P. Chrysler, Jr.'s cache of stamps and manuscripts. Compared to other antique markets, this one has yet to boom. But Bruce says it's on the edge, and already many a gentlemanly scholar with bucks to burn has entered the fray.

Don't be fooled by the jumbled, apparently nonchalant atmosphere of Bruce's establishment. Here, the letters strewn on the floor may have been written by signers of the Declaration of Independence. You may trip over pieces of manuscript by Henry David Thoreau, or have to step carefully to avoid planting your foot in the middle of an autographed picture of John Kennedy or Richard Nixon.

Lately, Bruce has had several especially interesting pieces in his cluttered inventory, including a document dicussing the purchase of slaves and signed by George Washington. It's on sale for $12,000. There's also a letter from Thomas Jefferson, written during his term as Secretary of State, and priced at $22,500.

Whether you're already a collector or you want to get in on the ground floor of a rising market, call Bruce for an appointment. You might also ask him about his appraisal services, and he will seek out special works for you like a letter by that distant cousin of yours who served in the U.S. Senate during the second half of the last century. But be prepared to pay his daily rate, which he will discreetly discuss with you over the phone.

Charterhouse Antiques Ltd.

115 Greenwich Avenue   (212) 243-4726
between 7th and 8th Ave.
New York, NY 10014

Now in its 27th year, this delightful shop is a veritable wonderland for collectors of 18th- and 19th-century English porcelain, silver, crystal, and glass. It's like walking into the attic of someone who's been accumulating copious amounts of such treasures for decades, all seemingly catalogued, right down to the dust.

If your buffet begs a porcelain tea set, speak to owner James Ray. His are especially complete with all the accoutrements foreign to modern versions, like slop pots. Indeed, most of his porcelains are English, particularly pearl and earthenware from about 1770 to 1830. Both tend to be blue and white copies of Chinese designs like the platter, circa 1790, by an Englishman named Heath, which replicates the Chinese Fitzhugh pattern and sells for $550. There are also some period pieces with historical motifs. A platter depicting the death of Nelson and also selling for $550 comes to mind.

Likewise his collection of American and Georgian flatware is incredible, featuring lots of rare and very beautiful serving pieces—berry and stuffing spoons from the late 1700s ranging from $200 to $300 a piece.

You'll also find what may be the city's best selection of Georgian and Victorian decanters. Decanters being one of our favorite collectibles, we were particularly taken by a three-ring number with a mushroom stopper from about 1800 and priced at $250. And James has got brass candlesticks "by the bucketful," once again primarily Georgian and Victorian, with an average price of $175 a pair.

If it has occurred to you that the Charterhouse's prices are definitely on the modest side, join the club. James spots uptown dealers shopping his store all the time, and it's always crawling with decorators who claim he has the best prices in town for this type of merchandise. James has also been known to rent items to pal Robert Isabell to lend extra panache to one of his fabulous party decors.

In addition to the serious "big ticket items," by Charterhouse standards, James specializes in lots of little decorative trinkets—bits and pieces of things, which may be slightly damaged but still look great. Victorian saucers make great ashtrays, frames come in unusual shapes and sizes and eras, mostly Danish from the '20s and '30s. All make great accessories for a countryhouse. If they're broken by partying houseguests or stolen by marauding vandals, you can shrug off the loss, and always go back to Charterhouse Antiques for more.   ❧

Circle Gallery

468 West Broadway   (212) 677-5100
between Prince and Houston
New York, NY 10012

We doubt many garage sales have founded multimillion-dollar enterprises, but Jack Solomon's sure did. Back the in early '60s the Chicago lawyer was making periodic trips to Europe to buy art for his own burgeoning collection of contemporary works. Friends started asking him to pick up pieces for them as well—one thing lead to another and Jack began selling art out of his garage. He was so successful at it that by 1964 he opened his first gallery, naturally called La Garage.

Twenty-five years later, having long since left lawyering behind, he and his dynamic wife, Carolyn, run a publicly held company called Circle Fine Art Corporation, with 33 galleries in the U.S. and Canada. Circle's art is indeed fine, but still accessible for most people. With their exceptional printing facility, their aggressive limited edition program, as well as original works, there's something in this vast two-story gallery for almost everyone—from a $25 poster to an $80,000 painting by the star of their stable, Victor Vasarely.

While the painting is fabulous, we were struck by another of Vasarely's works, a sculpture entitled Kezdi. Handpainted on wood, it's stunningly representative of Vasarely's unique color palette and ability to create intriguing optical illusions—a cube within a square in this instance. For $8,500, there's something very uplifting, refreshing, even powerful about the piece. It's part of a limited edition of 175.

Another Circle artist we like is René Gruau, the urbane Frenchman who for generations has been enchanting the world with his marvelous fashion illustrations. His art is just as fascinating. He is truly the master of suggestion—a single stroke says so much, never more than in "The Rose." In this charming painting, Gruau hints at a hat, implies a nose, and insinuates luscious lips, all bowed to a rose. It's a painting bound to give endless pleasure for $15,000.

We were also intrigued by a new artist Circle believes in, Juan Sanchez. And, of course, Douglas Hoffman's extremely realistic, photographlike work is always a treat to behold. There's a lot to see here. The space and inventory are equally large. So ask Sid to give you the grand tour. That way you'll be sure not to miss anything like the little jewelry boutique where Circle's limited edition works in precious metals and stones are sold. Made by artisans in Scottsdale to Circle artists' designs, they range in price from about $250 to $12,000. We're most fond of the Erté pieces, predictably fancifully glamorous.

If you want to start a collection on a modest budget or want to get a big visual bang for your buck, Circle is your kind of gallery.   ❦

Colnaghi, U.S.A., Ltd.

21 East 67th Street   (212) 772-2266
New York, NY 10021

If you're most comfortable in surroundings reeking of merry old England, try the high-tea atmosphere of the American branch of Colnaghi, ensconced in an Upper East Side (where else?) townhouse complete with a winding, elaborately banistered stairway and red flocked wallpaper. Colnaghi, founded in London in 1760, has graced New York's gallery world since 1982. Their specialty is master paintings from 1400 to 1900, with a pronounced tilt toward the Italian. We've seen original frames on fifteenth-century pieces here—honest!

The last time we attended a party here, we were pampered by liveried and gloved servants, who checked our coats, checked our names, and served quite respectable food and drink—all in this second-floor gallery complete with floor-to-ceiling windows. Nicholas Hall, president of Colnaghi, U.S.A., and Alan Wintermute, his right-hand person, are usually on hand to answer any questions. Still, in such a formal atmosphere, you might feel more comfortable having made an appointment. It's kind of like a visit to a royal palace; in fact, one of the best pictures in the current crop at Colnaghi is a portrait of the Queen of Naples, Caroline Murat, by the famous French artist Gerard. Executed in 1808 and priced well into the seven figures, it's perfect for the family (any family) portrait gallery.   ❦

Fanelli Antique Timepieces, Ltd.

1131 Madison Avenue   (212) 517-2300
between 84th and 85th Streets
New York, NY 10028

This enchanting store preserves and reveres a special part of our heritage from times gone by. The large wall clock over the doorway, a casting of an eighteenth-century church clock from Argentina, tells the story.

Cindy and Joe Fanelli have a passion for antique timepieces. Their store is filled with them—from watches to large commemorative clocks, including the original of the clock dominating their entrance. In fact, they have lots of originals—vintage wristwatches from 1910 to the 1950s, eighteenth- and nineteenth-century carriage clocks, bewitching grandfather clocks from the 1600s to the 1800s.

The best watches are from Vacheron Constantin, Philippe Patek, Audemars' Piguet, Rolex, and the European Watch Company, the outfit that made all the watches for Cartier. They run from $700 to $15,000 and up. They are all exquisite and cause for comment. Cindy is very selective about her inventory, and she makes sure they all work—well, like clockwork. And with a watchmaker on staff, the Fanellis will make sure any watch they sell keeps on ticking.

They also have a full-time clockmaker—a gentleman who goes to your home to set up your Fanelli purchase just to make sure it runs properly. He'll guarantee it for a year, and Joe maintains that if an antique clock runs well for twelve months, it'll go for the next twenty years. If home is out of town, you can still look forward to the Fanellis' taking care of all the legwork. They ship anywhere in the world and have a network of craftsmen whom they will pay to set up the clock and maintain the guarantee.

As for repairs, we wouldn't think of calling anyone else. House calls carry a $175 minimum charge, depending on the clock and the extent of the work required.

Their selection of clocks is as fascinating as it is large. Prices range from about $900 to $85,000. We were taken with a rare American tall case clock, made even more valuable by the fact that it was fabricated in New York City. Circa 1805 and part of the Van Wyck estate, it sells for $30,000. Nearby, we were mesmerized by the automated ship-and-wave action of a gilded bronze French mantel clock. Dated 1860, it is priced at $10,000.

In fact, we're so batty about the Fanellis' timepieces that every time we walk through the door we're overwhelmed by a vision of ourselves as a couple of even battier old ladies taking comfort from the ticking of dozens of clocks and the purring of an equal number of cats. We know— the cat part is a little horrifying. But it's our vision, and we just have to live with it! 🐦

Hirschl & Adler

21 East 70th Street   (212) 535-8810
New York, NY 10021

The hallowed-hall atmosphere of Upper East Side galleries may best be captured in this townhouse on the same block as the Frick Museum. Your Bentley will be comfy parked at the curb outside, while you'll enjoy the cozy, indirectly lit, low-ceilinged interior that feels like a drawing room in a private home. Hirschl & Adler is where you go for American, American, and more American—mostly nineteenth- and early-twentieth-century masters. We're talking Hudson River landscapes and masterworks by the likes of Charles Sheeler and Marsden Hartley at a cost of at least $750,000 to $1 million. There are also watercolors by Demuth in the $65,000 to $400,000 range.

Hirschl & Adler has also recently gone into American decorative arts, particularly Neoclassical pieces and twentieth-century arts & crafts—Stickley, Frank Lloyd Wright, and Greene and Greene. Given the extremely volatile state of the market, the Hirschl & Adler folks stay away from quoting much in the way of prices, and discretion keeps them from discussing their clientele, exept to mention that in addition to private citizens it includes museums and corporations.

Proprietor Stuart Feld is an old hand at sensing new markets. In fact, Hirschl & Adler is the only gallery that has successfully cloned itself, in a brotherly sort of way. Barely blocks away on the other side of Madison Avenue, we now have Hirschl & Adler Folk, featuring the highest level of folk art and managed by Frank Miele. There's also Hirschl & Adler Modern, which shows younger artists and masters of the late twentieth century. We've seen some great minimalism there, including Cy Twombly and Robert Ryman. Among the three locations, there is a work of art for every taste, provided there's a purse to match. Hirschl & Adler play in the big leagues. 🐛

Hudson House

555 Hudson   (212) 645-0353
between Perry and 11th
New York, NY 10014

First you're greeted by Maggie (Princess Margaret Rose), a very sweet little street whore dog, or mutt. Then you stumble over partners John

Eader and David Vallese. They, all three of them, usher you past the mini flea market out front (a cache of knickknacks and curios) into a shop full of furniture. Between the sidewalk sale (affectionately referred to by charming manager Sigrunn as "Shitz [sic] and Bits") and the serious merchandise inside you can find uniques and antiques priced from $1 to $100,000. Whoopi Goldberg's been known to browse the stall outside, while William Hurt likes to pop in to see what's new on the furniture front.

Done like a home, so the furniture is placed in its proper setting, the shop is small, but backed up by the inventory of an enormous 5,000-square-foot warehouse. Still, despite its modest size, John and David always manage to display at least four armoires, as well as plenty of parlor chairs, sofas, dining tables and chairs, night stands, mirrors, and commodes. Most arrive from France where John and David go six times a year to shop. They pride themselves on the quality of their finds in terms of design and craftsmanship, like the First Empire mahogany armoire (about 1800) with its flat crown and ormalu decorated posts flanking the doors valued at $8,500. Then there's the lovely mahogany demilune table dating from 1825. Folded, it's a half-moon shaped console table, which opens up into a round dining table for six and priced at $4,800.

If you don't fancy French, Hudson House is still worth a visit. There's usually a fair amount of Biedermeier on the floor, and John and David do have a penchant for Italian neoclassical. Besides, once you've passed Maggie's sniff test and gotten to know the two proprietors, or Sigrunn who's here during their frequent absences, you may be invited to tour the warehouse. It's well worth the effort, stocked as it is with what is probably the largest assemblage of antique furniture in the city.

It's hard to believe that something here won't capture your imagination, but if nothing inspires, ask to see the album of pictures of the stock in the Palm Beach store. They'll also show you sketches and snapshots of pieces bought during the last European trip, but not yet shipped to New York or Florida.

If all else fails, try to describe what it is you're looking for. They'll go out looking for it, and with their vast resources they're bound to find it. David and John make their antique buying service unique by accompanying you to see the piece of your dreams, wherever it may be in the world, and negotiate its purchase—assuming, of course, that its value is sufficient to make it worth their (and your) while. ❦

Knoedler Contemporary Art

19 East 70th Street   (212) 794-0550
New York, NY 10021

Remember Armand Hammer, the wealthy industrialist who had the run of Russia before anyone else, mostly because of his support of culture there? Well, he's a pretty big supporter of culture Stateside too. He sits on any number of boards of cultural institutions (most of which covet his personal art collection, valued in the hundreds of millions) and in the early seventies bought Knoedler Galleries, one of the most prestigious in New York, in partnership with longtime financial advisor, Dr. Maury Leibovitz.

Pietra serena frames Knoedler's entrance, as it does so many of Europe's great churches; indeed, this is a temple dedicated to blue-chip contemporary American art. Need a Frank Stella wall construction (he calls them three-dimensional paintings) for $350,000? How about a Richard Diebenkorn for about $400,000? This is the place to find the crème de la crème of current art—new works by artists whose earlier works are consistently breaking auction-house records.

The firm, founded in 1846 by French emigrant Michel Knoedler, may well be the oldest in New York. The Knoedler family owned it right up until its sale to the doctors Hammer and Leibovitz. The gallery has a well-earned reputation for presenting the important and the current; during his lifetime, it represented the quintessential American artist, Winslow Homer. Today, Dr. Leibovitz personally oversees the operations. He's usually on the premises, which now hosts such artists as Nancy Graves, Robert Rauschenberg, and the estate of Adolf Gottlieb.

If you're bent on collecting what's going on now, there is nowhere with a wider range of high-class materials, both on canvas and paper. 🐛

Leo Castelli Gallery

420 W. Broadway   (212) 431-5160
between Prince and Spring
New York, NY 10012

It is difficult to imagine the now-mighty Leo Castelli in his first gallery, which he opened in 1957 in his small Upper East Side apartment. He practically had to beg people to come take a look, and was forced to usurp his daughter's bedroom for hanging space. Thirty-three years later, the name Castelli is now synonymous with contemporary art, especially the seminal Pop scene which included Roy Lichtenstein, not to mention golden boys Andy Warhol and Jasper Johns.

An early pioneering fortress in the warehouse district known as Soho in the early seventies, the sprawling two-room Leo Castelli Gallery is now considered a historic monument. Indeed, it's not hard to wind up spending a monumental price for a new painting by Jasper Johns. After all, a Johns piece set a new auction record for a living artist by selling for $17 million at Sotheby's last year. Leo has represented Johns throughout his career, since the days when he had to bring all his considerable salesmanship to bear to convince someone to pay several hundred dollars for a Johns painting.

Looking for Leo is a popular game among the gallery's regulars. He travels so much these days that it's a real treat to spot him in one of his ever-so-tailored Italian suits, working away at a desk in the back. A velvet rope divides his work space and the rest of the gallery. And if the rope fails, there's always the protective Brundage sisters, Susan and Patty, who've helped him manage the gallery for years. Even if you can't get to Leo, there's always someone interesting to chat with here. The place is awash in a battalion of attractive young people, all eager to make their mark on the art world. They'd all like to be the next Roy Lichtenstein, whose new Reflections Series is available through Leo at about $750,000 each.

If you're in the market for slightly less expensive contemporary works, check out Castelli Graphics at 578 Broadway. Think of the collection at 420 W. Broadway as Castelli's couture line and the graphics gallery as his ready-to-wear. ❦

Martell & Suffin

67 East 11th Street   (212) 677-5708
New York, NY 10014

When asked how he got into the business, Wade Martell will tell you he grew up with antiques and put in some time toiling for a dealer. The pay was lousy, and he didn't think his employer had any lock on taste or smarts. It occurred to him, "as the Broadway tune goes, I can do that—I can do that!" At about the time, his friend Michael Suffin was grappling with the sad, true reality that it is impossible to live on a teacher's salary in Manhattan. He was ready to do something else. They joined forces to put together a successful business specializing in rather serious antique furniture—mostly late eighteenth/early nineteenth century of French and English origin.

Since their shop is small, and they go to pains to keep it from being cluttered, Wade and Michael are very selective in what they buy. Their discriminating taste shows in their stock and is greatly appreciated by decorators whom Wade describes as running from the sublime to the ridiculous. But its not just the likes of Parrish Hadley, Grady Cooley, Robert Metzger, and Tom Britt who count on their good taste. Other dealers, like Kentshire and Stair, find much to admire and to purchase at Martell & Suffin.

They all think of the shop when they're in the market for double- and triple-based dining tables. There's usually an interesting selection here along with sets of eight, ten, and twelve chairs. But we tend to be drawn to the showier pieces like the Italian faux-tortoise slant-front secretary. Signed and dated 1793 it sells for $18,000. Not quite what you consider serious? How about the Regency rosewood conference-sized table with a cabinet base, gadrooned (braided) bronze edging, and bronze claw feet for $40,000?

On the enchanting front, we liked the French Empire console with the gilded bronze mounts for $9,000, and we couldn't take our eyes off the mahogany Charles X $24,000 writing desk, its leather top softened by the patina of age.

Wade was right, he could do "that" and do it better than most! ❦

Mary Boone Gallery

417 W. Broadway   (212) 431-1818
between Spring and Prince
New York, NY 10012

Mary Boone is one of the great success stories of the eighties—a woman who blew in from Erie, Pennsylvania, to become one of the most powerful dealers in New York by the ripe old age of thirty. Mary's stable of artists virtually defines the last decade where action in art is concerned. David Salle, Eric Fischl, Brice Marden, and Ross Bleckner are household names among art aficionados. Their new work, which Mary handles with tender loving care, hovers in the low six figures here, while on the secondary market it can easily go for triple, even quadruple that.

But don't think you can just wander in off the street and purchase even a small drawing by one of these famous names—Mary's sales are as orchestrated as her Chanel wardrobe and Bennis/Edwards shoes. And waiting lists can be years long.

Don't let that stop you from making a point of visiting, however. The gallery usually has an interesting show. You see, Mary is married to German art dealer Michael Werner, so some European superstars, such as Sigmar Polke, Georg Baselitz, and Anselm Kiefer, show here.

Mary is as professional as she is manicured. If you show some particular interest, or arrive equipped with an introduction, she's likely to regale you with stories of the latest additions to her court, such as abstract artist Moira Dryer or appropriationist Sherry Levine. You'll be glad you brought some extra mad money, but not necessarily a lot. Mary's inventory has a very wide range of prices—$5,000 to $500,000.   ❦

Pace Gallery

32 East 57th Street   (212) 421-3292
New York, NY 10022

If Wildenstein Gallery, farther uptown, is a bit too Old Mastery for you, then trot down to Pace, which is almost like a vast department store for contemporary art. One of the top galleries in the Art Dealers Association of America, Pace has been in business for more than twenty years, and represents some of America's greatest artists and their estates. Have a hankering for a Louise Nevelson for your dining room wall? Pace is about the only place you'll get a truly great one.

Other artists in Pace's stable include Jim Dine, Dubuffet, and Lucas Samaras, not to mention Richard Serra, whose large steel sculptures and oil stick drawings command wide attention—and high prices. Average price of a work here? Plan on spending at least $30,000 to $40,000, and think about going as high a $1 million.

Pace has taken on bad-boy artist Julian Schnabel, but the gallery's greatest coup was the recent hiring away of Douglas Baxter from the well-regarded Paula Copper Gallery downtown. Now vice president at Pace, the slightly elfin and definitely delightful Douglas has strong ties to the Saatchis and to other fabulous collectors, who sometimes sell their art through Pace. So don't forget to ask to see what might be discreetly tucked away in the back room.

Also, be sure to go upstairs to the tenth floor to take a look at Pace Master Prints. Carlo Bella, whose mother runs Bella Stampa, one of the best galleries in Milan, has been building the inventory for the last five years. Here, you might be seduced, as we were, by a Goya print for as little as $3,000. Or you can take a walk on the wild side and dive into the African art collection housed on the same floor.   ❧

Peter Spielhagen Fine Arts

372 Bleecker Street   (212) 741-0489
between Charles and Perry
New York, NY 10014

Peter Spielhagen probably inherited his interest in and fine eye for antiques. He grew up in Berlin, the son of an antique buyer for a major department store. His childhood was spent surrounded by beautiful things, developing a keen appreciation for well-traveled, well-loved pieces passed down from generation to generation. As a result, his is a store with an old world look of faded elegance and tattered charm, featuring accessible furniture with a sensitive, earthy countenance, nothing prissy here, nothing with museum-quality price tags, just good, respectable furniture and decorations.

It's a popular and friendly shop, due in great part to the wit and charm of manager Vincent Verdi, who's almost always here—Peter often isn't as he's out scouring the world for his kind of antiques. The result of his ongoing search is an ever-changing inventory, which constantly alters the appearance of the store. One month it will be full of Biedermeier and Empire—the next, sixteenth- and seventeenth-century pieces take center stage. Indeed, the only generality that can be drawn about the store is that it features consistently high quality pieces from the sixteenth through nineteenth centuries at affordable prices. It's a place well-known to decorators, film stars, and Park Avenue types, along with dealers from all over the country, who come for good buys and occasional real finds.

A seven-and-a-half-foot-tall mahogany Biedermeier secretary falls into the find category. Valued at about $20,000, it's an extraordinary piece, very architectural with lots of columns and pediments, resembling a neo-classical building. Its desk top drops down to reveal all the nooks and crannies typical of its brethren, but with a difference. There's a little niche in the middle which resembles a tiny ballroom replete with mir-rored walls and parquet floors.

For a good buy, we recommend a Charles II seventeenth-century (about 1670) oak chest for $7,500. Completely original, it's a beauty with its recessed drawers and characteristic molded decorations flanking them.

If you're in the market for furniture, particularly sixteenth- and seventeenth-century pieces at something less than the upper seven figure range, don't miss Peter's place.   ❦

Sperone Westwater

142 Greene Street   (212) 431-3685
between Houston and Prince
New York, NY 10012

Gian Enzo Sperone is the European counterpart to Leo Castelli. He was the first to show major American artists on the continent with exhibitions in Italy in the early sixties. With partner Angela Westwater, he now represents a stable of high-level artists, dominated by the Europeans (with an emphasis on the Italian persuasion) including Chia, Clemente, and Mimmo Paladino—a group that was phenomenally successful in the late seventies and early eighties. In fact, they're still pretty well regarded. The last time Sperone Westwater launched a Mimmo Paladino show of major-scale works (3 meters by 4 meters), they fetched $175,000 and more.

If you're tired of the austere, minimalist ethic, this is the gallery for you. Sperone Westwater is devoted to expressionism, bold colors, and grand gestures. They also have a reputation for doing educational shows, like the much-ballyhooed exhibit last year of early pictures by superstar Cy Twombly, whose works are now bringing millions at auction. Interestingly enough, the early Twomblys most closely resembled works by Dubuffet. In fact, the educational shows have proved so successful that Sperone Westwater has taken another space across the street and down the block to house most of them. Gallery director David Leiber will gladly fill you in on what is going on or what to look forward to.

Lately, Sperone Westwater has taken on artist Ray Smith, an American of Mexican heritage whose work follows the expressionist ethic combined with that of the Mexican muralists. Sperone Westwater is so taken with him and his potential that they gave him a one-man show at the Chicago Art Fair in May 1989, where his larger paintings sold for $30,000 to $35,000.

So if you're interested in getting a serious dose of art education or a peek at what's considered blue-chip quality in Europe, stop by and be prepared to be dazzled by Gian Enzo. He looks like those great Italian movie stars of the sixties, right down to the day's growth of beard, and he's a charismatic charmer.   ❦

Treasures and Trifles

409 Bleecker Street   (212) 243-2723
between 11th and Bank
New York, NY 10014

The moment you walk into this smallish shop your eye is drawn here and there and everywhere—there's such an abundance of beautiful "stuff," seemingly haphazardly arranged. But rest assured. Partners Ned Kell and Robert McCarthy know exactly where everything is among all the clutter.

Of course, you can't miss the chandeliers. The ceiling is covered with them in all shapes and sizes, crystal, rock crystal, brass, and silver plate. We couldn't take our eyes off a stunning large crystal chandelier dating from about 1840 for $6,500. Several rock crystal variations on the theme from the mid-nineteenth century hover in the $7,500 neighborhood.

Everything here is very stylish, very glamorous, very showy, like the brilliant apple-green Japanese urn decorated with white cranes that's been turned into a lamp. The pottery dates from the nineteenth century, the wiring from the twentieth, and it sells for $1,200. Indeed, Treasures and Trifles has a very large collection of decorative lamps—lots of Chinese black and gold so popular with decorators of late. There are also a number of dramatic bronzes made into lamps, and the collection of Baccarat candlesticks and oil lamps transformed into modern electric-driven lighting fixtures is unparalleled.

Ned and Robert have also made a habit of bringing outdoor statuary indoors. Pieces originally meant to decorate gardens can look great in the corner of your living room or library. They'll show you how.

We should mention that there is furniture on the premises, but that's not why folks flock here. Just consider it a bonus that they have some very decorative French pieces, good contemporary copies of signed originals. Beautifully made by long-forgotten companies, they can dress up any room with a look that suggests considerably more expense than their real cost—one of Ned and Robert's reproductions of a chair might cost

$11,000 as opposed to $25,000 for the signed version. Virtually identical, they would even have been made within a decade of each other. Short of being so gauche as to flip it over and look for the tell-tale mark, we challenge anyone to tell the difference. So do Ned and Robert. 🐛

Vito Giallo Antiques

966 Madison Avenue   (212) 535-9885
between 75th and 76th streets
New York, NY 10021

You're forgiven if you momentarily wondered if this postage-stamp-sized store features a particular variety of antiques called Vito Giallo. In fact, Vito Giallo is the name of the engaging owner of one of the best haunts in town for unusual decorative accessories. In fact, "unusual" might be the courtly Mr. Giallo's middle name (we've never heard anyone call him Vito). It's certainly his favorite word. And in a nutshell, it describes his specialty—the rare, the unique, the singular, the uncommon.

He's relentless in his pursuit of objects that deserve such adjectives. Friends who have watched him at dealers' auctions report he'll outbid anyone for something he's never seen before. What's more, he'll sell it and sell it quickly—big time society decorators, with and without their rich and famous clients, and less well-known collectors shop his store weekly, contributing to a turnover of inventory that makes many other dealers very jealous indeed. The moral is, if you see it, like it, and want it at Vito Giallo, then buy it on the spot. Otherwise, you'll likely suffer the waffler's remorse—it won't be there when you go back for it.

Of course, Mr. Giallo will hold that lovely $1,200 and predictably unusual little Biedemeyer shaving mirror with ivory mounts for a day of two, if you ask. But be sure you pick it up when you said you would. Otherwise, it's by-by Biedemeyer. Of course, you can always console yourself with a piece of his extraordinary Chinese porcelain collection, some of it dating from as early as the eleventh century. Or maybe you need a cut crystal decanter for your, or someone else's, bar. They tend to start in the $300 neighborhood (considerably less than the porcelain prices) and have proved to be one of our most reliably appreciated choices as wedding gifts.

Mr. Giallo's treasure trove can also be counted on as a superior source of eighteenth- and nineteenth-century sterling silver serving pieces, with prices starting as low as $75 and ranging well into the thousands. He notes that, lately, collectors with truly educated eyes seem to be zeroing in on his punch ladles. Another recent trend that sends the in-crowd flocking to Mr. Giallo's door is the penchant for decorating dining tables with precious, little objets d'art. Each place setting is distinguished by its own piece—none better than his selection of little silver figurines of classical bearing. For $500 to $800 apiece, you can have the likes of Antigone and Bacchas adorning your table—more expensive, but certainly longer lasting than floral arrangements, and so in vogue that last time we visited, three people came in asking for them.

Andy Warhol used to drop by all the time. A collectors' collector, he wanted to make sure he didn't miss anything. Over the years, he bought most of his extensive hoard of rock crystal here. Lovers of fountain pens also make Vito Giallo a regular stop. There's always a beautiful array of vintage pens in the window, about $200 and up.

While there's no room for furniture, unusual or otherwise in the shop, there's plenty in Mr. Giallo's East Side townhouse, circa 1864. If you know to ask, he'll make an appointment for you to come by and wander through room after room of English, Continental, and American furniture, mostly 18th and 19th century. Our buddy, bank marketing whiz Cynthia Cole, once found a charming empire table for $1,700, which must be the cleverest piece of furniture we've ever encountered. On the one hand it can snuggle up all slender and compact along a wall, just right for a silver picture frame or two, and maybe a lamp. On the other hand it unfolds to comfortably seat six for dinner—with the additional leaves it can do ten or twelve.

Less versatile but suitably unusual is a pair of eighteenth century Italian tables with an olive wood veneer, about $5,000. We liked them, we wanted them, but didn't buy them. A week later, even at Mr. Giallo's by-appointment-only residence/furniture showroom, they were gone. 🐚

William Beadleston Gallery

60 East 91st Street   (212) 348-7234
New York, NY 10128

Talk about exclusive, discreet, and elegant—William Beadleston, one of the most distinguished galleries for Modern and Impressionist paintings and sculpture, is located in a marble-foyered townhouse somewhat off the beaten track, but close enough to Park Avenue to be convenient to some of its best clients. This is the place for Picasso (Beadleston had a show a couple of years back of seldom-seen material in conjunction with Jan Krugier) or for other work that has not been seen on the market in ages. Recently, with Coe Kerr Gallery, Beadleston managed to procure the Arnold Askin collection of Impressionist and Modern work. Is your heart's desire a Gauguin watercolor of a native girl for $1 million? Beadleston is your kind of gallery.

Bill Beadleston is a joyful, friendly man who loves talking about his work and about his ranch out west, a passion second only to a great piece of art. His right-hand person, Susan Seidel, handles the day-to-day workings of the gallery and is considered by some of the smartest inhabitants of the art world to be most well informed.

She can, for instance, tell you all about the Calder piece entitled *Red Disk,* circa 1947. More painted and wire sculpture than mobile, it is large (81 by 74 inches) and is perfectly balanced on a center of gravity on a wooden base. Interestingly enough, when Beadleston purchased the piece it came in the crate Calder had originally made to ship to its first owner. Susan says whoever buys it this time gets the crate too.

As a regular client, you might be invited to one of the famous Beadleston Friday lunches, where art honchos wheel, deal, and gossip over a gourmet meal in a private dining room overlooking a lovely oasis of a garden. Foie gras tastes even better when served in the company of some of Beadleston's masterpieces.   ❦

Wildenstein Galleries

19 East 64th Street   (212) 879-0500
New York, NY 10022

If a short jaunt to Paris, perhaps an hour or two, appeals, head for Wildenstein Galleries. The five-story townhouse on a particularly posh street on the Upper East Side was constructed especially for gallery use. The understated elegance of the crystal chandelier in the two-story entrance hall, the grand staircase with the graceful filigreed banister, the marble floors, the Louis XV consoles, and the eternally fresh flowers gracefully set off the many, mostly fresh, masterpieces.

But however enchanted you are by the Parisian splendor of Wildenstein (and you will be), never forget that this is a very serious gallery. Indeed, if $500,000 seems a bit steep as a starting price, don't bother to make an appointment to be taken into one of the exclusive viewing rooms on the upper floors. That's where Wildenstein shows the serious works—those it considers important enough to be shown in one of these rooms.

Basically, Wildenstein takes on, as one art-world aficionado put it, "anything that's great and worth a mint." Guess we have to take his word for it, because the powers-that-be here are loath to discuss anything in their inventory for publication. Of course, they'll be happy to talk to you in person, at length. And afterwards, you can step around the corner to La Goulue. It's a great place (especially in the spring and summer when the sidewalk café is open) to sit and have a drink or a meal. It will complete your illusion of having spent a day in gay Paree!   🐛

Zigi Ben-Haim

94 Mercer Street   (212) 431-4689
#5
between Spring and Broome Street
New York, NY 10012

There are some terrific artists, growing more important every day, who are not represented by galleries. Instead they center their artistic lives on studios in places like SoHo, where dozens of old factory buildings have been converted into everything from elegant living spaces for yuppies to artists' sprawling, often chaotic workplaces. Zigi Ben-Haim, a thoughtful, exuberant Israeli is one such artist. Known for his large-scale sculpture, Zigi's work has been shown in 57th Street galleries and in major museums. Furthermore, it has been acquired by some of the country's most prominent collectors, like California's Fred Weisman.

Zigi's work is as intelligent and kinetic as its maker, ranging in size from smaller table pieces to larger-than-life bronzes. Our favorite in the latter category is his group of dancers inspired largely by the genius of Matisse, and most recently shown as a complete project at the Herbert Johnson Museum at Cornell University.

In the past, Zigi has worked in cement and wire mesh, making the figures seem grounded, yet slightly precarious. "My work is the opposite of De Kooning, who takes a concrete shape, like a woman, and makes it abstract," says Zigi. "I take abstract shapes and ask a viewer to see the forms in them."

When we last visited Zigi, one room off the living quarters, just across from the freight elevator, was jam-packed with his work. We were taken with a large wire mesh sculpture resembling a pair of scissors. Three balls are lodged between its "blades." Prices run from $6,000 to about $100,000 for one of Zigi's outdoor bronzes.

But remember, this is a fun rather than stuffy artistic venue. It's likely you'll be invited to sit and chat about art history over a cup of coffee. And surely Zigi will show you his proudest creation—his four-year-old son, Yori! ❦

CHAPTER EIGHT

Beauty and Health

From ear to there

B ehind all the glitz and hype, the Hollywood mystique and the marble and mirrors, you can still get a pretty good haircut in New York—or a perm or a makeover. Not only that, there are lots of experts who'll be delighted to impart their deepest, darkest secrets of beauty, grooming, and fitness for a price.

As many ways as there are to feed yourself, clothe yourself, house yourself, or amuse yourself, there are at least as many ways to make yourself beautiful—be you male or female. In fact, if there's one big trend here in recent days, it's that New York's beauty establishment has discovered that men have money, and vanity too. So if you've come to New York as a couple, you really can do everything together now. That brief respite when the little woman goes off to the beauty salon—that one place of female refuge from the male species—is no longer. You may go in separate doors, but once inside, what they do to you isn't all that much different.

What they do is to make you feel good, as well as beautiful—all over. The secrets of Hollywood or Broadway, those magical substances dispensed from tiny bottles onto the world's most fabulous faces, are now available in beauty boutiques (even cosmetic counters) all over town. With health and exercise so "in," there's someone or something somewhere in New York to help you along from head to toe. There's an exercise regime for everyone, with and without machines. And plenty of masseurs to rub out the aching memories.

Then once you're whipped into perfect shape, it'll be just the right time to go out to one of those wonderful little restaurants just around every corner in this amazing city. . . and start all over again!

SUPPLIES

Boyds of Madison Avenue

655 Madison Avenue   (212) 838-6558
between 60th and 61st Streets
New York, NY 10021

At first glance, the window looks like the jumble often associated with all-purpose discount emporiums. On closer inspection, there's the mink headband or the fox boa, the collection of very fine natural bristle brushes, and a truly world-class selection of cosmetics and perfumes. Then there's all that very good-looking costume jewelry. And while you're pondering the mixed messages of the crowded window, Cher, Farrah Fawcett, Robert Wagner, Liza Minnelli, Richard Harris, Paul Anka, Diana Ross, Jackie Onassis, even the reclusive Greta Garbo might sweep by you on their way into the city's best source of personal hygiene and beauty products.

Albert and Arnold Fader are responsible for an inventory that specializes in things impossible to find elsewhere. They've owned Boyds for the past forty years and have frequented the far corners of the earth seeking unusual, but quality products. What they haven't been able to buy, they've had made for their private-label line by Europe's finest manufacturers.

Albert's wife, Carol, is the lady in charge. Pretty, blond, and vivacious, she always looks perfect and is happy to share her beauty secrets with you. She oversees twenty makeup artists, who will retouch or redo your face, in return for a $50 purchase—an easy requirement with Boyds' exceptional products.

Take the terrific German-made line filler pencil; for $10.75 it does a magnificent job of filling all those bothersome little lines around the eye and mouth. Then there's the most incredible collapsible hairbrush, actually capable of brushing even the thickest hair. It slides perfectly into a lady's evening bag (even into Judith Leiber's exquisite minaudière) or a gentleman's briefcase and only costs $3.75.

Ever wonder how Joan Collins's lipstick always seems to sit perfectly on those pretty, pouty lips of hers? Seems Carol introduced her to something called Sealed Lips; once applied, it keeps lipstick adhering to lips through eating, smoking, kissing, or whatever (especially whatever). For $6.75, how can you possibly beat it?

Carol's no doctor, but she swears by Eye Tucks—a $39.95 nonsurgical eyelift that really works. Carol won't say exactly who, but she proudly claims that any number of famous and beautiful faces benefit from its regular use.

Many of those faces also benefit from Boyds' exclusive line of Renoir cosmetics. Boyds' own private label, the Renoir products are first rate and well priced—lipsticks at $10.75, mascara (la Garbo buys no other) for $12.75, and foundations starting at $20.

As for hair, Boyds has everything necessary and accessory—Italian boar-bristle brushes so fabulous that fifty of the nation's best beauty salons work with nothing else, and ornaments—racks and racks, drawers and drawers, filled with them.

Needless to say, you'll need lots of time at Boyds—time to sort through all this, to make the right decision. So try confining your Boyds shopping to weekdays between 10:00 A.M. and 1:00 P.M.—they tend to be the least hectic hours. Boyds is open from 8:30 A.M. to 7:00 P.M., but the early mornings and the afternoons are crazy. Saturdays are nothing short of insane—from 9:30 A.M. to 6:00 P.M.

If your main interest is a makeover, call for an appointment. And keep in mind that plans are in the works for ever-new services—facials, for instance, and pedicures and manicures too. And don't forget the catalog, for your favorite supplies wherever you might find yourself in the world, like so many of Boyds' faithful.

Floris

703 Madison Avenue   (212) 935-9100
between 62nd and 63rd Streets   For Mail Order (800) J-Floris
New York, NY 10021

These days a stroll past any fragrance counter invokes a roll-call of luminous show business names like Elizabeth Taylor, Cher, Sophia Loren, Catherine Deneuve, and Dionne Warwick. Recently another name rich with Hollywood associations has joined this star-studded fragrance firmament—Niven. James Niven, son of the late, great English actor David Niven, has associated himself with not one but a whole line of fragrances marketed under the name of Floris.

There's nothing new about Floris. It was established in 1730 by Juan Famenias Floris, who had sailed to England from his native Spanish island of Minorca to seek fame and fortune. He secured both with the establishment of a shop on fashionable Jermyn Street dedicated to perfumes, then considered a novelty. Capitalizing on the traditional English love of gardens and possibly on the coincidental descriptive nature of his name, Juan's shop became renowned as a purveyor of floral-scented perfumes and toiletries. Seven generations later, the dynasty he founded still operates the business from the same extended premises at No. 89 Jermyn Street, where for over two hundred and fifty years they have served the fashion conscious ladies and gentlemen of the Court of St. James.

Thanks to Mr. Niven, just as suave and debonair as his father, an almost exact replica of the original shop now sits invitingly on Madison Avenue dispensing a tranquil breath of fresh English country air. The moment you enter the tiny shop lined with softly gleaming mahogany showcases your senses are awakened by the seductive scent wafting from the large bowl of English rose potpourri. It can work its magic in your home for $17.50 for 4 cups or $35 for 16.

You can also pickup a $15 room spray to mask any unpleasant odor or ingenious fragrance disks for $25 that use the heat from lightbulbs to spread the scent. But Floris built its reputation on scents for the person and they remain the specialty dispenser with a unique collection of perfumes, colognes, talcum powders, and bath preparations—for both sexes. Floris caters to masculine as well as feminine tastes and needs. Indeed, men seem to feel uncommonly comfortable shopping in this clubby atmosphere, where the staff is incredibly hospitable. Here they can assemble a complete fragrance wardrobe—hand soap, shaving cream, shaving soap (which comes in a wonderful wooden bowl), aftershave, deodorant, hair lotion, talcum powder, and toilet water, all in the classic No. 89 named after the address of the London shop. If 89 isn't your cup of tea, all these products are also infused with another Floris bouquet for gentlemen, Elite.

For ladies, there are 16 scents with names like Edward Bouquet, English Violet, Ormande, and Wild Hyacinth. Perfumes range from $50 to $90, while the toilet waters fit into the $27.50 to $47.50 slot depending on size and dispenser. As confirmed devotees of long luxurious baths, we're especially fond of the various concentrated bath essences. The elegantly boxed selection of six for $45 makes a terrific present.

Indeed, manager Donna Reynolds puts together marvelous gift wicker baskets of Floris' wares. The gift wrapping alone is as beautiful as can be. The selection, presented either in wicker baskets or in smashing Floris blue "hat boxes," depends on your taste and pocketbook. They start at $35 and Elizabeth reports that she's constructed several in the $400 range, but really the sky's the limit.

Even if your preference in perfumes leans toward the spicy Oriental scents rather than florals, we highly recommend a visit to this little oasis of British gentility. It's such a refreshing, soothing experience.   ❦

Kiehl's

109 Third Avenue	(212) 677-3171
between 13th and 14th Streets	(212) 475-3698
New York, NY 10003	FAX (212) 674-3544

It's not much to look at, this 138-year-old establishment. The linoleum floors are tacky, literally and figuratively, and the funny little chandeliers have a decidedly faded sparkle. There's just nothing fancy about this former apothecary, now a thriving cosmetics business—no elaborate packaging, no expensive advertising or marketing, just simple see-through plastic bottles containing beauty products that lure New York's most fashionable women to the store's less-than-chic East Village location.

Founded in 1851, Kiehl's was a typical neighborhood apothecary dispensing homemade preparations—aphrodisiacs, virility cream, and cures for baldness. In 1921 Irving Morse, a trained pharmacist, purchased the store from the founding family and began formulating the first Kiehl-brand products. His son Aaron took over in 1978. A pharmaceutical expert, Aaron had already enjoyed a brilliant career as the developer of the nation's first fluoride treatment and as a pioneer in the development of a drug instrumental in fighting tuberculosis. It was Aaron who conceived of many of what have become Kiehl's most popular products.

Yet another generation of Morses is now in charge at Kiehl's—Aaron's striking daughter, Jami. She's taken over and expanded Kiehl's market by selling their products to Barneys and to outlets in Europe and Japan. Her husband, Klaus, a former professional skier, has added a number of men's and unisex items geared to the needs of the athlete.

Still, the basics of Kiehl's haven't changed much, though they have stopped the practice of custom-blending fragrances, which used to be one of their great claims to fame. Unfortunate perhaps, but Kiehl's does offer 118 different scents, so it's difficult to complain too much.

As for their other claim to fame, there are some 350 Kiehl's skin- and hair-care products, based on a combination of the best homeopathic and herbal remedies, high-quality oils, and other natural ingredients, all mixed with a good dose of modern technology.

A lot of people (Cher, Tatum O'Neal, and a whole slew of models among them) swear by items like their gentle Washable Cleansing Milk for $11.50 and superb Ultra Facial Moisturizer at $14.50.

If the one hundred percent money-back guarantee doesn't convince you of Kiehl's quality, the fact that over one hundred of their products are on permanent display at the Smithsonian's Public Health and Pharmacy Exhibit in the National Museum of History and Technology probably will.

In any case, it's unlikely you'll buy anything that doesn't satisfy. The delightful staff, led by manager and chief skin-care consultant, Christopher Brosius, is very liberal with its samples. Indeed, Kiehl's actively encourages new customers to try samples before purchasing anything; it helps ensure that each will find the optimum regimen for his or her individual skin, scalp, and hair types. Besides, they know once you've tried their products, you're hooked!

Kiehl's may not be fancy, but it sure is smart!

Shu Uemura Beauty Boutique

241 Columbus Avenue   (212) 724-0684
at 71st Street   FAX (212) 724-0246
New York, NY 10023

Black, sleekly modern, almost austere, the Shu Uemura Beauty Bou-tique looks a little forbidding from the outside. There's no indication at all that this place is fun, even exciting. In fact, there's only scant evi-dence of what this rather imposing three-story structure might hold. The window displays have a stylized, stage-set look that suggests many possibilities, a photographer's studio among them, and Shu Uemura is hardly a household name.

At least, it's not all that familiar in this country, but Shu Uemura is a very well-known and respected name in Japan, where sixty-six boutiques proudly operate under it. The name and the boutiques belong to Japan's premier makeup artist, who once practiced his art in Hollywood. Frus-trated by what he considered the inferior quality of the cosmetics on the market, he worked with Japanese chemists to develop a line that would satisfy professionals like himself. Indeed, initially, fellow makeup artists made up the bulk of Shu Uemura's customers. But as he expanded, with the addition of skin-care products and applicators, consumer demand grew. Before long, he had boutiques all over his native country, plus one in Singapore and Hong Kong and two in Paris. Four years ago, he brought his concept to the U.S. and now has operations in Dallas and Los Angeles, as well as the New York headquarters.

What exactly is his concept, and what makes it so obviously success-ful? Typically Japanese, it is both simple and complex. The quality of the all-natural, preservative-free products is high, the prices are not. Healthy doses of cleanser, toner, day moisturizer, and night cream cost a total of only $120. The secret is the lack of advertising and expensive packag-ing; all containers are very basic, very practical.

The fun and truly unique aspects come into play, quite literally, when you realize you are not only invited, but actually encouraged, to sit at one of the testing counters and experiment to your heart's content, free of charge. You can spend all day at it, and solicit the advice of the li-censed makeup artists, or not. There's no high-pressure sales talk from the overly madeup vampires that inhabit so many other cosmetic counters. In fact there's no pressure here at all. It's all extremely relaxed and informal. Unless you initiate the conversation, the only question you'll be asked after the obligatory "May I help you?" is "May I get you some refreshment?"

We've found that a glass of wine helps our brushing technique. And at these prices, we don't have to worry about it loosening our inhibitions and causing us to spend too much. Brushes start at $11, eyeshadows at $9.50, while foundations are $12.50. We adore their $16 color correctors that even out skin tones, removing the yellow or red. They banish that sallow look that can occasionally affect even the most beautiful countenances, like those of Cher, Bianca, Jamie Lee Curtis, and Christie Brinkley.

Besides helping you learn to use their products as expertly as these glamourous Shu Uemura customers, the staff artists will apply makeup for $25, by appointnment only. Since Shu Uemura is open seven days a week, you should be able to book just before that important occasion. Hours are 11:00 A.M. to 8:00 P.M., Monday through Saturday, Sundays from noon to 6:00 P.M.

With movies creeping up to $7.50 and beyond, we've taken to entertaining ourselves on a lazy Sunday by settling down at Shu Uemura for an afternoon of makeup research and development. It's fun, free, and we look so much better when we finally emerge to face the world. 🐾

LADIES' SERVICES

Ame Salon

29 East 61st Street   (212) 371-1266
New York, NY 10021

Ame may be the best-kept manicure secret in New York. While tucked quietly away on the second floor of a discreet building on the Upper East Side, Ame is still first-rate and accessible—particularly to the traveler in need of a last-minute fix-up. Of course, regulars stop in at least once a week for owner Haydee's special touch. Quiet and pleasant, she gives the best manicure in town, but the worst interview.

That's probably why you haven't seen her written up in *Vogue* or *Elle*, and why her salon rates a prime spot in this book. She just can't be bothered. She and her three other specialists are too busy grooming the hands of the likes of Anna Bulgari and Joanna Carson.

She charges $18 for a regular manicure, $20 for French, and $40 for Juliette. That's all she said, and that's all we've written.   🐛

Elizabeth Arden

691 Fifth Avenue   (212) 407-7900
at 54th Street
New York, NY 10022

When you breeze through that trademark red door, you enter a whole new world, a sea of calm dedicated to pampering, to improving the tone and pace of your everyday existence—a world created by a feisty little Canadian redhead named Florence Nightingale Graham, who parlayed a jar of cleansing cream into a billion-dollar industry.

Encouraged to follow in the footsteps of her illustrious namesake, Florence attended nursing school during the early years of this century. There she developed an acute awareness of the direct correlation between the feeling of physical well-being, massage, and the maintenance of healthy-looking skin. A chance encounter with a biochemist working on formulating a cream that would soothe and heal skin blemishes led her to seize upon the notion of devising skin creams for cosmetic use. The rest, as they say, is history.

Florence popularized skin treatments that combined the use of massage with that of her cosmetic creams. She experimented with rouges and tinted powders and discovered that she had a flawless sense of color. Her metamorphosis into the world's leading beauty expert—Elizabeth Arden—had begun. It was completed with the opening of Elizabeth Arden salons in all the great capitals of the world and in cities throughout the United States.

Today, Arden's flagship in New York has six floors of services to take care of your every need. The main floor has an array of cosmetics and fragrances and some fashion items. Floors eleven and twelve are devoted to hairdressing and manicures. There are sixteen stylists and eleven assistants, trained and equipped to deal with the most sophisticated haircutting, styling, and coloring. If you have a sudden urge to try out a wonderfully whimsical hair ornament, there are plenty to choose from, and the stylists will show you how to manage them when you are on your own.

For nails, a staff of nineteen manicurists is ready to cater to any request, from a polish change to a soothing paraffin pedicure. A regular manicure costs $15.00; add a set of ten tips with wraps and you're talking $85.00.

The eighth and ninth floors house the Face and Body Departments, where you can indulge in a restorative facial or massage. The twenty-four facialists possess the secrets of what were known as Florence's "magic hands," while the fourteen masseuses are equally endowed with knowing just how to ease away all your tensions. For a special treat, have the excess creams and oils rinsed off with a Scotch hose. A regular old shower will never again suffice!

One of our favorite people here is Constantine, the makeup artist. Decked out in your signature Arden pink smock, you will be amazed by what Constantine's little tips can do for your appearance. He will teach you, as he has many of New York's smartest women, how to (literally) put your best face forward.

Should you wish to sample all the beauty wonders Arden has to offer, plan ahead and make arrangements to experience either the Miracle Morning for $175 or a Maine Chance Day for $225. As part of the package, you will feast on a light spa repast in the delightful lunchroom on the ninth floor. If you prefer, lunch can be brought to you on a tray, wherever you choose in the salon.

There is one aspect of this otherwise almost perfect world where we found fault—the Fashion Department on the second floor. Despite the presence of glorious furs by J. Mendel, enticing loungewear by Coty Award–winner Bill Tice, and one of New York's canniest Personal Shopping services in the guise of Ellen Schwartz, the days when Arden flaunted the best of the world's greatest designers are no longer.

Perhaps Eli Lilly, the international pharmaceutical giant that purchased Elizabeth Arden in 1971, just did not understand fashion, did not consider it an important component to the continuing success of the firm. We can only hope that Arden's latest parent company, Fabergé, will have a better appreciation of Florence Nightingale Graham's original vision of furnishing a sophisticated clientele with a beauty salon/clothing store they could truly call their own.

García

240 East 27th Street   (212) 889-3028
New York, NY 10016

Few people are as lucky as García, master makeup and hair artist. This is a man who loves his work—and his work loves him. It has fulfilled his dreams of traveling around the world, meeting and working with all the best people. One of them, the amazing Amalita de Fortabat of Argentina (you know, the cement heiress who had to loan the Argentine government her aircraft fleet for the Falklands War) counts on his services twice a day when she's in town—for daytime and evening looks. For her granddaughter's wedding in Buenos Aires, Amalita imported him for the duration of the festivities.

Likewise, Gayfryd Steinberg made sure García was the director of beauty services for stepdaughter Laura's wedding to Jonathan Tisch. García even did Laura's hair and makeup for her wedding-dress fittings with Scassi, so that the total look could be polished and refined to perfection.

García will gladly polish you as well. His goal is to develop your best features and bring out your personality, in the most uncomplicated and attractive way. For $300 he'll do your makeup and freshen your coif with hot rollers and comb-out. It makes no difference if he comes to you or you go to his studio—the price is the same. But if you want to take advantage of one of his $400 lessons, we think it best you go to the studio. Everything is at his fingertips there, and it's likely he can spend more time with you.

Like most makeup artists who are in demand by celebrity clients like Diandra Douglas and Ann Getty, and who have worked with the world's greatest photographers like Norman Parkinson, Horst, and Skrebneski, García has developed a line of products. The prices are fair, starting at $6 for a lip pencil, going up to $12 for a powder brush. But the best news is that, with typical grace, García has the good sense not to insist you use his line. If you're happy with whatever you've been using, that's okay with him.

Indeed the only thing difficult about the charming García is getting an appointment with him. Agent and business partner Charles Howard is the keeper of García's schedule. Call him and see what you can work out. You'll be very glad you did.

John Sahag

18 East 53rd Street (212) 371-4777
2nd Floor
New York, NY 10022

No doubt about it, as you wend your way to this second-floor salon, you are entering a very rarefied world indeed. Classical music wafts through the air of this coolly serene oasis—gray marble floors and soft gray leather contoured chairs. It's a place designed to help you relax as you put yourself in John Sahag's capable hands.

He really is a master, having trained in Paris and freelanced for the world's leading magazines for years. At thirty-six, John, with his own long, wavy mane and warm demeanor, has been in New York for nine years, where he's made quite a name for himself. Who else insists upon a consultation before touching your hair? It takes only about five minutes, but you'd better call at least a week before. And who else is constantly booked weeks in advance despite (or maybe because of) a $250 charge for a cut? Should his services be required at your hotel or home, the price tag jumps to a whopping $1,000! The regal presence of his greyhound, Baron, usually in graceful repose right next to John's station, adds to the alluring mystique of this establishment dedicated to the perfect cut.

Make no mistake, things are done differently here. John and his seven stylists cut hair *dry*. He likens it to sculpting stone, taking advantage of the natural shape and texture. It takes an hour or two, but the results are worth the time. The cut is custom-designed to suit the hair's inherent qualities and to flatter the face. Look at his success with Farrah Fawcett, Jacklyn Smith, Brooke Shields, Alana Stewart, and Demi Moore.

John feels a sincere and abiding responsibility to such visible heads. He knows how important hair is in defining a woman's total appearance. Laughingly, John claims, "It's probably easier to get into Harvard than it is to get a job here. I'm a fanatic about making sure the people who work for me are really talented and well trained." In fact, he requires a minimum of five years' experience to become an assistant in his salon. Only after serving an apprenticeship with John are the assistants allowed on the floor as full-blown stylists like Eiji, who trained under John for six months. Eiji's been very popular ever since he was promoted three years ago; he charges $150 and is booked six to eight weeks in advance.

Mark Schwartz offers another styling alternative at $125. Call him about three weeks before you need a cut. Lello and Mayumi are terrific too, and bargain-priced at $100.

Predictably, John's approach to coloring is uniquely his own. He bases it upon the cut, taking advantage of the shape to illuminate the texture. He applies at least two and often as many as five different shades to give hair a lovely luminescence, comparing the process to properly lighting a carefully assembled decor.

Clearly, John Sahag is not the kind of place most people go for a weekly wash and blow-dry. Still, some can't resist, so John allows his assistants to do the honors at $75 a clip. If you insist, by special request and a higher fee, one of the senior stylists can be engaged for the job.

But why bother? There are any number of places in New York to get washed and coiffed, few others that can guarantee a cut that's so undeniably you.   ❦

Leonardo

(212) 288-8060

Ever wonder who's responsible for the dazzling locks that frame those gorgeous faces staring out from the covers of all those magazines? One possibility is Leonardo, the Venezuelan who emigrated to New York fifteen years ago and has been working hair wonders ever since.

He operates on the "have scissors and hair drier, will travel" principle. Leonardo goes to you—hotel, home, or office. Even at $150 for a wash and blow-dry (including carfare), he's often booked at least a week in advance. He's just so popular.

In fact, there are those who simply cannot live without him. When summering in the Hamptons or at the Cape, many of his clients import Leonardo. Of course, when his services are required beyond the boundaries of Manhattan, he expects his transportation to be provided—limo or private plane will do!

When not keeping tabs on the glamorous manes of Lauren Bacall, Gena Rowlands, Mary Steenburgen, and any number of models, Leonardo is often occupied with wedding parties. He has developed quite a specialty—wedding dates are set pending his availability.

Leonardo takes weddings very seriously indeed. He consults with the bride months in advance, considers the gowns and headpieces, scouts the bridesmaids to determine the most flattering and complimentary styles. The results are gratifying, but costly—$250 for the bride, $150 for each attendant. With a $500 minimum for weddings, you might as well enlist at least two bridesmaids. Weddings, it seems, are very time-consuming, and Leonardo *does* stick around for retouches during the postceremony festivities.

Dream weddings just a dream for the moment—no man in sight? Leonardo to the rescue! Nothing improves your appearance faster or more dramatically than the perfect custom-designed hairstyle. Leonardo can perform the appropriate magic; a complete reworking of your coiffure will cost $175. Consider it an investment in your future! ❦

Linda Mason

29 King Street   (212) 929-5867
between 6th and Varick
New York, NY 10013

With her flaming red hair, bright blue eyes, and peaches-and-cream complexion, Linda Mason is her own best advertisement—testimony to her theory that even the most beautiful women can benefit from makeup. Granted, Linda takes a somewhat offbeat approach to makeup artistry. She considers the zodiac her cosmetics guide.

Whatever your opinion of the merits of astrology, it's difficult to argue with Linda's successful collaborations with the world's top fashion designers—Jean-Paul Gaultier, Issey Miyake, Perry Ellis, Chanel, Giorgio Armani, Yohji Yamamoto, Versace. During her years in Paris, where her career began, she created makeup to suit the colors and shapes of their clothes for shows and advertising.

Now firmly established in New York, she frequently works for *Vogue, Harper's Bazaar, Mademoiselle,* and *Vanity Fair.* Private clients who depend on her inventive style include Loni Anderson, Cybill Shepherd, Bette Midler, and Demi Moore. Even Rob Lowe's boyish good looks have been enhanced by Linda's touch.

In keeping with the title of her book, *Linda Mason's Sun Sign Makeovers,* published in 1985, Linda bases her makeup strategy on the four elments as defined by the zodiac—air, fire, earth, and water. Since she believes makeup should be an expression of personality, she chooses colors suited to the sign that defines an individual's nature.

In fact, Linda is so committed to this notion that she has developed three makeup kits for each of the elements, which sell for about $28 at

Barneys. Appropriately named Elements, each kit contains eye and face shadows, blush, and long-lasting matte lipstick. The color combinations are often surprising, even eccentric, and always exciting.

Visit Linda's loft tucked away on the 4th floor of an old schoolhouse building in Soho, and she'll show you how "impossible" it is to make a mistake with her palettes. She charges $350 for a two-hour lesson geared to teaching you how to make several different statements with makeup, statements that mirror your various moods. Feeling romantic or seductive? Linda will teach you to communicate the message more effectively with makeup.

For $500, she'll spend three hours helping you explore your moods in greater depth. If you want her to come to you, add another $100 to the charge.

She'll also take on weddings—in fact, she loves doing them. But she quotes price only on request, depending on location and whether her services are required just for the bride or for the entire wedding party.

Put yourself in Linda's capable hands and we guarantee you will learn something about yourself and the potential of makeup to change the image you present to the world.   🌶

Nathan

24 East 64th Street   (212) 838-5583
2nd Floor
New York, NY 10021

Few people are as specialized and talented as Nathan—he does hair color, period. He creates beautiful natural color for some of the chicest heads in New York.

Working in his sunlit salon on the second floor of a charming old townhouse, Nathan builds on and enhances his clients' inherent attributes—skin tone, eye color, and original hair pigmentation. He shuns fads and trends in favor of a classic genuine look, loaded with glamour.

He's truly a master colorist, having trained under the legendary Rosemary at Kenneth. When she retired, she passed the scepter to Nathan, who now reigns supreme.

His prices start at $175 and up, depending upon what is required. Nathan's special kind of custom coloring can be a lengthy process, particularly where streaking and highlighting are concerned. You may spend hours with him and drop several hundred dollars, but it will be time and money well spent. Your hair will look marvelous, making you look sensational. You should expect nothing less than perfection from Nathan, and you'll get it.

Nathan's calm, soothing personality and sympathetic nature are another bonus. A couple of hours chatting amiably with him is a great substitute for your weekly visit to the analyst.   ❦

Rex

77 Fifth Avenue   (212) 633-2091
between 15th and 16th Streets
New York, NY 10003

Rex—what a story! He's the little Dutch boy who went to Paris and became a nude dancer at the Folies Bergère. A freak onstage accident in 1969 left him paralyzed for two years, a time he devoted to practicing his first love, drawing. Exercise and determination restored his health, but he decided not to resume his dancing career. Rather, he determined he would exercise his newly refined talent.

At the time, a lot of advertising was still done with illustration. Thinking that he could avoid the starving-artist routine, Rex presented himself to the Elizabeth Arden Salon in Paris as the answer to all of their advertising prayers. They recognized talent, all right, but not for advertising. After reviewing Rex's sketches, Elizabeth Arden's sister decided that his future and his fortune could be made as a makeup artist.

The rest is history. During Rex's tenure as Elizabeth Arden's premier *artiste de maquillage*, he was discovered by the French magazines and became a favorite with French *Vogue,* leading to a connection with its American sister. That's how Rex came to New York—on a month-long assignment from *Vogue.* Somehow he's just never gotten around to going "home."

He's too busy here even to consider it. In constant demand, he is responsible for many of the exceptionally beautiful faces that strut down the runways of designers Calvin Klein and Donna Karan. His faces also grace the covers of every major magazine. You know who we mean. We're talking Paulina, Cindy Crawford, Iman, and Isabella Rossellini. He's also popular with Hollywood types, when they're in town. Diahann Carroll, Eva Gabor, Joan Fontaine, and Linda Gray all dial his number frequently.

Fortunately, you can too! Rex offers several ways to attain that polished look of the professional beauty. There's his book, for one—*Makeup by Rex* for $13. Not into do-it-yourself? Rex also gives group makeup lessons; groups are limited to five. Each series is three sessions, three hours each, $400 for the course, at his studio Monday nights 7:00 to 10:00 P.M. Private lessons are also available at $250 a shot for "an hour or so." Rex doesn't watch the clock. His goal is to make sure each student/client learns to use makeup properly to take the very best advantage of her looks.

No time for a series of lessons? Rex will set aside a weekend morning, and for $250, he'll spend several hours showing you the finest in makeup arts. Rex says it's like building a house—first lay the foundation, then concentrate on the decoration. Rex will build your face for that very special event. For $100 and about half an hour of time he'll go to your hotel or apartment to work his magic.

What better way to treat yourself and all your many admirers?

The Wayne Webb Technique

124 East 65th Street   (212) 772-0200
New York, NY 10021

Mirror, mirror, on the wall, who's the fairest of them all? You are, of course. Wayne Webb truly believes that every woman has the potential to be the fairest; she just has to learn how to make the most of what she's got.

Wayne, with his easy manner and love of beauty, is the man to do the teaching. Interested in "real people" with real lives, Wayne teaches them how to master their look and tailor it to their individual lifestyles. A single makeup lesson costs $175, an application $125. We recommend the $250 two-and-a-half-hour course to make a real difference in your life. The first hour and a half Wayne works with you, teaching technique in his makeup room, which is stark black with clear mirrors and bright lights (no colors to compete with that of your hair and face). Then he sends you off for a few days to practice. Return for the last hour to work out whatever problems you've been having. Once more, there's never any future charge for any question you might have; just call or drop by and Wayne will be only too happy to help.

Wayne's look is soft, classic. More importantly, he makes it your look. Before touching a new face, he sits down with the client in the lovely chintz-draped and mirrored boudoir-like outer room of his studio. He discusses how she wants to look and how much time she has on a daily basis to devote to that look.

His objective is not to push products, but he does produce a line and, of course, he uses nothing else. Having tested everything in the market, Wayne was dissatisfied. "Most cosmetics seem to be conceived by corporate committees or marketing people who never had to apply makeup to faces," Wayne points out. "Women must be discouraged with the fuss necessary to look right."

Enter Wayne Webb and Bob Unger, the pharmaceutical chemist with whom he worked to develop a line that is easy to use with true colors that hold their own through fourteen-hour days. Uniquely, each product comes with a professional applicator—foundations with sponges, blushes with full-size brushes, pencils with sharpeners.

Other than his opulent salon in an elegant East Side townhouse, Bonwit Teller at Trump Tower is the only outlet for Wayne Webb Cosmetics. The salesperson there is a makeup artist trained by Wayne. Even the purchase of a lipstick will get you a five-minute lesson in its proper application. Should you decide to throw caution to the wind, throw out your collection of assorted makeup components, and commit yourself exclusively to Wayne's line—it will cost somewhere in the $200 to $250 neighborhood—but you will get the benefit of lots of the clerk's time and expertise.

Some free advice from Wayne—whether it's his or anyone else's, throw out mascara after three months' use. The older it gets, the more it's exposed to air and the more likely it is to breed bacteria that can cause serious eye infections. Wayne also counsels against using any mascara claiming to be waterproof, unless of course you're Esther Williams. It drys out your lashes and is difficult to remove, potentially damaging the sensitive area around the eye. Wayne describes his mascara as "water resistant" and assures us that he makes his with a setting lotion like that used on hair. It coats and conditions the lashes and does not clot.

Wayne sees only four or five clients a day, and he's very popular, especially with a number of those ladies who appear daily in the social columns. They book him in the afternoon for their evening outings. So he generally reserves the mornings for lessons. He will come to you for a $250 minimum, but given the beauty of his salon and the perfection of the lighting there, why subject the two of you to less than ideal conditions?

UNISEX SERVICES

Georgette Klinger

501 Madison Avenue	(212) 838-3200
at 53rd Street	(800) KLINGER
New York, NY 10022	

978 Madison Avenue	(212) 744-6900
at 76th Street	
New York, NY 10021	

At seventy-three, Georgette Klinger is a pretty persuasive advertisement for her skin-care regimens and products. You recognize her immediately from her famous ads, featured with her daughter Kathryn, who's thirty-something. Clearly, for the whole family, beauty is another fine example of the Klinger philosophy. Together they operate an empire of seven salons and over 400 products with annual sales of about $16.5 million. No wonder the press often refers to Georgette as the Dean of Skin Care.

Born in Czechoslovakia, she studied skin care in Budapest, Vienna, and Zurich, before opening her first salon over her then-husband's objections. He was afraid people would think he couldn't support her. It became a moot point when the war broke out and they fled to London, but his protests resurfaced after they moved to New York and Georgette started angling to open another salon. She claims she had to sneak out, but through stealth, not to mention hard work, in 1941 she opened a six-room salon at 509 Madison Avenue.

In 1959, having shed Mr. Klinger, she moved to larger quarters at 501 Madison, a location which today sports three floors, with sixty treatment rooms, a hair salon, manicure and pedicure facilities, and serves as many as 250 clients a day. To address what she considers the active urban dweller's need for a scientific, total-care program offering comprehensive services in a private, relaxed setting, Georgette opened a second uptown New York facility at 978 Madison in 1986.

Manager Bonnie Bonilla oversees this luxurious sanctum, which acts as a restorative haven focused on the individual's total well-being—health, nutrition, personalized exercise, and appearance. Consider it a personal retreat in the city, where you can go to take advantage of regimens and treatments specifically designed for you. It's all very nurturing, from the private nutritional counseling by Harvard graduate Dr. Lilian Cheung, to the soothing massage by European-trained experts, to the private exercise instruction. The initial counseling session lasts over an hour and costs $100. Follow-up sessions are $75. The fifty-minute massages run $1 a minute and the exercise classes are $60 each.

Georgette is a firm believer in individual treatments, which is why she's developed so many products in her New York labs. She's adamant that every skin is different, and insists on careful analysis by her skin-care specialists before any product is recommended. They are all fragrance-free and sold exclusively in her salons, despite tempting distribution offers from major department stores. Careful records are made of your skin type and purchases. The client files are kept active for three years, after which it's time to reevaluate your skin. So a quick call from anywhere in the world to (800) KLINGER can ascertain your needs, and arrangements will be made to ship your selections to you. Her line also includes a group of skin-care products for men, which she launched in 1972.

Having anticipated the now huge market for preparations for men, she continues to cater to their needs at the uptown salon. There, she's created a masculine, wood-paneled environment decorated in vivid blues and reds. It has a private entrance and consists of a personal exercise room and designated areas for facials, body treatments, massages, hair styling, nutritional counseling, manicures, and pedicures. Indeed, just like the ladies, gentlemen can pamper themselves with a day at Georgette Klinger for $205 including a spa lunch in the solarium. Individual services range from $30 for a pedicure to $65 for a facial.

Prices for the ladies are comparable, although the Deluxe Full Day of Beauty is $260 and facials for females include makeup application. There's even a Full Year of Beauty for $500—six facials, four body massages, an hour-long makeup lesson, and a bottle of Georgette or Kathryn cologne. But the best bargain is Georgette herself. When she's in New York she's available and accessible. If you're having a special skin problem, call to book an appointment. She really cares, and she's delighted to use her decades of experience to solve your problem. The best part is that she doesn't even charge for her time.

Behind the signature lily of the valley–etched glass doors of every Georgette Klinger salon awaits a cool, calm oasis. It envelops you cocoonlike, separating you from the stresses, the demands of the outside world, and makes you concentrate on some wonderfully decadent, very restorative self-care. 🍒

Il Makiage

107 East 60th Street   (212) 371-3992
New York, NY 10022

Just when you think you've got it all together, fate has a nasty, though often fortuitous, way of stepping in and rearranging everything. Take the case of Israeli-born Ilana Harkavi. She was enjoying a successful life as a professional dancer when a taxi accident ended her career, or rather the career of the moment. Undaunted, Ilana decided to channel her artistic energies in another direction by attending beauty school in New York with the intention of becoming a special-effects makeup artist.

She continued to pursue that dream, working as a theatrical makeup artist in Europe, until fate stepped in once again on her return to the U.S. in 1971. This time it appeared in a more pleasant form, that of her future husband. Together, they decided to open their own business; Il Makiage was born in 1972.

Ilana and Il Makiage literally lit up the cosmetics industry. At a time when colors were confined to what was tried and true, Ilana experimented with a broad palette, producing an unlimited array. When hair colorings were mostly chemically based, she introduced natural henna as an alternative, and at a time when interest in skin-treatment products was practically nill, she helped to revolutionize the industry with collagen products.

Eighteen years later her products are distributed in over 500 fashionably upscale outlets worldwide. The Il Makiage cosmetics line is one of the world's most extensive, with over 400 colors, including 110 eyeshadows, 74 lipsticks, and 65 nail polish shades—and dozens of new color variations are added each year. Considered *the* makeup artist's makeup, it is very popular with those who march down runways or tread the boards of a stage.

Ilana's Avigal hair colors are the best-selling henna products on the market. Its thirteen shades are used in exclusive salons like John Sahag. And the formulations of her Shoynear skin-care cosmetics have won praise for their ability to supply maturing skin with natural collagen.

Of course, at the Il Makiage Salon, you can benefit from all of these products, made at Ilana's own factory on Long Island. The salon, Ilana's international headquarters, gives full head-to-toe service—haircut to pedicure, for men as well as women. At street level, you'll find the cosmetics counter, where you may run into supermodels Iman or Cindy Crawford checking out the huge assortment. Or you might see Rex, that other dancer turned makeup expert, stocking up.

Rooms for the $30 pedicures and $15 manicures are located just beyond the cosmetics, followed by the hair salon, which occupies what once served as a corner of the garden, now glass-enclosed. The greenhouse allows the stylists and colorists to take advantage of strong natural light. What remains of the garden is, during the warmer months, a delightful oasis for the drying of nails and toes.

The lower level is reserved for facials, waxing, and makeup application. Ilana will do your makeup, as she does for Diana Ross and Raquel Welch, and Sly Stallone when movie parts require it, for $350. Group lessons are given, limited to ten people, on Monday and Thursday evenings from 6:00 to 8:00 P.M. They're only $35, and you get a ten-percent discount on any of Ilana's products, plus a complimentary copy of her book, *I'll Make You Beautiful.*

The salon has another specialty, besides the quality of the products and the expertise of the personnel—conveniently extended hours. It's open from 10:00 A.M. to 9:00 P.M. on Mondays and Thursdays, from 10:00 A.M. to 6:00 P.M. on Tuesdays and Wednesdays. On Fridays, Il Makiage closes at 3:00 P.M., and Saturday is Ilana's day of rest. But that means she's open for business on Sunday from 11:00 A.M. to 6:00 P.M. (except during July and August, when no one in their right mind is in the city anyway). Those highly unusual Sunday hours have bailed us out on more than one occasion. Isn't it comforting to know they can do the same for you?   ❦

Kenneth

19 East 54th Street   (212) PL2-1800
New York, NY 10022

In a society dedicated to the chic of the moment, where hair stylists and the trendy coiffures they create come and go, Kenneth stands alone as an enduring institution. His fame and fortune firmly established by his care and feeding of Jacqueline Kennedy's widely copied bouffant hairdo in the early sixties, Kenneth has occupied his ornate five-story townhouse, committed to beauty, for twenty-seven years.

Originally the exclusive preserve of many of New York's most elegant ladies, Kenneth's services have expanded to include those for men and even children. Five years ago, Kenneth did a top-to-bottom facelift on his townhouse, done originally more than two decades ago by the inimitable Billy Baldwin and inspired by the lavish Brighton Pavilion. In the 1980s redo, Kenneth ripped out the ground-floor boutique and installed a decidedly masculine mirrored and tiled salon, complete with authentic barbershop chairs imported from Italy. Now, in privacy, totally separated from prying female eyes, men can have their hair cut, permed, or colored. Manicures and pedicures are also available, as is chest and back waxing. Haircuts run about $50, including shampoo and blow-dry. We were told prices for all other services are the same as those for women — we can't help but wonder if that includes the chest and back waxing!

Kenneth has reserved another space on the first floor, just off to the right of the lobby, for children up to seven years of age. There's no need for an appointment, just pop in; whoever is available from the main salon upstairs will be summoned to cut your child's hair for $20. Be forewarned, the service is strictly limited to cuts. No shampoo — they simply wet down the hair, cut, and blow-dry.

You'll also find on the first floor a counter with all Kenneth's excellent private-label cosmetics. So after benefiting from a $50 makeup instruction or $35 application in a private room upstairs, you can take home all the products responsible for the miraculous transformation.

An imposing staircase rather amusingly enhanced by a Chinese lamp on each newel post leads to the second-floor hairdressing salon. Here, as on each of the floors, a receptionist greets you and escorts you to your stylist. This is Kenneth's personal domain. No prima donna, he's a gentleman who treats women like ladies. A haircut by Kenneth costs $100; by any of his twenty stylists, it's $60. They're all great, although we particularly like Aldo, Gelia, Joel, and Alexander.

Despite the number of stylists and clients who might be here at any given time, there is nothing claustrophobic about the space, no sense of intrusion on your privacy. Indeed, the two styling rooms with their soaring ceilings seem enormous. They're separated by a rotunda boasting a domed ceiling awash in gold leaf. Beyond the rotunda is the lavishly draped tent room, set aside for drying or the occasional nap on one of the comfortable chaise lounges.

The whole effect, with chintz-wrapped mirror frames, richly upholstered chairs, swagged ceilings, and huge bowls of potpourri, is that of a very highly styled Victorian mansion. There's a studied cocoonlike quality to the place. Kenneth even shut out all outside views to emphasize an interior committed to conveying a sense of luxurious pampering. Coffee or tea, hot or iced, is always available, together with a superior supply of reading materials—*The New York Times, The Wall Street Journal,* and *W.* There's a telephone at every station so you can catch up on all those important phone calls as Sigourney Weaver, Joan Rivers, Lauren Bacall, Pamela Harriman, and Jane Pauley do.

No time for lunch? There's always time at Kenneth. They order two different kinds of sandwiches daily from William Poll and serve them on a tray with cookies and your choice of beverage—a terrific deal at $6.50. Should the sandwiches not quite suit, whatever you desire will, of course, be ordered from wherever you like.

Farther up that grand staircase you'll find perming, manicuring, and pedicuring services on the third floor. Permanent waves cost $100. Straightening can be done for $80. Manicures are $14, while pedicures are $30. Farther still (you'll be happy to know there *is* an elevator), the fourth floor is dedicated to coloring, waxing, and scalp treatments. For color, which ranges from a $7 rinse to $100 for double process work, ask for Chang or Marris.

Once colored, coiffed, waxed, and cured, you can be assured of maintaining the semblance of perfection for at least a little while. You can be protected from the ruinous onslaught of environmental forces like wind and rain by taking advantage of yet another Kenneth service—a chauffeur-driven station wagon that will take you to your next appointment, gratis. No reservations needed, just ask Donald, the doorman, if the driver is available.

One final note. Kenneth does have a last name. It's Battelle, but he never uses it. Why should he, when his first name, all by itself, is virtually synonymous with hair?   🌿

La Coupe

694 Madison Avenue   (212) 371-9230
New York, NY 10021

Talk about being born to a family business! It would seem that Charles Booth was destined to make a career of hairdressing. His earliest recollections include his mother's salon in London and pictures of his French grandfather cutting soldiers' hair during World War I. Still, Charles pursued a formal private education and was set to go to Oxford, when his mother pushed fate a bit by suggesting he take time for a brief internship with Vidal Sassoon in London.

It was the sixties, the height of Sassoon's explosion onto the hair-care scene. Recognizing talent, Sassoon made Charles his personal assistant and introduced him to an exciting new celebrity-studded world. Oxford fell by the wayside and Charles opened his first salon in Montreal in 1967.

La Coupe—"the Cut"—is the basis, according to Charles, "of all modern hair design." It reigns supreme at this chic black and white salon, staffed by twenty stylists, each the product of Charles's intensive training program. No matter where else in the world they may have worked, they must serve a one-to-two-year apprenticeship as assistants at La Coupe before Charles allows them on the floor as full-fledged stylists.

The dean of the current crop is Antonio da Costa Rocha, whose clients include Laura Pomerantz, Carolyne Roehm, Shirley Lord (beauty editor of *Vogue*), Kimberly Farkas, and Glenn Close. He charges $120 for a haircut, as does the other star in the stylist firmament here, Kim Lepine. She practices her craft on the likes of Eileen Ford, Mary Tyler Moore, Victoria Newhouse, and a host of other loyal fans who keep her booked two months in advance. Dustin Hoffman has expert stylist Kerry Resnick cut his hair and scores of businessmen feel as comfortable here as the women.

Kim's former assistant, Clare, was recently promoted to the rank of stylist and is a talent to be reckoned with, particularly at her current rate of $50 per cut. As the demand for her grows, the price will go up. In the meantime, she's the bargain of the year—almost. There is such a thing as a $10 cut here. Tuesdays after 5:45 P.M. are "model nights." The assistants take over the cutting chores under the supervision of a stylist. Call 355-9460 before 9:00 A.M. or after 4:40 P.M. to find out what technique they're practicing on any given Tuesday. If it sounds like your kind of style, try it. If not, they'll keep your name and number on file for when they're perfecting something more your style.

Many of La Coupe's very visible clients depend on the extraordinary hair-color genius of Daniel Galvin of London. He pops over for two weeks every couple of months or so and is booked solid for the duration. Daniel's fee starts at $250 for his "haute couture coloring" techniques, custom-designed for each individual.

Stop by for a consultation to determine what he can do for you—no need for an appointment and no charge either. Rachel, a veteran of Daniel's London color salon, is here full-time and is a very capable alternative when Daniel is not in residence.

If you're in the market for a manicure or pedicure, talk to Sophie, who subscribes to the old world Parisian school of nail care—lots of buffing and no cutting. A manicure takes about half an hour and costs $15. Plan on an hour and $35 for a pedicure.

Not quite satisfied with his mastery of the cut and the two salons that execute it so well, Charles Booth's entrepreneurial nature led him into the realm of hair-care products. In 1983 he introduced the first setting mousse in the U.S. Now his line, La Coupe Collection Privée, encompasses eighteen products. Because it has developed a reputation for quality and noticeable results, the line is licensed for international distribution at retail stores. Charles, not wanting to give up his ties to the professional world of hair products, has produced a new line called Charles Booth Professional, which is available at fine salons across the country.

At forty-two, the owner of a business grossing millions annually, we figure Charles is pretty happy about his fate having been sealed at birth.

GENTLEMEN'S SERVICES

Delta Men's Hair Stylists

992 Lexington Avenue   (212) 628-5723
between 71st & 72nd St.
New York, NY 10021

At least there's one place left in New York where a fellow can still get a good old-fashioned, simple but first-rate haircut, and a manicure too, if he's so inclined. It doesn't have all the trappings of the fancy hotel tonsorial parlors. It doesn't have the fake, old interiors of some of those other chichi places on and off the avenues, especially on the Upper East Side. It does have, purely and simply, six great barbers who give you a no-nonsense cut for $18, which may be the best bargain you'll find in this book.

We found out about this little mirrored jewel on the corner of 72nd Street from George Elliott who ought to know something about hair—he's been coiffing the rich and famous for years in his salon in Palm

Beach's fabled Bath & Tennis Club during the winter and on Fisher's Island, playground of the quietly rich, in the summer. But when George comes to New York, he heads straight to Delta to get his locks shorn.

When he gets to Delta, he heads straight for the chair of Peter, the amiable, soft-spoken Greek who's been cutting hair on this corner for two decades or more. Or he might (if Peter's on vacation) try Olga—an admittedly unlikely name for a perfectly marvelous men's coiffeuse. Helen is there to work on your paws and chat about anything, and everything, that catches her fancy.

Because of its location, because of Peter and his merry band, Delta has its share of New York notables who ring for the obligatory appointment (though if you're a regular Peter will do his best to squeeze you in—provided it's not Saturday morning in the middle of the social season). 🍒

Gio's Barber Shop

The Pierre Hotel   (212) 308-7600
2 East 61st Street
New York, NY 10021

It's hard to say what gets done more effectively at Gio's—megadeals or first-rate haircutting. The sign in the lobby identifies it discreetly as just "Gio's Barber Shop," but for men of stature, power, and wealth, who follow the stairs down to the basement, it's a cocoon of tan leather walls, soft lighting, and carrara marble floors. It's a place where movers and shakers can meet their counterparts from around the world, make their deals, and be pampered in luxurious, elegant surroundings.

Ryan O'Neal, Paul Anka, Al Pacino, Malcolm Forbes, Luciano Pavarotti, Lewis Rudin, Lee Iacocca, and Larry Tisch all depend on Gio's to tend to their locks, or what remains of them, when they're in town. There are five private rooms, each equipped with a phone, for business or pleasure.

Services range from cuts, perms, body waves, and scalp treatments to streaking, manicures, pedicures, and facials. Regular haircuts start at $35, manicures at $13, pedicures at $28. Coffee, tea, soft drinks, and cocktails are readily available from Gio's own kitchen, but what most clients love best is the endless supply of Oreo cookies.

Gio's operates on an appointment-only basis, Monday through Saturday 9:00 A.M. to 5:30 P.M., though with service of paramount importance here, don't hesitate to ask for special dispensation where hours are concerned, especially if you plead business reasons.   🐝

EXERCISE

Body Art Exercise Limited

1017 Third Avenue   (212) 593-5771
2nd Floor
New York, NY 10021

New to the fitness scene, this brightly sunlit studio is owned by Arthur Clyde, formerly with the New Jersey State Police Department. He's brought to New York the kind of training that keeps state troopers so fit and formidable. While one-on-one programs are Arthur's specialty, a broad range of classes are offered weekly to satisfy any exercise style—yoga to calisthenics to free weights—and fit any schedule.

Classes are by appointment and limited to twenty-five people, allowing instructors to deal with each individual's needs and hold down goofing off. The cost is $16 for each hour-long class—the same for the seventy-five-minute version, once you've worked up to it. A one-year unlimited pass runs $1,500. For those limited to lunchtime outings, there are forty-five-minute sessions at 12:15 and 1:00 P.M., specially priced at $27 for five—only $5.40 a pop!

So far, Body Art, dedicated to "the art of body perfection," is especially popular with women. It may have something to do with their Total Wellness Program, which includes a body composition test to determine your percentage of body fat. For a one-time $75 charge, the test also measures your level of water retention and metabolic rate. Given that information, fitness director Renée Jones can calculate how many calories you require daily to maintain, lose, or gain weight. She'll work out exercise programs to help you reach your goals, and for a $50 consultation fee, there's a registered dietician to help you get your nutritional act together. The program also has an all-important behavior modification component.

Body Art's floors have a cushiony flexibility, appropriate to a studio that emphasizes cardiovascular conditioning through a combination of high- and low-impact aerobics, calisthenics, and stretching. There's Nautilus equipment, too, but it's used as an ingredient in a total program, which relies more on moving the body than moving machines. The work is strenuous here. Arthur very sensibly strongly recommends taking your fitness test before engaging in any of the routines.

As for one-on-one training, it's done in private in a separate fourth-floor facility. Arthur or one of his staff concentrates on you and your fitness goals for a solid hour. What a relief (during warm weather) to plunge into a whirlpool on the terrace outside the training room. During the cooler months you can take a steam bath or sauna to relax after your workout.

The jury's still out on Body Art, since it just opened in February 1989, but we think Arthur and his studio bear watching.   🦋

Lotte Berke

23 East 67th Street	(212) 288-6613
2nd Floor	
New York, NY 10021	

If you wonder where all those beautiful bodies that grace New York come from, where those ladies go to stay so fit and trim despite the city's bountiful caloric temptations, chances are they are going to the Lotte Berk Studio.

A modest affair on the second floor of an old townhouse—no massage rooms, no sauna, no steam rooms—the studio owned by Lydia Bach is committed to hard work. It is work based on a method of rehabilitation exercise developed in London by Lotte Berke. Lydia adapted and further refined the method into what is now a combination of modern dance, yoga, and orthopedic, stretching, and strenghening exercises. Designed to be equally effective for men and women, the regimen yields truly remarkable results. Just look at manager Elizabeth and her husband, Fred.

Elizabeth grew up practicing the Lotte Berke method and credits it with her youthful, healthy, not to mention beautiful, looks. Fred, long and lean himself, is in amazing shape and has been teaching here for the last three years.

Classes begin at 7:45 A.M., and the regulars who show up everyday for the early class are all active, busy women. You know, the likes of Betsy Aaron of CBS, Sheila Britz of *Architectural Interior Designs*, and Patty Fischoff of Baxton. But don't worry, they have classes running all day. And there are evening and weekend classes as well, so that virtually anyone can fit them into their schedule. By appointment, and limited to twelve people, each session costs only $16, so there's no excuse for not keeping fit during a business trip or a New York weekend. You can sign up for a series to keep you occupied during longer stays at a slight discount.

However, you should bear in mind that this is serious exercise in a no-nonsense environment (yes, there are showers and some lockers, but this is not one of your high-tech fitness palaces). If you want a place to show off the latest in leotards or to socialize, look elsewhere.   🍋

Radu's Physical Culture Studio

41 West 57th Street   (212) 759-9617
Fifth Floor
New York, NY 10022

Radu! RADU! you can almost hear hordes of Huns chanting their leader's name. And believe us when we tell you there are any number of people in New York who would swear Radu makes Attila look like a wimp. Dubbed the "toughest trainer in town," Radu Teordorescu runs a tight ship based on hard work—human body work, not machine-driven work.

In fact, his studio bears no resemblance to the gleaming temples of exercise loaded with tons of expensive equipment that seem so popular these days. His classes are held in an unair-conditioned facility with minimal accoutrements—some familiar- and used-looking exercise apparatus, a few mats thrown around for good measure. The only glamour is the clientele, including Candice Bergen, John Kennedy, Jr., Tatum O'Neal, Bianca Jagger, Calvin and Kelly Klein, Faye Dunaway, and countless models. But with regimens that typically produce sweat in the first seven to eight minutes, whatever starlike charisma they bring with them soon fades as they huff and puff along with everyone else.

Radu studied physical education at the University of Bucharest in his native Romania, before emigrating to the U.S. in 1972. Having attended one of the most prestigious physical fitness schools in the world, he was shocked by the sorry state of Americans' training efforts. Everyone was jogging like mad, but without benefit of proper training. Orthopedists were reaping vast rewards.

Radu discovered his true calling—making people safe for sports. He opened his gym in 1977 and developed a routine heavily reliant on gymnastics. His theory is that if you are in top physical form, as defined by his routines, you can avoid many common sports injuries. Word quickly spread that his students got the quickest results in the shortest period of time. It also got around that he was merciless. Potential students stayed away in droves. Financially, things got so tight that for three years he and his wife lived in the back room of the gym.

Still, he persevered, never altering his program to suit the lazy masses. The financial situation is no longer so grim, his wife having graduated from medical school and begun practicing, but he still has, relatively speaking, very few regular devotees. Most people just can't take the strain and the verbal abuse he doles out when he's displeased with your efforts.

Of course, at his prices he's not running for Mr. Popularity, although he can be disarmingly charming. He's probably the best, and he certainly charges the most—$50 for a half-hour private session, $100 for an hour with the master. His staff trainers get $45 for half an hour, $65 for the full hour. Group classes run $15 each, but drop to $9.15 apiece if you buy a 120-class card for $1,100.

Quite a bargain for your own Hun to chase you around a room.

Vertical Club

330 East 61st Street   (212) 355-5100
New York, NY 10021

As the name suggests, this facility goes up, and up, and up—seven floors and 175,000 square feet of fitness nirvana. It's almost like a country club in the middle of the city with eight tennis courts (six indoors, two on the roof), five squash courts, three racquetball courts, a track, tanning rooms, a sundeck, and a lap pool. With upbeat music blaring throughout, the energy level here is phenomenal; if it could be tapped, the city would never suffer another blackout.

Not all that energy is totally committed to exercise. Sexual tension hangs in the air, almost tangibly. This is a coed club where many members are as intent on exercising their social skills as they are their muscles. Beautiful bodies abound, clad in show-off duds that explain published club policy banning swim suits and midriffs from the second-floor gym area—likewise the edict that "men must wear full short-sleeve shirts" in the gym. While the staff is friendly, encouraging, and helpful, the clientele can be a bit intimidating, particularly if you have reason to be self-conscious about your love handles or thunder thighs.

Take heart—the club's one-on-one training program at $20 per half hour can whip you into shape with maximum results in minimum time. It's just one of the many add-on options to the basic $750 initiation fee and $60 monthly dues, not including tennis privileges at any cost. Tennis memberships are available for $4,000 the first year, $1,000 annually thereafter. Full use of the club is incorporated in the fees, and there are no monthly dues.

Vice president Tom DiNatale is the man to see about either membership. If his dark good looks and easy-going charm aren't enough to convince you of the merits of joining, talk to Bill Cosby, Gay Talese, Maria Shriver, Brooke Shields, Keith Hernandez, Cher, John MacEnroe, Harrison Ford, Chris Everett, Sly Stallone, or Jimmy Connors about the club. They have all taken advantage of the immaculate facilities at one time or another.

The Vertical Club accommodates most schedules with long hours— 6:00 A.M. to 11:00 P.M. Monday through Friday, 9:00 A.M. to 9:00 P.M. weekends. Prime time for the tennis courts is defined by a $20 court charge from 5:00 to 8:00 P.M. weekdays, 9:00 A.M. to 6:00 P.M. Saturday and Sunday. Off-peak hours can be had for $10 each. In either case, you can reserve up to forty-eight hours in advance—the same for squash and racquetball. Court charges for both are $8 an hour.

If you're not into racquet sports, you can save a lot of money at the Vertical Club. There's a never-ending series of classes, all day every day for no additional charge. Many have provocative titles like "Legs & Buns," "Funky Fitness," "Dirty Dancing," "Abs & Upper Body," and "Rubberbands," which is defined in the helpful Definition of Classes as a "resistance-oriented workout with stretching included."

Most are held in the giant second-floor gym with the dress code. That's also where you'll find every piece of state-of-the-art exercise equipment known to man. A 1/9-of-a-mile track circles the room overhead. It's three lanes wide, with a rubberized surface, and we understand the birds-eye view of the action below is useful for more than breaking the monotony of running. It allows joggers to (literally) set their sights on the person they would most like to invite to the restaurant on the third floor.

Open for lunch and dinner and moderately priced, the restaurant has a view too. If conversation lags you can always pretend fascination with the tennis or racquetball games going on around you. Should a meal seem like too much of a commitment, you can opt for a drink at the juice bar on the lower level near the locker rooms.

And even as plush locker rooms go, these are quite nice. Towels, hair driers, and toiletries are available. On the same level you'll find the sauna and steam rooms, as well as the whirlpool. Rooms designated for massages are also located here. The staff masseurs charge $25 for a half-hour rubdown, $45 for an hour.

If you're visiting New York and want to experience what the Vertical Club has to offer, find a member and go as a guest. There are thousands of members scattered throughout the city, so with a tactful inquiry or two you're bound to come across one. There's a $20 guest-pass fee. Assuming you like what you see, try buying one of the books of ten passes for $150.

Whatever your approach to the club—whether you're looking for a meat market or a workout, as a regular member, tennis member, or regular guest—you're sure to enjoy its energy and be infused with a new sense of *joie de vivre*. ❦

CHAPTER NINE

Miscellaneous Services

"I can get it for you. . ."

S ome folks might be tempted to complete this phrase with the (heaven forfend) word *wholesale*. Not on your bippy. There are indeed people who can get just about anything for you in this city—or do anything for you—but it won't necessarily be wholesale.

There are people in New York who'll save you time or save your ties, immortalize your home, cater to your whims, redo your car, or even your helicopter. We're not talking mundane services here like dry cleaners and copy centers, though there are plenty of both. We're talking the important things in life, the things that make it easier, more interesting, and downright spectacular. And, indeed, New York is an Oriental bazaar—from the fabulous to the fantastic, and everything in between. A visitor or longtime denizen has only to think of a want or desire not yet satisfied and there's a clairvoyant unlocking a shop or hanging out a shingle to do just that—to gratify their wish. Satisfaction guaranteed.

Alice S. Mason, Ltd.

635 Madison Avenue	(212) 832-8870
between 59th and 60th Streets	FAX (212) 832-7634
New York, NY 10022	

The great smile is what you first notice about Alice Mason. Then there's her fabulous taste. Finally, you'd be mesmerized by the enormous double strand of white and black South Sea pearls, or some other magnificent piece from her ever-expanding collection of jewels. What you *should* realize immediately is that she is one smart cookie; therein lies the secret of her phenomenal success.

A native of Chestnut Hill, the tony Philadelphia suburb, Alice arrived in New York in 1952 at the tender but not unseasoned age of twenty, an aborted stab at college and one marriage behind her. She rented an apartment from a broker by the name of Gladys Miller, who also gave her a job. She worked for Miller's firm for five years before branching out on her own in 1957.

From the start, she broke barriers. At twenty-five, she was considered too young to be starting her own business, but that didn't stop her. Neither did the Social Registered co-op boards that spent their time denying applications of anyone they considered NOCD—Not of Our Class, Dear. Alice rightly recognized that there were a lot of NOCD types with a great deal of money to spend. She solicited their business, then set about becoming an expert on board psychology. Her success at getting the right clients into the right buildings became legendary.

In the process she built an extraordinary network of contacts, which she carefully nurtures with her fabled dinner parties. They became a tradition early in her career, when she realized how fascinating it would be (and how good for business) for such diverse clients as Alfred Gwynne Vanderbilt and Marilyn Monroe to meet and mingle. Those dinner parties, now faithfully chronicled by a gushing Suzy, helped her build a business that keeps twenty-two brokers very busy selling the city's best residential real estate.

The parties keep her network so well oiled that she doesn't have to do much advertising, and she often seems to know when an exceptional property is going to come on the market even before the owner knows he's decided to sell! Somehow, folks just seem to trust Alice with their secrets or their suspicions. They know she's the soul of discretion. She's proved it over and over again by refusing to reveal who paid how much for what, even though her interests might have been better served if she had been a little less discreet.

Naturally, Alice is in in her element at the top of the market, say $3 million or more. Indeed, she won't personally touch anything less, but she's got brokers on her staff who are as comfortable at the $200,000 level as she is in the megamillions. But if you want an invitation to one of her parties, you'd better be prepared to up the ante—considerably! ❦

Baxton, Inc.

(212) 832-6754

There is a fine art to gift giving and no better practitioners of its intricacies and protocol than Sarah Baxton and Patricia Fischoff. Their by-appointment-only operation is pledged to making your gift giving effortless and satisfying—no more ho-hum responses to your little tokens of appreciation, no more descriptions of your selections as "interesting."

They carry a wide and eclectic array of merchandise in an extensive variety of prices, from a $20 silver-plated pastry server to a $600 piece of antique art glass. More important, they are equipped with the experience and resourcefulness to fulfill any request, to find the perfect gift for any occasion. Both are well-traveled world-class shoppers with sources for unique items all over the globe. What's more, Sarah grew up in the gift business, so she has a particularly well-trained eye for what will please both giver and recipient. Your bank balance is really the only limit to these girls' imaginations.

We've found their $25 silver-plated cheese grater a much appreciated alternative to the all-too-standard bottle of good wine as a hostess gift. We've also started a couple of traditions with Baxton gifts; we gave our favorite bride a dramatic $100 black sandblasted ceramic bowl. Each time we visit the happy couple in their new abode we bring along one or two of Baxton's enchantingly colorful (and deceptively real-looking) glass candies to put in the bowl—$11 apiece. Other friends have begun to follow suit, and the focal point of the newlyweds' coffee table is coming along very nicely, thank you very much.

And thanks to Sarah and Patricia, we no longer waste time and energy agonizing over what to give. From office Christmas party trinkets to unusual treasures commemorating life's most sentimental events, we let their ingenuity make us look good. ❦

Charles D. Kelman, M.D., P.C.

The Empire State Building   (212) 736-9696
350 Fifth Avenue
New York, NY 10118

We hate to admit it, but of late we've had to deal with the fact that our eyes aren't what they used to be. As a result, our bags were bulging with glasses for reading, glasses for driving, and sunglasses for glamour. It was such a bother sorting them out—so embarrassing when we grabbed the wrong pair to make a boardroom presentation or rummaged endlessly to find the right pair to read the menu.

Thank goodness for the good doctor Kelman, who's solved our multiglasses problem, and can probably do the same for you. He's developed a technique that allows his patients to wear a contact lens in their dominant eye, permitting them to read. In the other eye, they wear a lens that gives them perfect vision for driving, movies, and theater. It may sound a trifle schizoid. But amazingly, the brain sorts it all out, puts it all together, and his patients see clearly at all distances.

It generally takes fifteen or twenty minutes to adjust to the system. Once you do, you'll look and feel years younger—just like Cindy Adams, Lionel Hampton, and Congressman Guy Vandergagt. At about $450, it's a lot cheaper and certainly quicker than plastic surgery. Even more important, you can throw away all those glasses—all except those ostensibly for the sun. 🍎

Dillinger-Gaines

325 Exterior Street   (212) 402-6700
Bronx, NY 10451

Exotic limousines are the specialty at Dillinger-Gaines. The company's visionary, Jack Schwartz, takes a plain old Chrysler or Cadillac sedan and dresses it up a bit. He's been known to put in a jump seat that converts into a bed, a hot and cold wet bar, projection TV, and lighting on a dimmer system. Of course, petal-soft Italian leather upholstery is de rigueur for clients who demand all the comforts of home in their cars—clients like Calvin Klein, Donald Trump, Larry Holmes, and Brian Marlowe.

No request, no fantasy is too much for Dillinger-Gaines. They can turn cars into offices with twin pilot seats in the back, serviced by two phones, a fax machine, a paper shredder, and a desk that emerges from the side. Lest the VIP have his or her hands full between the phones and the personal computer, the bar can be digitally controlled by an automatic drink dispenser.

In fact, the only thing Jack Schwartz and Dillinger-Gaines can't do with a car is make it fly. But not to worry—they customize helicopters too. Plan on the transformation taking six weeks to four months and costing at least $80,000 for a car. Count on $200,000 for the helicopter.

Herman Agar Co.

(212) 695-1135
(800) 932-0081

Herman Agar started his ticket agency in the Roaring Twenties, operating out of what is now the coat checkroom of what was then the city's most notorious speakeasy—the 21 Club. The establishment was as awash with Whitneys, Vanderbilts, and Astors as it was with illegal booze, and they all relied on Herman to secure their tickets for the era's most important events.

Herman is, alas, long gone, but the service he founded for the carriage trade remains intact under the experienced supervision of Paul Abramson and Phil Reisel. They've been in the business for decades and have thirty agents in their employ. For the right price, quoted on request and dictated by the degree of difficulty involved, we've never known them to fail to satisfy a client's request. And with clients like Bill Paley, the Bass and Hunt families, Estée Lauder, the inimitable Martha of Martha's fame and her daughter, Lynn Manulis, Douglas Fairbanks, Jr., and every serious investment house in the country, you can bet those requests have been pretty demanding, the right price pretty high.

Credit cards are accepted by the agency, but somewhat grudgingly. Paul and Phil prefer to deal with house accounts. It's so much more genteel, and no percentages are annoyingly subtracted from their profit. The only way to get an account, though, is to be recommended by an existing client. We suggest you roam through the Fortune 500 and see who you know.

Whether you're looking for tickets on or off the Great White Way, to the opera, the ballet (in Manhattan or any other city), or any sporting event in the world, you can count on the Herman Agar. In fact, for mega-events like the World Series or the Super Bowl, they set up an office in the host city and somehow manage to snap up the very best seats.

Once you become a regular client, they'll extend their services to obtain impossible-to-get last-minute reservations at New York's most popular restaurants. Rumor has it that members of the Rothschild family call Herman Agar to arrange all their Stateside activities, even before they book their Concorde flights. Maybe you should too. Remember, Paul and Phil are just a phone call away from making sure you're seen wherever you like. ❦

Jerry Kravat Entertainment Services

205 Lexington Avenue	(212) 686-2200
at 32nd Street	FAX (212) 689-9140
New York, NY 10016	

Having a party for two, twenty, two hundred, or two thousand? Producing a corporate or institutional event? Is there a trade or industrial show or perhaps the launch of a new product in your future? What about that benefit for your favorite charity? For anything that requires some form of entertainment, call the delightful Jerry Kravat. Founder of a completely unique service that matches talent to places and events, Jerry is relentless in making sure his clients' needs are satisfied.

And those needs are myriad. He regularly meets the entertainment demands of all the best places and people. Jerry's prestigious credits as entertainment director and regularly featured orchestra include the Waldorf-Astoria, the Pierre, the Plaza, and the principality of Monaco (among others) all at the same time. Jerry always seems to have a unique understanding of and appreciation for what makes each event special and what kind of clientele it attracts. He says it's like solving a jigsaw puzzle, putting all the pieces together to make a perfect fit—to wed location, ambiance, crowd, and entertainer(s). Jerry's marriages never fail. When perfectionists Barbara Walters and Merv Adelson threw their big wingding at the Pierre, they turned to the Jerry Kravat Orchestra to play for all their glamorous guests. The coming-out party for Rupert and Anna Murdoch's daughter Elizabeth as well as the internationally televised CBS show "Happy New Year America" featured Kravat's music and entertainment.

No affair is too small or too special; from a small dinner party to a wedding or a major event, anywhere in the world, Jerry Kravat has played a role. He's put together shows at the San Diego Zoo, Universal Studios in L.A., and Walt Disney World. In the process, he's hired the likes of Peter Allen, Bill Cosby, Cher, Ella Fitzgerald, Barbara Cook, Bob Hope, Lena Horne, Liza Minelli, Luciano Pavarotti, Chita Rivera, Joan Rivers, Kenny Rogers, and Bobby Short. He's equally creative at finding the perfect strings to stroll through your next cocktail get-together or the pianist to create that appropriately romantic background for a little *dîner à deux*.

Whatever you have in mind for any occasion, give Jerry a call to be sure it is a very special event indeed. ❦

Jill Gill

90 Riverside Drive   (212) 362-8440
New York, NY 10024

Jill Gill is into preservation—not wildlife, but our lives and yours. For twenty-five years she's made a specialty of preserving important parts of people's lives by capturing them in wonderful watercolor paintings—that glorious view from the office, a special garden in bloom, a room full of cherished memories. Lots of Jill's clients have her paint their townhouse to hang in their country house and vice versa. They also like to reproduce her painting as notes or Christmas cards; they make such a personal statement.

It all started with Jill's hobby of photographing, then painting, buildings and street scenes slated for demolition or radical change. After seeing some of these watercolors, friends asked if Jill would paint a portrait of their house, and a new career was born.

In pursuit of that career, Jill visits with her clients in the surroundings they want immortalized. She chats with them about their feelings, about what makes the place so special to them. Then she takes pictures, lots of pictures in both black-and-white and color. Armed with these, she retreats to her studio to immerse herself in painting, and about a month later emerges with the finished product.

Prices range from $1,800 to $6,000, depending upon size and scale; a facade is less costly than a garden or a room, which both require a three-dimensional approach. She only accepts one commission a month, so clients like American Standard, Kurt Vonnegut, Mrs. Drew Heinz, and the Russian Tea Room have to wait their turn. You'll wait too, but it's worth it to preserve for posterity your special piece of New York. ❦

Michel Thomas Language Center

60 East 42nd Street   (212) 688-8400
5th Floor
New York, NY 10036

The French government called on Michel Thomas as a star witness in the trial of Gestapo leader Klaus Barbie. After all, it was Michel, as a young leader of the French Resistance during World War II, who faced an interrogation by Barbie and lived to tell the tale. He's now put the language skills that got him past that little incident to work in a truly unique system for people anxious to learn a foreign tongue quickly and painlessly.

His way is really the only way to learn a new language, short of moving to its country of origin. In only ten days, Michel guarantees you'll be speaking, reading, and writing the language of your choice. He'll also find a teacher for any language in the world, though he specializes in the major tongues. And he's truly the master. Companies like Chase Manhattan, MCA, Boeing, and Westinghouse are terribly impressed with Michel and his system. He's taught any number of their top executives, not to mention Candice Bergen, Woody Allen, and Barbra Streisand.

Michel's system has one ground rule—"never try to remember anything. The responsibility for the learning and remembering is with the teacher, not the learner." Having exhibited absolutely no facility for languages until we ran into Michel, we now buy his seemingly improbable line—since we can now *parle Français* with the best of them.

$4,200 buys you 80 hours of instruction and a schedule tailored to your own needs. The first phase of the center's course concentrates on the basics of vocabulary, grammar, tense, and syntax. Then Michel tailors the program to fit your needs, whether personal or professional. Whatever your pace or your schedule, Michel can add a new dimension to your life by giving you the ability to communicate effectively in a language other than English. *Comprendez-vous?*   ❦

On Call Time Savers, Inc.

(718) 834-0304

Young, dynamic, energetic Amy McCloskey realized that anyone living, working, or even visiting New York is short of one commodity—time. Who has time to wait in line for a visa or to wait for the electrician? Who even has time to research finding a good electrician. . . or a good anything? For these and a million and one other little errands that need doing, at long last there is a lifesaver in Time Savers.

Amy and her firm will tackle just about anything, including standing in line to purchase tickets when the Lotto gets up to $50 million. It's a gamble at $35 for two hours, but it will keep you from suffering from the "what if. . ." syndrome. By the same token, Time Savers will pick up your airline tickets or do your grocery shopping. General errands run $13.50 to $20.00 an hour, depending on the nature of the business to be conducted. Secretarial work, catering, housecleaning—they'll do it all. Amy's crew will even mend that troublesome hem and replace the buttons robbed or mangled by the laundry.

If you have a problem, she's got the answer. Call her for an estimate of how she can make yours a life of leisure. Amy McCloskey and On Call Time Savers can help you get organized, so that you can truly enjoy all that New York has to offer. ❧

Premiere Ticket Service

(212) 643-1274

An opening-week ticket for Neil Simon's new play or for the latest Andrew Lloyd Webber musical extravaganza, a luxury box at the U.S. Open, orchestra seats for the Metropolitan Opera, tickets for the Metropolitan Museum's current spectacle of art and culture—none of these is a problem for Joanna Gutterman and Lyn Schwartz and their Premiere Ticket Service.

These two chic, sophisticated friends of ours have broken into a business that has traditionally been the preserve of men. There's sort of an old-boy network among ticket brokers that, until now, has successfully blocked female entrepreneurs from the business. However, Joanna and Lyn don't ever take no for an answer. Nothing could dissuade them and their perseverance has paid off. They've developed their own network that assures them access to the hottest tickets around.

They proudly claim, "Sold out is not a phrase in our vocabulary." In actual fact, we've never heard them say that anything was impossible. Still, it's best to call about the event of your dreams before you get to town, especially if it's Frank or Liza (or Frank *and* Liza) you hanker to see. But if you just aren't capable of planning ahead, take comfort in the knowledge that Joanna and Lyn work well under last-minute pressure. And once you've become a client, they'll send you a monthly brochure describing all the events in town and what's new on Old Broadway—no more excuses for not giving Premiere Ticket Service a little advance notice!   ❦

Spencer Realty

274 Madison Avenue   (212) 725-2440
between 39th and 40th Streets
New York, NY 10016

Fed up with hotels for long stays in New York and want a place you can really call home? For a pied-à-terre with character, charm, and at least a touch of class, call Brenda Spencer. Her business is rentals, furnished and unfurnished; her specialty is short-term leases. Whether you seek a turn-of-the-century brownstone, a prewar luxury apartment, or a loft in Soho, Brenda can find it for you. The whole of Manhattan's her inventory.

Monthly rates for a modest nest start at about $1,200, with the sky the limit. The minimum commitment is generally two months. A single month is possible, but difficult.

Corporate giants like First Boston, Chase Manhattan, Phillip Morris, and Morgan Stanley count on Brenda to locate homes away from home for visiting execs. She's popular too with entertainment-industry types in town to do a show or make a movie. Donald Sutherland and Keith Carradine regularly depend on her, as do any number of other world-class travelers who prefer private residences to hotels.

Brenda also provides free "settling in" services as a little bonus and to help make her clients comfortable as quickly as possible. They include arranging for maid service, cable TV, and garage space. She even maps out local restaurants, grocery stores, dry cleaners, and shoe repair shops.

Give her two or three weeks notice, if you're looking for a place in New York. Should you leave town for an extended period and wish to list your home with her, plan to do it two to three months before your departure.   ❦

Tiecrafters

116 East 27th Street   (212) 867-7676
6th Floor
New York, NY 10016

Andy Tarshis worries about neckties—not whether the red one goes with the gray suit, but whether the spot on the red tie will ever come out. For thirty-five years, Andy's been running one of New York's most unusual and most specialized businesses, one entirely dedicated to the proper care and feeding of ties. How many ties have you discarded because of stubborn stains or outdated widths? With Andy and Tiecrafters in your life, you may never throw a tie away again.

When it comes to cleaning, Andy's services may be the best in the world. He'll go to just about any length to remove that salad-dressing stain from your new Hermès. If necessary, Tiecrafters will open the back, release the stitching, clean the silk, and then resew the tie. All this, for $4 per tie, with a four-piece minimum.

As tie experts of long standing, Tiecrafters knows all the fabrics, all the styles. If you want to modernize your old wide ties by making them narrower, bring them in so Andy and his staff can work their magic. You'll have a new, fashionable cravat for only $6.50.

If you want to add to your wardrobe, as well as revamp it, remember Tiecrafters also makes ties—$30 each, including fabric. The charge is only $25, if you supply the goods.

And the best news is that you can take advantage of Tiecrafters services even when you're not in New York. Half their business comes from all over the U.S. and Canada via UPS and Federal Express. Cleaning and alterations usually take about a week if you drop off the ties or have Tiecrafters pick them up—it's more like a two-week turnaround if you're working through the mail.

But if you have a real tie crisis and can get it to Andy by 11:00 A.M., you can have it back that same afternoon. Isn't it wonderful that Andy worries so much about ties, so you don't have to?

Ultra Smith Systems, Inc.

554 West 38th Street   (212) 695-3342
New York, NY 10018

Barry Smith is in the business of creating dream cars—taking that old clunker, or more likely that Lamborghini Jeep or Porsche Turbo, and adding all sorts of goodies that make it worthy of a Hollywood star. He'll put in custom leather door panels, trimmed with ostrich, or he'll use exotic leathers to cover seats and steering wheels. Then there are the electronics—the 500-watt stereo with CD player and nine (count 'em, nine!) speakers, the portable cellular phone system and the window and lock systems that can be operated a hundred feet away from the car.

Barry's cagey about exactly who requests his services, but we imagine it's an interesting crew. How many people do you know who are interested in disappearing taillights? Barry explains that at night a push of a button could force a pursuer to break off the chase as the telltale lights vanish. Another item aimed at discouraging followers, or even just tailgaters, is the zap light mounted behind the license plate. Its super high-beam blinds the guy behind you, sending a very definite message to back off!

Less sinister and virtually standard equipment for an Ultra Smith System transformation are TVs and VCRs, not to mention the custom-sculptured Wilton carpets, bound in leather, and the high-powered European lighting systems.

Barry does only about 350 cars a year, so plan ahead—two weeks for an appointment, four to six weeks of work on the car. And count on a starting price tag of $50,000, depending on your vehicular fantasies. But remember, the fifty grand does not include the original price of the car!

Acknowledgments

To Passport Books' Bill Pattis for breakfast at the Palace where the idea for this new series was born.

To Mark Pattis for his soft-spoken guidance and direction in making this book a reality.

To my editor, Michael Ross, who always had time, encouragement and serenity even when I did not.

To Floria Lasky for being there time and again and again.

To all my pals in New York, Beverly Hills, Los Angeles, San Francisco, Houston, and Vancouver for their encouragement, their belief, and most of all for their friendship, which has always been a constant source of happiness to me.

Thanks.
F.W.K.

To David Andelman for his editorial expertise, his devotion of untold hours to making sure our book would be a good read, but more importantly for his unqualified belief in me and in the project.

To Ferne, the established author, for taking a chance on a novice.

To Ed Callaghan and Barton G. Weiss for their patience during the home stretch.

To all my family and friends who make my life so very special, who help sustain my joie de vivre, which allows me to relish New York on a $1,000 a Day...or a $1 a Day, before lunch.

Eternal thanks.
S.M.C.

Index

ABOUT THE AUTHORS

Ferne Kadish

Born in Chicago and raised in Beverly Hills, Ferne Kadish is now bicoastal, dividing her time between New York and California. She attended Boston University and the University of Southern California and has recently served on the faculty of the New School of Social Research in New York City. An avid world traveler, Ferne is much in demand as a speaker to women's groups throughout the U.S. and has written on the subject of travel for numerous magazines. Her successful writing career also includes a novel, *The Golden Circle*, of which she is co-author. Drawn from her various experiences and expertise in travel, fashion, marketing, and design—as well as her intimate knowledge of the lifestyles of the rich and famous—*New York on a $1,000 a Day (Before Lunch)* and *London on a £1,000 a Day (Before Lunch)* are the first two titles in Ferne's new travel series. ❧

Shelley Clark

Born in Lewes, Delaware, and raised in both Delaware and Maryland, writer/publicist Shelley Clark has had an eclectic career. After graduating with honors in history from Kenyon College, Shelley gained hands-on experience in a variety of fields, including tape editing, sales, marketing, and public relations. Following a stint with the first Reagan inaugural, Shelley joined a D.C. consulting firm, where she was responsible for organizing conferences and special events for the National Institutes of Health. Her skills as a writer and publicist caught the attention of Hanae Mori, for whom she became director of communications based in New York City. Today, Shelley works for an independent public relations and marketing firm, specializing in fashion. When not meeting the press or organizing parties, Shelley enjoys cooking, sailing, and traveling. ❧